John Sayles, Filmmaker

John Sayles, Filmmaker

*A Critical Study of the
Independent Writer-Director;
With a Filmography
and a Bibliography*

by

JACK RYAN

McFarland & Company, Inc., Publishers
Jefferson, North Carolina, and London

Frontispiece: John Sayles on the set of *Passion Fish* (1992). Photo by
Bob Marshak.

Library of Congress Cataloguing-in-Publication Data

Ryan, Jack.
    John Sayles, filmmaker : a critical study of the independent
writer-director ; with a filmography and a bibliography / by Jack
Ryan.
        p.   cm.
    Includes index.

    ISBN 0-7864-0529-5 (cloth : 50# alkaline paper)

    1. Sayles, John, 1950–   — Criticism and interpretation.
I. Title.
PN1998.3.S3R93   1998
791.43'023'092 — dc21   98-29150

British Library cataloguing data are available

Manufactured in the United States of America

McFarland & Company, Inc., Publishers
    Box 611, Jefferson, North Carolina 28640
        www.mcfarlandpub.com

For my father, John E. Ryan, an old union man
who enjoyed *Matewan*, the last movie he ever saw.

Contents

Acknowledgments   viii
Preface   1
Introduction   3

 1. A Storyteller: From Literature to Film   9
 2. New World Pictures: Training, Fun, Profit   19
 3. Screenwriter-for-Hire: Revisions, Additions, Originals   35
 4. *Return of the Secaucus Seven*   53
 5. *Lianna*   72
 6. *Baby, It's You*   85
 7. *The Brother from Another Planet*   97
 8. *Matewan*   115
 9. *Eight Men Out*   137
10. *City of Hope*   156
11. *Passion Fish*   174
12. *The Secret of Roan Inish*   192
13. *Lone Star*   213
14. Contributing More   242

Filmography   247
Bibliography   257
Index   267

Acknowledgments

Like me, this book found a life in Cleveland, Ohio, and I owe thanks to many fine people from that wonderful place: Judy Oster, who taught me more than I thought possible; Bill Siebenschuh, whose insouciant wit and appreciation for life's pratfalls helped me more than once; Roger Salomon, who gave me a start and stuck with me as I learned the ropes; Mayo Bulloch, who offered her finely tuned sense of humor and generous support. My appreciation also goes to Mary Grimm, Park Goist, and Lila Hanft for reading the original manuscript of this book and offering constructive suggestions toward its refinement. I'd also like to thank Doug Clarke, Tony Whitehouse, Steve Bulloch, Ruth Walter, Peter Royston, Jean Ryan, John Vourlis, and all of my colleagues at Gettysburg College for their generosity and encouragement. My children, Nicholas, Emily, and Gabriel, deserve credit for being extremely delightful people. Thanks to Camille Spaccazento, Karyn Kusama, and Dan Rybicky, John Sayles's production office staff in New York, who answered my questions, and thanks to John Sayles for the concise notes and the "Twilight Zone" challenge. Finally, I'd like to thank Gettysburg College for its generous help in the form of a research and professional development grant, which allowed me to complete this project.

Without the backing of three special people this book would not exist. My mother, Elizabeth Ryan, gave her support, love, and ceaseless encouragement. Louis Giannetti supported my initial idea for this book, then read, criticized, and helped edit my original manuscript. Elizabeth I. Walter, Ph.D., is my wife, my first reader, and my best critic. Nobody has lived through the oscillations of this book more than she. She has boosted sagging spirits, challenged my quick drafts, demanded my best labors, and reminded me that this was a worthwhile project. I only hope this book justifies her faith and her love.

Preface

I set out to write this book for two simple reasons: I am simpatico with the values reflected in the movies of John Sayles, and I had the great good pleasure to become Louis Giannetti's friend while I lived in Cleveland, Ohio. The book is an introduction to the work of John Sayles, and it is written for a general audience. Film terms in the text have been clearly defined. I have not attempted to dazzle the reader with theoretical jargon or arcane insights. Each film chapter explains the production history, provides a story summary, discusses various cinematic elements, and suggests some characteristics that set Sayles apart as a filmmaker. This book can be used by teachers of literature, history, or film; above all, however, it is meant for people who, like me, are fans of John Sayles's brand of filmmaking.

Introduction

Mr. Shine, the protagonist of John Sayles's short story "Children of the Silver Screen," is the manager of a neighborhood movie theater about to drop classic Hollywood pictures in favor of Russ Meyer–type skin flicks. At the conclusion of the story, Mr. Shine commits an act of material and cultural subversion: He shows *On the Town*, featuring Gene Kelly, free of charge to his matinee regulars, a diverse collection of urbanites. Shine deliberately ignores his distributor's extra screening royalties policy because he knows that his regulars are losing the singular experience that brought them together: watching good movies on a big screen, in a real theater. The last image we see in the story is of Mr. Shine, lost in the infinite light on the screen, caressed by the "pulse and flicker of life."

It used to be that movies mirrored American life. The public went to the pictures because the pictures had meaning for their personal lives. Today, however, the movies are mostly about money — how much the film cost, how much the star made, how much the box office took in on the opening weekend. Instead of intelligent reviews, we are pounded with box office numbers. The market dictates success. The box office hits are multimillion-dollar productions with superstar actors and generic plots. Audiences keep coming because of the glitz and glamor, not the stories painted in light on the screen. However, like Mr. Shine, John Sayles seeks something different from the cinema, something more substantive.

Sayles is perhaps America's best-known independent filmmaker, willing to sacrifice large profits for creative freedom. He writes, directs, edits, and often acts in his own low-budget, independent films. Sayles's prolific independent output is unequaled in the history of the commercial American cinema. Though Sayles's own pictures have not been box office hits, they have consistently made money and generated favorable reviews. A Sayles picture is skillfully structured, well acted, morally complex, and full of complicated characters. His only solid connection to Hollywood has been writing screenplays and working as a script doctor for various production companies since 1978 when his first script, *Piranha*, was produced by Roger Corman's New

World Pictures. Sayles uses the profits he makes from his lucrative screen-writer-for-hire career to finance his independent projects. But unlike the Hollywood productions that fuel his independent projects, a John Sayles picture captures in light the poetry of real people.

To date Sayles has completed 11 feature-length movies, written five books (three novels, one short story collection, one work of nonfiction), worked in the theater and television, acted, and contributed both short fiction and journalism to major periodicals. His list of Hollywood screenwriting projects is long and impressive, including uncredited rewrites for *Apollo 13* and *Mimic*. Two of Sayles's original screenplays, *Passion Fish* and *Lone Star*, have been nominated for Academy Awards. Remarkably, despite enormous difficulty in securing financing, Sayles has remained independent, making the films he wants to make, telling stories that appeal to him rather than to a room full of Hollywood producers. After the success of *Lone Star*, Sayles could have worked on a commercial, studio-backed production, the traditional goal for most independent filmmakers. However, he decided to make a film about political malfeasance. Set in a nameless Latin American country, *Men With Guns* (*Hombres Armados*) is presented in Spanish with English subtitles. Combining contemporary politics with foreign language may seem quixotic, but Sayles's production company, Anarchists' Convention, Inc., and Sony Pictures Classics brought this challenging drama to American audiences. There are few filmmakers working today who would take on such unlikely material, especially after being recognized by the Hollywood film establishment. However, *Men With Guns* (*Hombres Armados*) extended Sayles's track record for producing quality films without commercial potential. Also, Sayles now has two works of nonfiction.

Sayles's story topics change from picture to picture, jumping from the insecurity of the sixties generation to a lesbian coming-out story, from baseball's most famous corruption scandal to a children's tale to a film border culture. He defies popular critical labels, except to say that he is a realist concerned with quotidian lives. Sayles makes conscious choices to represent, through a variety of filmmaking techniques, certain aspects of American life never reflected in other contemporary films. He fuses dialogue, editing, camera angles, sound, and mise-en-scène, among other cinematic devices, to make the world of his films appear real. His own theories on filmmaking are decidedly populist, and he seems to enjoy the collaborative process of making a movie. Sayles's superior storytelling does, however, demand audience involvement. A Sayles film is not entertaining eyewash.

Sayles's independent projects resonate with cultural issues, both societal and personal. In almost all of his films individual will and consciousness are locked in a battle with ideological forces. In *Matewan*, *City of Hope*, and *Eight Men Out*, this struggle is easily recognizable because of obvious separations in class and power. In these films, Sayles's own politics stand out, even though none of his characters actually transcend the economic conflict in which they are engaged. These films are conflicted, unsentimental, as are all of Sayles's pictures. *The Secret of Roan Inish* might seem the exception to this rule, yet even these characters opt for the hardworking life of the sea. For the most part, Sayles's films examine communities and the multitude of problems that arise when a variety of people interact. An uncommon decency marks all of Sayles's work, making him anathema to the current hedonistic world of popular film, where B movies are now A movies. Without apology, Sayles offers a cinema influenced by his left-wing politics; he is, moreover, a humanist. As the film scholar Gerald Mast observed, Sayles confronts the figures and forces that often make the United States a difficult place to live. Simply put, Sayles cares about people. Even his repellent characters have reasons for being who they are. Thematically, his films revolve around justice, responsibility, and integrity; he is against prejudice, injustice, and the abuse of power. In his work, Sayles examines people and how their lives are influenced by the world around them, which can take so much and give back so little. Sayles is skeptical of palliative rhetoric, especially from politicians or intellectuals. He keeps his stories at ground level, focusing on ordinary people and their communities. He is open-minded, compassionate, and quietly emotional in his observations. Yet he is far from solemn. Sayles appreciates humor, and his best work is full of it. His democratic idealism resonates through his ensemble casts, and characters drive his stories. His stories are smart and complicated, never relying on simple answers.

Sayles's work does come with flaws. None of his films is totally free from melodrama. His early work suffers technically. However, the integrity of Sayles's collected work far outweighs its defects. By reviewing Sayles's film work since 1980, we can witness the growth of an extraordinary filmmaker. As he learns to use cinematic grammar, his films become more visually sophisticated; as his expertise increases, so do his budgets. Still, numerous critics have found Sayles's work lacking, especially visually. The standard critical line on Sayles is that what he says is more impressive than how he says it. He is a writer-director — emphasis on the former. Pauline Kael, never one for films of social relevance, started the trend by calling Sayles the thinking man's shallow filmmaker. Michael Sragow followed up by claiming that Sayles is an uninspiring film director whose work lacks kinetic talent. Stuart Klawans finally admitted to readers of *The Nation* that he finds Sayles's work pedestrian to the point of indifference. Even Andrew Sarris (who would later retract this assessment) observed that Sayles's emphatic integrity and his moral sensibility overwhelmed both his visual style and his dramatic instinct.

Sayles readily admits that he is not interested in form or style for its own sake. Rather, he is interested in the materials he has to tell a story; therefore, he avoids a signature visual style, removing himself from the world of rapidly moving cameras and jackrabbit cuts. Sayles has worked with a variety of recognized cinematographers in order to ensure that the look of each film reflects the story being told. Still, as Sayles's screenplays become more complex, so too do his mise-en-scène and the choreography of his camera movements. Indeed, *Passion Fish*, *The Secret of Roan Inish*, and *Lone Star* were actually praised by a handful of popular film critics for their visual style.

In order to ensure artistic integrity, Sayles runs his own film company on a shoestring budget, albeit with considerable help from a loosely affiliated group of regular collaborators, particularly Maggie Renzi. Quietly, he has accomplished the dream of filmmakers from Charlie Chaplin to Francis Ford Coppola: Creative control rests in his head, hands, and eyes. Of course, Sayles's collective is extremely talented. Starting with Renzi and spreading outward to include actors, technicians, and production people, Sayles's collaborators know their business and seem to enjoy the process of making remarkably unassuming films.

Maggie Renzi has been Sayles's partner and collaborator for more than 20 years, having produced nine of his 11 films and acted in nine. Renzi anchors Sayles's productions, handling all the unexpected problems, keeping the crew focused, and making sure the film progresses as planned. She is experienced in all areas of producing, from fund-raising to public relations. Renzi can make a production look far more expensive than a typical Sayles budget allows. *Millimeter* magazine once named Renzi one of America's "50 Top Producers." In addition to working with Sayles, Renzi has produced a dance film, *Mountain View*, for public television's *Alive—From Off-Center* and three videos for Bruce Springsteen, one of which, "Glory Days," won an American Video Award. Renzi also acted in Jonathan Demme's *Swing Shift* (1984).

Actors who have regularly worked with Sayles include David Strathairn, Joe Morton, Chris Cooper, Mary McDonnell, Vincent Spano, Stephen Mendillo, Nancy Mette, Kevin Tighe, Josh Mostel, Tom Wright, Michael Mantell, Elizabeth Peña, Gordon Clapp, and Angela Bassett. Several well-known actors have worked with Sayles because they believe in his projects, including Christopher Lloyd, Rosanna Arquette, and James Earl Jones. For the most part, however, because he is a naturalistic filmmaker, Sayles prefers not to distract attention from his stories by using well-known actors.

On the technical and financial sides of the filmmaking process, Sayles has collaborated with Haskell Wexler (cinematography), Sarah Green (production), Barbara Hewson Shapiro (casting), Cynthia Flynt (costume design), Peggy Rajski (production), Nora Chavooshian (production design), Dan Bishop (art design), R. Paul Miller (production), Mason Daring (music), and John Sloss (executive production). Because he is familiar with them, their specific talents, and their strengths, Sayles can relax on the set and concentrate on his duties as the director. They know and support each other, and they work well together. Sayles takes pleasure in the collaboration of filmmaking, auteur theory notwithstanding.

Sayles describes himself as a conduit for people's voices, a handy metaphor for the script rewrites he does for other productions. Getting those voices into theaters via his own films is more difficult. Like many peripheral filmmakers, Sayles finances his movies independently, guaranteeing him artistic control. Sayles understands that paying the bills and sponsoring the film guards against studio interference. Even though he willingly takes studio script work, Sayles's real desire is to make movies that audiences would not normally see. Sayles is a talented, prescient, and motivated filmmaker whose work demands wider attention.

1

A Storyteller:
From Literature to Film

I always wanted to write, not to be a writer.
— John Sayles (Bonetti)

John Sayles takes pleasure in telling a good story. Flashy style, abstract language, and narrative experimentation are not his concerns. Sayles is a realist, traditional and unabashed. As the novelist Vance Bourjaily has pointed out, Sayles's type of realism is a mixture of Jack London's "reportorial vigor" and Stephen Crane's "sweet impressionism" (33). In all of his writing, Sayles empathizes with a variety of character types and displays an unerring ear for American speech: male and female, gay and straight, jocks and intellectuals, old and young. These people come from all walks of life — they are dishwashers, dog breeders, cowboys, truck drivers, anthropologists, college professors, football coaches, temporary workers, builders, coal miners, baseball players, cops, and even Cuban expatriates.

Sayles turned to independent feature filmmaking just as his second novel, *Union Dues* (1977), was nominated for both the National Book Award and the National Book Critics Circle Award. Sayles invested his own money in *Return of the Secaucus Seven*, his first film, which was commercially released in 1980. Sayles saw the movie as an audition piece, a Hollywood calling card, never expecting a theatrical release. The film, however, became a grassroots success story, spreading across the country thanks to solid word-of-mouth reviews and, eventually, smart marketing.

Return of the Secaucus Seven is noteworthy because it carries all the hallmarks of Sayles's later, more assured work. His characters are smart and funny, speaking with colloquial vigor. *Return of the Secaucus Seven* focuses on a group rather than on a single character, and women are as important to the story as men. The film is also politically savvy, revealing an understated social relevance. Sayles shows disagreements among members of the group, yet he does not come down on one side or the other; he is not doctrinaire in his political

9

leanings, allowing his audience to come to its own conclusions. On a limited budget, using a plain visual style, Sayles establishes a sense of community, friendship, and honest reality in this rueful, winning first effort. Since then, Sayles has become one of the country's best-known independent filmmakers, free from studio dependence or interference. As Sayles told George Hickenlooper in 1991, "I always say, 'Fuck the studio, don't let them make your movie. Do something else. Make a cheaper movie'" (309). His films are individual, offbeat, and generally noncommercial. Because he has remained almost completely independent from any Hollywood production system and because of his strong literary background, John Sayles is an unusual contemporary American filmmaker.

Many American movie directors begin as independents, scraping, borrowing, and begging for money to produce small, off-beat films. Few remain independent. If they are lucky, they graduate to big-budget studio assignments. John Sayles, however, is of a different type. Before making his first feature, Sayles had never looked through a movie camera. He happily says that he came to the movies from out in left field. Yet, Sayles loved the movies, especially those that seemed to capture a sense of real life, so he taught himself how to make a motion picture — learning how to write screenplays, shoot and edit film, run a film crew, and how to direct — all in a remarkably short time. Sayles's command of the film medium has steadily strengthened. Now he is an assured filmmaker, whose overall style can be described as low-key, unobtrusive. As his film narratives have grown in complexity, so too have his visual compositions. As the 1990s draw to an end, Sayles stands alone as a truly independent, commercially successful filmmaker, one whose perceptive, thoughtful, unerring stories explore how ordinary people live.

Because he was uninterested in traditional career goals, Sayles's work background is eclectic, including stints as a hospital orderly, plastic molder, meat cutter, and day laborer. His association with people from all walks of life is clearly reflected in his fiction and in his films. Since the publication of his first novel and the success of his first film, Sayles has also written for television and theater, and worked as a journalist and an actor.

Sayles was born on September 28, 1950, in Schenectady, New York, an upstate industrial town dominated by General Electric. His parents, Donald and Mary Sayles, were both educators, one generation removed from their working-class roots. They were not movie buffs. Instead, they encouraged their son to read, which he did when not watching television shows or playing sports. They also seem to have fostered an incredibly strong sense of independence in Sayles because they wanted him to avoid the trap of dispiriting work, which permeates old industrial towns. "They didn't lay any big trips about, 'This is what you are supposed to do,'" he explains. "Enough people in my family did things they didn't like, and they didn't want us to do that. I wanted to be a pitcher for the Pittsburgh Pirates" (Dreifus 33). Sayles never pitched professionally; he went his own way instead, avoiding GE, the Vietnam draft, and a traditional career path. Oddly, in 1968 he landed at Williams College, an upscale liberal arts college comfortably hidden away in the Berkshire Mountains, a move that does not seem to fit with Sayles's working-class sympathies. As so often when talking about himself, Sayles offers little explanation. Speaking to an interviewer, he explained how he ended up in college, a choice he was ambivalent about: "I had a guidance counselor say to me, 'Here's two places I want you to apply — Williams and Colgate.' I ended up feeling like, if I went to Colgate, they'd make me play serious football, and I played too much serious football in High

John Sayles on the set of The Secret of Roan Inish *(1995). Photo by David Appleby.*

School already" (Dreifus 32). Although Sayles majored in psychology, not English, he did take a few creative writing courses because "they graded on poundage, and I wrote long stories, so I got A's in that, which brought my average up to C for my other courses, which I mostly didn't go to" (Chute 57).

What Sayles did do in college was read: "I'd never read Faulkner or Hemingway or any of these American guys, so even though I took almost no English classes, I just started reading everybody — James Baldwin, Mark Twain" (Davis 23). Sayles also took a film class in college, attended some anti-war rallies, found an interest in acting — playing "large, brain-damaged people" (Zucker 329) — and established some important friendships, with Maggie Renzi and David Strathairn in particular. Typically, Sayles makes his time at Williams sound unremarkable. Yet he is not what he seems. Indeed, as Upton Brady, his original editor at Atlantic Monthly Press described Sayles, "He comes on like the village idiot, but behind that is one of the great storytellers — and a very, very sensible character" (Osborne 32).

After graduation in 1972, Sayles had a massive unpublished novel and no prospects. He traveled and wrote, blindly sending stories out to any and all magazines as he went (American Audio Prose Library). He worked as a day laborer, meat cutter, and hospital orderly, in factories and nursing homes, all jobs and settings that would reappear in his fiction and films. While working, Sayles continued sending out his stories. Unlike many writers, he simply enjoyed writing. He did not want to be a writer. That is, he suffered from no romantic illusions about the job — there were no long, smoke-filled nights in the garret sweating and scribbling away. Sayles wrote and mailed. The rejection slips piled up.

In 1974 Sayles mailed a long story to the *The Atlantic Monthly*. Someone turned the story over to the Atlantic Monthly Press, where editor Peggy Yntema suggested Sayles expand the manuscript into a novel. As he tells it, the story was originally a movie idea: "I started with a couple scenes that I saw dramatically, saw the setting, imagined a certain graininess to the image, heard a country-Western soundtrack compressed through a tinny box speaker" (*Thinking in Pictures* 4).

In 1975 the book was published as *Pride of the Bimbos*. "It was a real jeu d'esprit," observed Upton Brady. "There aren't many books you read about a dwarf private detective in drag playing baseball" (Osborne 33). Although he was still working odd jobs or collecting unemployment, Sayles had arrived. He then published a short story in *The Atlantic Monthly*, "I-80 Nebraska, m.490–m.205" (1975), which won an O. Henry Award for short fiction; his 1977 story "Golden State," also published in *The Atlantic Monthly*, also garnered an O. Henry Award. His second novel, *Union Dues*, was published in 1977 by Little, Brown and Company, a division of the Atlantic Monthly Press.

Then, in an improbable twist for a successful fiction writer, Sayles went to work for Roger Corman's New World Pictures writing drive-in schlock. He went into the entertainment industry to immerse himself in filmmaking: "I wasn't interested in getting a big house. All I was interested in was, I think it would be really great to make movies. This is the kind of storytelling that I really like. How do I get to do that and do that on my terms?" (Dreifus 33). Working for Corman proved to be fun and educational. Sayles acquired the knowledge necessary for making movies cheaply, efficiently, and independently. For Corman, Sayles wrote *Piranha* (1978), a *Jaws* parody that was his first Hollywood job, *The Lady in Red* (1979), a character study of John Dillinger's mistress, and *Battle Beyond the Stars* (1980), which sends the "magnificent seven" into outer space. He also scripted *Alligator* (1980) and Joe Dante's *The Howling* (1981). For *Alligator*, Sayles's screenplay followed the mutant creature from the sewer as it ate its way through the socioeconomic food chain: "It comes out of the sewer in the ghetto, then goes to a middle-class neighborhood, and then to a real kind of high-rent area" (Chute 58). *The Howling* is a werewolf satire that is both funny and gruesome. In the film's most hilarious sequence, a copulating couple are transformed into werewolves, reaching orgasm as they howl at the moon. Sayles's writing adds humor, verbal textures, and character touches that make these films much more interesting than they really should be.

While Sayles is best known for his film work, his fiction is also impressive. Like his movies, Sayles's fiction writing covers a lot of ground, revealing his eclectic interests. *Pride of the Bimbos* is a comic novel with a dark side about a five-man softball team that barnstorms the South. They call themselves the Brooklyn Bimbos. The Bimbos play in drag, and their star shortstop is a midget named Pogo Burns, who used to be a big-city detective and is on the lam from a giant black pimp named Dred. As in countless first novels, the theme of *Pride of the Bimbos* is manhood — masculinity and maturity. However, the book is actually a satire of American machismo. Here, Sayles's writing is rich and controlled, showing an original talent for articulating place and dialect.

Sayles's second book, *Union Dues,* tells the story of the death of sixties radicalism by dividing its attention between a seventeen-year-old runaway from rural West Virginia, Hobie McNatt, and his father, Hunter, who leaves his mining job to find his youngest son. The book examines the social and political climate in the United States in the late 1960s. In *Union Dues,* Sayles displays a sympathy for all sorts of political affiliations while keeping some critical distance.

The Anarchists' Convention (1979), a collection of short stories Sayles sold to raise money for the production of *Return of the Secaucus Seven,* shows Sayles's extraordinary ability to capture American speech. This book contains a series of Brian McNeil stories, as the high-school basketball player and dropout travels from place to place in true picaresque fashion. The title story displays Sayles's low-keyed humor, as a group of old-age radicals prepare for their annual reunion, carrying resentments and political feuds into one of their final gatherings.

Sayles's work as an independent filmmaker interrupted his steady flow of literary fiction, although he did not stop writing. *Thinking in Pictures: The Making of the Movie Matewan* (1987), Sayles's single nonfiction book, recalls every aspect of *Matewan*'s production and details how he makes films outside the Hollywood machinery. It was a major publication during a busy movie making period. But throughout the 1980s, in addition to his other work, Sayles did find time for smaller writing projects, contributing stories to *The Atlantic Monthly* and *Esquire,* reviewing William Goldman's *Adventures in the Screen Trade* for *Film Comment,* and covering the Republican National Convention for *The New Republic.* In the latter essay, a collage of revealing voices and telling descriptions, Sayles displays his ability to perfectly capture American oddities: "Detroit is like a theme park open just one week. Everything — the friendly cops, the ethnic food festival, the sunny weather and clean streets — is a special little time and reality warp, untouched by the world. It is the perfect environment for the Republican convention" (20). Sayles also exposes his political leanings in this essay.

Los Gusanos (1991), Sayles's latest novel, explores the Cuban exile community in Miami—the people Castro called "worms" upon their exodus—and their lost homeland. The novel is, among other things, highly political. As Randall Kenan pointed out in his review, "Sayles points an angry finger at the machinations of the F.B.I./C.I.A./Tio Sam, which we are led to believe still persist, a sinister ballet of entrapment that is one of the mainsprings of this novel, as people are deceived, manipulated, and eliminated" (858). *Los Gusanos* also contains numerous passages in Spanish, Sayles's reminder that America is a multilingual country, especially in its large urban areas. The structure of *Los Gusanos* parallels the structure of the films *City of Hope* and *Lone Star*, in which a large cast of people make up a community that is divisive, supportive, and corrupt.

Sayles's recent editor at HarperCollins, Terry Karten, compares him to Don DeLillo because of his politics, and to Gabriel García Márquez because he weaves multiple individual stories on a single narrative thread. Although the Márquez comparison seems a bit of a stretch, Sayles has great admiration for the Nobel Prize winner's fiction. Márquez indulges in the supernatural, or magic realism, which Sayles used definitively in two films, *The Secret of Roan Inish* and *Men With Guns* (*Hombres Armados*). The writer Thulani Davis suggests that Sayles can be compared to Robert Stone, for they are both concerned with the "idea that the ordinary individuals, with their dreams and hopes, play their parts but are damaged by the 'big picture' of powerful international forces" (21).

Sayles credits Nelson Algren's hobo novel *Somebody in Boots*, about a poor white Texas boy's itinerant life and criminal behavior during the depression, as the book that planted the germ of writing in his mind. "Algren wrote from neck-deep in the trash of American culture," Sayles remarked, "the only place I was ever likely to be" (Simpson 64). This quote underscores Sayles's contradictory nature—he is a savvy mixture of low culture and high culture, and embraces most of the cultures in between.

In addition to his fiction and film work, Sayles also explored theater and television. Sayles's two plays, *New Hope for the Dead* (1981) and *Turnbuckle* (1981), met with decidedly mixed reviews. What is interesting about the plays, however, is that they were staged outdoors on a Hudson River pier in New York City. While this fact may seem insignificant, it does indirectly connect Sayles with a forgotten American literary figure, Paul Green. Green, who practically invented outdoor drama in the United States (his 1937 play *The Lost Colony* is still produced annually on Roanoke Island), spoke to the failures of democratic ideals, a major theme in much of Sayles's work. Green, like Sayles, also observed and wrote about our stratified society and dealt with large themes in American history. For a time, Green attempted to live in Hollywood writing screenplays, but he found the commercial film industry to be debilitating. In the end it is the theater that connects Green and Sayles.

Unlike Green, however, Sayles found Hollywood to be more welcoming, especially for a writer of his talents, because he had no trouble giving studios exactly what they wanted: "Depending on the mandate from the producers hiring me, I either forget about the previous drafts and go back to scratch with the original concept, as in *Piranha* or *Alligator* or *The Howling*, or I try to improve the existing script in the direction they want to take it.... I was asked to come on to *Apollo 13* fairly late in their production — they had already cast the lead and had started building spaceship sets. The process was not so much damage control as bringing the story back toward the source material" (Mary Johnson 6–7). Sayles is a swift, efficient, and practical rewrite man. "Sometimes I've written a script and just not sent it in for another week," Sayles revealed to David Kipen, "just so people won't feel like, ho, this guy just dashed this thing off. If you just hand it in two weeks, [Hollywood producers] feel like they didn't get their money's worth" (Kipen 6). Sayles wrote a draft of John Frankenheimer's *The Challenge*, a modern-day samurai picture, over a long weekend, and dashed off *Alligator*, a Spielberg sendup, while waiting for the New Jersey Transit bus in the harmonious New York Port Authority bus terminal (Kipen 6).

Sayles's early successes allowed him entry into the world of commercial television. He feels that the film world has "ceded the real-life-problem drama to TV" (Davis 50), a condition reflected in programs such as *Hill Street Blues*, *St. Elsewhere*, *Homicide*, *ER*, *NYPD Blue*, and *Chicago Hope*. It is only natural, then, that Sayles would try his hand at television. His teleplays *A Perfect Match* (1980), an adaptation of Grace Paley's *Enormous Changes at the Last Minute* (1983), and *Unnatural Causes* (1986) revolve around left-leaning subjects and regular people. His short-lived weekly series *Shannon's Deal* (1989; series run, 1989–90) provides a good example of Sayles's varied talents. The protagonist, Jack Shannon, is a washed-up corporate lawyer trying to shake a gambling habit and a failed marriage. He is unorthodox in his approach to the law, an outsider trying to regain his bearings. But Shannon lacked glitz; in fact, the protagonist seldom saw the inside of a courtroom, settling his cases out of court, a bit of realism that probably cut into the show's ratings. It died quietly. As is his fashion, Sayles had some key collaborators working with him on this television program, including musician Wynton Marsalis. He also had a quirky team of writers and directors — John Byrum, Tom Rickman, Lewis Teague — and an excellent supporting cast, including Elizabeth Peña, Richard Edson, and Jennifer Lewis.

What stands out in *Shannon's Deal* is the storytelling, especially in Sayles's pilot episode. The characters are idiosyncratic and their speech flavors their individuality. Sayles takes the same narrative sense to all his projects. The three Bruce Springsteen videos he shot — "Born in the U.S.A.," "I'm on Fire," and "Glory Days"— are all enhanced by the visual story that Sayles created to go along with Springsteen's lyrics. In each case, Sayles was able to produce a sense of character, even within the limited space of a rock–TV video. Although not a musician himself, Sayles has composed songs for his own films: "Homeboy" and "Promised Land," for *The Brother from Another Planet*; "I Be Blue," for *Eight Men Out*; and "Calle Loca," for *City of Hope*.

Sayles also works as an actor, popping up in most of his own films, where he usually plays an unctuous jerk, freeing himself from any emotional investment in his character. Sayles has appeared as Howie in *Return of the Secaucus Seven*; Jerry in *Lianna*; an intergalactic bounty hunter in *The Brother from Another Planet*; the hardshell preacher in *Matewan*; Ring Lardner in *Eight Men Out*; and Carl in *City of Hope*. In addition, Sayles has acted in film and television. He appeared briefly in *Piranha* (1978); played the dopey morgue attendant in *The Howling* (1981); filled out the role of Don, an intellectual, philosophical drug dealer in *Hard Choices* (1986); exchanged sexually provocative lines with Melanie Griffith in Jonathan Demme's *Something Wild* (1986); entered the foreign language market in David Ferrario's *La Fine de la notte* (1988); showed up in *Little Vegas* (1990); took on the role of the military high commissioner, who rides around in a chauffeured limousine accompanied by a large fat pig, in Go Takemine's *Untamagiru* (1990); was Guy Girardi in *Straight Talk* (1992); worked as an FBI agent for Spike Lee in *Malcolm X* (1992); showed us what marginal producers are really like in *My Life's in Turnaround* (1993); and returned to work for his old colleague Joe Dante in *Matinee* (1993). Recently, Sayles appeared in Londie Curtis-Hall's *Gridlock'd* (1997), which, as he told Leonard Maltin, made Sayles "the only actor who ever worked with Tupac Shakur and Dolly Parton." Ken Burns asked Sayles to comment on baseball history for the PBS miniseries *Baseball* (1994). Perhaps Burns contacted Sayles because of *Eight Men Out*; or perhaps Burns saw Sayles play Roy "Lefty" Cobbs, an unusual pitcher, on *Mathnet* (1992), public television's mathematics show for children. Sayles started his career as an actor, working summer stock throughout New England, and all his film work reflects the appreciation he has for the actor's craft.

Sayles's approach to filmmaking constitutes a radical break from Hollywood's blockbuster, star-driven mentality. Like his sprawling novels, Sayles's films tackle whole worlds, not one point of view. What comes through in all of his films is his strong sense of story, character, politics, class, and the desire to wrap all his interests in a realistic package that makes for literate, informative viewing.

Indeed, the film subjects Sayles explores are shown to be rare among American directors: *Return of the Secaucus Seven* (1980) is a witty elegy to members of his generation as they face turning 30; *Baby, It's You* (1983), his first industry-backed feature, is an antiromantic high school coming-of-age film with a class-conscious romance at its center; *Lianna* (1983) is a film of homosexual awakening that refuses to degenerate into cheap sensationalism; *The Brother from Another Planet* (1984) explores with sly humor the problem of race in America (among other things); *Matewan* (1987) depicts a neglected

Matinee *(1992): Sayles often acts in his own films, usually playing an unsavory or stupid character incapable of emotional or intellectual change, which, according to the actor, limits his preparation time. Here Sayles is reunited with Dick Miller, part of New World's stable of actors, and Joe Dante, who directed two of Sayles's screenplays. Sayles (left) and Miller (center) portray Bob and Herb, members of a right-wing Christian organization who protest the opening of the latest horror-fest by Lawrence Woolsey (John Goodman, right) in Key West, Florida. In reality, Bob and Herb are two blacklisted screenwriters who Woolsey, a.k.a. the "Master of Movie Horror," hired to help him promote his film. Photo by Dean Williams, courtesy of the Museum of Modern Art Film Stills Archive.*

piece of American labor history; *Eight Men Out* (1988) is a baseball film that exposes the sticky romanticism of the game which had some industry financing; *City of Hope* (1991) is one of the few honest films ever made about big city politics; *Passion Fish* (1992) is a lyrical, poetic story about two emotionally damaged, independent women who unexpectedly discover that they must rely on each other in order to get by; *The Secret of Roan Inish* (1994), a children's tale set in Ireland, explores culture, spirit, myth, and the physical world; *Lone Star* (1996) is a historic murder mystery set in Frontera, Texas, where the Anglo-Mexican border offers a rich, complex metaphor that Sayles examines with dramatic and visual intensity; and *Men With Guns*, a film in Spanish, set in Latin America, is about a doctor who discovers that many of his students, whom he has sent out to treat the rural poor, have been murdered by the government. Currently, Sayles is working on *Limbo*, a film set in Alaska and starring David Strathairn which deals with commercial fishing, generational change, and two people with opposite ways of looking at the world.

In 1983 Sayles received a MacArthur Foundation grant, the so-called genius award given to selected Americans in diverse fields for innovative work. Sayles won his for artistic achievement in film. The award provided him with a tax-free $32,000 grant every year for five years. Since he was always walking a financial tightrope during his early filmmaking years, the grant allowed Sayles to work with a net. Since then Sayles's movies have been recognized at a variety of film festivals, on commercial Ten-Best lists, at the Independent Spirit Awards, and, finally, by the Academy of Motion Picture Arts and Sciences, which nominated his screenplays for *Passion Fish* and *Lone Star* for Best Original Screenplay awards. Sayles now jokingly refers to himself as an "ex-genius" (Minsky 40).

Sayles still publishes stories, including "Peeling," a rollicking piece revolving around a group of Louisiana crawfish workers, for *The Atlantic Monthly* in 1993, and "Keeping Time," a rock 'n' roll story, also published in 1993, for *Rolling Stone* magazine. But the movies take up most of his current writing life. Speaking of Sayles's relationship with Hollywood, producer Peggy Rajski remarked to Thulani Davis, "Are they after him to write scripts? Yes, all the time. Are they beating down his door to direct? No" (50). But this condition does not seem to bother him. Sayles's screenwriting trade still pays the bills and he is in real demand. His status as an outsider is shifting, however, and he is beginning to receive notice as a director. Recently, Sayles joined the Directors Guild of America because the DGA's Terry Casaletta adjusted the organization's rules and regulations to help independent film directors (Asinof On Line. Internet 4). In November 1997, the Library of Congress added *Return of the Secaucus Seven* to its National Film Registry. Sayles now works as an advisor for Next Wave Films, the finishing fund company for emerging filmmakers formed by the Independent Film Channel. And Sayles's Anarchists' Convention production company provided financial backing for writer-director Alejandro Springall's *Santitos* (*Traveling Saints*), a tale of a woman's journey from rural Mexico to Los Angeles (Kelley On Line. Internet. passim). Still, Sayles is best known for the characters he creates, and his list of awards continues to grow. In April 1997 he received an Imagen Award, which recognizes film and television programming portraying Latinos in a positive light, for *Lone Star*. And, in 1998, the University of San Jose presented Sayles with its John Steinbeck Award. The Writers Guild Foundation, an affiliate of the writers' union, recognized Sayles with its 1998 lifetime achievement award. Sayles tempered his acceptance of the award: "It's great to be honored by other writers, but I honestly don't feel like I've been out there long enough to get that, and I have things I'm still doing" (Sterngold 6).

As a filmmaker Sayles is difficult to categorize, although popular critics attempt to do so with the release of each new film. Uncomfortable with the word *artist*, Sayles calls himself a storyteller, plain and simple. He is, of course, far, far more than that. In a stunning reappraisal of Sayles's film work in *Film Comment*, Andrew Sarris positioned Sayles in his taxonomy of American film directors: "In an age of cynicism and derision, John Sayles emerges ... as a cinematic poet of consonance and goodwill, and heaven knows we need him" (30).

2

New World Pictures: Training, Fun, Profit

> The transition I was able to make from writing fiction to making movies was a case not of graduating from one to the other, of moving up or down, but of eventually having the practical means to do another kind of storytelling I'd always been interested in.
>
> — John Sayles (*Thinking in Pictures*)

In order to get *Union Dues* published, Sayles acquired a literary agent, someone "who had business connections with an agency in Hollywood" (Chute 57). Because he was always interested in screenwriting, Sayles sent his agent's contacts on the West Coast a letter of inquiry and a sample screenplay, his treatment of Eliot Asinof's *Eight Men Out*, the story behind the Chicago Black Sox scandal of 1919. The heady script, however, only worked as a Hollywood calling card because the film rights to Asinof's book were already under contract and unavailable to Sayles. Still, the agency, Robinson, Weintraub, Gross and Associates, Inc., decided to represent Sayles, provided he move to the West Coast for a while, which he and Maggie Renzi did, settling in Santa Barbara.

Through the agency, Sayles was contracted by Roger Corman, who directed Edgar Allan Poe tales for American International Pictures before founding his own company — New World Pictures — the renowned B picture training ground for countless moviemaking personnel during the late 1960s and throughout the 1970s, including Monte Hellman, Francis Ford Coppola, Peter Bogdanovich, Joe Dante, Paul Bartel, Martin Scorsese, and Ron Howard. Indeed, Corman, according to David Thompson, "seized what was a dying form, reestablished its worth, and managed to introduce its crazy disciplines to the indulgent perceptions of underground cinema" (149). Sayles wrote three low-budget films for Corman and New World and learned how to make commercial features on a tight budget with little time.

"The first decent offer I got," Sayles recalls, "was the rewrite on *Piranha*" (Chute 57). Sayles credits Frances Doel, Corman's story editor, for helping him secure the job because "she read fiction for pleasure (a rarity in Hollywood)" and was familiar with his work (*Thinking in Pictures* 5). As originally conceived, *Piranha* (1978) was to be a *Jaws* parody, chock-full of B genre conventions, including nudity, bloody deaths, and seat-grabbing suspense. Until he went to work for New World, Sayles had no formal screenwriting training, although his fiction resonates with crisp dialogue, the bedrock, according to most critics, of any good screenplay. "Basically," Sayles notes, "I was self-taught. I had seen a lot of movies — that was my film school" (Schlesinger 2). Corman told Sayles, "Forget this script, keep the name *Piranha*, we've test marketed it, it tested very high, and keep the idea of piranhas in North American waters. Make it something like *Jaws*" (Auster and Quart 330). *Piranha* fulfills generic expectations, like most of the New World library, but has a sociopolitical twist, the Sayles touch. *Piranha*, as film historian Gerald Mast notes, takes a "violent nibble at the military, the Vietnam War, Bob Hope, and capitalist priorities" (*Short History* 547). In other words, *Piranha* is drive-in fare for a sophisticated audience.

Corman provided an end point for Sayles: the carnivorous fish would descend on a summer camp, where children would be happily frolicking in the water. In addition, Corman wanted the thrills packaged into a 90- to 100-minute block. Sayles designed a fish attack or the threat of a fish attack for every ten minutes of screen time. Yet the movie idea that Sayles inherited from Richard Robinson, who wrote the original story, had one logical flaw: "If you know there are piranha in the water, why not stay out of the river?" (*Thinking in Pictures* 6). This formal problem supplied Sayles with *Piranha*'s central image: people poling down a piranha-infested river to warn others about the flesh-eating fish. Sayles contrived a schematic to flesh out the film's narrative:

> I drew a picture of a river and a lake ... but there's no point where the people are going to have a rest. So I drew a dam in the middle of it: the first half of the movie is getting to this dam; the second half of this movie is the piranhas getting around this dam, and then it started taking shape before I had any characters. [Schlesinger 3]

Initially, Sayles kept the script "actor proof," and, because no director had been chosen while he was writing drafts, he wrote the script as if he were going to direct the film himself, "a full shooting script with each cut away detailed and nothing left for a director to fill in" (*Thinking in Pictures* 6). Sayles's early approach to screenwriting underscores his cinematic sensibility:

> Most critics figure that the dialogue is the screenplay, but I write shooting scripts, I write images. I always try to do things with as little dialogue as possible. Especially on an action thing, like *Piranha* ... I think about how I would tell the story if it was a silent movie, so that Japanese people could

understand it without subtitles. I have a lot of pictures in my head, and I reinforce them with dialogue. [Chute 59]

Joe Dante eventually directed *Piranha*, and, as Sayles notes, he "did more than fill in the action described in the screenplay, taking it as suggestions he was free to use or not use as he saw fit" (*Thinking in Pictures* 6). With little money and uncompromising logistical problems, part of life at New World where films were made quickly and cheaply, Sayles and Dante debuted with a solid piece of filmmaking, which made money for Corman and guaranteed both the writer and the director more film work. *Piranha* put people in the river and they were eaten, and that, as Sayles recalls, was his job: "That's basically what they paid me ten thousand dollars for. The film came out well and made lots of money for them" (Auster and Quart 330).

Sayles's characters are noteworthy because while they do things normally associated with B genre schlock — die shocking deaths, occasionally remove their clothes, utter saucy double entendres — they are also witty people with identities and histories, as Sayles pointed out to Tom Schlesinger:

> I'm very concerned with what people do for a living. So in *Piranha*, I had a guy who used to work in the mill that had been flooded in order to make a resort. He had a grudge against this lake. He almost hated the river and hated the lake because it had taken his job away from him. The girl was a skip tracer, and it was her job to find people as it was his job to hate the lake and sort of drink. So immediately, when they were on this river, there was something about it — she was always looking for someone and he was always grumbling. [4]

Moreover, Sayles's B film work contains political and philosophical slants that stretch generic convention. Writing in *Film Comment*, Andrew Sarris says that Sayles's early "screenwriting lifted the horror genre to a level of wit and humor and irony that startled mainstream critics" (29).

Indeed, not only did Sayles learn about moviemaking working for the New World factory, he enjoyed an appealing freedom: "Once you agree on a premise — like, this is about piranhas eating people in North American waters — you could pretty much do anything you wanted" (Chute 57). And Sayles did just that, even though he toed the line in order to appease Corman, who, Joe Dante believes, "is not interested in character," at least not when it comes to his exploitation films (Chute 58).

Piranha's opening sequence straddles the line between B film conventions and cinematic homage, often part of the New World look. The film starts like *Citizen Kane*: We see a NO TRESPASSING sign, and then the camera rises up and over a fence. We have entered secret territory, but not the baroque, psychological world of Charles Foster Kane. Rather, we are swept into the libidinous world of teen horror pics, which is more fun. It is midnight, and two characters, a man and a woman on a backpacking trip, venture into the no trespassing zone, where they find an inviting swimming pool. The young woman entices her partner into taking a swim by removing her clothes and jumping in. Her partner follows without hesitation. Then we see a point-of-view shot from below. Before the credits appear on the screen we have witnessed two deaths connected to the promise of sex, a time-honored horror film tradition. The screams of the dying couple are juxtaposed with a shot of the moon, which recalls the midnight swim sequence that opens *Jaws*. This shot, however, also recalls Luis Buñuel's surreal *Un Chien Andalou*— or just about any horror film made between 1940 and the present, where sexual imagery takes on absurd connotations. As *Piranha* makes abundantly clear, not only do Sayles and Dante know movies, they also know how to appeal to a diverse crowd. In fact, most Roger Corman B productions pop with outrageous narrative and insider film jokes, making for deliciously decadent viewing.

B movies came of age in the mid–1930s with the invention of the double bill, an audience magnet, particularly during the depression, because the double feature appeared to give ticket buyers a good deal. The B movie, made at a much lower cost than the A film, was never intended to do anything except economically fill up screen time. Corman learned how to make these low-end films at American International, but his pictures were designed to stand on their own merits. Films like *Piranha* are more appropriately called exploitation films, not secondary fillers. Corman's films appeal to the drive-in crowd, young thrill seekers, and film-savvy folks seeking subversive pleasures. In fact, according to David Thompson, "in 1970, the enterprising Edinburgh Film Festival ran a program of Corman films to crystallize the growing interest in his work among avant-garde critics" (149). Yet even intellectual exploitation films demand certain elements, like the sexual invitation that opens *Piranha*. The liberating quality of exploitation films, of course, lies just below the image we see on the screen, beyond what Stephen King calls "oogah-boogah," that moment when the audience is invited up the stairs into the forbidden room and then scared to death (37). This shock, as James Twitchell observes, must be "short-lived and cannot be stretched out or the effect will be lost" (45). *Piranha*'s thrills, indeed, come with deadly efficiency. Everyone, it seems, experiences a fish bite, even if they do not die. More often than not these attacks are played for comic effect, not dreadful pleasure. What makes *Piranha* fun is its leftist politics, as Sayles willingly points out: "In *Piranha* the horror is caused by the military, and I hope that there's some kind of awareness, from the characters themselves, that we've been down this river before" (Chute 58).

Within this context, one sequence in particular stands out. Here, Paul Grogan (Bradford Dillman), the unemployed, heartbroken sodden mill worker, Maggie McKeown (Heather Menzies), the skip chaser, and Dr. Robert Hoak (Kevin McCarthy), the academic research scientist now working for the military, find themselves together on Sayles's centerpiece, the wooden raft. Sayles's dialogue illustrates his humor, politics, and ability to link a disparate group of people.

> MAGGIE: The government paid you?
>
> HOAK: Of course they paid. Whether it's germ warfare, the bomb, chemical warfare, there's plenty of money. Special agencies. They pay. They pay a lot better than they do in private research.
>
> GROGAN: For raisin' fish.
>
> HOAK: No. It's a matter of genetics. Radiation. Selective breeding. They called it Operation Razor Teeth.
>
> MAGGIE: What was it for?
>
> HOAK: To destroy the river systems of the North Vietnamese. Our goal was to develop a strain of this killer fish that could survive in cold water, and then breed at an accelerated rate. We had everything. Blank check. And then the war ended.

Maggie's character fills a role that will become familiar in most of Sayles's scripts: she is our guide, asking the questions needed to make sense of the bizarre situation in which these characters find themselves, because she, like us, is new to the territory. Grogan, the laconic, dissolute mountain man who seeks a mission to revive his life, adds sardonic humor to the mix, complaining in a voice often heard in working-class bars. Dr. Hoak, a twisted, misunderstood research scientist right out of central casting, supplies comic, politically telling dialogue. Hoak's experiments should raise questions about morality, government, and the very nature of human life. Yet Hoak considers himself to be free from all blame because of his profession, a form of work taken for granted even by his employer:

> GROGAN: You sound disappointed.
>
> HOAK: They poisoned the water. After all that work. Poisoned the water.
>
> MAGGIE: But some survived.
>
> HOAK: We developed a lot of mutants, and a few of them were able to resist the poison. They ate their own. Their own dead. And then they began to breed like some wild species. Suddenly there were hundreds, maybe thousands.

Cleverly, Sayles has established the invisible threat from within, a condition created by the military-industrial complex. What Hoak does not realize, however, is that a disgruntled military official, passed over for a higher rank, who oversees the doctor's experiments, has hooked up with Buck Gardner (Dick Miller), a Bob Hope–like glad-handing real estate investor, to create an adult getaway on the river, and nothing, not even the threat of man-eating fish, can interfere with the resort's grand opening. Once the presence of the mutant fish has been logically established, we follow a bloody, watery trail to the film's conclusion, underwater carnage at the resort. But, as this early scene demonstrates, Sayles gets his digs in whenever and wherever he can:

> GROGAN: Our tax dollars at work, huh?
>
> HOAK: Well, that's science in the service of the defense effort.
>
> GROGAN: Sure. Spreadin' strains of bacteria in the subway system.
>
> MAGGIE: You put them in the river where they could kill people, including civilians and little kids swimming in the rivers.
>
> HOAK: I never killed anybody. If you want to talk about killing you talk to your politicians, the military people. Oh, no! I'm a scientist.

Rather than editorialize scenes, in the manner of Sam Fuller or Larry Cohen, or completely give in to the indulgent ideas, Sayles returns to his primary plot by introducing fresh drama, refocusing our attention on the river.

> GROGAN: Kids in the water.
>
> MAGGIE: What?
>
> GROGAN: The dam. They let the water through every couple of days, you know, to keep the level steady on the new lake. The resort's down there, summer camp. All those kids. Come on!

Through dialogue, Sayles pumps tension back into the scene, which has provided a bit of relief after two unexpected killings. Sayles understands that the pace of any film is an important script ingredient:

> It's more important how you handle the time period as far as the audience's relief and tension is concerned. I think that people like Hitchcock are the best at that because they'll have some stupid little scene and if you looked at it on paper you'd ask, What is this scene for? But he put it there because he's sort of lulling people so that he can shock them or give them a break after a big suspense sequence. [Schlesinger 3–4]

Even in an early script like that of *Piranha*, Sayles's expertise in creating the rhythm of a film is unmistakable. The piranha attacks are fierce and shocking, a pattern reminiscent of Hitchcock's *The Birds* (1963), which set the standard for the natural horrors that gobbled their way through the 1960s and 1970s. Moreover, Sayles's *Piranha* was a shooting script, indicating shot numbers and editorial transitions. Therefore, after making his audience aware of the fishy threat that the military bankrolled and science created, Sayles's script suggests a cut to a long shot of children splashing in the water at the Lost River Summer Camp, a place to keep the kiddies while their parents frolic at the new resort development. The piranha, it seems, will not go hungry. The setup is predictable, a bit of guilty fun designed to keep the audience waiting for the big feed. Sayles then returns to the raft, where Dr. Hoak begins to come to terms with his own culpability:

HOAK: I was pure research. No scrounging for grant money. No academic politics. You don't know what that means to a scientist!

MAGGIE: You fed them! You kept them alive!

HOAK: I continued the experiment. There was so much more I could do with the species. So much further I could take them ... [pause]. You're not holding me responsible?

[Cut to individual reaction shots.]

HOAK: I think you are. You pulled the plug and you're holding me responsible. You're blaming me. Incredible!

Hoak's moral detachment will be short lived; he has provided the audience all the information he can — now he is piranha chum. Hoak has reminded Maggie that she too must share some of the responsibility for releasing the deadly fish into the river. What is telling here, however, is the amount of information Sayles packs into a small space. On-screen the lines are funny, emotional, and, for a horror film, almost believable. In many ways, *Piranha* is a better film than *Jaws* just because of its unrelenting political assault and the giddy confidence of Sayles's script.

Sayles, of course, does not take his exploitation work too seriously, as he remarked to an interviewer:

> Somebody from one of the more "intellectual" film journals was talking to me about *Piranha* and how horror movies are always an allegory for something and I was trying to convince him that *Piranha* was actually an allegory to the cultural revolution in China and the piranhas were the Red Guard, and the four bad guys were the Gang of Four, and the heroes were actually Mao having let these things out accidentally and trying to get them back in. It works, but almost anything works when you look at it that way. [Schlesinger 3]

Still, *Piranha*'s politics are unmistakable. At the conclusion of the film, we witness a scene that recalls the evacuation of Saigon more than the Chinese cultural revolution. The piranha bring tumultuous havoc to the Lost River Resort, ruining its kitschy opening, much to the displeasure of its investors and promoters. When Buck Gardner hears from his right-hand man that the fish are causing a problem, he snaps, "What about the goddamn piranha?" His lackey responds, "They are eating the guests, sir." Because there is a great deal of money involved in the Lost River Resort, Gardner elects to go on with the program, conveniently ignoring the fact that his guests are being devoured by renegade fish. The Colonel, Gardner's partner, finds himself on a houseboat in the middle of the manmade lake surrounded by happy customers floating, swimming, and paddling. When the fish attack, people frantically try to climb on board the houseboat, much the way South Vietnamese refugees attempted to board American helicopters leaving the U.S. Embassy in Saigon. The military man pushes people off the houseboat, back toward certain death in the bloody, churning water. The Colonel, however, is outnumbered, and soon he finds himself overboard, where a uniform offers little protection against hundreds of razor-sharp teeth. He falls prey to his own military operation.

Sayles also slips in a wry bit of environmental criticism here. The real estate speculators have redesigned the river for profit. The river, in turn, exacts its revenge as the conduit for the man-eating fish. The fish, of course, are also the result of tampering with the natural order, a classic literary theme that Sayles blends with popular horror. Sayles's script upholds the tradition established in American science fiction films of the 1950s, such as *Them!* (1954), *Invasion of the Body Snatchers* (1956), or *The Blob* (1958), which, as Gerald Mast notes, "surveyed a universe with no limits whatever on our knowledge or potential for either creation or destruction" (299). *Piranha* is about the creation of monsters, human and marine, and the gruesome destruction they cause.

Sayles's script does not end with the death of the bad guy, however. The frantic action, generated by surreal military thinking fused to real estate flimflam, continues unabated. Our hero, Grogan, a victim of the real estate marketplace when the smelter where he used to work was closed and then submerged in the Lost River Lake, contrives a suitable death for the unstoppable fish. Because this mutant strain of piranha can survive in salt water and because the Lost River empties into the ocean, the marauding fish pose a threat to the entire planet, not just to the bucolic river community they are buzzing their way through. Grogan's solution is to "pollute the bastards to death" by opening the underwater tanks filled with toxic residue from the smelter. To that end, Grogan ties himself to a length of rope strapped to the bow of a boat, dives into the river, swims into the submerged smelting plant, and opens the chemical tanks, even though he is under constant assault by the piranha. Maggie remains in the boat counting to 100, per Grogan's instructions. When she reaches her goal, Maggie opens the boat's throttle and zooms away, pulling Grogan away from both the toxic release and the munching fish. Sayles's comic deus ex machina is so bizarre it works.

Of course, as James Twitchell correctly points out, this type of ending "may make an interesting social exemplar," but it provides little in the way of fright (47). Yet it is difficult to believe that Corman, Dante, and Sayles actually set out to scare people; rather, they made a smart, funny film that some members of the audience might mistake for serious horror. New World never camouflages its mixture of vulgarity, humor, and chronic lack of detail. Nothing got in the way of the fun. In fact, Sayles, upholding a valuable exploitation tradition, opens the gates for a return of the fishy man-eaters, matching the regenerative power of the shark from *Jaws*. Sayles, however, sends his mutants into roman-numeral life with a horrific twist featuring famed femme fatale Barbara Steele, of Great Britain's Hammer Films. Steele plays Dr. Mengers, a scientist tied to the military operation and cover-up. As she stands on a beach being interviewed by a news crew, the interviewer asks her if there is any chance that the fish could survive the toxic release and actually make it to the ocean. The doctor looks directly into the camera and responds, "There is nothing left to fear." Horror film aficionados, of course, know better. Steele's presence adds fiendish delight to *Piranha*. Her remark deliberately recalls the apocalyptic undercurrent in most horror films, especially those that recycled monsters for more box office returns.

Sayles also makes a brief, uncredited appearance in *Piranha*. He plays an MP designated to guard a tent holding Grogan and Maggie, incarcerated because they know that the Brazilian river munchers are heading toward the Lost River Resort. Grogan tells Maggie to "seduce" the guard, so they can get on with the business of saving innocent lives, a difficult task as they always arrive after a piranha repast. The stalwart Maggie agrees, but pauses to ask a question seldom considered when movie women seduce movie men: "What if he's gay?" "Then I'll seduce him," Grogan replies, which is hardly appropriate for an American action hero. Outside the tent Maggie confronts Sayles's MP, clearly a half-wit. Maggie immediately blurts out, "Are you gay?" The MP is flummoxed, asking Maggie what she means by that question. Quickly Maggie moves around the guard, forcing him to turn his back to the tent. Then Maggie does what any young, B movie heroine would — she tears open her shirt. The MP loses himself. Grogan then throws a bag over the MP's head and ties him up. This scene presents an ironic movie in-joke: the screenwriter, usually a marginal player after shooting begins, gets an intimate view of the leading lady.

Piranha, because it is parodic, subverts convention with giddy confidence. For example, we never actually see the piranha; instead, we see a lot of red dye in the water, some Maytag agitation, and we hear a sound effect that resembles an overworked circular saw. These low-rent effects add a sneaky charm to the film, making it more than a routine gorefest; this is a film that takes tongue-in-cheek pride in itself. The film's cast is also dispatched quickly, especially cameo performers like McCarthy, Keenan Wynn, and Bruce Gorman, all of whom die with comic zest. Casting these recognizable actors helps to move Sayles's script along because they deliver the dialogue professionally. Wynn, for instance, plays the river rat Jack, a good neighbor who delivers booze to Grogan on a weekly basis. His function is twofold: We wonder why Grogan needs so much liquor, and Jack, always accompanied by his faithful dog, is someone we can relate to. Like so many doomed monster movie characters, Jack has charm, so when we see him sitting on the edge of his dock talking to his dog with his feet hanging in the water, our first impulse is to scream at him, "Pull your feet up!" Of course Jack, like the other causalities, is a stroke too slow to escape Sayles's hungry school of predators.

Interestingly, *Piranha* is a movie in which one of the heroes, rather than some twisted scientist, unleashes destruction on the world; it is a movie in which the heroes cannot prevent a high body count; and it is a movie in which the raging menace survives. *Piranha* also undermines the family — these fish gorge themselves on a lake full of innocent children, a sequence even the most grotesque horror films avoid. Sayles's script moves with speed and efficiency. After the film ends, we have to stop and think about the crackpot tale he has foisted upon us. What stands out are his characters and their language, unique to the image-driven exploitation picture. Even if they are slated for early disposal, Sayles's characters move the story forward by communicating essential facts. His characters are real, spontaneous, normal folks caught up in bizarre circumstances.

Discovering the unexpected in the everyday, of course, is what Sayles does best. *The Lady in Red* (1979), his second New World film, strives for more realism, at least on paper: "*The Lady in Red* didn't turn out the way I wanted because they just didn't have the budget to make the movie right. I wanted that to be a real breathless, 30s, Jimmy Cagney everybody talking-fast type movie. It turned out a little more like Louis Malle" (Schlesinger 3). Indeed, much of *The Lady in Red* is well managed, even cautious like much of Malle's work. Still, Lewis Teague, Corman's director, did not allow caution and good taste to completely smother Sayles's depiction of Prohibition-era Chicago.

The Lady in Red tells the story of Polly Franklin (Pamela Sue Martin), the woman who, according to folklore, betrayed John Dillinger, one of America's most famous criminals. Her heart set on a singing and dancing career, Polly sets out for Chicago, fleeing her strict father. She then progresses through a series of jobs that describe her character and the social conditions that limited a young woman without money or education. Sayles sees the story in terms of work: "She started out as this farm kid who worked for her father, who was an asshole. She ends up working in a sweat-shop, being a dime-a-dance girl, being in prison and doing work there, then becoming a prostitute and then becoming a bank robber" (Schlesinger 4). Polly's progression creates an episodic structure for the movie, much like *Piranha*. After being branded by the press as the infamous "lady in red," Polly turns to crime, and as the movie ends, she heads toward the California dream coast with a bag of money and a bit of hope. In keeping with the exploitation tradition, *The Lady in Red* presents plenty of sex and plenty of blood.

We follow Polly over three years of her life, often a dark, moving story that fuses personal politics with the then dormant gangster picture. In fact, Sayles remarked to David Chute that after extensive period research, with the help of the Chicago Historical Society, the script became one that "he might have enjoyed directing himself" (58). The rich social observation that still filters through on the screen connects to Sayles's social and political sensibility. After all, Polly, a woman mythologized by the media, only sought legitimate, steady work, and she lived with the choices that she was forced to make. Sayles, however, suggests that his script went even deeper:

Lady in Red, which did not turn out very well, and probably will not be seen unless it's on Home Box Office, was a revisionist gangster film. It was basically a very political film about why the FBI was chasing after this hick bank robber, John Dillinger, instead of looking into Lucky Luciano, who was taking over prostitution in Chicago. However, by the time the film was made, some performances weren't what they could be; most of the scenes that explained why things happened were gone, and so what was left were scenes where people shot each other. [Auster and Quart 331]

Clearly, Sayles did not like the final version of *The Lady in Red*, because most of the film's political spine was removed. He learned that once you turn a script over to a studio, even an enlightened one like New World, it becomes their property. Although an ambitious company, New World always kept an eye trained on the bottom line. *The Lady in Red* reveals the production limits that New World worked within. Still, *The Lady in Red* marks a somewhat ambitious turn for New World, considering the film's feminist perspective and sociopolitical commentary.

Because bloody shootouts punctuate the film from beginning to end, the film satisfies the generic requirements of an action picture. What makes it quirky is Sayles's portrait of Polly Franklin. In true antiheroic fashion, we root for her from the start of the film. When her taciturn father grumbles, "You'd better hustle your tail back here. You have those pullets to tend to," we want her to stay out all night, which she does. Polly is full of desire and imagination, and Sayles's script quickly makes us privy to her private life: She dances and sings while tending to her chickens, and she steals photo stills from the local movie marquee. Clearly, she is a rebellious youth, cut from the same cloth as Marlon Brando's character in *The Wild One* (1953) or James Dean's in *Rebel Without a Cause* (1955). Polly rebels against rural conformity. But Sayles's script blunts rebellious romanticism. Polly is used as a shield by a gang of bank robbers, who leave the main street of her hometown wet with blood. She is held on the running board of the getaway car by a stylish gun moll (Mary Warnov), in a "Perils of Pauline" manner. Polly becomes famous for a moment, and an oily newspaperman, who is looking for a story, seduces her. When she finally returns home from her life-changing adventure, her father beats her for disobeying him. So Polly takes to the road, in the American tradition.

Chicago initiates Polly into the world of politics, economics, and sex. She is befriended by Rose Shimkus (Laurie Heineman), a character loosely based on Emma Goldman. Rose is politically committed to unionism. When she offends her boss, Patrick (Dick Miller), by tending to his mistress, who is bleeding because of a botched abortion, he turns her over to the Industrial Squad, police goons who handle union organizers. Polly then instigates a floor revolt, a fracas involving all the sweatshop workers, after which she loses her job. Soon she and Rose are reunited in prison. In order to gain her own release and to protect Rose, whose health is poor and who remains incarcerated, Polly agrees to work as a prostitute for the prison matron, Tiny Alice (Nancy Anne Parsons). The Chicago bordello, run by the classy, connected Anna Sage (Louis Fletcher), is upscale, serving politicians, gangsters, and assorted swells. It is here, in a Dickensian coincidence, that Polly meets the heartless newspaperman who took her virginity and then turned his back on her. Seeing her in the bordello, he says, "Always glad to see a young girl find gainful employment." Needless to say, Polly's situation has spiraled downward, yet she displays relentless grit and determination.

Though muted and truncated by New World, Sayles's script deftly circumscribes generic conventions here: unionism, economic oppression, and political power. The bordello scenes also allow Teague ample opportunity to run low-budget riffs on scenes from Malle's *Pretty Baby* (1980), which captured its bordello interiors from the point of view of a child, a mise-en-scène strategy *The Lady in Red* deliberately avoids. The prostitutes, for example, are used in a bizarre nude tableau across a Chicago mobster's lawn, adding a decadent seasoning to a raucous party. This bacchanalia, however, is disrupted by a gangland killing, sending mobsters, women, and waiters running for cover. Polly, who has slept with the killer, recognizes him but conceals his identity from the police. In the end, the hitman, Jake Lingle (Robert Hogan), returns the favor by executing the imperious newspaperman, which illustrates Sayles's desire to connect seemingly unrelated characters.

The narrative linkage that Sayles attempts to achieve in all of his film work follows from the screenwriting formula of Allan Dwan, a well-known silent-era screenwriter who wrote *Sands of Iwo Jima* (1950), among numerous other films. Sayles described Dwan's technique to John Schlesinger: "If you draw lines of emotional connection between the characters, you have to have at least two coming from every person" (5). The connections among the characters in *The Lady in Red* are rather overt. Tiny Alice, for example, exerts power inside the women's prison in the same fashion that the Mob and politicians do on the outside. She, in fact, has Mob and political connections. Yet Sayles allows the social order inside prison to be challenged by the inmates in a scene that recalls the sweatshop revolt. Rose is killed by Tiny Alice, but, in a show of solidarity, the other inmates kill Tiny Alice by sticking her head in a hair dryer and then drenching her with water. Polly sees that Rose's coffin is draped with a red flag, complete with hammer and sickle. Furthermore, the slimy newspaperman is no better than the violent characters he pursues for the sake of his job. He only hides behind the mask of objective reporting. Jake Lingle shows more integrity by killing the newsman for Polly, because his is an act of honor, a payback, not simply a self-serving gesture. For the most part, every character in the film, even minor figures, has significance. This design appeals to Sayles, and it becomes his screenwriting signature.

Usually, peripheral characters stand only in service to the plot. But Sayles attempts to add some level of meaning to all of his characters. As an illustration Sayles explains the function of a minor character from the picture: "There was a cop named Hennessey who at first we see as a bag man for the mob, and then he had another line, sleeping with the Madam, and then he also had a connection to the FBI" (Schlesinger 5). Although seemingly insignificant, playing just another corrupt Chicago cop, he is indeed well connected. He is, in fact, "the spider in the middle of the web," according to Sayles (Schlesinger 5). The multiple characters in *The Lady in Red* serve as a structural model for Sayles's ensemble approach to screenwriting.

Sayles's script, because it focuses on people and images, tempers New World's frantic visual momentum. Characters such as Pinetop (Rod Gist) and Pops Geissler (Peter Hobbs), two honorable men who work for Anna Sage, are drawn with emotional understanding. The choices they make ring true. Even Christopher Lloyd's murderous, deviate Frognose makes sense. Still, this is an exploitation picture meant to entertain. And Sayles knows how to appeal to a popular audience, even when he injects scenes with his own rueful awareness. "Steven Spielberg and George Lucas do not sit around wondering, 'What's good product, what will those suckers go for?' That's what I respect about those guys," says Sayles. "I have different taste, and maybe different values, but I never feel condescension there. The most successful movies, no matter how schlocky, have that quality. Like Russ Meyer, who said, 'Americans like square chins and big tits, and so do I'" (Aufderheide *Cineaste* 15). Much like Meyer, the king of exploitation sex films, Sayles produced work for New World that had the requisite number of breasts, but the films also had an intellectual sense that pushed the genre.

For example, John Dillinger's death sequence resonates on multiple levels. Dillinger (Robert Conrad) enters Polly's life unexpectedly, and she thinks that he will be the man she can settle down with, but after he is gunned down outside the Biograph Theater, where they watched *Manhattan Melodrama*, she discovers his true identity and that he had been lying to her all along by saying he worked at a "commodities exchange." But his grisly death and not his companionship will change Polly again, making her a renowned figure. Dillinger is slaughtered in bloody slow motion, a low-rent Sam Peckinpah death scene. After Dillinger is killed, however, the press with its power takes over. We see Polly captured in numerous camera flashes as we hear the word spread that the dead man is John Dillinger. People then begin to sop up his blood, which is running everywhere, with newspapers, handkerchiefs, and cups, anything that will hold the bloody proof that they attended the spectacular public death of a folk figure. Certainly Sayles implies that the press and the FBI had as much to do with Dillinger's celebrity as the bank robber's own actions did. After all, Anna Sage was the real betrayer, a fact that most people are not aware of, but Polly is branded the infamous "lady in red." Clearly, Sayles attempted to tell a different version of the death of John Dillinger, one from the point of view of his notorious girlfriend, who turns out to be someone rather ordinary. Indeed, it is the small, obscure story that intrigues Sayles, as he remarked to Eric Foner: "One of the things that I feel is useful about making a small movie is that film can provide a voice for people who are not being heard and not being seen on the big screen" (Carnes *Past Imperfect* 24). On paper, Polly Franklin was one of those people.

Sayles's last New World script would shift genres, moving from Chicago gangsters to outer space, where androids, humanoids, robots, and monsters lurk. "Corman is very frank with exactly what has to be in the movie, and basically, after that, he leaves you alone," Sayles told *Cineaste* magazine. "In the case of *Battle Beyond the Stars*, all Corman did was come to me and say, 'We want to write a science fiction picture that's the *Seven Samurai* in space'" (Auster and Quart 330–31). Sayles neglects to mention that New World, always business savvy, wanted to grab onto the coattails of the George Lucas–produced *The Empire Strikes Back* (1980), his sequel to *Star Wars* (1977). *Battle Beyond the Stars*, directed by Jimmy T. Murakami, merges a *Star Wars* look with a story about how the defenseless cope with marauding barbarians, Kurosawa's plot device. Yet, as David Thompson explains, *Seven Samurai* "is as exciting as a good Western: its leading characters are distinct and appealing; the situation is contrived but compelling…. But it is almost twice as long as a good Western, and its social theme — that the samurai are disapproved by the village they protect — is made monotonously" (410). Sayles reduces the length of his version of the *Seven Samurai*, and he cuts out the social theme, which allows more time for fun and guns. *Battle Beyond the Stars* also allows its female stars to keep their clothes own, injecting sexual hijinks through words, not images. Sayles's final New World script crackles with parodic, good-natured laughs, starting with the opening credits, which look exactly like these in *Star Wars*.

Sayles's screenplay moves the samurai from sixteenth-century Japan to the future but with his own special twist: "Even hack work is about something. *Battle Beyond the Stars* … is about death, different life forms' attitudes toward death. It's no big heavy thing, it's just something to base the characters around" (Chute 58). Sayles's warriors are willing to die for a cause that means little or nothing to them. Yet each gladiator has good reason to take up arms against an intractable foe. Perhaps the Nestors (Earl Boen and John McGowans), five clones who count as one mercenary, sum things up best when they reveal why they want to join the group: "We are becoming bored to death." No price is too large to pay. Sayles also borrows from John Sturges's American, testosterone-fueled version of Kurosawa's film, the 1960s' *The Magnificent Seven*, by echoing the lines of specific characters, particularly those of Robert Vaughn's eerie, cowardly gunfighter. Vaughn, in fact, pops up here as a tight-jawed killer who is a loner, as was his aging existential cowboy in Sturges's film.

Sayles's plot is familiar: A harmless planet is threatened by Sador (John

Saxon), who possesses the deadly stellar converter, which can reduce an entire planet to cosmic dust, akin to the Empire's Death Star, and his vicious, genetically addled gang of interstellar bad guys, who travel in a spacecraft large enough to create a solar eclipse. Sayles introduces the terrible Sador by having him to blow two smiling weathermen, sent aloft to ensure a good agricultural harvest, out of space. The planet sends out an emissary, Shad (Richard Thomas), an untested soldier, to find mercenaries. He succeeds. Ultimately, there is a battle in which the invaders die, as do five of the mercenaries, which, of course, proves their integrity.

The script also contains a love story, between Shad and Nanelia (Darlanne Fluegel), derived from Shakespeare's *The Tempest*, a deliberate literary conceit that allows Sayles some gooey dialogue on birth, death, and the fun of procreation. Nanelia, who has grown up knowing nothing of the vast universe beyond her own stormy planet, parallels Miranda. She works for her father, Dr. Hephaestus (Sam Jaffe), the cerebral presence in charge of an android repair operation. When Shad arrives, Nanelia tells him that her father has changed a bit. And indeed he has. Because his body has atrophied, Dr. Hephaestus's head floats over a robotic platform, which keeps his brain alive. Since he lacks a heart, objective decisions come easy, so he immediately assigns Shad to impregnate his daughter and to settle in for an eternity at the android station. Shad, however, seeks a more abundant life, one that includes death. Like Miranda, Nanelia naively offers herself to Shad without hesitation — theirs will be a limitless, artificial existence marked by the pitter patter of little feet and conversations with broken androids. Shad, however, displays a thirst for real life, and he tells Nanelia a story about a communal birth on another planet in which birth and death are witnessed simultaneously. Against pleas from her android guard, Nanelia elects to travel back to Shad's planet in order to discover the pleasures of a mortal life. Needless to say, both Shad and Nanelia are pure, innocent characters. But like Shakespeare's Ferdinand, Shad quickly evolves into a spirited fighter capable of making serious decisions. When *Battle Beyond the Stars* ends, Nanelia and Shad survive to continue a life together.

Still, *Battle Beyond the Stars* is not just a romance. The fun comes from the supporting characters, who add a zany multiculturalism to Sayles's cosmic spoof. These characters are full of attitude, which allows Sayles to stretch his wiseacre sensibility. Robert Vaughn's Gelt, for example, is a tough-as-plutonium hired gunman who is "looking for a place to hide and a meal," but ends up dying for "a minor planet in a third rate galaxy." Fittingly, Shad has Gelt buried with a five-course meal. Space Cowboy (George Peppard) carries scotch, soda, and ice in his space belt, and plays Western music on the tape deck in his spacecraft. Cowboy, who is a space trucker, puts a dissolute spin on Harrison Ford's overly serious Han Solo. John Saxon's Sador is a hilarious bad guy, especially when he utters his final line, "But, I wanted to live forever." His hubris knows no bounds. In fact one mercenary, a scaly snake who runs around the universe with two creatures called Kelvins (who communicate through thermal energy) and a mute muscle man, screams at Sador, "I'm going to kill you. You overage degenerate." These characters are lightly drawn, but they are comic, especially when juxtaposed with their testosterone cowboy predecessors.

The best lines, however, are saved for St. Exmin (Sybil Danning), a busty Valkyrie whose libido rises along with her battle lust. Defining her life philosophy to Shad, she recalls the famous line uttered by Nick "Pretty Boy" Romano in the 1940 film noir picture *Knock on Any Door*: "Live fast, die young, and have a good-looking corpse." St. Exmin delivers a deliciously dirty double entendre as she explains her brand of sex to Nanelia. Gripping a long crystal shaft, St. Exmin describes how she would handle Shad: "I could do wonders for that boy. I would recharge his capacitors. Stimulate his solenoid. Tingle dingle, dangle his transistors. You know: Sex." Shad would never be the same, but he is far too pure for the likes of the Valkyrie, who goes out with a bang.

Sayles also throws in a good computer, NEL, who stands in complete opposition to Stanley Kubrick's malevolent HAL, the killer computer in *2001: A Space Odyssey*. NEL controls a true mothership, which, in fact, looks like a flying uterus, and she wants nothing more than to see the all-male bad guys blown into stellar dust. NEL convinces Shad that the Varda, his planet's bible, which declares, "That which is organic must not harm that which is also organic," is full of "some damn stupid rules." She preaches aggression, especially in the face of certain death. Like the rest of the film's gallant heroes, NEL too dies, although she is instrumental in Shad's growth from a boy to a man.

Clearly, *Battle Beyond the Stars* plays for more laughs than Sayles's other New World scripts. His writing, however, enlivens a familiar and often cynical genre. Sayles breathes a bit of comic optimism into a tired form. At this point in his screenwriting career, Sayles had mastered the slightly campy, slightly tongue-in-cheek genre script. Next, he set out to make his own film, *Return of the Secaucus Seven*, which would signal his literary ability and his filmmaking talent. But Sayles never strayed too far from the pay associated with Hollywood productions. As Gavin Smith points out, Sayles would find an "autonomous niche between the studio major leagues and the indie minors" (57). Since 1980, Sayles has made a good living rewriting scripts, writing scripts for hire, and polishing bits and pieces of scripts for large Hollywood studios.

3

Screenwriter-for-Hire:
Revisions, Additions,
Originals

In *Alligator* or *The Howling* I try to bring them into the twentieth
century, to make them a little more consistent. The tension that is
interesting to me is taking something totally fantastic and sticking it in a very realistic setting. I try to say, "OK, what would really
happen if you walked outside, and there's this giant alligator there?
Who would try to catch it, who would react with fear, who would
just say, 'Great, let's go see the giant alligator!'?"
— John Sayles (Chute)

For Corman, Sayles displayed a comic sensibility, scripts full of interconnected characters, knowledge of film history, and a literary flair. In 1981
Sayles began to branch out, to move away from the New World Pictures factory, and he brought his writing touch to two genre pictures, Joe Dante's *The
Howling* and Lewis Teague's *Alligator*. Both exploitation pictures are black
comedies full of cult allusions that embrace the Corman tradition: They are
smart, funny, and full of precise social observations. If exploitation films are
necessarily rigged, required to appease audience expectations, Sayles's scripts
bend convention, offering rich, illuminating subtexts that make his "hack
work" exceptional.

The Howling is ambitious, exploring contemporary themes such as television New Age groups and wrapping everything up with the ageless terror
of lycanthropy, the magical ability to transform oneself into a wolf. Writing
in *The New York Times*, Vincent Canby observed that "*The Howling* is ridiculous but it's not stupid" ("Lycanthropophilia" 10). Although Sayles wrote the
script with Terence H. Winkles, credit has gone largely to Sayles. *The Howling* offers something for everyone, for it reaches high-brow, mid-brow, and
low-brow audiences without condescension. Clearly, Sayles learned well from
Corman. *The Howling* acknowledges Corman early on; he appears as a dap-

per fellow who patiently waits outside a telephone booth as Karen White (Dee Wallace), a member of the Update News team and the film's heroine, receives a call from a man who may be responsible for a series of grisly crimes. Although Corman says nothing, his presence frightens the reporter and provides a few laughs for his fans. Sayles and Dante establish their low-budget cinematic signposts quickly. Together they amplify an old story by adding both spoken and visual puns to their story of werewolves, television, and redemptive therapy.

Sayles still enjoys the opening of *The Howling*, which he says is his favorite among the screenplays he has written: "What you try to do is tell the people what world they are entering. Because a movie is a world, and it should live and die by its own rules.... Yes, it is the world of werewolves, but it's not Transylvania, folks. These guys are hip to the media" (Smith 68).

The film's credits appear in blood-red ripping through a black background. Next we see and hear a fuzzy television set, full of static and horizontal and vertical lines. A quick cut provides us with glimpses of a television studio, which establishes the contemporary setting for Sayles's script. We hear people talking about a television show that promises to examine the mind of a psychotic killer. "But," someone says, "you know, it focuses on the beast in all of us." The blurred television screen comes into focus and we see Dr. George Waggner (Patrick Macnee), a psychologist, being interviewed by a television talk-show host. We hear snatches of their conversation, as the picture pops in and out of focus. "Repression," Waggner says, "is the father of neurosis"; and "We should never try to deny the beast, the animal in us." Cleverly, Sayles establishes the two tracks his script will follow, weaving the primal world of the man-beast, represented by Dr. Waggner, with the civilized world, represented by television. Film fans will recognize Macnee's character, named after the director of the 1941 film, *The Wolf Man*, a film that Dante refers to twice in *The Howling*.

Dr. Waggner is a fraud. He manipulates the television audience into accepting man's atavistic side while attempting to integrate a group of werewolves into the civilized world, in order to keep the ancient race alive. A community of werewolves, of course, would naturally be full of strong, subversive personalities, not all of whom are interested in finding their human side. James B. Twitchell, author of *Dreadful Pleasures: An Anatomy of Modern Horror*, contends that films like *The Howling*, though flawed, are as interesting as traditional horror films because they speak to a particular generation, one that demands old genres that comment on their reality. Therefore, in *The Howling* "the chief werewolf was a Dr. Get-in-Touch-with-Yourself from Esalen Institute," a well-known New Age spa still in operation in Big Sur, California (Twitchell 54).

The problem with these topical characters is their immediacy, as Twitchell points out: "You run the risk of losing the next generation audience in a much more abrupt way than with other [film] forms because objects of contemporary obsessions, especially political ones, have a half-life of about five years" (54). However, today the Dr. Waggner character sounds a bit like Robert Bly, without the poetry of course. And, in fact, the self-help movement is stronger than ever. Sayles's characters, in fact, still hold up; it is the werewolf film that has flagged. As David Chute discovered, "Joe Dante himself contends that werewolf movies are 'a dead genre,' and, with Sayles, he settled upon a fun-and-games approach to *The Howling*, piling on de-mystifying natural flourishes, and movie in-jokes that set up a winking complicity in disbelief between filmmaker and viewer" (58). Of course, every culture has its werewolf story, because the tie to "the werewolf transformation [and] a clearly sexual scenario" (Twitchell 219) remains strong, and Sayles exploited that connection early on in his screenplay, using one of the unruly werewolves to make his point.

Eddie the Mangler (Richard Picardo), a werewolf who stalks Karen, sardonically plants "smiling face" stickers throughout *The Howling*. Eddie has no desire to get in touch with his humanity; instead, he uses his lycanthropic strength to satisfy his sexual desire and his urge to kill. Eddie talks on the phone to Karen, who is inside a phone booth emblazoned with a "smiling face" sticker, directing her to an adult bookstore. There she takes a seat inside a tiny, pitch-black peep show booth where Eddie is hidden in the shadows behind her. Suddenly, a pornographic movie begins to run, showing a group of men sexually assaulting a woman. Eddie assures Karen that the woman is enjoying herself. Then he says, "I'm going to light up your whole body, Karen," as he orders her to turn around. Karen obeys, and we see Eddie from her point of view, which, because of the light from the projection booth, is blurred. All Karen can make out is long, coarse hair, and an unshaven face. Then we see a reaction shot of Karen's face, from Eddie's point of view. Obviously, something is happening. We see only the reaction in Karen's eyes. All of a sudden, a police officer appears and Eddie is shot dead. Karen, covered with blood, cannot remember what has occurred.

Here Sayles's screenplay branches off. Two of Karen's co-workers, Chris (Dennis Dugan) and Terry (Belinda Balaski), make their way to Eddie's apartment, which is grotesquely decorated with newspaper accounts of the Mangler's murder spree and self-portraits of an angry animal-like Eddie. Terry remarks that "he could design the Marquis de Sade coloring book." The reporters are not sure what to make of Eddie's room, so they visit the morgue, where the Mangler's body is being held in cold storage.

Meanwhile, Karen's boss, Fred Francis (Kevin McCarthy) cannot wait to get her in front of the cameras, where she will tell her audience about her encounter with Eddie the Mangler. "We'll make ratings history," he says, sounding like a Paddy Chayefsky character from *Network* (1976). But Karen has been suffering from nightmares, and she blacks out on camera, instead of delivering a tantalizing piece of television journalism. Karen is directed for psychiatric help to Dr. Waggner, who suggests a weekend at his northern California retreat, The Colony, where the fun really begins. Sayles's script allows Dante to create "scenes of traditional horror, as well as campy nuances" (Broeske 210). All he has to do is get everyone to The Colony, the center point of his screenplay.

Karen and her husband, Bill (Christopher Stone), a former athlete who is a vegetarian and is in the health spa business, set out for a restful weekend. Karen tells Bill, "I hope these people aren't too weird." Of course we anticipate that they will be extremely weird. In the next shot we see Erle Kenton (John Carradine) howling as other guests try to prevent him from directing his wild call at the moon. Bill and Karen are right in the middle of a rather odd community, which Dr. Waggner wants to humanize. His desire establishes a thematic link to the plight of Larry Talbot, Lon Chaney, Jr.'s character in *The Wolf Man*, who understands his curse and wants to be separated from society to prevent further killing. Dr. Waggner's group, however, does not take to self-help programs well.

While Karen and Bill are trying to figure out the odd people at The Colony, Chris and Terry make a startling discover at the city morgue. The morbid morgue attendant (John Sayles) tells the couple about his job, recalling how one night he was talking to another man at a shift change, when not an hour later he came back dead "with water pouring out of both his ears." This morgue veteran has seen it all, at least until he opens Eddie's freezer compartment. The stainless steel body drawer bears dents and scratch marks that suggest "dead" Eddie made a forced exit. This strange occurrence sends the reporters to an occult bookstore, where the topic of werewolves arises. The owner (Dick Miller) says that werewolves can be killed only with "silver bullets or fire. That's the only way to get rid of the damned things. They're worse than cockroaches."

Back at The Colony, Karen sits in on a group therapy session. A young woman says, "EST, Scientology, T.M., primal screaming, I did it all. I figure another five years of hard work, and maybe I'll be a regular person." This scene is shot in bright daylight. Other more mysterious scenes are shot either in the shadowy woods, which come right out of Hawthorne, or at night, when horror and camp merge effortlessly. Bill, who is presented as a dedicated husband to Karen, falls victim to the night, but not in the typical manner. After killing a rabbit, Bill is instructed to take it to Marsha, a gratuitously erotic member of The Colony who wears leather, animal teeth necklaces, and an inviting expression. Clearly, her urges are primitive, beyond Dr. Waggner's rational approach. After skinning the rabbit, Marsha throws herself on Bill, who rejects her. As he is walking home at dusk, Bill is attacked and bitten by a mysterious creature. He gets back to the cabin where Karen tends to the bite, but soon Bill's darker impulses begin to emerge.

Meat becomes part of his diet, he starts reading *You Can't Go Home Again*, by Thomas Wolfe, and he now has a strong attraction to Marsha. Karen, who is still ill, sees Bill's flirtation, but looks the other way. Finally, Bill becomes Young Goodman Brown and enters the woods at night, where a fire and Marsha are waiting for him. Here Sayles's script appeals to generic expectations. Marsha, who looks like Barbara Steele, and Bill remove their clothes and writhe on the ground in front of the fire. We witness Bill's furious arousal in the form of hair emerging from strange places, guttural sounds emerging from his throat, and all the excitement he had contained breaking free. As their lovemaking reaches climax, Bill sprouts fangs and begins to salivate. At the end of the sequence, the lovers, now fully formed wolves, howl at the moon. It goes without saying that Sayles and Dante clearly had great fun imagining and creating this scene. Traditionally, horror films kept their sexual content submerged, allowing the audience members to figure things out for themselves. Here, however, we see a comic version of horror's true intent. "Horror monsters may frighten," writes James Twitchell, "but that is partly because they are acting out those desires we most fear. When they come out in the nighttime, as monsters always do, they must move around using a body that has become a sexual weapon, a body full of power but so lacking in control" (68–69). Sayles and Dante play off Bill's lack of control for comic effect, not Freudian dreams.

Chris and Terry, who are back in the city, in bed watching the scene in *The Wolf Man* where Gypsy Queen Malvena (Madame Maria Ouspenskaya) tells Larry Talbot, "Whosoever is bitten by a werewolf and lives, becomes a werewolf himself," receive a frantic call from Karen, who says that Bill has changed after being bitten. Terry, who now believes that werewolves are indeed real, drives to The Colony to be with her friend and to investigate The Colony. She discovers Eddie's room at the retreat, but Eddie discovers her, and in a bloody, bone-crunching sequence she is killed. Chris, meanwhile, returns to the occult bookstore to retrieve the silver bullets. Karen searches for Terry, only to find her mangled body in Dr. Waggner's office, where Eddie awaits her. Their reunion is a bit of special effects wizardry, as we watch Eddie transform before our eyes into a huge, two-legged wolf. But Sayles's macabre humor also punctuates the scene. Eddie, angry at Karen's earlier betrayal, says, "I want to give you a piece of my mind." As Pat Broeske describes, Sayles's dialogue foreshadows a horrendous transformation:

> The words have a literal meaning — for Eddie reaches to his forehead, which bears bullet marks, and pushes inward through the wound. His flesh gives way, allowing him to grasp a handful of slushy substance which he grimly hands to Karen. This is but a prelude to Eddie's transformation, as his cheekbones and forehead begin to throb, his chest heaves and expands (shredding his clothing), and his jaw begins to protrude. Giving Karen a wicked smile, he holds up his hand, allowing her to watch as claws sprout from his bloodied

nails. When the change is complete, a massive wolf, standing upright, moves menacingly toward her. Karen is able to escape only after she throws a vial of acid into his face. [211]

The Howling's smart words and concise direction are complemented by Rob Bottin's special effects, even though the film was made for less than $1 million, making it a marvelous example of low-budget filmmaking with a high-budget sensibility.

Sayles handles Karen's escape by burning the werewolves, who are locked in a barn. Still, he plays things up a bit, and he enhances the film by attaching an empathetic ending to the film. Chris arrives just in the nick of time armed with a rifle full of silver bullets. The Colony's patients have all arrived at the barn, where they are about to turn on Dr. Waggner and his humanity program. Chris shoots Waggner, who thanks him as he falls to the ground. The rest of the pack begin to chant, "Humans are our prey." Chris shoots a few of them, forcing the rest into the barn, which Karen sets on fire. In a nice montage sequence, Dante underscores the monsters' will to live by showing the creatures battling against the flames. However, at a roadblock set up by Sheriff Sam Newfield (Slim Pickens), a werewolf who enjoys eating Wolf Chili right out of the can, Karen suffers a bite.

Sayles cuts to an interior shot of the television studio, where Fred Francis is again anticipating big numbers because Karen is about to recount the story behind the deaths and the fire at The Colony. But she veers away from the script to talk about a plague from which there is no escape. As she pleads for compassion and understanding, Karen begins to transform before her television audience. Unlike Eddie's metamorphosis, Karen's is sad. Her snout quivers slightly as a tear runs down her cheek, for Chris, who knows about the newscast, stands aiming the rifle at her and fires. Karen's call for understanding, however, is lost in the chaos on the set. Sayles inserts reactions from typical viewers. Some children squeal with delight, "Wow, the news lady's turning into a werewolf!" A couch potato channel surfs though the bizarre scene. A bar patron exclaims, "The things they do with special effects these days!" Another patron says that the anchor did indeed turn into a wolf. The bartender, who is cooking a hamburger for a customer, glances at the television, then yells over his shoulder, "How do you want that burger cooked?" The camera glides over to Marsha, who sits next to a drinker, her breast heaving glory. "Rare," she answers with a wisp of anticipation. As the closing credits roll, we watch her burger cook on the grill.

The Howling is a rollicking film that mixes social commentary with the horror genre and a celebration of low-budget filmmaking. The movie is full of visual and spoken references too, but its major strength is Sayles's script, which realizes that the werewolf is not as important as the threat of the werewolf. The film is filled with cameos: Roger Corman; Kevin McCarthy;

Alligator *(1978): Like many well-known contemporary filmmakers, Sayles started his career working on B-movies, particularly for Roger Corman at New World Pictures. Quickly, Sayles established a name for himself and started working for other studios. Even then, Sayles attempted to create scripts that worked on as many levels as possible.* Alligator, *directed by former New World colleague Lewis Teague, started with the old urban alligator myth, but Sayles needed to take it to another level: "I started to think of it as a social ill. And like most social ills, nobody pays attention until they reach the upper middle class. So while the alligator's eating poor people, it's like 'Isn't that too bad, your cousin got eaten,' but when it finally gets to the suburbs, that's when the SWAT team arrives" (Ferrante 8–9). Here Sayles's protagonist interrupts an upscale wedding, the final stop on his journey through the socioeconomic food chain. Photo courtesy of the Museum of Modern Art Film Stills Archive.*

Forrest J Ackerman, the editor of *Famous Monsters of Filmland*; Ken Tobey; who survived *The Thing from Another World* (1951); John Carradine; and Slim Pickins. We also see Chris reading Allen Ginsberg's *Howl* and watching *The Three Little Pigs* on television. Sayles also underscores the artificiality of television and the idea that a TV nation quickly loses the ability to discern between fantasy and reality.

Horror, film history, and comedy are the mainstays of Sayles's generic scripts. *The Howling* is no different, although it is, as Gerald Mast points out, "a tragicomic and sardonic tale of werewolves, the media, and psychological fads," which makes it more than a monster movie, and another testament to Sayles's amazing screenwriting ability.

Sayles's next screenplay rewrite, *Alligator* (1981), was also a New World reunion, this time with Lewis Teague, who directed *The Lady in Red. Alligator* is as relentless and as comical as *Piranha*, and it even resembles Sayles's first feature assignment. Clearly, *Alligator* parodies *Jaws*, as well as *Them!* and

Piranha itself. *Alligator* takes up where the fish left off. As in *Piranha* and *Jaws* the horror comes from below, but this time from the sewer. Sayles uses an urban myth as his starting point: The sewers of large cities contain alligators that started out as pets, grew too large, and were flushed down toilets, ultimately finding a home in the dark, wet subterranean space below ground. Sayles, of course, put a twist on the folk tale. What if, Sayles asks, the alligator had a food supply pumped up by a chemical company experimenting on growth-inducing hormones? The answer is a 32-foot, one-ton, mean-tempered creature named Ramon, who needs to eat, and eat a lot.

Alligator does not speed up or cloud over bone-crunching deaths. Instead, Sayles and Teague let us see how an alligator chews its prey. While *Alligator* lacks *The Howling*'s production values, Sayles brings the same political attitude, splashed with humor and film savvy, to his screenplay. *Alligator* is a meditation on a youngster's nightmare with an adult sense of humor. Once again, Sayles proves that he knows exactly what he is doing.

The renegade alligator starts out in Florida and ends up in a typical American city, which is probably Chicago, even though we see a sign that announces Missouri, and some of the sewer scenes look like Los Angeles. Place, however, matters little. Sayles places something totally fantastic in a realistic Midwestern setting. Conceptually, Sayles's plot called for the alligator to eat its way through an American socioeconomic chain: "It comes out of the sewer in the ghetto, then goes to a middle-class neighborhood, then out to the suburbs, and then to a real kind of high-rent area" (Chute 58). Unfortunately, budget limitations forced the removal of a number of scenes, so Ramon's progression is somewhat truncated. Still, most of Sayles's political in-jokes remain on screen. The alligator emerges through the sidewalk in the inner city and by the end of the film he is happily munching his way through an upscale wedding on a large, rural estate. Sayles had to write four endings for *Alligator*, because he wanted to destroy the large reptilian model used during the shooting, but BLC, the film's production company, wanted it for a publicity gimmick. Sayles had to settle for a conventional explosion to kill off the beast.

Alligator lacks New World's panache, yet it is still a competent piece of generic filmmaking. Sayles's screenplay recalls the science fiction bug extravaganza *Them!*, in which mutant ants, the result of military nuclear testing, threaten Los Angeles. Indeed, one exterior shot Sayles wrote comes right from *Them!* As in the 1951 film, the shot takes place in the storm drain of the Los Angeles river. David Madison (Robert Forster), Sayles's hero with a troubled past, convinces a combat battalion of police and National Guard troops to wait for the huge alligator to take some bait placed near the entrance to a runoff tunnel. Just as in the antecedent film, *Alligator*'s result is the same: Nothing happens, leaving an embarrassed Madison to explain to the small army about the giant reptile all over again.

Like *Piranha*, *Alligator* uses *Jaws* as a stepping stone. We see shots from the creature's point of view as it silently races toward its victim, which enhances the terror. Then we see a reaction shot, the horror the victim feels just before the alligator's massive jaws clamp hold, which plays out with good dirty fun. These attacks are also cinematic descendants of Hitchcock's *The Birds*; in fact, while Hitchcock uses Tippi Hedren's callous behavior in the pet store as part of the explanation for his film's premise, Sayles nods toward Hitchcock by creating a malicious pet store owner who is to blame for feeding Ramon. He, of course, must pay for his crimes, and the alligator has him for lunch.

As a piece of generic filmmaking, *Alligator* delivers. In his laudatory review in *The New York Times*, Vincent Canby contends that *Alligator* "simultaneously demonstrates the specific requirements of the formula while sending them up with good humor" ("Long in the Tooth" 12). Low production values create some of the fun that *Alligator* delivers. We know, for example, that we are watching a baby alligator scurry through miniature sets; this is not the work of Ray Harryhausen, but it is not bad either for a low-budget action film. Unlike *Jaws*, this film did not have money available to construct a lifelike creature, as Canby notes: "*Alligator* is a sort of underprivileged *Jaws*, made by people who clearly don't have the financial resources to spend half a million dollars fabricating a lifelike, machine-operated, 32-foot Ramon, about people who cannot afford to vacation on Long Island, Cape Cod, Nantucket or Martha's Vineyard" (12). As Canby suggests, *Alligator* is a low-budget, blue-collar version of the glitzy *Jaws*, definitely Sayles territory.

Alligator is plot driven, following generic expectations enriched by Sayles's sense of humor. In an essay he wrote to defend his praise for the low-budget formulaic *Alligator*, Canby pointed out that "the film meets its classic narrative obligations as carefully as the composer of a sonnet meets his obligations to a form" (17). On vacation in 1968 the Kendall family, Mom, Dad, and young Marisa, visit an alligator farm in Florida. There an alligator wrestler is severely mauled by an alligator. Most of the people watching assume that they are seeing a prank, a carny sideshow stunt — except Marisa, who recognizes the creature's primal power. She buys a ten-inch baby gator as a pet, and then takes it home with her. Dad Kendall becomes fed up with Marisa's attachment for the reptile, which she calls Ramon. Announcing, "We'll tell her we found it dead, just like the hamster," Dad flushes Ramon down the toilet. Here, Sayles's script calls for a point-of-view shot from the toilet, so we can empathize with Ramon's plight. With a gentle plunk, Ramon lands in a dark, cavernous, wet sewer and scurries away.

Twelve years later, body parts start turning up in the city's sewer system — arms, legs, even a thumb. The *National Probe*, the local newspaper, begins to run a page-one headline that keeps track of Ramon's body count. The police chief (Michael Grazzo) assigns David Madison to the case, who has moved to this town because of trouble on his old job — he was wrongly accused of his partner's death. After the alligator eats a pet store owner, Madison starts investigating Slade Laboratories. The company owner, Slade (Dean Jagger), is a rich, powerful, nasty old man who has the mayor (Jack Carter) in his pocket. Keeping city officials away from his secret operations will not be any trouble, as he tells his future son-in-law: "It's not the police we have to worry about; it's the damn yellow journalists." The mayor contacts the police chief, telling him to stay away from Slade Laboratories. Madison, of course, pursues the case with a vengeance, for it does not matter to him who is involved. Any good formula film has a hierarchy such as this one. Madison, who does the grunt work, is the blue-collar hero, so full of integrity he will do whatever it takes to solve the mystery. The police chief simply clings to his job. But the mayor is beholden to Slade, who is as slimy as he is rich. What makes some formula films so much fun is the fact that bad people always pay for their sins, usually in a delightfully grotesque manner.

After a sewer worker is reported missing, Madison and a rookie partner investigate the sewer. There the rookie is attacked and eaten by the alligator, which allows Madison to see the huge animal face-to-face. No one, however, will believe him, which is also a standard device in most formula films. Finally a newsman in pursuit of the story falls victim to Ramon; he at least has the good sense to photograph the beast as it eats him alive. Enter Dr. Marisa Kendall (Robin Riker), a pretty, world-famous herpetologist. As expected, she and Madison fight a bit before they fall in love. Soon Ramon surfaces for all to see, and he eats his way toward Slade like the Frankenstein monster in pursuit of his creator. The mayor turns the hunt over to a Hemingwayesque big game hunter, Colonel Brock (Henry Silva), who is so sexist and racist that we know he will not have much screen time. Soon Ramon bursts through a sewer grate in front of the Slade mansion, where Slade's daughter is being married to the same doctor who purchased puppies and kittens from the pet store owner in order to conduct the hormone experiments. Ramon's vengeance is swift: He eats the mayor alive and crushes Slade as he cowers in the back of his limousine. Finally, Madison lures Ramon back into the sewer where the creature is blown to bits, but not before Sayles pokes fun at the monumental coincidences that he has used throughout *Alligator* and that are part of any formula film. Madison, who has set the charges in the sewer, plans to escape through a manhole, but a little old lady pulls up and parks on the cover. Our hero is locked in the sewer with the ticking bomb that will set off a supply of methane gas and blow up the alligator, which is snapping at his legs and feet. The car moves, of course, just in the nick of time.

Alligator sounds more ridiculous than it is. As Canby observes, the film is not a parody but rather a genre picture with a real sense of humor (12). While the exploitation film actresses Sue Lyon and Angel Tompkins cameo as news reporters, *Alligator* does not have as many visual jokes as *The Howling*. Here Ramon is the star, and Sayles and Teague use him for all he is worth. Although both *The Howling* and *Alligator* were rewrites, Sayles received much of the writing credit. His next major assignment, John Frankenheimer's *The Challenge*, would require a "marathon, three-day rewrite" (Chute 59). For this film, Sayles primarily reworked dialogue.

The Challenge (1982) is a contemporary action film that revolves around the clash between modernity and tradition. Set in Kyoto, we follow a somewhat dull-witted sparring boxer, Rick Murphy (Scott Glenn), as he is drawn into a private battle between two brothers, Toru Yoshida (Toshiro Mifune), the older and more traditional brother, and Hideo Yoshida (Atsuo Nakamura), the young industrialist who puts machines ahead of ritual. The brothers engage in a private war over an ancient sword, and Toru hires Murphy to carry the sword into Japan. Murphy is trapped between the two camps the moment he enters the country. After a time of indecision about the two groups, Rick becomes a disciple of Toru, a samurai who believes a tough, grueling path is the only means of gaining true wisdom and the combat skills necessary to skewer your opponents. By the end of the film, old Japan takes on new Japan, and old wins, but not without the help of the converted sybaritic Westerner. For the most part, Frankenheimer's film follows a safe path, one that appeals to an audience schooled in the action genre. *The Challenge* at times can be vicious, but some of Sayles's dialogue gives considerable depth to the characters.

The one character who delivers snappy lines is Ando (Calvin Jung), an Americanized bad guy who works for Hideo and talks as if he has seen too many movies. Indeed, his character's most savage moment recalls Richard Widmark's Tommy Udo from Harry Hathaway's 1947 thriller *Kiss of Death*. After pushing Toshio (Sab Shimono), his boss's wheelchair-bound nephew who was crippled for life by his uncle, out the back of a moving van, he explains to Murphy the significance of the sword: "You mess with someone's blade, you mess with his soul." Murphy, of course, cannot fathom the fanaticism over the sword, but he does know that he has made a big mistake getting involved, especially after Ando delivers him to an ultramodern industrial complex to meet Hideo. "So what does the man do for a living, when he's not waiting for the sword?" Rick asks. Ando is happy to tell him:

> He's chairman of the board here. That's no ordinary board. No. That board runs the length of the building and out the far end. Who's sitting on either side of that board waiting for the good word from him? The President of the next fifty biggest companies in Japan. When you go below them, into the fine print, you're looking for General Motors.

Sayles's means of defining enormous is humorous and telling. But it is the comic, casual cruelty of Ando's business-as-usual attitude that truly marks Sayles's work here. After the film is over, it is Ando's deadly professionalism that stands out.

While the sequence that closes the film is stunning to look at, it delivers little in terms of story. It is played for blood and special effects. As Janet Maslin noted in her *New York Times* review, *The Challenge* is "a hard-boiled action film with great hopes of becoming something more" (8). The most interesting contribution from Sayles is seen in the dialogue, which depicts how power is used and abused. CBS Theatrical Films controlled too much of *The Challenge*, which did not fare well at the box office, and its unevenness is the result of studio interference. Still, working with a recognized director like Frankenheimer elevated Sayles's name further in Hollywood. He was becoming known as a quick and dependable script doctor. His next screenplay, however, would be more indicative of the type of independent films that Sayles was making himself.

Enormous Changes at the Last Minute, a set of stories by Grace Paley, was adapted for the screen by Sayles and Susan Rice. The film looks like an independent project: Its production values are low, the episodes are uneven, and some of the acting is second rate. Still, this independent project does have illuminating moments and a strong literary sensibility. The film's rocky production history is, perhaps, the primary cause of its obvious weaknesses.

The three stories that make up the film involve Virginia (Ellen Barkin), Faith (Lynn Milgrim), and Alexandra (Susan Tucci), each of whom experiences an enormous change in her life. Other than that, these women have little in common, although they are linked from time to time in master shots throughout the film. In the first and strongest segment, Virginia attempts to come to terms with her life after her husband, Jerry (David Strathairn), leaves her and her three children. John (Ron McLarty), whose mother is Virginia's landlady, quickly appears. Virginia, however, wants nothing to do with an overweight, balding guy who now lives in New Jersey with his wife and children. John is undeterred, having been in love with Virginia since high school. Virginia reluctantly allows John into her life out of loneliness. Thursday night becomes John's Night, when he brings gifts and entertains Virginia's children. Eventually, they make love, and Virginia points out to John that "for a guy who sends out the Ten Commandments for a Christmas card, you're pretty quick getting those pants off." Virginia accepts the fact that her life has little without John's presence, as poor an arrangement as that it is.

Faith's story, the second installment, is also about a woman alone. Faith is a divorced mother of two who visits her father (Zvees Schooler) and mother (Eda Reiss Merin) in a Brighton Beach nursing home. After talking with her father, who reveals to Faith that he and her mother were never married, and that they were idealists and therefore different from her, Faith comes to realize that her own existence has been mundane. She runs along the beach and has her children bury her in the sand, an act that seems to allow an emotional release.

Finally, Alexandra, a divorced but financially secure social worker, has an affair with a young cabdriver, Dennis (Kevin Bacon), who is also a would-be musician. Dennis falls for the older woman, after picking her up as a fare and then dropping her off at the hospital where her father is a patient. Dennis is quirky, naively charming. At one point, he asks Alexandra if she has ever heard of his band, The Atomic Pile. She responds that she has not. Then Dennis explains why she has not heard of the group: "They're into anonymity; that's what they are known for." Alexandra cannot understand why she finds the young man so attractive. Like John in Virginia's episode, Dennis provides Alexandra emotional support, even if he is not aware of his role. Soon, however, Alexandra learns that she is pregnant. Her father belittles her when she tells him of her condition. Dennis, on the other hand, is happy; Alexandra is confused. By the end of the episode, Alexandra, who has explained to Dennis that he cannot become a permanent part of her life, opens up her house to an interracial group of unwed mothers. In the end, Alexandra finds and provides emotional comfort, and she is looking forward to having a child.

Though rough around the edges, *Enormous Changes at the Last Minute* is a more typical example of a John Sayles film than any of his early screenplays. The film presents a quilt of multiethnic and multiracial urban voices. We meet highly educated women, teenaged mothers, street kids, a blue-collar Romeo, and a couple of retired radicals. There is a gritty realism on display here, as there is in Paley's stories. Sayles uses Paley's words and characters well. These are ordinary people who lead ordinary lives. The film was codirected by Mirra Bank and Ellen Hovde, who raised money to continue the picture after showing footage of Faith's story to prospective backers. Eventually, they raised funds to complete the picture, which was begun in 1978 and released in 1985. Clearly this was a labor of love. In addition to Strathairn, who plays a marvelous lover who is tired of having children, Mason Daring, Sayles's musical director, worked on this picture. *Enormous Changes at the Last Minute* is a regional, independent film that served as a training ground for some talented filmmakers.

The low point of Sayles's screenwriting career is *Clan of the Cave Bear* (1986), his adaptation of Jean M. Auel's successful novel about a Cro-Magnon child who is raised by a tribe of Neanderthals. In fact, Auel considered the film so terrible that she sued the producers, Jon Peters and Peter Guber, for creating such an inaccurate portrait of her novel. The film was directed by Michael Chapman, the cinematographer for *Taxi Driver* (1977) and *Raging Bull* (1983). Darryl Hannah, who plays Ayla, the female protagonist of Auel's story, looks as if she has just stepped out of the gym by way of the dentist; she is horribly miscast as a prehistoric woman.

The dialogue for the film consists of grunts and hand gestures, enhanced by subtitles. The sophistication of the text makes the visual gesticulations unintentionally comic: "The Mogurs say you are of the Others. You will anger the spirits"—which sounds part literary theory, part New Age revival. Warner

Brothers had hired Sayles to adapt Auel's *Valley of Horses* also. But after the swift box office death of *Clan of the Cave Bear*, the next installment in Auel's trilogy never made it out of the planning stages.

Sayles's next screenplay, *Wild Thing* (1987), also has a prehistoric conceit. As this was also a rewrite assignment, Sayles felt that he could improve on the existing script, which he inherited from Larry Stamper. Sayles described his version of the script as "an urban Tarzan story" (Aufderheide *Cineaste* 15). The Wild Thing (Rob Knepper) is orphaned in the inner city, after his parents are killed in a drug deal gone sour. Their child, who escapes by diving into a sewer runoff, becomes the ward of a benevolent bag lady, who introduces the Wild Thing to street people and the craft of survival. As a teenager, the Wild Thing is an urban legend who swoops down from abandoned buildings to save innocents from street thugs and to give street kids and old drunks food. He lives in a part of the city called "The Zone," which is known for its crime, and is clearly a part of the city given up as lost. Jane (Kathleen Quinlan) is a social worker who is left in the wrong part of "The Zone," where she is accosted by two thugs who work for Chopper (Robert Davi), the overlord of "The Zone" who killed Wild Thing's parents. Needless to say, *Wild Thing* follows a generic arc.

Some of Sayles's political bent comes though in the title character's design. A "wild child," Wild Thing is a hippie love child. His parents drive a VW bus and listen to the Jefferson Airplane's "White Rabbit." Following their deaths, the child is forced to live off the land, which is, of course, concrete and extremely dangerous. Wild Thing lives in an urban jungle, swinging though the air silently but with the vigor and moral intent of Spiderman. Max Reid's film, however, is standard fare, an action film that, perhaps, once enclosed an interesting message. Wild Thing, like Ayla, speaks in grunts and hisses, although he reveals his ability to speak on an elemental level at the film's midpoint. Sayles did give the film some lively comic dialogue. A street kid who lives in a halfway house inside "The Zone" explains his condition effectively: "My Dad wanted me to play tackle for the Packers. I wanted to play keyboards for the Circle Jerks. The rest is history." For the most part, however, the script is standard action genre material: The bad guys control "The Zone" and the police, but Wild Thing will save the day. At the end of the film, when everyone thinks Wild Thing is dead, we see his sneakers planted firmly on the top of a tenement building, still on guard.

Breaking In (1989), directed by Bill Forsyth, the Scottish filmmaker, whose droll, dry sensibility can be both funny and melancholy, was an original screenplay of Sayles's, and it follows the old-fashioned buddy movie genre. Forsyth, who directed *Gregory's Girl* (1981), *Local Hero* (1984), and *Housekeeping* (1989), matches Sayles well. They created a film with substance. Vincent Canby noted that the film is "an accumulation of wonderfully buoyant, sometimes irrational details that would be throwaways in more conventional comedies" ("Of Shaggy Dogs…" 18). Pauline Kael had a differing opinion, calling John Sayles "the thinking man's shallow writer-director" (*Movie Love* 191). Kael ridicules Sayles for his narrative construction, which she considers to be devoid of drama and just an accumulation of notions. Social realism, for the most part, never appealed to Kael. Sayles actually wrote the script for *Breaking In* ten years before it was filmed. He liked the story but was reluctant to direct the material himself. Moreover, he did not want simply to sell the script — until, that is, Forsyth signed on to direct the film.

As the film opens, we see two different people break into the same house. Ernie Mullins (Burt Reynolds) is a professional thief; Mike Lefebb (Casey Siemaszko), a local kid who works at the tire shop, breaks in to "eat, watch a little TV, and read the mail." After a while, Ernie takes in the young upstart, to educate him in the trade of thievery. Mike learns how to make use of and detonate explosives. There are a few charming scenes that develop the connection between teacher and apprentice. Ernie, who lives anonymously in a nondescript house on the edge of Portland, Oregon, and thus avoids calling attention to himself, tries to educate Mike to the ways of a professional thief. But Mike is a slow learner. Ultimately, after a series of successful thefts, Mike settles into a large, expensive apartment, buys a large car, and lavishes presents on a prostitute, Carrie (Sheila Kelly), Ernie introduced him to. Needless to say, the police catch up to Mike quickly. In a display of loyalty, Mike takes credit for all of Ernie's jobs. Mike goes to prison, and Ernie pays for the kid's protection on the inside.

The breaking-and-entering story reveals Sayles's observation on generational distinctions. Ernie retains and upholds his values. Mike covets material goods, although he learns about life by the end of the film. *Breaking In* shows signs of Sayles's sense of humor. For example, Ernie tells Mike about his old partner in order to teach the kid how to act once he has completed a successful robbery: "He drank like a fish, smoked three packs a day, and he chased women. He wasn't a serious person." In order to help him along in his new career as a thief, two of Ernie's card-playing buddies, Johnny Scat (Albert Salmi) and Shoes (Harry Carey, Jr.) decide to give Mike a nickname. Because he is from Castroville, California, Johnny Scat wants to call him the Artichoke Kid. But Shoes tells him "a guy from Detroit used it. Liked to eat 'em." In the end, Mike becomes the "Firestone Kid, where the rubber meets the road." Mike tells Carrie that he has enough money to keep her off the street. Carrie tells him, "I have to make it on my own, so I can hold my head up." In another telling bit of dialogue, Mike's lawyer, Tucci (Maury Chaykin), explains to him that if convicted to ten years, one serves six, and if sentenced to six, one serves two. "It's like logarithms," says Tucci. Perhaps the funniest scene in the film belongs to Carrie, as she recites an ode she wrote to Mike's testicles. The film's credits, however, point out that Sayles did not compose the poem. Overall, *Breaking In* is a funny, easy-going film, made with a tone

Apollo 13 *(1995): "The worst case of anonymous work going unacknowledged is John Sayles on Apollo 13," the novelist and screenwriter Richard Price told interviewer Steven Rea in 1995. "Ron Howard [the director] said this guy rewrote everything, and he didn't get a credit" (7). According to E. Deidre Pribram, an independent filmmaker and scholar, Sayles included a short, bold note with his third draft revision: "Please precede [sic] with your preparation of the movie based on this draft of Apollo 13. This is it. It really is. No kidding. Good luck" (12). Sayles dramatized the screenplay and incorporated some of Tom Hanks's ideas, yet the screenwriter's Guild denied him a credit. Brian Grazer, the successful producer of the film, paid Sayles a screen-credit bonus anyway.*

similar to that of Sayles's own directorial work.

Lately, Sayles's name has appeared on a number of different films, some good, some bad. *Men of War* (1994), an action film starring Dolph Lundgren, began its film life as *A Safe Place*. Sayles's original screenplay was about "a guy who's a mercenary. He runs into Stone Age people, and they seem pacifistic. He starts rethinking his life, and decides to defend the place, and of course there's a big fight at the end" (Aufderheide *Cineaste* 15). The film's credits now include two other screenwriters, Ethan Reiff and Cyrus Voris. While Sayles's story line is still evident, the film itself is a testosterone dream. Now the film stands as a weak copy of John Irvin's *Dogs of War* (1980). Many of the actors in the film, including Don Harvey, Anthony John Denison, Tom Wright, and Kevin Tighe, have worked with Sayles in the past. But the film lacks the humor of the old New World picture reunions.

Sayles has established a rewarding side career as a script doctor. For instance, Sayles fleshed out Gene Hackman's character in *The Quick and the Dead* (1994), to "Americanize" the villain's language (Turan 1). He rewrote a film entitled *Passing Glory* for Disney. But Sayles's best-known uncredited work was on Ron Howard's Oscar-nominated *Apollo 13* (1995). "The way I make my living, basically, is by writing screenplays for other people which usually means rewriting screenplays that somebody else tried," Sayles explained to an audience at the Independent Feature Film Marketplace, "and so I read a lot of screenplays and I'd say the biggest fault that I find with them is that they're not dramatized" (Pribram 13). What

Sayles did with the screenplay written by William Broyles, Jr., and Al Reinert, which was based on James Lovell's *Lost Moon*, was to make the story more personal, to enhance the moon mission's history, a story most filmgoers would know, by revolving around the figure of Jim Lovell (Tom Hanks).

As the film opens, the Lovells are hosting a party to celebrate Neil Armstrong's walk on the moon. Lovell, according to the screenplay, badly wants to reach the moon. As he says, his career is "like climbing Mt. Everest and stopping ten yards from the top." Sayles makes viewers empathize with Lovell and his wife, Marilyn, who understands her husband's desire yet fears his going into space again. The emotional connection established between these two people early on gives the film a personal quality that adds excitement to an old story. *Apollo 13* is, after all, a tale of heroic endeavor. We witness an individual putting his aspirations ahead of his family, only to return to them after his quest has failed. *Apollo 13* is big Hollywood entertainment. With the possible exception of Jack Swigert (Kevin Bacon), every individual here performs his job with strength and intelligence, even as the pressure to save the three trapped astronauts seems, at times, beyond human possibility.

According to Sayles, the producers of *Apollo 13* "were very, very technically accurate. I got to talk to astronauts, and my job was to translate what they were saying into language that nonscientists could understand" (Carnes *Past Imperfect* 19). As E. Deidre Pribram observes, "Without this 'translation,' the suspense and excitement of the rescue efforts — which dominate the film — would be rendered virtually meaningless to a general audience" (14). Sayles creates easily consumed metaphors. Gene Kranz (Ed Harris) announces, "The lunar module just became a lifeboat." Or, as an engineer explains the power needed to complete a successful re-entry, "They could run this coffee maker for eight hours." Using common objects to fill in for technical jargon helps to keep the suspense high and the story understandable. Sayles's unadorned dialogue made *Apollo 13* the mass success it became. But rather than revel in his success, Sayles moved on to other projects.

Recently, Sayles completed drafts on a script for Rob Reiner focusing on the 1960s. Sayles adapted a Doris Lessing novel, *The Fifth Child*, for the screen. He also worked on a science fiction film titled *Brother Termite* for James Cameron, the director of *The Terminator* (1984), *Aliens* (1989), and *Titanic* (1997). Sayles's explanation of his work on this film sums up his attitude concerning the difference between his Hollywood assignments and his own work:

> With my own stuff, it's, "This is the story I want to tell." And that's the line I always use when one of my films is test-marketed, and it tests lower than they wanted it: "But it's the story I wanted to tell." Whereas, when you're working for other people, it's a different ballgame. I was just working on a giant cockroach movie, and the assistant to the public health guy in the story transformed from a pudgy Jason Alexander type to being a black street kid

who happens to like bugs, only because this or that producer was telling me
what to do. It doesn't matter to me, I can make them both work. It's their
story. [Lippy 196]

Sayles's quote indicates that he is flexible when it comes to studio work, which
is not the case when he is working on his own material. He also points out
that he can create any type of character and any type of voice, revealing the
confidence he has in his own writing skills. Clearly, Sayles understands that
there is more at stake when he is writing, directing, editing, and acting in his
own films.

4

Return of the Secaucus Seven

> If I'm going to make something outside the industry, it might as
> well be something that the industry isn't going to make.
> — John Sayles (Popkin)

In the fall of 1978, after a few years of writing screenplays for other people, Sayles decided he wanted to write, direct, and edit his own project, an
audition piece outside Hollywood's commercial limitations. Sayles had
$40,000 in start-up money, gained from his three New World Pictures screen-
plays and the sale of *The Anarchists' Convention*, a collection of short stories,
so a 16-millimeter feature seemed possible.

Because the financing for *Return of the Secaucus Seven* was all out-of-
pocket, Sayles understood that he "had to back up a bit and stop thinking in
pictures," part of his job description as a screenwriter-for-hire, and "start
thinking in budget" (*Thinking in Pictures* 5). After finishing the screenplay,
Sayles completed principal photography in five weeks. Because he was working with an inexperienced crew, he exceeded his own expectations: The film
was a success, albeit a slow-moving one, reaching a niche audience of filmgoers looking for real people and recognizable human behavior on-screen. *Return
of the Secaucus Seven* established Sayles politically, thematically, and aestheti-
cally. This seminal film introduces Sayles's pragmatic, realistic cinematic
approach, marked by economical camera work that is subservient to the story,
the play of his characters.

Before considering *Return of the Secaucus Seven*, Sayles understood that
access to the director's chair would be difficult, especially for someone with
no formal training: "I realized that it was going to take me a long time to
break into directing by the usual route, which is to write a hit for a studio
and then say, 'I want to direct the next one'" (Chute 54). Sayles saw "a good
five years of writing screenplays" ahead of him before he might be considered
as a director; he wanted to speed up the process (Auster and Quart 326). So

Return of the Secaucus Seven *(1980): John Sayles's first film displays his amazing ear for dialogue and his meticulous, pragmatic, evocatively realistic style of filmmaking. Sayles's ensemble cast deliver solid acting jobs, making it hard to believe that they are really a group of summer stock friends who set out to help a buddy make his first movie. Sayles's characters are bright and articulate, with a strong sense of irony. The movie succeeds because of its language and actors. Even though Sayles never intended to release the film commercially,* Return of the Secaucus Seven *went on to spawn a genre all its own. As Tom Stempel observed, the children of the* Secaucus Seven *are everywhere: "Sayles's emphasis on dialogue showed young writer-directors the way to make a major impact on a low budget was through great, dramatic, funny, often raunchy, dialogue. Without* Secaucus Seven, *would we have had 'Please baby please' and the sequence of pick-up lines in* She's *Gotta Have It, the explanation of 'snowballing' in* Clerks, *the discussion of the meaning of Madonna's 'Like a Virgin' in* Reservoir Dogs, *or, speaking of Madonna, the sales pitch for her pap smear in* Slacker?" (Creative Screenwriting 98). *What sets Sayles's characters in* Return of the Secaucus Seven *apart, however, is their emotional and intellectual richness—they seem human, ordinary people with ordinary triumphs and failures. Moreover, they all connect with one another, a theme that Sayles explores in all his films. This is a group photograph of the cast and crew on location in North Conway, New Hampshire. Sayles is seated at the far right holding a baby. Photo courtesy of the Museum of Modern Art Film Stills Archive.*

he set out to teach himself how to make a movie — one he would want to see: "I figured whatever I did or learned about directing I would have to finance myself" (Chute 54).

Although a do-it-yourself filmmaking education seems an expensive and foolhardy endeavor, for Sayles the result was a pure American success story.

While *Return of the Secaucus Seven* opened and closed in New York in the fall of 1980 to little fanfare, in Boston, Los Angeles, and Washington, D.C., it drew sizable art-house audiences. Soon the *Secaucus Seven* was generating critical praise. The film won the Los Angeles Film Critics Award for Best Screenplay, found its way onto numerous "top ten" lists, and introduced John Sayles as a formidable new filmmaker, with talent as both a writer and a director.

Produced, in the end, for $60,000 of his own money with $125,000 covered by deferrals, a ludicrously small amount by film industry standards, *Return of the Secaucus Seven* caught the attention of film aficionados, critics, and studio executives because, according to critic David Osborne, it "tapped a warm vein of nostalgia among Sayles's contemporaries, longing for some public confirmation of their strange journey through the seventies" (31). The film, however, hardly wallows in nostalgia. *Return of the Secaucus Seven* contains shrewd observations about human nature, reveals conflicting class and gender viewpoints, and is full of sly humor.

Like all of Sayles's early screen work, *Return of the Secaucus Seven* appeals to the ear rather than the eye — speech governs image. Sayles, however, readily admits to the commercial and entertainment values of his first feature, which was conceived originally as an audition piece for the Hollywood studios: "I wanted to walk a tightrope between making something they'd never make, but having production, writing, and directing values that they would recognize as good for their purposes, too" (Chute 54). It was, however, Sayles's literary elements, story and characters, that attracted an audience.

Return of the Secaucus Seven is straightforward, a film in which nothing much happens, a slice-of-life story. Seven college friends, 1960s leftists and antiwar activists, all approximately 30 years of age, gather at a New England summer home for an annual reunion weekend, where they eat, drink, smoke, talk, and look toward the future with adjusted but not diminished ideals. For the most part, the film lacks dramatic action, eschewing traditional plot dynamics — the story is not chock-full of drama, leading to a climax and definitive resolution. Instead, the film unfolds episodically — a trip to a summer playhouse, a volleyball game, a basketball game, a cookout, a swim in an old quarry, a boozy night at a local tavern, a group arrest, and a hungover Sunday morning — events that combine to give the film a documentary, lived-in quality, cinema verité, a look Sayles does nothing to disguise. "Sometimes a line of dialogue," Sayles points out, "can save you a lot of shots that look great but don't tell you much" (Auster and Quart 330). Unlike the work of his contemporaries Oliver Stone, David Lynch, and Spike Lee, memorable, elaborate imagery does not dominate Sayles's early film work, especially *Return of the Secaucus Seven*.

Since the beginning of his film career, Sayles has never been seduced by style for style's sake. Film's broad canvas can be manipulated with a visual élan almost unattainable in other art forms. But when style smothers substance, the viewer is left with little after a trip to the theater except the fading memory of an attractive eyewash rich in light and color. Sayles's film stories grow from his populist conviction that a filmmaker should not become "either a caterer to the elite or a panderer to the masses," but should attempt to "pick and build" his or her "images so that anybody can get into the story on some level, so that maybe people are drawn in deeper than they thought they could or would want to go" (*Thinking in Pictures* 8).

Realism is Sayles's stylistic trademark. The literary critic Wallace Martin suggests that the best realistic narratives startle us "into an awareness of the real"; they capture "a truth of experience that we knew, however dimly, all along" (58). In other words, realism, when done well, can illuminate the mundane details of the day-to-day world, telling us about ourselves, as we experience people whom we know or could have known. In *Return of the Secaucus Seven* Sayles presents typical people who participated in a much criticized and revised period of American history in order to demythologize or debunk clichéd notions about those involved in the sixties movement. He creates ordinary people who believe in the power of community effort. In so doing, Sayles provides a view from ground level, free from the glitz and the glitter of ostentatious stylization and heroic posturing. None of these people is larger than life. Sayles dredges common experience out of the seemingly extraordinary sixties.

In response to a question that described the characters in *Return of the Secaucus Seven* as less ideological and sectarian than many of the people connected with the sixties movement, Sayles defined his approach to his characters and his audience:

> They are people who went to marches, not those who planned them. They're people who did not go just to see what the action was, but who really felt very strongly about their commitments. They were issue oriented and very concrete in their goals, not hard-liners or Marxist-Leninists who had a perspective that colors all their thinking. But I didn't want this to be an in-group film. I wanted my characters to be more accessible to an audience that did not participate in the "movement," and which might not like the characters if they met them in real life. I want the audience to come see the film, and possibly reconsider their own perspective on these people and the "movement." [Auster and Quart 327]

By constructing an unglamorous group of people who actually participated in the counterculture movement, Sayles offers an alternative portrait of a community of friends who share a political and social linkage without sentimentality or apology, even while some of their lives are becoming more middle class, more stable, more mainstream status quo.

Return of the Secaucus Seven divides its attention among seven old friends (four women and three men), one invited guest, and two working-class "townies." The Secaucus Seven are Mike (Bruce MacDonald) and Katie (Maggie

Renzi), high school teachers who rent the summer home that is located in Mike's hometown; Jeff (Mark Arnott) and Maura (Karen Trott), an estranged married couple whose split adds a trace of drama to the reunion; Francis (Maggie Cousineau-Arndt), a medical school student; J.T. (Adam Le Fevre), a down-on-his-luck folk singer; and Irene (Jean Passanante), a speech writer for a Democratic senator. Into this mix Sayles blends Irene's lover Chip (Gordon Clapp), a straight-arrow the others do not know, and Mike's two "townie" friends, Ron (David Strathairn), an ex-jock gasoline station attendant, and Howie (Sayles himself), the perplexed father of three who works two jobs just to keep his family afloat. All the actors, people Sayles "knew from having worked in summer stock as an actor and director" (Rosen 183), played their parts superbly. Many film critics credited the actors for their improvisational spontaneity, which missed the mark but stood as a testament to their ability to carry off Sayles's lines.

Return of the Secaucus Seven revolves around the lives of these people and their relationships. The Secaucus Seven gained their name on a trip to Washington, D.C., for an antiwar rally. The group was arrested at the Secaucus, New Jersey, turnpike exit and spent the night in jail for possession of marijuana, a charge dropped the following day due to police bungling. The group contains a variety of personalities, sixties-generation cohorts, who break up into twos and threes as the events of the reunion weekend occur to recall the past, to talk about turning 30, and to make fresh plans. These sequences serve as opportunities for sizing each other up, for sharing confidences, for brief love affairs, and for ending a marriage. In short, it is a fairly typical gathering of old friends.

This multicharacter, episodic format interconnects like a collection of short stories sharing the same characters, such as Sherwood Anderson's *Winesburg, Ohio*, but without its dark rumblings. We hear and see people talking to and about their friends with humor, warmth, and rueful understanding, providing the film an authenticity not usually associated with American cinema. Sayles's film recalls the Swiss director Alain Tanner's *Jonah Who Will Be 25 in the Year 2000* (1976), a film that examines a diverse group of French and Swiss friends while commenting on the cultural and political changes after the revolutionary events of 1968 in France. Both Tanner and Sayles present committed people with a shared history attempting to make their way in a society that provides few leads. As in *Jonah* the vitality of *Return of the Secaucus Seven* comes from Sayles's characters. Not unlike the characters in Anderson's short fiction or Tanner's film, these people attempt to come to terms with the direction of their lives.

For Sayles, however, it is John Cassavetes, the late American actor and maverick director, who provided the creative impetus for Sayles to move beyond the limitations of his paycheck screenplays and to set out on his own. In describing Cassavetes's work for the *New York Times* Sayles notes an awareness shared by many would-be filmmakers who saw *Shadows* (1962) or *Faces* (1968) or *A Woman Under the Influence* (1974) for the first time:

> This is an American movie, but I know these people. It isn't a Technicolor dream or a cartoon with live actors; it doesn't drip with studio mood music or theatrical problem-drama dialogue. There is recognizable human behavior, adult human behavior, happening up on a movie screen. ["Cassavetes's Sources" 17]

Cassavetes's work was emotionally honest and risky. Like Sayles, Cassavetes ignored heroic endeavor and melodramatic longings, which lie at the core of many American films. Cassavetes, however, also sacrificed consistent, planned narrative development, which is anathema to a Sayles film. Though his plots drifted, the focus of Cassavetes's films was realistic characters. Indeed, the often unpleasant honesty with which Cassavetes explored the reality of people's daily lives, reminiscent of neorealist films of the 1940s, puts to shame most mainstream American films dealing with similar domestic traumas.

In addition to the honest subjects Cassavetes explored, Sayles also points out that Cassavetes's "other legacy lies not in the content or style of his films, but in the mere fact of them" ("Cassavetes's Sources" 21). Cassavetes was a prototypical independent filmmaker who told the stories he wanted to tell outside the mainstream industry. "His career as a director," Sayles writes, "was a great, subversive act, and you never got the feeling watching his movies that he expected any thanks for it" (21). Cassavetes's brand of cinema dealt with the private domain, examining themes of a more personal nature: emotions, relationships, and family structures. He did not create tight commercial packages. Instead, Cassavetes brought his own particular point of view to the screen, and in doing so asked his audience to re-examine the conventions of traditional American filmmaking.

According to Sayles, it was Cassavetes who showed aspiring filmmakers that the "natural moment" was not the property of the Europeans. Cassavetes and Sayles share a common desire to capture what Andre Bazin described as "a fragment of concrete reality" that in itself is "multiple and full of ambiguity" (37). Sayles's characters spring from the same unadorned reality, but they are buffered by his humanism and the wry, ironic wit of his pen.

Moment by moment, *Return of the Secaucus Seven* captures the characters living their lives — the camera simply documents their actions. Sayles used a 16-millimeter camera to photograph *Secaucus Seven*, resulting in a grainy image when the release print of the film was blown up to 35-millimeter, adding an unpolished, gritty authenticity to its images. It was Sayles's intention to ensure that the characters "come across very real, that you don't feel you are watching actors" (Chute 56). By using unknowns, actors free from critical typecasting, Sayles had an advantage that allowed him to be more natural in his approach, an impossibility with slick, recognizable actors. Viewers, according to Sayles, "would think they must all be playing themselves, even though none of them are" (Chute 55). The actors do not appear more organized or purposeful than life allows. Sayles's cast members were non–Screen Actors Guild actors, all around 30 years old, whom he knew from working in a summer stock company called the Eastern Slope Playhouse in New Hampshire, which is where the *Secaucus Seven* was shot. According to David Rosen and Peter Hamilton, authors of *Off-Hollywood*, "The project grew out of [Sayles's] experience working with Jeff Nelson," a producer of the film, at Eastern Slope (182). Nelson told Rosen that the film was made "to culminate and memorialize our work together" (182–83). Not only do these unknowns look right for their roles, but as professional actors they understood how to make their characters believable and, more important, how to deliver their lines as written.

Overall, the acting in *Return of the Secaucus Seven* carries an ease usually realized by seasoned professionals. Each performer accentuates his or her written role with nonchalance. Their acting is natural, seemingly effortless. Much of the credit for this successful transference from script to screen must go to Sayles for his writing and his directorial belief that actors bring life to their written roles: "Even though there is no ad-libbing in the picture, it still is not a living thing until actors come there and make something out of these characters. Each actor is the star of their own movie" (Schlesinger 7). Furthermore, as Nelson observes, the film was completely scripted: "The improvisational tone achieved is the result of John's approach as a director, and of the actors, including John, having worked together for years in summer stock" (Rosen and Hamilton 184).

Traditionally, a screenplay is a story told with pictures, but the *Secaucus Seven* depends primarily upon talk. As Sayles notes, the film "is a story about complex relationships of human beings," and "human beings do most of their communicating verbally" (*Thinking in Pictures* 6). Yet for an independent filmmaker, deciding to make a film with a large ensemble cast is unusual. Typically, first features focus on one or two characters because the cost of production limits the scope of the script. But Sayles explores many themes in the film: friendship, love, political commitment, and the malaise of middle-class reality. This reunion of old friends allows Sayles to deal with all these issues and more, and the event has a natural beginning and ending. But the film does not seem overly schematic or structured. "I did," Sayles says, "what I knew I could do best"—which is write (Auster and Quart 330).

In the opening sequence, as Mike performs toilet maintenance, muted music can be heard, then Katie's voice: "We should put Irene and this guy in here." Mike responds, "Yeah, we probably should. You know where the dustpan is?" Then Sayles cuts to Katie as she smoothes out a freshly made bed: "They just got together, they'll be at it like rabbits. Behind the refrigerator." A cut to Mike as he whispers to himself, "No, it's not," while he gazes into the slow-running toilet. Then he replies loudly, "Yeah, like when she and J.T. first got it on, when we lived on Mass Ave." Again a cut to Katie, who is now testing the gauge and squeak of the box-spring mattress: "Or maybe out on the porch?" Talking while prepping the house for weekend guests is hardly flashy; in fact, it is downright plain, and representative of Sayles's low-key approach. The dialogue, however, has the mercurial quality of everyday speech, weaving carnal speculation with the mundane trivia of household chores. By splicing conversational topics and establishing crosscurrents, Sayles cleverly renders what lies at the heart of *Return of the Secaucus Seven*: how individuals intertwine through shared history and work to form a community.

The Secaucus Seven overlap, connect, miss each other, yet cleave to the group through shared histories. As Katie and Mike continue to plan the sleeping arrangements for the weekend, the dialogue reveals this past and the fluctuation that marks the lives of these old friends. Again the characters are separated by their positions in the house. Katie stands framed by a doorway, clutching a pile of linen; Mike squats, peering into a vanity cabinet full of cleaning materials:

> KATIE: How did we ever fit everybody when Jeff and Maura came?
> MIKE: Well, for a while Irene and J.T. were sleeping together, which made it more convenient.
> KATIE: Yeah, but that was when Frances was with what's-his-name.
> MIKE: The one nobody could stand.
> KATIE: Jeff liked him.
> MIKE: No, no. Different guy. The one nobody liked was before the one that only Jeff liked.

Skillfully, Sayles introduces the "seven" through Katie and Mike's dialogue. By discussing the various partners each character has had, Sayles speaks to the old free life of the "seven." This interconnection reflects Sayles's desire to move away from a single focal figure whose story commands control of point of view, toward a more realistic examination of group interaction, involving multiple perspectives.

Sayles's written depiction of his female characters illustrates the fact that the Secaucus Seven are a politically aware bunch. These women reflect ordinary lives: They are not model beautiful, maniacally depressed, or perky television types. Instead, they are strong, normal-looking, independent women who work and think for themselves. Feminism is firmly established as part of their lives. In Sayles's words, "These are women who have gone through the 'movement' (feminism) and come out the other end, and, now, it's part of everything they do" (Auster and Quart 328–29). They talk about their problems, their work, sex, birth control, the possibility of having children, and offer solutions with informed intelligence. For example, when Katie and

Frances discuss the negative aspects of "the pill" early on in the film, the scene is, in typical Sayles fashion, both funny and serious:

> KATIE: I saw you came prepared.
> FRANCES: Huh?
> KATIE: The old plastic clam in the overnight bag.
> FRANCES: Oh, yeah. I decided to get off the pill.
> KATIE: What was it doing to you?

Frances's response is couched in medical school terminology, describing the possible side-effects of oral birth control on women. As the list of adverse reactions grows — nausea, vomiting, bloating, bleeding, suppressed lactation, hirsutism, nervousness, fatigue, mental depression — Katie and Frances roll their eyes and smile. The list alone is enough to cause depression. But Katie ends things on an upbeat note when she reminds Frances that she brought her diaphragm for a purpose.

Times, of course, have changed. But taken in the cultural context of the late 1970s and early 1980s, Sayles's female characters are the sort Molly Haskell lamented not seeing on the Hollywood screen in the 1970s when she noted that "nothing in movies came close to conveying the special quality of women's relationships on a day-to-day working, or living, basis" (377). Sayles, unlike most of his contemporaries, does not ignore or subjugate women; rather, he endorses feminism. His female characters are their own people: Katie is a teacher, Frances is completing medical school, Irene is a speechwriter, and Maura, who is breaking away from a suffocating marriage, directs inner-city children's theater groups. Each is relatively comfortable with herself. They understand that they can make choices in their lives. Still, Sayles's dialogue would never have made it into a more commercial script. Therefore, his female characters countervail the film images of women's inferiority, which Haskell describes as the "big lie perpetrated on Western society," a staple of most contemporary American filmmakers even today.

Like Cassavetes before him and Ken Loach today, Sayles attempts to capture people who not only look real, they sound real. There is nothing theatrical or melodramatic about Sayles's characters. The ability to capture the texture, pitch, and sound of everyday speech, spoken by a wide spectrum of characters, is an uncanny gift Sayles possesses, and one that he downplays, calling it a trick akin to "being able to bend your fingers back" (Chute 56). Sayles does not suffer from the endless introspection that dominates much of modern literature, but instead keenly observes the world and reports on it both literally and figuratively. In *Return of the Secaucus Seven*, the dialogue is pitch perfect, a solid, believable record of people talking; it has to be, because the pace of the film is structured around cuts between dialogue-rich scenes: Characters drive the narrative.

Sayles's writing, in both his fiction and his films, reveals a wry, natural sense of humor. His characters are funny without seeming contrived, eliciting from the audience smiles of awareness and knowing chuckles, not guffaws. When a line is funny, it is the character who gets the credit, not the screenwriter. For instance, Katie lies wide eyed in bed analyzing relationships as Mike groggily responds, trying to fall asleep:

> KATIE: Everybody breaking up. It makes me nervous.
>
> MIKE: Who's everybody? Just Maura and Jeff.
>
> KATIE: Maura and Jeff and J.T. and Irene and Irene and Dwight and Frances and Phil. And my parents.
>
> MIKE: I don't think your parents are good examples of anything.
>
> KATIE: How many people do we know who have been together for any length of time?
>
> MIKE: Lots. Look at the people we know at school — the Whites...
>
> KATIE: The Whites are born-again — they don't count.
>
> MIKE: Karen and Dick.
>
> KATIE: I mean people we like.
>
> MIKE: That must be it — everybody we like is hard to live with.

Katie is comparing herself to their friends; Mike wants to sleep. Of course, Katie's concern is valid, and maintaining a long-term relationship is an issue broached by the film. But Sayles's approach is nonchalant; this is bedroom talk, not a dramatic event. On one hand, Katie sees the world as threatening, always on the verge of chaos; on the other, Mike accepts the day as it comes, and tries to get by with wit and, as he sees it, critical intelligence. Because the dialogue is humorous, it is entirely possible to miss the underlying point of the conversation, which is Katie's unstated desire for more security, a symptom of turning 30. This, however, is Sayles's method: Only upon reflection do the film's seemingly miscellaneous, talk-filled events take on larger meaning.

The subtle veracity of Sayles's writing makes his work both rich and concrete. His screenwriting here presents varied ideas in honest speech. The relationship among Ron, the gas-pumping mechanic, Howie, the family man, and Mike, the only member of this high school basketball playing trio who got away from their hometown, illustrates Sayles's class consciousness, which is an essential part of all his work.

By crossing and examining class boundaries, Sayles's political bent becomes clear. Early in the film, members of the reunion party are sitting in the backyard, soaking up the sun, preparing for a cookout, and gossiping about their friends. The phone rings. Mike tells Katie, who elects to answer the call, that "if it's Ron, tell him I'm out shopping." J.T. asks him, "What's wrong with Ron?" Irene says, "I saw Ron in town; he tried to wipe my windshield with his body." Mike replies, "That's Ron. I like Ron. We just don't have anything in common anymore. High school was ten years ago. I teach high school now." The degree of intellectual distance between Ron and Mike is obvious. Ron speaks in a provincial, clichéd argot, the often sexist, often funny, speech of working people. For the most part, Ron avoids expressing his thoughts and feelings, relying on brash witticism and goofy mugging instead. Mike, on the other hand, likes to display his education and intelligence through his language, performing a mock display of his role as high school history teacher for the group, using the Socratic method to explore the Boston police strike of 1919, which had its roots in class antagonisms. He sees himself as the de facto leader of the group.

Yet Mike sees no link between his leftist intellectual leanings and Ron's position in their small New England hometown. In fact, he considers Ron to be a yahoo, telling the group that the last time Ron traveled to Boston was for a snowmobile convention, a sign of cultural impoverishment. Mike thinks he shares little with Ron, conveniently ignoring their own past, which is an odd choice for someone who teaches history from a working-class perspective. Here we see a solid example of Sayles's trenchant, layered irony.

The relationship between Ron and Mike fits a pattern that runs through Sayles's work — people whose lives, while connected, are separated by culture and class. In his narratives, Sayles makes few critical judgments about his characters, allowing them to speak for themselves, and allowing his audience to make its own judgments.

Sayles recognizes that college negates high school's democratic mixture of people from different classes. Sayles examines this separation, giving equal credibility to each character. Thus, Sayles makes Ron appealing, even with all his shortcomings. Ron, as played by David Strathairn, is funny and charming, a delightfully sexist garage-jock fully aware of who he is and why he stays in his hometown pumping gas and working on cars. Unlike many of the Secaucus Seven, Ron understands why he does what he does.

During the bar sequence, for instance, after Frances asks Ron why he does not think of moving away, his response underscores his self-knowledge: "I fix cars; that's what I do. In town here, if somebody's car is running a little rough, brakes are shot, thing won't start, they say, take it to Ron." Frances tells him that his position sounds like that of the family doctor, and Ron likes the analogy. He says, "But if I move, say, somewhere else, the city or something, I'd be just another guy in a grease monkey suit." Ron's need to be appreciated for his work and his abilities is obvious, and even if his choice may not satisfy the appetites of Sayles's audience, Ron's logic is sound: His character exemplifies Sayles's genuine leftist values by showing the integrity and decency beneath Ron's workingman's exterior.

Howie, who appears briefly, plays a slightly different role. He has children. The kids cause Mike to wonder, with a slight touch of envy, what life would be like with his own children. Katie, on the other hand, delivers her attitude toward a family: "There but for the grace of Ovulin 21 go I." None of the Secaucus Seven has kids, a fairly typical choice for these early baby boomers, and only Irene declares that the thought of having children is appealing. Sayles allows Howie to use two small-town-male passions to define life with children: cars and Main Street. He recalls a former high school classmate, "Ace Campana," who in eleventh grade bought an old Thunderbird automobile with a lightning bolt painted down the side: "Every day after school he was down at the Texaco station pumping gas to pay for the insurance, and every minute of every weekend he's under the fuckin' thing." Howie's point, however, is the pride Ace took when "he bombed down Main Street." For a brief small-town moment, Ace was a "king." Howie says, "You thought of Ace, you thought of that old T-Bird. Like one of those Greek things. Horse ones." Mike interjects: "Centaurs." Howie agrees, "Centaurs. Half man and half T-Bird. Anyway, that's what it's like having kids." Mike contends that having children cannot be as bad as Howie's strained analogy suggests. In truth, Howie is proud of his children, even though he complains about them. He enjoys taking his wife and children out, showing them off, as Ace did with his car. Yet he works two jobs to support them; this is no Capraesque family. Still, Howie, unlike the other characters, has at least one concrete thing in his life, his family. Intellectually, Mike and Howie are miles apart, but Mike still wonders what life would be like if he were married and had children, decisions Howie made when he was 19. As always, Sayles does not didactically advocate one choice over the other.

Being smart and committed, however, is not the secret to a successful existence either. Jeff, who like many of the others served as a VISTA volunteer, remains the most radically committed of the Seven; he is also the most confused character in the film. As written, Jeff is an upper-middle-class man captivated by activism. Even though his parents can, according to one of his friends, "cater the entire state of Delaware" for their family reunion, Jeff has the most politically progressive job of them all. He works in a detox-rehabilitation center, displaying his activism for all to see. Much can be gained from examining what Sayles's characters do for a living. Sayles, who himself spent time working in hospitals, describes detox centers as the frontline, "one of the best burnout places you can be in" (Auster and Quart 328). Maura, Jeff's estranged wife, calls his crumbling psyche "sympathetic withdrawal." To underscore the point that Jeff is lost, Sayles has the character carry a small bag of heroin for the entire film. Jeff is unsure whether the narcotic is a gift or an acknowledgment that one of his patients has kicked his habit. Metaphorically, the drug represents the ruinous effects of Jeff's sixties involvement. Jeff is drunk on high-profile activism: He cannot let go of the narcotic because its potential is too great. Jeff, in Sayles's words, "is somebody who got hooked on activism, rather than on the spirit and ideas behind it, and he misses the limelight of activism" (Auster and Quart 328). The detox center provides no satisfaction; it is a burden like the small package in his pocket. Jeff has lost his way by anesthetizing himself against the realities of the present. He does not use his past as part of his process of growth. Like the junkies he works with, Jeff discovers a narcotic release in his form of activism.

During the course of the film, Jeff reveals nothing about himself. All of his friends talk about their work, their worries, and their feelings, adding depth to their personalities as they learn from one another. Generally, Jeff confronts people and tries to dominate the conversation with clever rhetoric or shouting. In the bar sequence, he mystifies a pretentious female "rock critic" with his analysis of progressive rock, telling her that "even the back beat is full of nuances," which makes no sense but certainly sounds good. Later on, he yells at Maura, silencing the entire bar with his rage. Sayles also presents a single, quick, telling shot of Jeff in the bar: He stands alone, looking confused, framed in black. Clearly, Jeff is the most troubled of the Secaucus Seven. As the film ends, Mike finds a note from Jeff saying, "I'm sorry." Jeff's cryptic note suggests that he is apologizing for his disturbed behavior, but his problems run much deeper.

Yet even though Jeff cannot release himself from his past, and must suffer for it, Sayles still treats him sympathetically. As Jeff rattles off his arrest record — an arm-long list that would do any left-wing radical proud — for a police officer late in the film, he longingly looks at Maura with the realization that this list, this spoken testament to his turbulent commitment, was shared with the woman standing near him, and without her his seemingly heroic achievements will come to nothing. As Sayles says, "The problem was not that he was a radical, it's just that he was hooked on the wrong part of it [the movement] to be happy now" (Auster and Quart 328). This reaction shot is a touching visual moment from a director not then known for his mise-en-scène.

Indeed, Sayles's ability with a pen draws praise while he is criticized for perfunctory visuals, yet he clearly understands the importance of the visual field, and how it influences the success of a picture. Part of the problem, of course, is money. Sayles tailors his films to the resources he has at hand, a pragmatic choice for any sober, independent filmmaker. For example, *Secaucus Seven*'s opening credits feature mug shots of the group, from front and side, as if they had just been pulled from a police file; these images are spiced with the heroic flavor of dramatic, guitar-driven malaguena music, forcefully building to a climax. As Sayles points out, "It could be a movie about terrorists. And it could be a thriller" (Smith 68). This snappy, charged mixture of photography and music is undercut by a less than heroic shot of a toilet plunger, the first real shot we see. Juxtaposing the outlaw figures of the credit sequence with an innocuous, necessary household chore is deliberate; it establishes a mock-heroic tone. Sayles reminds his audience that life is not grandiose but mundane: "These kids had this inflated expectation of how they were going to change the world" (Smith 68). Still, the mug shots and the household chores are interrelated; each shot represents a part of the lives of the people whose stories are about to unfold before us, which contain more toilets than highlights. "They had their moment in the sun," Sayles remarks, "and their publicity, it turns out, was a mug shot. Not the cover of *Time* magazine — a mug shot in Secaucus, New Jersey" (Smith 68).

From its opening shots, *Return of the Secaucus Seven* signals an independent, unromantic sensibility at work. Plunging a toilet is not the most enticing way to open a film, especially one meant to appeal to Hollywood executives, but that is what Sayles shows us: a plunger at the ready, about to be used on a rust-stained toilet bowl. Nothing could be more pedestrian — or, in a slyly ironic way, more comic. Any expectations that the Secaucus Seven were somehow a magnificent but overlooked bunch from the fringes of the counterculture movement are immediately dashed. Quickly, Sayles has communicated via images that this film deals with the ordinary, prosaic affairs of regular people, and not a group whose collective title suggests great daring.

Sayles defends his visual plainness by reminding his critics what his work is about. "My main emphasis," he says, "is making films about people. I'm not interested in cinematic art" (Auster and Quart 330). Certainly the bathroom shot is not beautiful, nor is it meant to be. Yet as Sayles denigrates cinematic art, the reality he captures reveals his own film aesthetic. Indeed, his essential style presents visual facts from his characters' lives. Sayles's group of seven are regular folk, and the opening of the film says as much. However, when dialogue blends with the opening scene, Sayles's fascination with people and their interrelatedness becomes concrete.

Because Sayles's writing is so strong, the suggestion that his visuals are a bit crude has become a constant critical focus. But circumstances explain that Sayles makes do with what he has. In spite of a limited budget, a tight shooting schedule, poor equipment, and lack of experience, Sayles did not deny the mise-en-scène of *Return of the Secaucus Seven*. While his visual composition is low-key, a consequence of independent filmmaking and his unadorned style, Sayles shows concern for the pictures that make up his films. *Return of the Secaucus Seven*, which was conceived as flypaper for studio executives, does not neglect its visual components. In this first film, Sayles's sure, formal approach to composition is refreshing, avoiding seductive, flashy visual technique, the dominant visual aesthetic of contemporary cinema.

Sayles understands the distinctions between visual communication and verbal communication, but he is skeptical of purely visual communication. In *Thinking in Pictures* he defends *Return of the Secaucus Seven* as a film that could not be told only in visual terms: "to make these characters mute would be to reduce them to stereotypes" (6). While his defense stretches credulity (no critic demanded that Sayles make a silent film), he does go on to make a point that illustrates the type of film he wants to make and his desire to reach a general, literate audience:

> This goes against most concepts of "pure cinema," but pure cinema is at its weakest when trying to deal with human beings in narrative form. Stories, cartoons, and even the best of the silent comedies and dramas, or the visual metaphors become so complex in themselves that you have to do an incredible amount of mental translating into highly literary language to understand what is going on. [6–7]

On the surface, television commercials or MTV videos with high production values can be more viscerally stimulating than the mise-en-scène of *Return of the Secaucus Seven*, yet commercial images tend to be painfully simple, the message easily forgotten once the glare and the flash fade.

By contemporary American standards, Sayles's visual style is plain. Sayles insists, however, that filmmaking is a multifaceted process, combining writing, mise-en-scène, sound, and editing. For example, when J.T., the down-and-out folk singer, is introduced, Sayles sets up a master shot with considerable awareness, for multiple elements combine to tell us about this character. This long shot reveals J.T.'s physical appearance and his personality. He has the uniform of a folk singer, including a vest, denim shirt, blue jeans, a rucksack, and a guitar case. But J.T. is more than an image, and Sayles's shot goes beyond stereotyping. J.T. is in the foreground, and the open road, his place metaphorically and literally, is to his back. When he spots an oncoming car, he raises his thumb with hopeful anticipation. To comment on the image and the character, Sayles adds an upbeat folk guitar track. As a car approaches, the buoyant music matches the look on J.T.'s face; when the car passes, the music stops, and J.T.'s grin fades. This shot illustrates a hitchhiker's lament, pricking the memories of the audience; it also visually describes this character. J.T.'s life, we will come to find out, has been inflated and deflated since he dropped out of college, and he has missed more rides than he has caught.

Sayles's naturalistic mise-en-scène communicates much about J.T. He is, for example, the only member of the Secaucus Seven without roots of some kind; he still hears the call of the open road, the dream of something better down the line — in his case, Los Angeles. Sayles displays his understanding of visual metaphor here. Yet the image is not overly complex, abstract to a fault; rather, it is approachable, easily consumed, and does not require a professorial translation in order for the viewer to understand its meaning. Sayles's mise-en-scène is straightforward; his visual imagery deliberately celebrates the ordinary. J.T. appears as he is, alone, hoping to catch a ride, seeking more than open space.

The weakest scene of the film, one that provides critics fodder for their attacks on Sayles's visual constructions, is the basketball game, a scene created to show studio executives on-screen action. Before the game begins, J.T. admits to Jeff, who arrived unexpectedly, that he had slept with Maura the previous night. Jeff and J.T. then express their sexual jealousy on the court, while poor Chip displays how inept he is when it comes to physical activity. The problem with the scene is that it goes on too long before any payoff comes. Sayles's editing is at fault, not just the shot selection — the pace of the entire sequence lacks unifying rhythm. Incredibly, Sayles had no experience editing before *Return of the Secaucus Seven*: "I learned how to work the editing machine by reading the manual they gave me when I rented it" (Osborne 32). Still, Sayles seems to have recognized the problem himself. He cuts to shots of Frances, Irene, Maura, and Katie talking about their relationships, jobs, children, and J.T.'s plight while the men play out their aggression on the basketball court. The juxtaposition of men not talking, yet acting out their aggression, and the women discussing real issues points out their differences. Sayles's editing here actually enhances the sequence.

Part of the problem with the basketball sequence is its veracity. The actors are not good at presenting believable stunts. When Jeff pushes J.T. into the support pole that holds the basketball backboard and hoop, he does not actually hit the pole. We are, however, asked to believe that he had suffered a blow to the head. To complicate the problem with the sequence, Sayles drapes a nearly inaudible pulsing beat over the action; this sound, which is meant to accentuate the anger building on the court, creates an aural distraction, like an insect buzzing in one's ear. Thus, the basketball sequence becomes superfluous, visually retelling information we already know. Sharper editing, stuntmen, and more fluid camera work, which all cost money, would have strengthened the credibility of the sequence.

In contrast, the swimming hole sequence demonstrates considerable visual flair. In the hands of a more commercial director, this portion of the story would have signaled the obligatory female nude scene. Sayles, however, turns the tables on the traditional and presents the men nude. For the most part, we see everything from the point of view of the women. Katie delivers explicit, comic comments about various pieces of male anatomy. In addition, diving off rock cliffs into a cool blue-green swimming hole is visually more appealing than a bunch of slow guys playing a game of pick-up basketball. Moreover, adding an ersatz alpine yodel as background music works much better than the electronic buzz of the basketball game. Both the physical setting and the musical choice blend to create an appealing yet straightforward sequence.

Sayles presents a more sophisticated mise-en-scène example at the conclusion of the film. As the Seven begin to depart for home, Jeff goes off by himself to cut wood behind the house, where no one can see him. We know Jeff suffers from his inability to recapture the thrill of sixties-style activism.

Sayles intercuts quick, medium shots of Jeff, furiously chopping, with long shots of various people departing. Jeff is photographed from a low angle; he is threatening, confused. His aggression countervails the friendly good-byes of his friends. Finally we see Jeff in a full shot, his back to the camera and his head leaning toward the ground, sitting on the chopping block with the detritus of his work spread before him, representing the fragmentation of his life. Jeff is trapped, a victim of his own inability to deal with people and events on an everyday level without the charged feel of a grand cause. This concluding shot is dominated by open sky, but Jeff is cut off by the splintered wood that surrounds him. We recognize Jeff's pain and loss, sympathizing with him while realizing that he is the root of his own unhappiness: He is not at ease with the ordinary circumstances of his life.

Return of the Secaucus Seven perfectly illustrates Sayles's methodological, formalistic approach to filmmaking and his ability to bring quality work to the screen. Sayles acknowledges a link between *Secaucus Seven* and "movies they made during World War II about a bunch of guys going through basic training and then into the army" (Schlesinger 7). The structure of a buddy film helped Sayles by keeping costs down, a priority for any independent filmmaker. Such films tend to be dialogue bound and contain multiple perspectives rather than that of one prominent individual. In addition, using an ensemble cast allows for numerous, rational cuts among various groupings of the cast, a technique Robert Altman used with success in *Nashville* (1975) and many other films. For Sayles, however, these cuts were not about style but about efficiency. Knowing the limitations of his budget, Sayles made a deliberate choice to "cut a lot," which keeps the audience's eyes moving and compensates for the lack of action. Metaphorically, however, the ensemble cast offers more than just a reason to keep the film flowing; it reveals Sayles's democratic philosophy, the multiple voices suggesting a pluralistic society rather than a single perspective, an approach Sayles uses in all his films.

Sayles realized that his budget would limit him to a finite location and time. Having established the New England setting and restricted the action to a single reunion weekend populated by friends all of whom are about to turn 30, Sayles then created believable people, giving each character something to talk about, the sort of language friends share. Formally, *Return of the Secaucus Seven* has what Sayles calls "a sort of molecular structure" (Schlesinger 5), a linkage system in which everyone has two or more connections to the other characters: These people know each other on physical, emotional, and intellectual levels. As Timothy Johnson observes, "Each individual compares himself or herself with the others and thus comprehends the choices he or she has made and the consequences of those choices" (486). Sayles presents nine fully realized characters in this film, people who talk with candor, wit, and intelligence in recognizable voices. His use of language is, in fact, so subtle that, because we are watching a film, the nuances he achieves can be easily overlooked. Sayles's story introduces his audience to a group of friends who exist in a nonheroic world where disillusioned yet noncynical adulthood has replaced the glamour of the sixties movement.

Before Sayles made *Return of the Secaucus Seven*, there was no such thing as a reunion film exploring the interaction of a group of old friends, once young together, who reveal their histories, as they revert to youthful behavior, to make sense of their present conditions. Now it is a genre, indeed almost a cottage industry. Sayles's depiction of people who were involved in the sixties movement and who now have their own problems was immediately picked up by Hollywood. Lawrence Kasdan's *The Big Chill* (1983) was the result. Since then television delivered *Thirtysomething*, and Hollywood returned with *Peter's Friends* (1992) and *Indian Summer* (1993).

Even with its low production values, *Return of the Secaucus Seven* compares more than favorably with all its offspring because of the creative force behind the film. Sayles created a group of smart, humorous, generous people, and he gave them unique voices and lives; they are not Hollywood "types." Sayles's Secaucus Seven display what was worthwhile about the sixties movement — his characters are still politically and professionally idealistic — without indulging in sentimental nostalgia or caving in to cynicism.

Moreover, *Return of the Secaucus Seven* now stands as a contemporary independent classic, because of its low budget and Sayles's writing, directing, acting, and editing. *Secaucus Seven* also marks the first feature Sayles made with people who would become regular collaborators: actors Gordon Clapp and David Strathairn, composer Mason Daring, and producer and actor Maggie Renzi. As David Rosen points out, "By all accounts, the making and marketing of *Secaucus Seven* was a successful venture. Not only did it launch John Sayles's directorial career, but it helped create an innovative marketing approach for independent films" (Rosen and Hamilton 195). Sayles's pragmatic, unconventional approach to feature filmmaking captured an unintended audience response, as well as a look from Hollywood producers. Sayles likes to say that *Secaucus Seven* catapulted him from "total obscurity to relative obscurity" (Smith 68). The film showed that an independent film could be made with integrity and could achieve box office success.

During the 1980s, a decade dominated by Ronald Reagan and a conservative agenda stressing a return to traditional values, Sayles would commit his own brand of Cassavetes-like subversion by making films about homosexuality, unionism, political corruption, and racism. Sayles could not have picked a less opportune time to begin a film career dominated by the desire to present serious, adult issues. But rather than follow the typical career arc, turning solely toward big budgets and studio control in Hollywood, Sayles continued along his own path, working as a studio rewrite whiz while making his own politically astute films. His next two pictures, *Lianna* (1983) and *Baby, It's You* (1983), stand in contrast — one being a completely independent production, the other, a film made within the Hollywood system that does not lose sight of conflicting class and gender issues. Both films are artistic, moving examples of how Sayles involves his audience with solid, intriguing characters and their concerns while remaining relaxed in tone and straightforward visually. Typically, each film is serious, witty, and ironic, and displays a decidedly left-of-center attitude.

5

Lianna

Once again, the film is called *Lianna* and not *An Unmarried Gay Woman*. She's got things wrong with her, but she's not made to represent all gay women.

—John Sayles (Popkin)

Return of the Secaucus Seven brought Sayles commercial recognition but not creative control. Typically, aspiring filmmakers begin with a low-budget, independent effort and then, with luck, move on to a big-budget Hollywood studio assignment. After the success of his first feature, Sayles sought investment for a screenplay entitled *Lianna*, a feminist coming-to-consciousness story with a lesbian love affair at its center. Sayles wrote *Lianna* (1983) four years before *Return of the Secaucus Seven*; however, after offering the script to various Hollywood studios, he realized that a story about a woman who leaves her husband and children for another woman was not commercial material.

Moreover, the film's subject matter made raising independent production money difficult, because, as Vito Russo observes in *The Celluloid Closet: Homosexuality in the Movies*, even the "smallest step toward positive depiction of lesbians and gay men on the screen is cause for alarm" (295). To illustrate this claim, Russo quotes Sayles aping the reaction of potential investors when they learned that *Lianna* concerned lesbianism: "Oh, no! Not another one of those!" (296). In other words, traditional investors would not sink their money into a film dealing with homosexuality. Therefore, Sayles's producers, Jeffrey Nelson and Maggie Renzi, raised production money through a public offering, a unique, grassroots approach. About 30 nontraditional investors — people who had never backed a film before — financed the picture. *Lianna* cost $340,000 to make, with deferments to crew members; it was filmed in 16-millimeter and shot in 36 days.

Despite the difficulties in financing his second independent production, the time period between the successful release of *Return of the Secaucus Seven* and the filming of *Lianna* was fruitful for Sayles. Hollywood's doors opened for him. He signed two studio contracts, one to write a science-fiction script, *Night Skies*, for Steven Spielberg at Columbia, the other to write and direct

Blood of the Lamb, a contemporary take on *The Man Who Would Be King*, for the Ladd Company. Sayles used some of this Hollywood income to make *Lianna*.

Lianna is outside the mainstream and is therefore a comfortable fit for Sayles. He scripted, directed, acted in, and edited the film. Once again, he employed a large, ensemble cast, and all the actors deliver natural, believable performances. Since the film was shot mostly with a handheld camera, the color cinematography is grainy, giving the film a realistic look that complements Sayles's screenplay. While the production values for *Lianna* are low, its humor, drama, and realism are anything but. The film is a wholehearted attempt on Sayles's part to bring another portion of America's disparate subcultures to the screen.

Lianna bolsters Sayles's endorsement of feminism. The film tells the story of Lianna (Linda Griffiths), an academic's wife with two young children. Her husband, Dick (Jon DeVries), is a professor seeking tenure at an unnamed Eastern liberal arts college. As the film opens, Lianna is at a crossroads in her life without realizing where she is. Her marriage does not satisfy her because Dick offers little emotional support, communication, or encouragement. Her main source of ballast is her friend Sandy (Jo Henderson), whose husband coaches football at the college. Although Sandy's marriage seems intact, she also suffers from intellectual ennui.

Both women are trying to enhance their lives. Together they take a college night class to stay intellectually challenged and to counterbalance the boredom of their daily lives. Lianna feels attracted to the female professor who leads the night class, and their affair sets her new life in motion. Although many films show us people who make changes in their lives, *Lianna* is among the few that show us the consequences of those changes. To his credit, Sayles avoids the simple, melodramatic story of a woman who comes out of the closet with a grand, liberated flourish, showing us instead what happens after Lianna comes to a deeper awareness of her own sexuality and social position, and her efforts to responsibly face the consequences of her choice.

What makes *Lianna* so specific and compelling are the regular people at its core. Sayles, however, took a great deal of criticism precisely because of the film's ordinariness, and for the fact that he is a male director dealing with women's issues and issues of lesbianism. In *Jump Cut* Lisa di Caprio wrote of the film's "absence of any real passion" (45). In *Off Our Backs* Angela Marney suggested that *Lianna* is about "how homosexuals aren't really all that different ... about and not for lesbians" (18). The same review found Sayles's bar and street sequences, which involve the exchange of evocative glances, to be "lecherous" and worried that such scenes might keep some lesbians in the closet. However, *Lianna* is not simply about the physical or cultural components of lesbianism; rather, it is the story of a life being reshaped outside the constraints of socially acceptable sexual behavior and prescribed domestic roles. Fur-

The story of a married woman's coming out as a lesbian, Sayles's self-financed Lianna *(1983) generated both controversy and praise. In the film, Sayles surrounds his protagonist (Linda Griffiths, in the pool) with an assortment of regular people, allowing him to present a variety of reactions to Lianna's affair with Ruth (Jane Hallaren), an older, sophisticated woman who teaches at the same college as Lianna's husband.*

thermore, Sayles does not suggest that *Lianna* tells every lesbian's story. The film is a complex piece of domestic realism with a controversial subject as its dramatic impetus.

In his essay "A State of Being," Vito Russo noted that "gay visibility has never been an issue in the movies. Gays have always been visible. It's how they have been visible which has remained offensive for almost a century" (32). Indeed, many critics of *Lianna* address Sayles's depiction of lesbian life. In fact, Sayles acknowledges that making a film about a woman's sexual choice is presumptuous. "You're presuming you know something that other people should hear," says Sayles. "There is more pressure, more public eye on it, because it's a film, and so few films get made about anything that's vaguely controversial" (Osborne 32). *Lianna* was released in 1983, the year of *Making Love, Personal Best, Tootsie,* and *Victor/Victoria,* all commercial properties with homosexual content, characters, or themes. Yet these Hollywood films tell little about the reality of the homosexual experience in America. *Lianna,* on the other hand, does not acquiesce to commercial standards of acceptable taste. The film presents homosexuality in a direct, natural manner.

Like *Return of the Secaucus Seven, Lianna* concentrates on interpersonal dynamics. Time, money, and experience once again held Sayles back from visually invigorating his film. Mainstream critics again complained about his plain visual style. In his negative review of *Lianna* in *The New Republic,* Stanley Kauffmann suggested that the most "disturbing element in Sayles's critical reception is the suspicion that he is being hailed as a filmmaker because he has shown gifts outside film" (24)—the implication being, of course, that Sayles displays little visual talent; his strength is writing, not filmmaking. As Sayles acknowledges, however, he tried "to keep the technical end simple and competent" (*Thinking in Pictures* 4), budget limitations being his foremost concern. In fact, the film's grainy, soft look gives *Lianna* a credibility that more production money might have obscured. Sayles follows his characters through a series of episodes, using music, dialogue, and cutting to fill in for camera movement.

The opening sequence is emblematic of the film's approach to its subject matter. *Lianna* just begins. Without any introduction, we see and hear two women—Lianna and Sandy—discussing the condition of their lives. Lianna sits on a child's swing, listening to and commiserating with Sandy, who is standing. These visual signs indicate a distinction between Lianna, who is still unsure of herself, and Sandy, who is fully aware of herself and her position in the world. Speaking of her husband, Sandy says, "I've gone places since I have married him. He's, you know, still Bobby-Ballgame." Immediately, Sayles establishes two important themes: one, the adolescent approach toward life that many men in this picture will take; and two, Lianna's search for a mentor in her life, which is indicated by her position on the child's swing, as she listens to Sandy's opinion on husbands and marriage.

As we enter into her life, Lianna inhabits the circumscribed world of a housewife, which, as Molly Haskell points out, "corresponds to the state of women in general, confronted by a range of options so limited she might as well inhabit a cell" (159). Here, being a mother and a housewife defines Lianna as a person, one who adheres to prescribed codes of conduct that provide her husband room to navigate both his intellectual, academic pursuits, and his affairs with female students, which he does with regularity. Dick's job at the college is the focus of his life. Everything else revolves around his position there, including dinner conversations, which serve as a sounding board for his troubles. In one witty scene, Sayles has Dick explain to Lianna that he knows he will be denied tenure because he is slated to teach an entire course on William Dean Howells, the neglected American realist whose characters typically grappled with ethical problems, an ironic twist the boorish Dick ignores. He then quickly leaves the table to watch the movie *Battleground,* a film by William "Wild Bill" Wellman whose sadism toward women was well known, on television, because, he says, "I have to teach it next week." Lianna is left alone to clean up and to take care of their daughter. Sayles's talent for capturing realistic dialogue and situations is evident here. Without being told, we know that what we have witnessed is a nightly occurrence.

Lianna herself exists in an enclosure, a condition Sayles reinforces by framing within a variety of constraints — a swing set, a car, a classroom, a kitchen, a bedroom — that visually define the limits of her world. After Lianna begins to acknowledge her sexuality, however, Sayles does not wipe away aspects of closure in his mise-en-scène, because she is still a woman faced with real economic and social restrictions.

The emotional pain of Lianna's domestic situation resonates in her interaction with Dick. From the back of his classroom, Lianna watches as Dick demonstrates Heisenberg's Uncertainty Principle to debunk the "purity" of documentary film for his class, which consists mainly of women. He concludes his lecture by saying, "Anything that doesn't fit with our idea of what the story should be ends up on the cutting-room floor." Dick dismisses the class, avoiding eye contact with Lianna as his students file out the door. No form of recognition crosses his face; he does not even greet her.

Sayles establishes the oppressive tension between these characters by shooting Dick in the full-front medium shot, as he gazes into the foreground, his face registering anger and disgust. Lianna is shot in profile, which carries less emotional weight. Here, however, just the opposite occurs. Lianna waits for Dick to make eye contact, which underlines her emotional struggle, the dominant shot element. Abruptly we realize that Dick would prefer to edit his wife out of his life, especially on campus. Lianna caustically responds to his emotional detachment and anger by asking, "What's the matter, afraid to let them see you playing husband?" Dick turns his back to her and walks away. Clearly, their marriage is in serious trouble.

Although Lianna knows her marriage is falling apart, she tries to keep her domestic life in order by fulfilling the role of dutiful housewife. When we first encounter Lianna, her options have stalled, and she has mutely accepted her subordinate position and Dick's philandering. She cares deeply for her children and takes care of Dick, providing him with comfort both in the kitchen and the bedroom, albeit without much enthusiasm. Lianna is at her most animated, however, in Dr. Ruth Brennan's (Jane Hallaren) child psychology class. There Lianna is attentive, asks questions, and even quotes Professor Brennan in conversations with both Sandy and Dick. In fact, Sandy actually declares that Lianna has "a crush" on Ruth. To be sure, Ruth's class causes Lianna to re-evaluate her life.

The academic settings of *Lianna*— classrooms, campus, athletic fields, faculty parties — underline Lianna's process of self-discovery. Sayles links Lianna's messy journey toward personal truth to teaching throughout the first half of the film. Ruth, for instance, is a childless child psychologist whose area of expertise suggests her role in Lianna's maturation. Lianna is her student, her would-be research assistant, and finally her lover. As Lianna tells

Ruth, she started out as an English major and ended up a wife. She was once and now is again a student listening to lectures. Now, however, she is ready to apply her new knowledge to her life.

Lianna confronts lesbianism as a simple love story, and in doing so illuminates the world we all share. Sayles portrays lesbian relationships as typical, a fact of life, without the titillation commercial films demand. As Christine Holmlund points out about Robert Towne's *Personal Best*, "The constant close-ups of women's crotches, asses, thighs, legs, and breasts led many critics in both the mainstream and the alternative press to comment on the film as voyeuristic, even to label it soft core pornography" (155).

The single, key love scene between Lianna and Ruth begins with Lianna trying to get her daughter off to the baby-sitter's house while deciding what to wear for a working dinner at Ruth's apartment, where they will discuss Ruth's next research project and Lianna's role as her assistant. When she meets Ruth, the atmosphere is at first awkward but relaxed, as the two women chat over dinner. The discussion is typical — the children, the past, married life. The conversation moves to the couch, and a series of close shots showing the women drinking wine and talking. At Ruth's request, Lianna describes her first crush, which was on a female camp counselor. Soon they begin to kiss, and the scene shifts to the bedroom, the traditional location for cinematic exploitation.

Sayles, however, represents lesbian sexuality gracefully. The bedroom is bathed in blue light, which seems to come through an open window in the background. The open window suggests a release from the enclosed space that has described Lianna until this point in the film. By backlighting the scene and shooting it through a blue filter, Sayles creates an ethereal image, notably missing from other shots in the film, to underscore Lianna's new awareness. Sayles films their lovemaking with close-ups of various body parts and heightened physical reactions to demonstrate the tenderness and charged sensuality. The blue filter accentuates the fragmented body parts; it adds mysterious, soothing eroticism to the scene. Sayles uses a soundtrack of soft bedroom whispers in French, extracted from Alain Resnais's *Hiroshima, Mon Amour*, to heighten the exotic nature of this sexual encounter (Merck 173).

This scene stands in stark contrast to a heterosexual love scene that precedes it. Here Dick uses Lianna's enthusiasm for the psychology course she is taking with Ruth as an impetus for sex. "How about working some of that energy off with your old man?" he asks. The diffused high-key lighting used in the scene washes out any erotic possibility. We are witnessing a routine, tired come-on. Lianna, whose face registers annoyance with Dick's tired request, replies without any trace of interest, "Let me go put the thing in," and leaves for the bathroom and her diaphragm. In the end, we do not see them make love, nor do we have to because Sayles has effectively communicated the dull, pedestrian nature of their physical relationship.

Were Sayles a less complex filmmaker and writer, he would structure his fictional universe so that honest fulfillment would provide happiness and contentment for his characters. However, while Lianna's homosexual awakening provides a brief liberation, Sayles's film suggests that this transcendence from the ordinary should be viewed for what it is: a heightened moment in an otherwise bland, confusing world. While Sayles provides a broader context for Lianna's lesbianism — that it is a state of being, not simply a chosen activity — and recorded the unrestrained pleasure she takes in her recovered sexuality, the rest of the film explores the effects of her choice on not only herself but on those around her.

As a coda to Lianna and Ruth's lovemaking scene, Sayles shoots the women in bed talking. Lianna admits to Ruth that this experience was her first sex with another woman. Ruth's response is registered with a happy, yet slightly shocked "No!" She asks Lianna how she is feeling while embracing her warmly. Lianna, obviously still enjoying the restorative pleasure of their encounter, casually asks the time. Ruth tells her that it is 3:30 A.M. Lianna bolts upright, rapidly assessing all the things that might have gone wrong at home. Sayles uses a close-up to intensify her worries: Lianna is in the foreground, the blue light no longer illuminating her. Her face registers fear; Ruth appears in profile behind her, half hidden by deep blue shadows, a bit of memory rather than current reality. Here the erotic blue flame of Ruth's bed is extinguished by domestic responsibility. Lianna, therefore, has only briefly escaped from her traditional enclosure.

When Lianna returns home she finds Spencer, her fifteen-year-old son, who has spent his free evening investigating *Hustler* magazine, still awake. He defends himself by telling her that he was watching late movies on television, while reminding Lianna of the late hour. She responds, "These research projects get pretty complicated sometimes. Professor Brennan had a lot of details to explain to me. We got pretty wrapped up in it." Here both Lianna and Spencer lie to cover up their sexual explorations. Lianna's words, however, actually define the structure of the rest of the film because she has indeed entered into a research project, one that will define the rest of her life. Moreover, Lianna functions as a surrogate who makes it easier for Sayles's audience to spend time with people and in places they ordinarily would not experience.

Indeed, as Cindy Rizzo points out in the *Gay Community News*, *Lianna* represents a "perfect collage of coming out scenes" (7). Of course coming out differs from individual to individual, and nowhere in the film does Sayles suggest that Lianna's self-awareness is meant to be a catch-all depiction of lesbian life; it is, simply, Lianna's story. Yet some critics found *Lianna* to be pallid, precisely because it lacks unrestrained lesbian love: "Several alternative reviewers faulted Sayles for his choice of situations like falling in love, loneliness, and boredom to which anyone, gay or straight, could relate" (Holmlund 162). But his depiction of lesbianism comes close to meeting Richard Dyer's call for the development of positively valued gay types:

> This is the representation of gay people which, on the one hand, functions against stereotypes, for it does not deny individual differences from the broad category to which the individual belongs. But it also does not function just like "rounded" [i.e., E.M. Forster's literary definition] characterizations; it does not diminish our sense of a character's belonging to and acting in solidarity with his or her social group. [293]

Unlike the gay and lesbian characters who populated the commercial cinema in the early 1980s, Lianna and Ruth interact within the context of a lesbian community. In *Lianna* lesbianism is neither an aberration nor is it silenced. We witness Lianna's first steps into a new community. Again, Sayles's approach met with criticism. Writing in *Film Comment*, Marcia Pally suggested that "*Lianna* is the most popular of the welcome-wagon films — those that try to persuade audiences it's okay to have lesbians on the block" (37). Such a comment misses Sayles's central point: While *Lianna* does indeed have a lesbian affair at its core, the affair does not subvert the larger concerns of the film. *Lianna* is not so much about homosexuality as it is about the life of someone who happens to be gay. According to Vito Russo, "The few times gay characters have worked on-screen have been when filmmakers have had the courage to make no big deal out of them" ("A State of Being" 33). To his credit, Sayles makes "no big deal" out of Lianna's homosexuality except to show how her new choices will erase her old, more traditional existence.

The heart of the film is the consequences of Lianna's coming out, the attendant difficulties that accompany any large life decision. Sayles mixes humor and irony, and avoids melodramatic proclamations to show us Lianna's acceptance of her homosexuality. For example, we see her in the library looking for books on lesbianism. Lianna mutters to herself traveling through the *L*s in the card catalog. When she finds the term *lesbian*, she practically shouts the word, much to the embarrassment of an older woman who shares the frame with her. Jerry Carlson (Sayles himself), film professor and department wolf, arrives at Lianna's new apartment, after she has left Dick, ostensibly to see how she is doing. His intention, however, is obvious: He wants to get Lianna into bed. Jerry asks Lianna what she is reading. She replies, "*The Well of Loneliness*," Radclyffe Hall's well-known lesbian novel. Jerry, who does not recognize the title, immediately asks her to go to bed with him. Lianna also recalls erotic moments from her past that involved other women, checks out the bar scene, gazes at women, and finally stands in front of her own reflection and declares to her own mirrored image, "Lianna Massey eats pussy." Sayles treats all these scenes with the same style and tone that he does all his work. His characters are not embellished yet are truly engaging because of the complexity in the reality of their lives.

Sayles's art introduces his audience to people and situations commercial films tend to ignore. Witness Lianna's introduction to the heretofore invisible gay community, depicted in the My Way Tavern sequence. Lianna is, naturally, nervous, even shy about being in a gay bar. She tells Ruth that women are staring at her. Indeed, several women do look at her, but looking is part of any bar scene. Soon, Lianna is relaxed. She dances with other women, drinks with Ruth, and seems to change from private person to public person before our eyes. Sayles quickens the pace of the sequence with rapid editing and a pulsing, upbeat disco song whose feminist lyrics — "Women of the world, at last you know that you are free"— celebrate the exhilaration Lianna obviously experiences as she enjoys herself in the company of other women like herself. Medium two-shots and rapid long shots of women laughing, dancing, drinking, smoking, talking, and hugging are intercut with Lianna's frenzied dance and close-ups of an unidentified pair of eyes gazing at the unfolding scene. Or Lianna. Sayles's shots are a collage of bar activity. Here, Sayles's mise-en-scène camera work, editing, and soundtrack effectively show us that Lianna has found a new community, one in which she can act and be herself.

The sequence that follows shows Lianna walking down a street, obviously happy. The security and camaraderie she discovered in the My Way Tavern now extends outdoors, away from the protective, closed space of the bar. Everywhere she looks, she sees women: women alone, women with other women, women with babies, women getting out of cars, women who acknowledge Lianna's gaze with a smile or a nod; the whole world, it seems, is full of women. Sayles uses open forms here to celebrate Lianna's freedom, her escape from a life that was not her own, and to register unlimited sexual possibilities from Lianna's point of view.

Sayles builds a sobering transition into this sequence, however, which reminds the viewer once again that he is an unsentimental, realistic observer of life's small moments. In a medium shot, serving to bring the characters close together, Sayles films the elated Lianna running up to Ruth, who is exiting her apartment. Lianna hugs Ruth from behind, telling her how happy she is to see her. Ruth reminds Lianna to take it easy, because "It's the real world out here." Lianna's joy fades. Breaking off her embrace, Lianna casts her eyes toward the sidewalk. Here we witness a generational difference between Ruth and Lianna. Lianna wants to feel good about her choice. Ruth, who is older and professionally established, is more circumspect, especially in public, a hint that Lianna's new life will not be as liberating as she had hoped.

Decidedly, there are endless social consequences involved in Lianna's realization of her lesbianism. At first, Sayles takes us through the reactions of Lianna's old friends to her coming out. For the most part, their views on homosexuality are stereotypical. Sayles, however, leavens the drama, slipping some humor into a dramatic situation. As he said to Daniel Popkin of *Cineaste*, "I don't believe that people, no matter how bad their straits are, are totally humorless" (39). Sandy, who struggles to understand Lianna's choice, after being told by Lianna that she and Ruth had had an affair, quizzically asks, "What did you do?" Jerry Carlson declares, "I'm from California. That sort of thing doesn't faze me." Lianna's precocious fifteen-year-old son, Spencer says, "So my old lady's a dyke. Big deal!" Sandy's husband, Bob, recalls one of his own football recruits who was gay: "He was a black kid. I didn't even know they had 'em that way." And Dick belittles Lianna by asking, "How was it? Like a drugstore paperback?" Still, Lianna's choice creates problems she could not anticipate, and at first her old friends offer her little support.

In an interview with the *Gay Community News*, Sayles calls *Lianna* a lesbian film that is also "about divorce, about growing up" (Rizzo 8). For a woman who has previously accepted the vacuum of a purely domestic existence, being cut off from her home, her children, and her financial source, finding a job or a place to live can be a devastating experience. Lianna is an outsider in more ways than one. Although *Lianna* is about sexual choice, the homosexuality issue does not obscure Sayles's own observations, which stem from shared human concerns. By creating a multifaceted film about a lesbian, Sayles undermines Hollywood's ability to create more acceptable illusions of ourselves. Vito Russo noted that these illusions are detrimental to common understanding and acceptance:

> Hollywood is yesterday, forever catching up with what is happening today. This will change only when it becomes financially profitable, and reality will never be profitable until society overcomes its fear and hatred of difference and begins to see that we're all in this together. [*Celluloid Closet* 323]

As Sayles's work indicates, his essential philosophy is egalitarian, pluralistic, not divisive — he attempts to capture an honest picture of contemporary life.

Visually Sayles communicates Lianna's transitions in plain cinematic language. The enclosures that trap Lianna early on in the film are all domestic, representing both her lack of freedom and her unappreciated social position as housewife and mother. For the most part, these interior shots emphasize the discord between Lianna and Dick: the passionless request for sex, Dick's packing for a film festival, and Lianna's confronting him with the fact of his latest infidelity. Each of these shots occurs in their bedroom, where Lianna and Dick are separated by open space within the frame. Dick, however, always assumes a dominant position, either looming over Lianna in the background or the foreground. These scenes lead to their final, violent argument, the precursor to Lianna's leaving her home. Here Sayles used a hand-held camera to reinforce Lianna's domestic problems with documentarylike precision, the camera recording the event in jerky, claustrophobic detail. Dick and Lianna hit each other, break objects, and scream without remorse. This scene comes as close to the raw passion of Cassavetes as Sayles will get. The two actors capture the angry pain of a serious domestic dispute.

When Lianna leaves Dick, she is faced with a series of fresh difficulties: locating an apartment, hooking up utilities, and finding a job. Without a husband, she has no money and no social status. Paradoxically, Lianna only becomes aware of her diminished position after she assumes responsibility for herself.

Sayles's visual setup at Lianna's new apartment effectively illustrates this point. Framed by a long floor-to-ceiling shot, Lianna walks toward the rear of the white, empty apartment into a space flooded with light. She turns, walks back toward the landlady, who stands fixed at the front door, reminding Lianna that "there are no men allowed here." Leaning against a colonnade, staring into a small, unadorned living room, Lianna mutters, "No, no men." The shot represents Sayles's take on Lianna's condition: The apartment is at once open and fresh, and tubular and confining. The sound of the landlady's voice and Lianna's shoes bounce off the walls to produce a cavelike echo; this is a new place, yet it is empty, devoid of life. In contrast, the kinetic mise-en-scène of Dick and Lianna's final bedroom confrontation is overly dark, the walls almost enveloping the couple, bringing them closer than they want to be. Yet, while the latter scene illustrates a repressive situation, the apartment sequence does not celebrate Lianna's new existence. Instead it depicts an oppressive emptiness. Sayles, then, communicates the fact that Lianna faces formidable obstacles in her new life.

Of course separation from her husband forces Lianna to participate in her own growth and development, which stands in contrast to the pupil-teacher relationship developed early in the film. Therefore, Sayles adjusts the mise-en-scène as well. In a seemingly insignificant scene, Lianna is photographed in a medium shot, on a dirty, noisy, busy inner-city street corner. She shouts into a phone to be heard above the din of a jackhammer and other street sounds, requesting a gas connection for her apartment. She is told that there is no record of her ever having used the utility in the past, a bit of information that leaves the former homemaker baffled. For years she has been identified only as Mrs. Richard Massey; thus, she has no credit record, no history.

While *Lianna* at times resonates with romance, the film casts a skeptical eye on the restorative power of love and demonstrates the inability of the human heart to fulfill its desires. After Lianna tells Dick about her affair with Ruth and her willingness to leave their home, her world becomes chaotic, confused, far from liberated. Seeking solace from Ruth, Lianna approaches her teacher near the college. As Lianna acknowledges to Ruth that she has indeed told Dick of their physical relationship, Ruth glances about furtively. Clearly, she is concerned about Lianna's decision to tell Dick about the affair, and she is worried about Lianna's unrestrained speech in public. Ruth says, "Right now I want to put my arms around you. If we were straight friends, I would have. But that's not the way the world works." Lianna is perplexed; she believed that new love and a new identity would alleviate her pain. "I thought," she tells Ruth, "when I found somebody, everything would be all right." Of course, love is not a tonic. Lianna is free, but she is also lonely, filled with guilt, and afraid. As a gay woman, Lianna faces a double set of difficulties: loneliness, and coping with her sexuality.

In *Return of the Secaucus Seven*, Sayles explored the limits of personal freedom. Many of the characters in that film search for a meaningful existence, one that will match their social and political ideals. In *Lianna*, Sayles confronts the theme again. Lianna herself must decide where her personal freedom ends and her responsibilities begin. When Lianna tells Ruth that she always wanted a room of her own, as they cuddle watching television and eating Chinese take-out food in her spare apartment, the moment is ironic. Echoing Virginia Woolf should be a bright moment, but in Lianna's case, having a room of one's own means utter loneliness. She has, in fact, lost her family, her life, her identity — everything. Dick threatens to expose her and Ruth if Lianna tries to take the children. The children, who played a pivotal role in the beginning of the film, are caught in a vicious tug-of-war between Lianna and Dick. Lianna, however, continues on with her new life, recognizing that she cannot support two children on a grocery clerk's income.

In the end, Ruth decides to return to her female lover of many years, and Lianna seeks comfort from Sandy, who still does not understand her friend's sexuality. Using a hand-held camera, panning between these old friends, Sayles highlights the emotional bond between Lianna and Sandy. Sayles then cuts to a close-up of Lianna to reinforce the emotional difficulty that sexual choice and love lost bring to her. But he also reminds us that Lianna is still a member of her old community, that she has friends who love and care for her, and that she has come to terms with the loss of her lover and grown because of it. Yet she is still a lesbian, still herself.

Lianna does not focus on the physical aspects of sexuality or celebrate liberation to the exclusion of economic and social realities — Sayles is too savvy, too honest a filmmaker for that. *Lianna* tells one woman's love story with perception, tenderness, and sober vision. It typifies Sayles's desire to examine people and society, and to tell stories overlooked by Hollywood. *Lianna* contained too controversial a subject to generate studio interest, so Sayles's producers looked elsewhere for financial backing. Sayles, then, made the film his way: He used his own production crew and musical consultant, and he cast unknown actors to flesh out his characters. The naturalness of the film works well — we feel as if we are part of a catty academic community, one of Lianna's friends, and, like Lianna, experiencing the gay subculture for the first time. Sayles shows here that he is an actor's director, a compassionate filmmaker, and a man with an open mind.

Still it is unreasonable to expect aspiring filmmakers to sacrifice the excessive rewards offered by Hollywood for the risky path of independent productions. Filmmaking requires money, a commodity the studios have in abundance. Yet the industry is all too often unwilling to take risks for business reasons. For his next film, Sayles accepted an offer to direct for a major studio, an opportunity he had been looking for since before the success of *Return of the Secaucus Seven*. But with a studio's money come the studio's ideas — scripting, casting, and final cut control are usually lost. The production history of *Baby, It's You* illustrates why Sayles subsequently resolved to avoid Hollywood — except for lucrative screenwriting jobs — for creative independence.

6

Baby, It's You

There are things in *Baby, It's You* that I regret having cut, but I
was trying to run some kind of middle ground between making a
commercially viable movie and making the movie I had written ...
there was a richness in the peripheral characters that just didn't
make it to the screen. About forty minutes of really good stuff...
With a different system or different moviegoing habits, we could
have stuck with a two-hour-and-ten-minute movie.... So of all
the movies I've made, that's the one that is least about a group of
people.
— John Sayles ("Dialogue on Film")

After seeing *Return of the Secaucus Seven*, Amy Robinson, an actress and
producer, brought a semiautobiographical coming-of-age story to Sayles's
attention. The project included a writing-directing deal from Twentieth Century–Fox. Robinson's story, *Baby, It's You*, intrigued Sayles; it revolved around
a wrong-side-of-the-tracks high school love story with class and gender
conflicts, while magnifying the often strained transition between high school
and college. The story was set in the late sixties, a period that helped Sayles
form his own ideals. After several screenplay drafts, however, Twentieth Century–Fox and Sayles parted ways over the structure of the story. But Robinson and her coproducer Griffin Dunne knew they had a solid commercial
property. They raised $2.9 million from independent film investors, and inter-
ested Paramount Pictures in distribution of the finished picture.

A rough cut of the film convinced Paramount that changes were necessary, especially in the second half of the picture, which Sayles felt cut against
the grain of most high school nostalgia pictures. According to Sayles, the film
"gets interesting and complex in the second half, which is why Paramount [did
not] like it" (Osborne 36). In a recent interview with Eric Foner, a professor
of history at Columbia University, Sayles recalled the incident: "I made *Baby,
It's You* for Paramount, which was a bad situation at the end of the day. I finally
got the cut I wanted, but there was a lot of me getting kicked out of the editing room, put back in, and all that kind of thing" (Carnes *Past Imperfect* 14).
Grudgingly, Paramount bought the distribution rights to the film but then

inexplicably withheld *Baby, It's You* from commercial distribution. Sayles described the situation as a creative disagreement: Paramount "wanted it to be only about high school ... but it was a much more serious film than they had planned on. They wanted to cut down on the college part ... I wanted a very balanced film" (Valen 11). Paramount called the whole affair "a tempest in a teapot" (Osborne 36). Even though Sayles said at the time that the final cut of the film was definitely his, in *Thinking in Pictures* he writes: "Only on *Baby, It's You*, the studio picture, did I not have complete cutting control and that turned into a major fight" (39).

Baby, It's You points up Sayles's desire for creative control. In 1983, after the film was completed, an interviewer from *Newsweek* magazine asked Sayles if he could ever return to low-budget filmmaking again. Sayles replied, "I'm willing to trade having a lot of money to have total creative control" (Ansen 78). Of course practically every independent filmmaker has uttered some form of this clichéd declaration. Sayles, however, stuck by his words. After finishing *Baby, It's You*, he tore up his Screenwriter's Guild card (Laermer 105).

Baby, It's You looks better than *Lianna* due to its increased budget, yet neither film carries the patina of a Hollywood picture. Commercial movies, of course, are a marriage of commerce and art, a glamorous experience designed to remove the audience from its everyday existence. In this context, Sayles's approach to filmmaking is unorthodox both technically and in narrative content. He attempts to articulate ordinary experience:

> I'm more interested in people than literature. I didn't major in English. I don't want people to leave my movies thinking of another movie, but of people they know. Technically, I'm not good at anything. I'm primitive. But I have a good ear for dialogue and can empathize. [Ansen 79]

Technically and visually, *Baby, It's You* is superior to *Lianna*, but Sayles is still angry at the Hollywood system for reducing the human scope of his third film.

Class issues are subtly woven into *Lianna*; *Baby, It's You* demands that we look at class as fundamental to the American experience. For Sayles, high school represents "the last bastion of true democracy in our society, where you have classes and eat lunch with the guy who's going to be picking up your garbage later in life" (Osborne 36). *Baby, It's You* presents the love between two young people as they prepare to leave high school. The film traces the emotional development of Jill Rosen (Rosanna Arquette), an ambitious, upper-middle-class young woman who wants to be an actress and who sees high school as a place to get good grades, where being straight makes you popular. At college, however, just the opposite holds true, especially at Sarah Lawrence in the late 1960s. Albert Capadilupo, a.k.a. Sheik (Vincent Spano), the son of uneducated, working-class parents, who gets kicked out of high school just as Jill gets accepted to Sarah Lawrence, lives in the 1950s — sharkskin suits and Frank Sinatra lyrics, buoyed by the exotic lure of Miami Beach. They are a mismatched couple, their union doomed to fail.

Made immediately after the completion of *Lianna*, in 1983, *Baby, It's You* begins inside high school's polyglot culture, where two disparate people like Jill and Sheik could meet and fall in love, and it ends in the cultural confusion of the late 1960s on a tony college campus, where such a romance cannot possibly survive. Structurally, the film is divided into two distinct parts following the impossible arc of Jill and Sheik's romance: senior year of high school in Trenton, New Jersey, in 1966, and the year following graduation. "One of the interesting things about *Baby, It's You*," says Sayles, "is that it's a plot you've seen before with this sort of upper middle class girl having a relationship with this working class guy, but usually the class has been erased so that it's just June Allyson and Cary Grant and although he may be her chauffeur, he's just as witty and educated and, in fact, smarter in some ways" (Popkin 39). In *Baby, It's You*, Sheik is never smarter than Jill; he has no real plan to do anything with his life. But because public high school resembles a classic melting pot, their early relationship is possible. Later, the film shows how class differences make a lasting relationship between the two impossible.

The $2.9 million budget for *Baby, It's You*, which is well below Hollywood standards, was a huge jump for Sayles and allowed him unaccustomed indulgences. For example, Sayles used young, up-and-coming actors in the film: Vincent Spano, Rosanna Arquette, Robert Downey, Jr., and Matthew Modine. Sayles's first priority, as he says, is "with the acting and the believability of the characters" (interview, *American Cinematographer* 86), and this group delivers.

Arquette drew critical applause for her portrayal of Jill Rosen. A year earlier, in the television adaptation of Norman Mailer's *The Executioner's Song*, Arquette was memorable as Gary Gilmore's lover, Nicole Baker. For Sayles, she had to make a necessary transition, jumping classes, religions, and economic conditions to play the smart, ambitious Jill Rosen. Taken together, these performances show a wide range in her acting ability. *Baby, It's You* comes with a large perk: Arquette plays a young, would-be actress. That is, she gets to try on a variety of personalities — she looks for new experiences and new identities, which makes her romance with Sheik plausible. For example, Arquette shifts between the plain, unsure, real Jill Rosen to an imitation of a gum-snapping working-class high school dropout she meets in a bar with Sheik to a pot-fogged college freshman. Arquette makes Jill's tentative search for assimilation believable, especially during the second half of the film when her behavior becomes erratic, unsure. This role confirmed Arquette's acting talent.

Vincent Spano's character does not seek acceptance; he is looking for a position outside social restraint, like his hero Frank Sinatra. Sheik, who is nicknamed after a condom, wants to achieve his own "style," a romantic notion of freedom beyond the confinements of home, school, and Trenton, New Jersey. Spano is an actor Sayles likes to work with. In fact, Sayles had to fight to get Spano cast in the role of Sheik. The studio wanted John Travolta, a choice that Sayles disagreed with because of the actor's older age and star power. Spano's sharp features make him stand out from the rest of the cast, an asset that adds to Sheik's personality. Sheik has one role, to call attention to himself, effectively lifting himself above his environment. His sharp suits alone make him an unlikely looking high school student. At least on the surface. Sheik is as vulnerable and as confused as Jill. Playing Sheik requires a look and a swagger that Spano has, but it also requires the ability to generate emotion. By the end of the film, we must feel Sheik's frustration when he becomes aware that he is living a hollow life, lip-synching jukebox songs in a backwater bar in Miami Beach. When Sheik reaches his crisis point, Spano brings his character's pain to the surface, making the audience feel for this likable character. Spano is an underrated actor who adds a degree of emotion to characters audiences might otherwise turn their backs on.

The studio backing for *Baby, It's You* allowed Sayles to increase his production budget, enhancing the sound, editing, and cinematography for the picture. American audiences expect their eyes and ears to be in one place when viewing English-language films. A good sound mix provides the listener with subtleties of tone and ambiance that, if done well, go as unnoticed in a film as they do in real life. According to Wayne Wadhams, Sayles's sound technician for both *Return of the Secaucus Seven* and *Lianna*, when working on a limited budget, "the advantages of recording sound via a boom microphone are as plain as day" (83). He notes, however, "the wireless mic ... insures the cleanest, most crisp dialogue obtainable" (82). Wireless equipment, of course, inflates a production budget. *Return of the Secaucus Seven* and *Lianna* rely on an authentic documentary treatment of characters, so the boom mike satisfied Sayles's dramatic, realistic needs. But *Baby, It's You*, with its studio budget, uses more locations and wide shots, making boom recording difficult if not impossible. Therefore, Sayles had to rely on wireless sound pickup, which enhances the overall quality of the film.

Sayles selects music for his films wisely. But working with a restricted budget does not allow access to a wide variety of music. In his first two films, Sayles employed his friend Mason Daring as a composer and a consultant. Working with Daring's own material and some inexpensive, unknown folk songs, they created admirable musical soundtracks. Music, however, plays a dominant role in *Baby, It's You*. The music selected to accent the first half of the film is vintage: "Woolly Bully," "Cherish," "Shout," "Chapel of Love," "Stand by Me." Indeed, golden oldies are associated with Jill's high school persona in the opening section of the film. Light and innocuous, these recordings add a flavor of nostalgia to the film without suffocating its narrative con-

Sheik (Vincent Spano) performs his lip-synching act in Baby, It's You *(1983). Photo courtesy of the Museum of Modern Art Film Stills Archive.*

tent. While lip-synching the Supremes' "Stop! In the Name of Love," Jill is every high school teenager, living an imaginary life through the sounds from her phonograph, trying to escape the world of her parents. Later in the film, however, while smoking pot in her college dorm room, the pessimistic lyrics and angry guitar work of Lou Reed and the Velvet Underground performing "Venus in Furs" describe Jill's transition, indicating not only a change in historical time and culture but a change in her character as well. The straight, popular high school girl is replaced by an angry, confused, alone, and frightened woman.

Sheik's life desires are, according to him, defined by the music of Frank Sinatra. The boy feels he belongs to the elegant world of big bands and lush orchestration, not electric guitars and girl-group vocals. Sheik is consumed by his quixotic desire to be the new Sinatra. In Miami Beach, he mouths Sinatra songs for aged customers when not washing dishes. As Sheik becomes aware that he will never escape his roots, fantasy gives way to hard reality. In Sheik, Sayles created a character out of time. His desire to be like Sinatra would seem plausible in the 1940s or 1950s but is wildly out of touch with the youth culture of the late 1960s. Sheik's lack of awareness makes his semigreaser characteristics believable; it also prefigures his downward spiral.

Sayles took time selecting music to define his main characters. In fact, he spent $300,000—10 percent of his budget—for music rights. Music was a part of both *Return of the Secaucus Seven* and *Lianna*, but the songs had neither popular appeal nor broad audience recognition. For *Baby, It's You* Sayles wanted music to play a larger role in his storytelling: "I'm not musical at all, but it's very important to me. When I wrote the script, I inserted lines from songs so people could visualize the scenes better" (Lawson 118).

Of course too many vintage pop songs would imbue the film with a sock-hop nostalgia, contradicting Sayles's realist aesthetic. To countervail sentimental high school nostalgia, Sayles chose several tunes by Bruce Springsteen, rock 'n' roll's working-class Steinbeck. Sayles selected Springsteen because his work "was so perfect for New Jersey, cars, kids, that kind of thing" (Valen 12). In contrast to Sheik's vision of himself, Sayles uses Springsteen songs to describe Sheik, the outsider who finally comes to angry awareness. Sheik wants to live in the mythic, elegant world of Frank Sinatra; what he gets is the unromanticized New Jersey of Bruce Springsteen.

Sayles also uses Springsteen's rock music as a device to link Jill and Sheik. For example, returning home from school one afternoon, Jill delivers perfunctory hellos to her parents, then climbs the stairs to her room. She enters her room, drops Dusty Springfield's mawkish "You Don't Have to Say You Love Me" onto her 45-rpm record player, and lies on her bed to listen to the tale of love gone bad, obviously lamenting her own lack of companionship. Sayles then quick-cuts to a shot of Sheik staring at his own reflection in a window while combing his hair, teenage narcissism in full color. The sound track registers the faint sounds of an acoustic guitar as Sheik practices his hard, tough look. With a grand flourish, Sheik bursts into the high school cafeteria, looking around with magisterial confidence. Springsteen's "It's Hard to Be a Saint in the City," the story of a young man trying to achieve status through his clothes, walk, and appearance, fills the soundtrack. This driving rock song describes Sheik's condition without sentimentality; it offers none of the hope that his favorite song, Sinatra's "Strangers in the Night," does. Instead it is an anthem to the impossibility of teenage bravado, complete with references to a hard upbringing, mean streets, and the swagger of Brando. The character in the song is trapped in an urban hell. Like Springsteen's protagonist, Sheik stands out like a peacock in a flock of pigeons. The other students are awed by his appearance: his snazzy, adult suit, his apparent self-confidence, and his brazen swagger all link him to Springsteen's narrator. But the song underscores how deceptive a youthful, romantic image can be: "It's so hard to be a saint when you're just a boy." Sheik, as we will discover, is indeed a boy dressed in a man's suit.

Baby, It's You also uses music as part of its narrative structure. In fact, the center of the film — Jill's prom night and Sheik's reckless attempt to rob a tuxedo store — relies on music almost exclusively to move the narrative forward. This sequence, which occurs at the center of the film, revolves around the insistent rock 'n' roll lyrics of Springsteen's "She's the One," a tune that emphasizes love's frustration. Here Springsteen's music brings high school innocence to an abrupt end, underscoring the fact that as high school students prepare to enter college, class alignments begin to develop.

In his book *Thinking in Pictures* Sayles points out how music works with film's edited images:

> Music added to the images can reinforce, underline, counterpoint or deny what is happening on the screen. Music can be treated as "source" or as "score," as something that comes from the world on the screen or as something the movie-makers are adding from the outside, an editorial comment. When it works movie music is like a natural voice, like the only sound the picture up there could possibly make. [109]

In the prom night sequence, Jill goes through the formal rite of passage for any traditional high school student. Sheik, who was expelled from high school and forbidden to attend the prom, acts with the desperation of a mock-hero. The soundtrack punches up this pivotal transition within the story.

Sayles begins the sequence with an interior shot of a profoundly bad prom band covering "Cherish," which marks the corny scene perfectly. Cutting to an exterior shot, Jill enters the prom with her date. Standing on the street, Sheik announces himself, walks toward Jill, and kisses her on the cheek, saying, "You won't be seeing me." Jill yells Sheik's name as the camera pulls away, visually establishing the growing distance between them.

Sayles cuts to an interior shot of the prom where Jill is dancing lifelessly. In the background Frank Sinatra's "Strangers in the Night," Sheik's song, fills the room full of shuffling couples. Jill's date then asks for a return of all the money he has invested in the evening because, as he says, "You obviously don't want to be here with me." Indeed, Jill would rather be with Sheik, even though she knows that he does not fit into her future plans, because he represents impossible teenage love.

Sayles cuts to a parallel interior shot, looking out on a dark street far removed from the prom scene. Sinatra's benign crooning is replaced on the musical soundtrack by the muted sound of an electric guitar. We have moved from the ersatz elegance of prom dinner dress to the streets. Sayles's musical selection changes the film's tone. The prom ritual is accented by the music of an older, stodgy generation. These young people look out of time shuffling around to the music of their parents. But, in fact, high school graduation marks the transition into the world of their parents. Springsteen's electric guitar riffs announce change. We are cast into the world of rock 'n' roll, the world of the outlaw, a street-level perspective that has nothing to do with propriety and everything to do with emotion. The prom and its music are lifeless in comparison. As the volume of Springsteen's music increases and Sheik rifles a cash register, drama and anticipation of the unknown are thrust into the sequence. Springsteen's music builds, matching Sheik's heart rate; the situation is anything but dull. Suddenly, the overhead lights come on. Sheik's partner, Rat, spins around and assumes a shooting stance; his gun pointing directly at the store owner, who has surprised the robbers. Sheik and Rat flee the crime scene in a large roadster, complete with brilliant red flames covering the sidewalls as "She's the One" pours from the soundtrack.

Darkness, which dominates this sequence's mise-en-scène, reinforces Sheik's desperation. He cannot escape these city streets, nor, as Springsteen's song about love's tenacious grip indicates, can he escape his desire for Jill. The police pursue Sheik and Rat. As the percussion and guitar reach a crescendo, Sayles cuts to Jill laconically driving her prom crowd around the city. The desultory look on her face registers the boredom of the evening, contradicting the driving soundtrack. A police cruiser passes, visually connecting her to Sheik, while Springsteen sings his protagonist's lament: "I wish she'd just leave me alone." Sayles photographs Sheik running into the night, money swirling around him as the musical vocals prefigure the pain Sheik's love and need for Jill will bring. Jill's ennui and Sheik's desperate act show the end of their innocent lives and a clearly defined social distinction that separates them.

Sayles's musical comment here reminds his audience that this story extends beyond the historical limits of the narrative. Springsteen's music is full of trenchant observations on city life, love, and friendship. It extends beyond the time frame of *Baby, It's You*, yet the music connects Jill and Sheik's story to the 1980s, where class distinctions are even stronger, and teenage romantic love is for innocents. Without the increased production values that come with a large studio budget, Sayles would not have been able to afford Springsteen, Sinatra, or the golden oldies songs that comment on and enhance the narrative quality of *Baby, It's You*.

Increased production values also bring technical specialists to a film that an independent moviemaker like Sayles could not afford. Sayles wrote, directed, edited, and acted in his first two features. With each new film Sayles evolves technically, gaining cinematic knowledge. Despite the overall good look, however, some of the editing in *Lianna* and *Return of the Secaucus Seven* is obviously the work of an unskilled cutter. In contrast, the addition of an experienced editor, Sonya Polonsky, for *Baby, It's You* is evident. The final cut displays a crisp, energetic, often fast editing technique missing from his first two films. Sayles managed to use action sequences, which require a great deal of editing, to energize the flow of the film, although none of the narrative content is sacrificed.

Editing determines the visual syntax of any film, but movies begin and end with pictures. For the first time, Sayles was able to employ a first-rate cinematographer, Michael Ballhaus, best known for his work with Rainer Fassbinder and now Martin Scorsese. In addition, *Baby, It's You* was shot entirely in 35 mm, a first for Sayles. Both *Lianna* and *Return of the Secaucus*

The visual arrangement of Sheik's efficiency apartment in Baby, It's You *(1983) describes the two loves of his life: Jill, and Frank Sinatra. The mise-en-scène also reveals an emptiness that suggests Sheik's actual condition: He will never become the "Chairman of the Board," nor will true love allow these young people to transcend their class differences. Photo courtesy of the Museum of Modern Art Film Stills Archive.*

Seven were filmed in 16 mm and then blown up to 35 mm. From a narrative standpoint, these films reduce the need for elaborate visual techniques. *Baby, It's You*, on the other hand, is about high school kids who, Sayles says, are "not that articulate." Therefore the film's narrative structure relied more on visual expression.

There are a number of beautiful shots in *Baby, It's You*, but they are not gratuitous and do not interfere with the film narrative. For example, when Sheik and Jill say good-bye to each other at the Miami airport, the shot records their reflected images, suggesting the actual distance between them and their emotional state — not a typical Sayles shot. Here Ballhaus's influence is evident. In addition, there are numerous night shots that would not have registered with such clarity on 16 mm film blown up to 35 mm. For instance, the night shot in *Lianna* showing Lianna as she cuts through her neighbor's backyard only to find her husband with his pants off in a sandbox with one of his students is almost impossible to read. The night shots in *Baby, It's You* are crisp and clear and reflect the eye of a skilled cinematographer.

Ballhaus's photography of Sheik in particular illustrates what increased production capital can do for a film. Sheik provides an outsider's point of view for *Baby, It's You*, especially during the first half of the picture. The cafeteria

shot, filmed with a hand-held camera to underscore Sheik's swaggering presence, shows how Sheik thinks himself to be above his youthful peers. Far more
telling, however, are the shots of Sheik alone — standing in a high school hall-
way, on a street, or on a playground. Sayles films this last shot from a distance in a high angle, capturing Sheik's insignificance. While the visual style
of *Baby, It's You* remains unobtrusive, holding to the tenets of film realism,
Sayles uses a variety of setups in this picture that provide a more complex
mise-en-scène, which enhances his story. His style is visually rich.

Witness a brief example from the scene where Jill returns home from
high school and goes directly to her room to listen to records, ignoring all her
homework. The setup is fairly typical: Jill enters the house framed in a
medium shot; the camera follows her through the dining room and then to
the second-floor stairs. Sayles's film language here is straightforward. The
running conversation between Jill and her parents is a series of one-shots.
Visually this approach is pedestrian. It is evident that Jill is in no mood for
predinner chitchat. Jill begins to climb the stairs while her mother follows
her. From the bottom of the stairs, Jill's mother inquires about a role Jill auditioned for in the school play, adding, "The object isn't to have the biggest part."
Jill quietly responds, "Yes, it is." Here Sayles's shot selection takes on a fresh
complexity, prefiguring Jill's confusion, an aspect of her personality that we
have not been privy to. She is photographed from the bottom of a stairway
in her parent's home, leaning over the second-floor banister to reply to her
mother. What the audience sees is Jill's face framed by lines running willy-
nilly through the shot, suggesting both confusion and confinement, revealing a lack of self-confidence equaling Sheik's lack of self-awareness. This shot
also displays Sayles's understanding of mise-en-scène, even though it is a shot
that can be easily overlooked.

Camera movement also plays a larger role in *Baby, It's You*. Sheik tries
to impress Jill with his driving skills by taking her on a roller-coaster ride
down one-way streets, over bridges, under bridges, and through parking lots
at breakneck speed. This sequence is filmed with the elan of an action director. Sayles's musical selection, "Surfer Bird," with its silly, repetitive lyrics and
speedy instrumentation, points up the absurdity of Sheik's bravura performance. Toward the end of the film, after Sheik realizes that Jill is leaving him
behind and he realizes that she is all he has left, Ballhaus photographs the
Statue of Liberty from inside Sheik's stolen, speeding car. The symbol of freedom and possibility is blurred by the dirty windshield framing the industrial
wasteland of Sheik's native New Jersey. The shot captures Sheik's reality, the
glamour of Miami Beach having given way to the working-class world of
Trenton, New Jersey. These shots are more stylized than is usual for Sayles,
although their message is clear and direct, demonstrating how studio backing can affect the look of a film.

Sayles notes that cinematography "is a good model for the entire process of making a movie. It's a constant barrage of choices to make, each choice creating and defining the next" (*Thinking in Pictures* 71). In fact, one of the best sequences in the *Baby, It's You* contains little dialogue, in contrast to the common description of a Sayles film. Sheik and Jill escape the confines of their high school for the Jersey Shore, specifically Asbury Park. Closed for the winter, the deserted park offers a perfect setting for their impossible but ineffable love. The shots of the ocean surf seen from the deserted boardwalk are crisp and clean. The blue sky and white sea spray are captured in painterly precision, establishing a lyrical, romantic quality to their day away from the regimentation of high school. Shots of empty, red concession booths combine with the natural whites and blues of the sky and the surf to add to the romantic feel of the sequence. Ballhaus uses a deep-focus shot of Jill and Sheik walking hand-in-hand along the deserted boardwalk toward a huge green building where fading letters announce Asbury Park's thrills and rides. Traditionally, amusement parks are a place for fantasy, escape, and equality — every race and class shares the same need to escape into the unfettered world of the imagination. For an afternoon, the boundaries of class can be ignored.

Jill and Sheik are, as the mise-en-scène indicates, momentarily free. Sayles, however, is no romantic. Later in the film Ballhaus uses the same color scheme after Jill and Sheik have had sex for the first time in Sheik's cheap efficiency motel room, decorated with pictures of Jill and Sinatra, his obsessions. The red and blue colors of a neon sign flicker on and off against Jill's pale, tear-stained face. The natural beauty of the seashore and the possibility offered by the amusement park have been wiped away by the gaudy, red, white, and blue reality of Sheik's Miami Beach.

Sayles brings *Baby, It's You* to an antiromantic conclusion. Sheik confronts Jill at Sarah Lawrence. The details of her new life send him into a frenzy: birth control pills, posters of rock stars, books, clothes. Jill, however, is having just as much trouble as Sheik dealing with her post–high school life. Jill has restructured her personality, at least on the outside, to fit into the culture she finds at college, a culture that has broadened her perception. Sheik, who recognizes this change, understands that Jill and he will never "be married and have babies." Jill wants something more, something undefined but definitely not a hometown marriage.

After a verbal battle where they make their positions known, Jill asks Sheik to take her to the college dance because none of her preppie college boyfriends will. The dance is, of course, the prom Jill and Sheik never had, but it is bittersweet. Sheik asks the long-haired rock 'n' roll band to play "Strangers in the Night." The with-it college students in the ballroom, decked out in red, white, and blue bunting, are nonplussed, and they begin to snicker. Quickly, however, everyone is dancing to the updated version of this antique music from their parents' era. Sheik does not fit into Jill's future; he has nothing left to pin his hopes on. We watch their last dance. As the camera pulls away from overhead, the rock version of "Strangers" begins to fade until it is drowned out by Sinatra's version.

After *Baby, It's You*, and all the battles he had with the studio over parts of the film, Sayles decided to direct projects he wanted to make and not be beholden to the whims and wishes of Hollywood studios. In January 1983 Sayles's work received the added boost of a five-year tax-free "genius award" from the MacArthur Foundation, which guaranteed him at least $30,000 per year. His decision to focus on his own fiction writing and filmmaking freed him from, in his words from an *American Film* interview, having to "deal with those fuckers" ("Dialogue on Film" 15)— Hollywood producers. Sayles reconnected to his own production staff, technicians, actors, and material. Fully understanding the financial sacrifice of his decision, Sayles simply felt more comfortable working with his own people, on his own terms.

Still, his expertise as a filmmaker grew making *Baby, It's You*. After three films, Sayles had established a reputation as an idealistic, politically left-of-center filmmaker out of step with the growing conservatism in America, a filmmaker unnoticed not by the critics but often by the public, a filmmaker whose matter-of-fact approach and literary sensibility obscured his cinematic talents. Typically, he did not let the whims of the marketplace stand in the way of his creative objectives.

His next project would be more ambitious. Shifting to a different genre, the historical period piece, Sayles set out to film *Matewan*, a story of a West Virginia coal miner's strike and massacre, inspired by the research for his novel *Union Dues*. However, even with a relatively low starting budget of $4 million, *Matewan*'s funding never came completely together, and he had to turn to other projects. He invested his own money from writing screenplays for other people into the story of a runaway extraterrestrial slave, filming *The Brother from Another Planet* on location in New York's Harlem with a small crew, little time, and a limited budget. Sayles came away with a charming, trenchant view of American society as witnessed by an escaped black extraterrestrial slave.

7

The Brother from Another Planet

> *Brother from Another Planet*, to me, is not so much a political state-
> ment, but about America and our life in this country and about
> waste. The waste of human potential caused by racism and clas-
> sism. So, by the end of the movie, you've realized what an extra-
> ordinary guy this visitor from another planet is, but because of
> what he is he's going to have to hide a lot of those talents.
> — John Sayles (Johnson *Creative Screenwriting*)

The Brother from Another Planet (1984) is a social fable disguised as a science fiction comedy. Ignoring generic science fiction trappings — elaborate
space vehicles, powerful technologies, monstrous aliens — *The Brother* revolves
around a mute extraterrestrial (Joe Morton) who is also a fugitive black slave.
The Brother crash-lands into New York Bay, swims ashore on Ellis Island,
and makes his way to Harlem, one of America's largest and most famous black
communities. Except for his odd feet and special powers, which few Earth-
lings see, the Brother acts like any other new immigrant to the city — lost.
The film follows this charmingly enigmatic figure as he wanders from one
telling vignette to the next with the resilience of a Buster Keaton hero, learning as he goes, staying upright in a topsy-turvy new world. *The Brother* also
parodies some well-known Hollywood films, including *E.T.*, *Splash*, and *Invasion of the Body Snatchers*, among others. Overall the film is a typical Sayles
production — smart, engaging, humane, and accomplished on a skinflint's
budget.

The Brother happened because financing for Sayles's ambitious period
piece *Matewan* fell apart. Sayles produced *The Brother from Another Planet*
out of pocket, at an initial cost of $250,000. He wrote the script, based on a
dream, in six days, and shot on location in Harlem for 24 days with a completely integrated cast and crew — black and white, experienced and novice,
women and men. In addition to his production team and musical composer,
Sayles employed a group of lesser-known black actors from the local Frank

Silvera Drama Workshop. He also hired a young cinematographer, Ernest Dickerson, whose major credit was Spike Lee's celebrated thesis film, *Joe's Bed-Stuy Barbershop: We Cut Heads*, as his director of photography. "We knew we had to make it with the people of Harlem," Sayles remarked, "and we knew we wanted to work with a largely black crew. The only hard part so far has been that everyone wants to work on it, and you wish you could employ them all" (Aufderheide *Film Comment* 4). Sayles calls *The Brother from Another Planet* a "low budget–high concept movie" (Laermer 105). It grossed $4 million.

Oddly enough, keeping the production in New York saved Sayles money: "You don't have to pay for board, you don't have to pay for dinner; they [the crew] just have to show up on the set, and then they go home" ("Dialogue on Film" 14). New York City also adds a gritty background to the visual composition of the film. We are always aware of place in *The Brother*, unlike *Lianna*. There is nothing anonymous about the film's setting. But New York presented problems. "I actually had a pretty good time shooting," says Sayles, "but the producers, Maggie Renzi and Peggy Rajski, said never again will they shoot a movie that fast in an urban area" ("Dialogue on Film" 15). Even with a relatively small crew, filming in a city the size of New York was extremely difficult. Problems with logistics and security could not be anticipated. For example, on the first day of shooting, the crew locked their keys inside their van. A Good Samaritan helped them break in, but his bag, which contained his methadone, vanished. Renzi spent the entire day filing a police report so that the man would not be without his treatment (Aufderheide *Film Comment* 4).

Writing in *Film Comment*, Pat Aufderheide described *The Brother* as "science fiction with a twist: this time, the alien comes home" (4). *The Brother from Another Planet* is an adult variation on *E.T.: The Extra Terrestrial*, without the special effects, but with a recognizable version of home. *The Brother from Another Planet* pokes fun at Steven Spielberg's alien for good reason: Sayles worked on *E.T.*, but, according to Gerald Mast, "he was dropped from the project because he disagreed with the direction it should take" (*Short History* 533). At the film's end, the Brother points skyward with his thumb, a gesture he uses throughout the film to indicate his home, mimicking Spielberg's creature. Another escaped slave from outer space, who helped rescue the Brother from two cosmic slave hunters, reverses the thumb gesture, indicating that a new start is possible on Earth: Harlem is home. As Terry L. Andrews makes clear:

> [Sayles] often presents the view of Harlem that one would expect in a socially concerned film: an image of a largely chaotic ghetto suffering from the social ills of poverty, crime, and drug addiction. Less predictably, however, Sayles also shows Harlem's surprising neighborliness, protectiveness, and pride. [119]

Once again, Sayles takes his audience into unfamiliar territory to meet characters not usually featured in mainstream productions. Indeed, in the

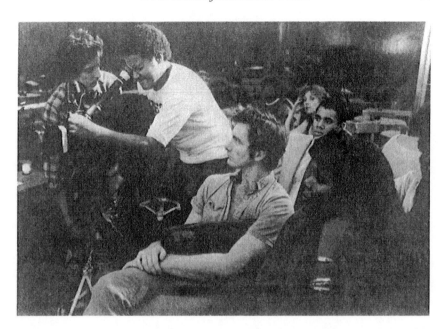

Since he started making his own films, John Sayles has faced one constant piece of criticism: He is not a visual artist. In fact, Sayles has worked with some of the best cinematographers in the business, including Ernest Dickerson, here shown setting up a shot for The Brother from Another Planet *as Sayles looks on. As Sayles's moviemaking skills have grown, so have his control of the camera and the design of individual shots. Sayles deliberately avoids leaving a unique visual stamp on his work, preferring instead to use all the language systems that go into making a movie work to enhance the story he is trying to tell. Sayles still cleaves to one guiding principle: "Talk is cheap; action is expensive." Photo courtesy of the Museum of Modern Art Film Stills Archive.*

early eighties *The Brother from Another Planet* was one of the few films that gave African Americans greater visibility and dealt with black-white tensions. Even Sayles's crew found the shoot to be an education. "I think coming up here [to Harlem] opened the eyes of some whites" (Aufderheide *Film Comment* 4), remarked script supervisor Marco Williams, whose autobiographical documentary *From Harlem to Harvard* chronicles his own cultural journey. While the Brother seeks his own freedom, Sayles puts the viewer in touch with "other people's lives," in his words, to "help us see beyond our own experience" (*Thinking in Pictures* 11), which is the Brother's function: it is directly related to his ability to observe and listen with empathy.

The plot of *The Brother from Another Planet* is straightforward. After escaping from captivity, Sayles's Brother arrives on Earth. At first, he is baffled and terrified by his new surroundings. The Brother, however, fits right into the heterogeneous city. In New York no one is completely out of place, even a man wearing torn and tattered space garments that give him the appearance of a jester who was just mugged. He wanders into a Harlem bar, where he is adopted by the regulars after repairing a broken Space Invaders game (the simple application of his palm revives exhausted machines). There he meets a social worker for the city. Soon he has shelter, clothes, and a job repairing machines in a Times Square video arcade. His new world, however, remains confusing, and to complicate matters, he is pursued by two robotic, white alien slave hunters (John Sayles and David Strathairn). Eventually the Brother is recaptured. But a heretofore invisible community of other escaped alien slaves rescues him. In the end, the Brother takes the A-train uptown, returning home to Harlem. Sayles's plot structure allows plenty of room for episodic asides, which are full of wonderfully original characters and situations.

The Brother from Another Planet presented obvious technical problems for Sayles. On a strict budget, commercial special effects were impossible. Yet Sayles needed to establish the fact that his protagonist traveled an intergalactic underground railroad to his new world. Sayles opted for a bit of parodic hijinks, drawing on both his background in B films and his creativity.

Most films that feature space travelers ostentatiously display the complex, futuristic design of space vehicles, whose detailed mechanical design comes with a large price tag. Nora Chavooshian, in her first job as full production designer, created the film's sets to fit the budget. In order to compensate for the lack of money, Sayles used an interior shot with no visible light source except the ship's control panel. We see whirling, blinking red dots and bars, and strange blue digital readouts; we hear mechanical sounds increasing in speed. An image of the Earth centers on a coordinate viewfinder, the Wal-Mart version of the elaborate landing technology used in Stanley Kubrick's 2001: A Space Odyssey. A creature inside a spacesuit attempts to steady this craft, which is shaking wildly out of control (an effect produced by rocking a hand-held camera from side to side). Background music builds to enhance the tension. Sayles cuts to a master shot of outer space. A dot of light flies across the screen from right to left accompanied by a cartoonish whizzing sound and an abrupt, small splash.

Sayles's set design is patently cheap and fake; it is a comic put-on, a burlesque of Hollywood's culture of special effects, done with bargain basement flair. The Brother's opening sequence recalls the worst 1950s science fiction films, while celebrating its own low production values and needling Hollywood's infatuation with toy technology. "The exterior of the spaceship," according to Sayles, "cost twelve dollars, and outer space was created with black construction paper and a pin" (Stempel FrameWork 237).

As always, Sayles's chief concern is with people and their struggles, not machinery or stylistic illusions. The Brother welds B-filmmaking with adult drama, Sayles's preferred film genre. Sayles acknowledges the connection: "It's a very serious movie, it's about racism and the economic system in America, and at the same time it's a very low-budget science fiction movie" (Valen 12).

Staging a high-tech opening in such a low-tech fashion appeals to Sayles's wry sense humor. While *The Brother* addresses serious subjects — race, drugs, crime, poverty, work — it does so in a friendly way, without rancor or pedantic finger wagging. Sayles's opening sets the tone for the entire film — serious fun.

However, Sayles's mise-en-scène reveals a definite subtext. A red, white, and blue color motif accents the frame during the opening sequence, reflected off the Brother's face shield, obscuring his face, making him unreadable, invisible. The laid-back, comfortable tavern the Brother feels so at ease in is also accented by lights that represent America. Other markers, which, as Bill Nichols puts it, "serve as a narrative thickening agent lending density or weight to its development" (85), include a natty blue suit, red tie, and white beret the Brother wears in the final quarter of the film, and the large, street-level windows of the social services office that are an ostentatious red and blue, and spackled with white handbills. With this tricolor motif, Sayles indicates that this film is about some of the social problems Americans and America face, not a fantastic world of make-believe.

While Sayles's narrative construction is praised more often than his low-key approach to directing, his subtle, economically sound approach to filmmaking reveals a careful, maturing style at work. For example, the core of *The Brother from Another Planet* is black and white, and Sayles uses this color scheme with dexterity. Race relations dominate the film but not in a stridently confrontational manner. Sayles is too meticulous an artist to indulge in a simplistic dichotomy. White men, however, signify unthinking authority as cops, slave hunters, and drug suppliers. In *The Brother*, white skin, for the most part, means trouble, a concept that flies in the face of traditional Hollywood stereotypes. As the slave hunters enter the Brother's neighborhood bar, the frame fills with a harsh, grainy white light, washing out all other color. When Mr. Vance, the businessman–drug dealer, is justly punished for trafficking in heroin, he is smothered in a bag of the white powder as the screen fades to white, lost like Edgar Allan Poe's Arthur Gordon Pym. White people cause the Brother anxiety early on in the film. Still, Sayles portrays the harmful separation of blacks and whites with humor and biting clarity.

The mute Brother's facial expressions and body language indicate that whites have caused him much pain and suffering. Even in the film's antic scenes, such as the encounter between the Brother and a rapid-talking Caucasian card manipulator, the Brother's discomfort is telling. The card trickster (Fisher Stevens), who is not portrayed as a white authority figure, performs a baffling card trick for the Brother, who is riding the subway home from work. Underground, the Brother is trapped, and his fear and confusion are obvious. He moves away from the trickster, looking at him with disbelief, not understanding a thing he is doing. As the card player cuts the deck for the terrified Brother, his speech accelerates because he is under a time restraint. When he finishes the card trick, the train pulls into the Fifty-ninth Street, Columbus Circle, stop, and the trickster performs one more perplexing trick, one full of big-city truth. He says, "Want to see me make all the white people disappear?" The train doors open and passengers get on and off. The brakeman's voice announces, "Uptown A express; 125th Street next." The camera pans the subway car interior. All the passengers are black or Hispanic. The card trickster flashes a knowing smile as he leaves.

The Brother, who learns by observation, is perplexed by his interaction with white people. When the film opens, he is afraid of every white person he sees because of his past, but he grows to understand that white people are not all oppressors or out to get him. Not every white person is a slave master. The Brother does, however, come to Earth with a certain set of assumptions that hold true. White men in uniform, for example, are to be feared. The slave hunters, dressed in black uniforms, represent an alien police force. Sayles plays to this conceit when he places the Brother in a scene with a rookie cop who has drawn Harlem as his first assignment. The Brother is visibly nervous being near an authority figure whose language is tinged with racist assumptions. The cop asks, "How long you been up here? You a native or what?" His partner, he relates, told him that in Harlem he was going to be cooked and eaten alive. The cop articulates small-minded attitudes toward blacks, yet he hears no irony in his words, nor does he mean any harm; this is, after all, normal speech for him. Sayles's hero just gets up and walks away. He does not seem to understand the racist substance of the cop's speech, but too much talk, especially from an authority figure, bothers him. The Brother recognizes the cop as a symbol of oppression. Still, the scene presents a typical Saylesian paradox: The cultural assumptions of both the rookie and the Brother make their characters unconventional — they add an increased level of understanding to the narrative.

The Brother is an unfamiliar character, yet he carries with him some of the traits that describe the traditional American hero, a figure that enjoyed a muscular rebirth during the Reagan years. Sayles does not miss the opportunity to mock the macho hero's return. On the one hand, the Brother is the quintessential man alone, facing long odds, a typical American movie protagonist; on the other hand, he is gentle, mute, lost, a healer, not a destroyer, and a runaway slave free from violent impulse. Worse, the Brother is black, homeless, and an illegal alien, wandering the streets of America's largest city, hardly representative of Reagan's conservative agenda. Typically, *The Brother from Another Planet* is a covertly political film, full of witty liberal conceits, for it displays a social concern decidedly lacking in most mainstream films of the 1980s.

By using a central character who cannot talk, Sayles relied more on visual communication than he had in the past. Part of his rationale, of course, was economic: If the lead character "doesn't talk you can shoot a lot of MOS

Brother from Another Planet *(1984): In this intergalactic immigration tale, Joe Morton (center) starred as the "Brother." Here the "Brother" is recaptured by an oddball pair of bounty hunters, played with robotic perfection by David Strathairn (right) and Sayles himself (left). Photo courtesy of the Museum of Modern Art Film Stills Archive.*

[silent] footage, which is much cheaper, especially on New York streets, with the horns and the breaks and the airplanes overhead" ("Dialogue on Film" 15). Ernest Dickerson's film aesthetic aided *The Brother*'s success. Like Michael Ballhaus, Dickerson has a fine eye for realistic detail and an expressionistic pictorial skill, which combine to enhance Sayles's narrative. Unlike Ballhaus, Dickerson did not arrive with much filmmaking experience. Sayles saw Lee's thesis film and hired Dickerson. As Dickerson tells it, things were not as straightforward as Sayles thought. "I lied when he asked me if I had ever shot 35-millimeter before," said Dickerson. "I figured a camera is a camera. All the camera is a recording device. You have got to see it first in your mind's eye, manipulate the image to make it look like it does in your head" (Ravo 19). Dickerson's brassy confidence paid off. *The Brother*'s poetic, realistic look fits its setting, and adds visual ballast to Sayles's narrative.

Cities produce sensory overload, especially New York. Simultaneously liberating and intimidating — the romance of bright lights juxtaposed with the hard reality of neglect — New York's cityscape is in constant opposition; it offers a ready-made metaphor for the brother's struggle. Dickerson's imaginative eye captures the conflicting aspects of modern urban life. For example, many of the buildings and subway trains we see are covered with graffiti, which, according to some, suggests the decline of quality of life in the city. However, for the anonymous citizens of lost neighborhoods, graffiti is an announcement of self, a signature statement, the only means of recognition, no matter how limited, at their disposal. As the Brother passes graffiti-stained walls, he looks as if he is reading an impossibly obscure text, trying to break a code.

Eventually he sees a recognizable sign, a specific mark of graffiti, signifying that he is not alone on this new planet, and he willingly leaves a reply written in his own blood. There are others like him here, but they, like graffiti artists, are invisible, anonymous. At the end of the film, his ability to read graffiti ensures his salvation. But Dickerson's graffiti shots are not elaborate stylizations, the sort of stuff one might find framed in a chichi art gallery. They are ordinary, actual tags, the names of hundreds of unknown people.

As Carol Cooper remarks, "Dickerson's camera is acutely sensitive to the beauty beneath Harlem's creeping squalor" (18). Dickerson's shot selection keeps *The Brother* at street level. His imagery holds a comic film in necessary balance: The shot selection intensifies the obvious, the way things are, which, in turn, underlines the honest condition of the film's setting. Like Sayles, Dickerson uses his artistic talents to add dimension to our contemporary scene, to show us that the obscure names on the wall have meaning.

Dickerson chooses his shots well, displaying his photographic talent throughout the film. As the Brother climbs ashore on Ellis Island, black dominates the mise-en-scène. Only the Statue of Liberty stands out in the background, but it is out of focus. We see fear on Joe Morton's face in the foreground, the dark waters of New York Bay in the middle ground, and the blurred statue in the background. This shot indicates the struggle ahead: The Brother is trapped by blackness, with the hope for liberty available to him in the dim indistinct distance. The shot virtually duplicates the opening of Ron Howard's *Splash*. But *The Brother* is no sentimental love story, and Morton is no ephemeral sea nymph. The mise-en-scène here is dyed with fear, the mystery of the unknown.

Next the Brother is photographed from a low angle, with the turret of the dilapidated, vaguely Byzantine, brick and limestone immigration hall looming above him like a Gothic cathedral. Here the Brother is dominated by history, although Ellis Island was not a stopping-off point for the overwhelming majority of blacks. When the brother enters the immigration building, he is photographed against a harsh, black backdrop. The cavernous hallways and vaulted ceilings of the immigration center are confining, tomblike. Sayles, however, lights the Brother from above, letting the audience know that this illegal alien has a unique sensitivity.

As the Brother touches the pillars inside the echoing chambers of the deserted immigration hall, his body "feels" a cacophony of foreign words, cries, and shrieks. He understands the pain of other travelers to this new world. But his empathy is overwhelming. A rapid montage of interior shots, all dimly lit, show the Brother's internal fear and confusion as his face contorts into a scream before he passes out from psychic overload. Metaphorically, Sayles suggests that awareness of the past, of what America once stood for, is lost, and along with it the ability to empathize with the plight of new immigrants. Like many immigrants before him, the Brother will not be welcomed with open arms. The abandoned immigration hall, which resonates with echoes, visually represents our neglected past. Dickerson's photography illuminates Sayles's ideas. Moreover, many of the night shots in the film deliberately suggest a sense of urban Gothic, especially the descent into the hellish nighttown of Harlem.

Structurally, *The Brother from Another Planet* uses a dialectical approach to make its points. Sayles juxtaposes night and day in his script, and Dickerson balances his night imagery with an Edward Hopper–like appreciation for the city. After his horrific introduction to New York, the Brother takes in the early morning splendor of the city. Dickerson's deep focus pan of lower Manhattan offers a quiet beauty. The tight, confining shots that dominated the beginning of the film give way to an airy openness as the Brother sets off with an inquiring gaze into Manhattan, landing at 125th Street, Harlem's main artery. Here Dickerson's camera captures the start of a new day — shops open, work starts, people begin filling the street. The camera registers the Brother's point of view for us, capturing the small, overlooked activities that build a day.

Sayles also juxtaposes noisy, empty speech with concrete imagery. For instance, the Brother is a creature of silence and an uncanny observer. He does not, however, need spoken language to survive. Until the Brother enters the immigration hall, the film has been unnaturally quiet. Not only have we been seeing through the eyes of the Brother, but we have also been listening through his ears. As his self-assurance grows, the Brother comes to understand how language functions, especially when it is misused. After all, everyone the Brother meets wants to define him and tell him his or her story. Once the Brother enters his new world, he cannot escape sound. How noise is used, then, is important to an overall understanding of *The Brother from Another Planet*. For example, at the end of the film, the Brother puts his hand over the drug dealer's mouth, stopping any more deal-making talk. Vance babbles with unconvincing rhetoric, the sort of bombast one might hear from a politician. By silencing him, the Brother gives Vance the opportunity to see. Placing his recording eye, an extraterrestrial trait, in Vance's hand, the Brother forces the drug dealer to see and feel the destruction his heroin has caused, replaying for Vance the image of the overdosed junkie kid lying dead in a detritus-filled lot in Harlem.

By filling the frame, Dickerson's camera brings volume to Sayles's words.

In the nightmarish journey through Harlem's netherworld with a friendly, stoned Rastafarian named Virgil, Dickerson's camera records the bleak conditions without distancing the audience through preachy, traditional images of urban squalor. The most poetic shot in this sequence is of a black dancer whose kinetic struggle articulates the problems of the entire community. The scene is lighted in lurid reds and blues. The dancer throws himself against a corrugated metal storefront, trying without success to break free. Virgil's speech accents the desperate image, a combination of Sayles's ability to capture authentic voices and Dickerson's eye, exploring the horrors of neglect.

Fire and smoke from a 55-gallon drum separate Virgil and the Brother. Virgil offers the Brother a spliff (a large marijuana cigarette, common to the Rastafarian culture), telling him to "take the ship home to the promised land," to escape the wickedness of "Babylon." The Brother chooses to cross over, taking the ship home. Here Dickerson presents desperate images of the disinherited of Harlem. The hellish nightmare lying just below the surface of an otherwise friendly film comes to full visual force in this sequence. Harlem's night struggle countervails the freedom the Brother seeks.

Despair could, of course, erode the tone of the film, but Sayles pulls back. The heavy beat of the Jamaican music that dominated the journey into the netherworld of drugs gives way first to silence and then to the celestial steel drums that mark the Brother's presence on screen. It is daylight. The frame is filled with a close-up of the Brother's massive, clawed feet, his shoes gone. Like Aeneas, the Brother, following the paradigm describing a hero's magnification, descended into the underworld, crossed the river of the dead, and returned to his work in the world. However, even a hero returning from hell is not immune to the needs of the disenfranchised, a wry comment on urban realities. Harlem's disrepair loads the frame as the Brother makes his way home, but the outrage generated by Virgil's tour is blunted by the Brother's missing shoes. Yet Sayles's graphic mise-en-scène underlines the desperate environment that the Brother now calls home.

Visually, Dickerson captures both the possibility of America and the American nightmare; he captures the poetry of the city. We see it through our hero's eyes, experiencing its foreignness and oppressiveness, its beauty and openness. In collaboration with Sayles, Dickerson makes everyday appearances extraordinary. He balances hope and despair with artistic precision.

Sayles uses a number of literary techniques in *The Brother from Another Planet*, putting his own spin on each. The hero descending is just one example, although Rastafarian Virgil gaining insight through an oversized joint is pure irreverence toward literary tradition, but it fits the bittersweet tone of Sayles's film.

The Brother is also a bildungsroman and a picaresque adventure. When the Brother first arrives on Earth, he is terrified, constantly fearful. After his baptism in New York harbor, the Brother emerges renewed, ready to seek a new life. But he is overwhelmed by the size of the raucous city. Walking down a street in silence, the Brother hears the loud sounds from a boom box, a common urban prop, and he quickly runs for cover, freezing with fear in a doorway. His fears, however, are overcome with the help of compassionate members of the Harlem community. Eventually, the Brother gains confidence and grows. By the end of the film, he is able to walk without fear into the skyscraper that contains and protects Mr. Vance, the film's one real villain. He is, in the end, able to make his own decisions, and he is able to take care of himself. Morton's precise acting style captures this growth with grace and precision. Using only his physical tools — face, gesture, body — he shows us the Brother's metamorphosis from innocence to maturity.

The Brother also satirizes American society. As Gerald Mast noted, the function of this type of character in film or literature is to "bounce off the people and events around him, often, in the process, revealing the superiority of his comic bouncing to the social and human walls he hits" (*The Comic Mind* 7). Charlie Chaplin, of course, is America's most famous film picaro, and Sayles, it seems, is completely aware of his main character's historical lineage. The Brother is a physical, comedic character for our modern age who bumps into strange people and strange events as he attempts to make sense of his new world.

The Brother from Another Planet is full of solid acting performances. With a silent protagonist, everyone else in the cast must play off him, revealing more about themselves than they normally might. As always, Sayles provides solid, unadorned dialogue for his actors. His ability to capture the nuances of various voices stands out. Even though *The Brother* focuses on a single character, Sayles presents a large, varied supporting cast. From the stoned Rastafarian to the Korean grocery store owner, from muggers to grandmothers, from barflies to street hucksters, Sayles created realistic lines. And his actors breathed life into his writing.

Joe Morton's task was, perhaps, the most difficult of the entire cast. Not only is he the focus of the film, but he must remain mute. Without dialogue, Morton must convey all his feelings physically. In a way, *The Brother from Another Planet* is a return to the silent era, exploring the kinds of scenes that have not been possible since movies started to talk. Morton exhibits fear, concern, innocence, disbelief, anxiety, understanding, love, hate, and glee without uttering a word.

One sequence in *The Brother* that displays Morton's abilities is particularly Chaplinesque. It concerns, not surprisingly, money. Tired and hungry, the Brother looks longingly at some pears in bins outside a market. The camera lingers on the fruit, letting us know the Brother's desire. A cut to the interior of the store frames the Korean grocer behind her store's cash register as she makes change for a customer. In the background, the Brother picks up a pear and greedily bites into it, furtively glancing about. A close-up of his face shows both his need for food and his fear. The shopkeeper runs outside, grabs the half-eaten pear, and castigates the Brother in Korean for stealing her goods. The Brother is perplexed but undaunted.

Still hungry, he watches as a customer completes a transaction. He sees cash exchanged for product, the American economic system in microcosm. The camera records his observation: To acquire fruit you need money; money comes from cash registers. He can open these simple machines with a concentrated touch of his palm, and he does so, snatching a handful of bills. As he turns to select another piece of fruit, the shopowner sees him gripping her money and the open cash register. Of course, our innocent hero only wants food. Outside, he extends the cash with one hand, while clutching the pear in the other, to the screaming shopowner. He uses multiple gestures to indicate his desire, growing more and more anxious with each shout for the "police." The shopowner ignores his attempt at payment. Turning, the Brother sees a policeman, a white man in uniform. The Brother's fear is overwhelming. Sayles quick-cuts to a point-of-view close-up of the cop's hat and his badge, reinforcing the image of authority. Running away, the Brother drops the money and the fruit as the officer makes chase.

The quick-shot that follows recalls Chaplin's *The Kid*. With the cop in hot pursuit, the Brother escapes with a deft, athletic maneuver. The police here, as in the Chaplin classic, protect the interests of the status quo, the propertied shopowner. Like Chaplin, Morton does a masterful job registering a number of feelings and emotions in this short sequence: hunger, desire, thought, panic, fear. He embodies the distinctive Chaplin blend of spunk, poetry, and enigmatic presence. We root for his escape. Sayles uses the situation not only to tip his hat to Chaplin but also to reveal something about economics and attitudes. It is evident that the Brother has no intention of stealing either money or food; rather, he is hungry and desperate. None of the other characters in the sequence attempt to communicate with him. After all, he is black, dressed in rags, and stealing — a criminal. Chaplin's Little Tramp confronted similar difficulties. Both characters are preoccupied with survival, food, and shelter. Both face respectable citizens and cops. Ultimately, these characters work by kicking the audience in the seat of their pants. And, like the Tramp, the Brother understands the economic forces of this new world.

While this sequence recalls Chaplin, Morton draws on many sources to create an aura of thought and free-floating emotion. The Brother also recalls Buster Keaton's implacable deadpan. Indeed, Morton's Brother has Keatonian resiliency. That is, he goes about his business by exercising his abilities and free will, confronting whatever comes his way. Integrity drives the Brother. Like many Keaton characters, the Brother gets into trouble because of his openness, his innate emotional and intellectual curiosity. The scene with the Korean store owner is a funny bit, even though its underlying meaning is serious. What gives this scene its comic lift is Morton's gestures and facial expressions; after all, he did what he was supposed to do, so why call the cops? The Brother approaches his journey with the unblinking, knowing passivity of a Keaton hero. He understands that this new world is full of impediments, but he will continue undaunted.

Joe Morton plays the Brother with expressive charm throughout the film. Like many of Sayles's actors, Morton is experienced in both stage and television. Like many of Sayles's actors, Morton wanted the work because of Sayles's reputation as an intelligent filmmaker, and because of the limited number of good roles for black actors. "It's almost impossible to find roles in the movies for a black actor," said Morton. "And most science fiction is like what Richard Pryor said about *2001*—they must think there won't be any blacks by then" (Aufderheide *Film Comment* 6). In addition, playing the part of a mute intrigued Morton. The other characters in the film create their own expectations of him—imagining who he really is and what he really wants. According to Morton, "The role makes the audience look at Harlem from both white and black perspectives. It's Harlem seen not as a jungle but from the eyes of an innocent" (Aufderheide *Film Comment* 6).

Morton's talent and passion for acting are both evident. In a quick scene after the cop chase, Morton's ability to communicate with his eyes and his face are beautifully illustrated. He reflects on a small statue of Christ nailed to the cross, blood dripping from his wounds. Across the street, he sees a cop place a young black kid up against a car in a similar position. His new world is steeped in violence, both symbolic and literal. Morton scores the Brother's anxious fear by averting his eyes from each image and walking quickly away. When a Hispanic video-game wizard laments her desperate condition using space invaders as an analogy for her life, the Brother brings her orgasmic pleasure by speeding the game up. Morton plays this bit straight—we understand the pleasure he takes in helping the young woman find brief solace from the empty monotony of her life. Morton's uniquely expressive face, body command, and self-deprecating gentleness infuse the role with believability.

In *The Brother from Another Planet*, Sayles wrote parts for specific actors. For example, Randy Sue, a white woman from Alabama who lives in Harlem with her black mother-in-law and her young mixed-race son, was written expressly for Caroline Aaron. Sayles wanted "someone who was very strong and tough and from the South" ("Dialogue on Film" 14). Aaron is memorable for these traits, and for her nonstop chatter, compassion, and naturalness. It also helped that she worked for scale, which is essential to any low-budget filmmaking project.

Also effective are Sayles and David Strathairn as the Brother's intergalactic pursuers. This comic tag team has a much easier time getting to Earth than does the Brother; in fact, because we never actually see them land, it seems as if they come with the territory, which, in a manner of speaking, they do: We see Sayles, dressed in black, arise from below screen on an escalator like a commuter from hell, clutching an *English as a Second Language* textbook. Strathairn, dressed identically, meets him at the top of the moving stairs with a picture of the Brother, whom they call "Three Toe." Even though these two have absorbed some American idioms, they wholly lack the escaped slave's gift for communication and his ability to pass without regard among the citizens of New York.

Sayles uses this daffy couple to parody television shows, Westerns, and kung fu movies. At times, the Sayles character sounds like Joe Friday from the old television series *Dragnet*, talking in a dull monotone, assured that his command "Just the facts, ma'am" will bring the desired results. It does not. Their dress mocks bad guys from B Westerns — all they lack are black hats — and their mad karate kicks and punches do Bruce Lee no justice at all. In fact, their tough guy personas are hysterical; they are so odd, people watch every move they make.

When they enter Odell's bar, obviously aware that they are on the right track but unaware how to follow their own leads, they are hilariously out of place. Their entrance is announced with a bath of bright white light that engulfs Walter and half the interior of the bar. They order, "Beer ... Draft ... On the rocks." When they ask for the Brother, Odell asks for an ID, because, as he says, "If you're dicks ya got badges." Strathairn's man-in-black responds without irony, "What makes you think we are Dicks?" From offscreen Fly says, "I could answer that," sending the regulars into hysterics. When the pair turn to leave, Smokey notes, "White folks get stranger all the time."

In the Sayles system, economics often drives casting, but not at the expense of quality acting. As Sayles put it, "We always have so little time to shoot that I usually work with people who have worked in the theater because they can retain two pages of dialogue with no problem" ("Dialogue on Film" 14). Stage actors work cheaply, and they welcome the opportunity and exposure film provides. In the main, Sayles does not work on the star system. Actors, however, do take priority in a Sayles film. Because he is more concerned with the real world than with the glamour of the movies, Sayles wants his cast to look and sound real. Having a good casting director helps. Barbara Shapiro cast both *Lianna* and *The Brother from Another Planet*. According to Sayles, "She knew us well enough to be able to interpret our sometimes vague feelings and comments and we knew and trusted each other's taste in acting" (*Thinking in Pictures* 48).

The Brother's bar family makes a good example. Odell (Steve Jones), the owner and bartender; Smokey (Leonard Jackson) and Walter (Bill Cobbs), two regular drinkers; and Fly (Darryl Edwards), who plays Space Invaders relentlessly, are quality actors. They spice up the bar scenes. Their characters span generations and descriptions. Odell has no use for anything below 110th

Street; he likes Harlem, and he enjoys running his tavern. Fly, the youngest member of the group, is the quickest with a line, which may or may not have thought behind it. Smokey, as his name implies, is the drinker in the group, accounting for the fluctuation in his awareness and for his willingness to believe in the supernatural. Walter is a world-weary philosopher, an existentialist who ruminates on space garbage, immigrants with exotic diseases, and the lamentable loss of community in Harlem. Their repartee is excellent, as they kid each other with the kind of cutting, sarcastic quips that only true friends can command. Sayles's ear for dialogue and some sharp editing help to make these scenes funny and provocative, but the actors infuse the scenes with a sense of reality that makes their time on screen memorable.

Odell's is the Brother's essential place. It fits neatly into Gerald Carson's definition of the American saloon as "a forum and a community center, a place for genial self-expression, and, for the traveler, a home away from home" (25). The Brother feels secure there because of the warmth, hospitality, and goodwill the bar patrons display toward him. For example, facing down the robotic slave chasers, Fly uses his arms, hands, and fingers to register his outrage when they ask him for his green card. "Green card! Man. Whats you talkin', sucker?" he yells at these strange creatures. "Ever been to South Carolina? My people built that." From off-screen Walter remarks, "Can't build a state, man." Fly becomes even more outraged and strives to prove his point: "All I knows, when they got off the boat weren't nothin' there. Now there's shopping malls, and, what's that shit, miniature golf." Though comic, Fly's outrage cuts to the bone of the racist mentality expressed by the alien creatures. To them, blacks are fodder to be used for profit and then discarded. In the end, Odell's patrons will defend their silent Brother with all the force they can muster.

Later, when two Midwestern graduate students looking for Columbia University and the "Self-Actualization Conference" realize that they are in Harlem and now in the minority, they sheepishly enter Odell's looking for directions. They sit next to the Brother, the only man in the bar who cannot speak. A few boozy hours pass. "I wanted to be Ernie Banks," says one of the lost students. "Mr. Cub," chimes the other, as if auditioning for a sports talk show. "And it never really dawned on me that he was black," responds his friend. Talking to a black man who does not respond to their observations seems to abate their nervousness. This dialogue, albeit funny, serves to show the gulf between the white Midwesterners, who are not even sure if there were any blacks in their hometown, and the urban world of the Brother. Ironically, the Brother is so fearful of them that he is afraid to get up to leave, even though he finds their talk to be nonsensical. Ernie Banks means nothing to him. None of the other characters in the bar even bothers to look at this lost pair, let alone speak to them. But the graduate students think that they have accomplished much by "communicating" with a black man who cannot respond.

The music for *The Brother* further illustrates how Sayles produces quality films without elaborate expenditures. When we first see the Brother, Sayles uses steel drum music, the sound of the Caribbean, to announce his character. The drums are analogous to an operatic signature, marking the Brother and other aliens throughout the picture. When the Brother discovers the slave tag graffiti, the steel drums fill the soundtrack with a shower of exuberance. Moreover, as the bounty hunters leave the welfare office, we hear the melodic sound and see an African American man who later is revealed to be a member of the underground alien community, physical proof that the Brother is not alone in this new world. At the end of the film, as the Brother pursues Mr. Vance, the drums sound as the camera comes to rest on a member of the night clean-up crew running a floor buffer, telling viewers that the Brother is not alone in his quest for justice.

Because the sound of the steel drums is so distinctive, Sayles's choice to use the instrument has significance. When he started making *The Brother*, the State Department had begun to crack down on illegal aliens arriving from the Caribbean, particularly Cuba and Haiti, a policy the Reagan administration toughened before the film was completed for distribution. The Brother is simultaneously constructed as a space alien, a runaway slave, and a Caribbean immigrant — he wears his hair in short dreadlocks, and the sound of Caribbean drums is his musical marker throughout the film. Sayles's musical selection, then, points up the hypocrisy of placing governmental restrictions on immigrants, especially those with dark skin, by constantly recalling the sound of the Caribbean. In addition, although the steel drums originated in Trinidad in the first half of the twentieth century, their roots can be traced to the drum music of Africans imported into the West Indies as slaves. Therefore, Sayles's inexpensive soundtrack enhances the film both musically and thematically.

Indeed, music punctuates Sayles's narrative, accentuating the mood and spirit of the film as a whole. In collaboration with Mason Daring, his musical composer, Sayles uses blues, jazz, soul, funk, and gospel music to give the picture a distinctly urban, distinctly black sound. Daring and Sayles wrote two songs in the film score. One, "Homeboy," is sung off-screen by Joe Morton. The other, "Promised Land," which concludes the film, celebrates the Brother's freedom, growth, and entrance into the community of runaway slaves. This concluding song, sung by The Labors in the Vineyard All Community Choir, reminds us that African Americans created beauty out of the ugliest of situations, human bondage. Dee Dee Bridgewater, who plays the Brother's love interest, Malverne, performs two songs Daring composed for the film, one of which, "Getaway," anticipates the night she and the Brother will spend together. Sayles also uses a Little Anthony and the Imperials song, "Two People in the World," during a montage of female images gleaned from a variety of sources — newspapers, billboards, magazines — to characterize the

Brother's desire for a female companion. For the most part, the score of the film remains low-key, unobtrusive, yet it burnishes the Brother's story. The jubilation with which Sayles ends the film acknowledges the Brother's presence in his new world. The trepidation and fear with which he once approached this new place are gone. The Brother is confident, self-assured, and, it seems, free. In the words that begin Ralph Ellison's *Invisible Man*, he is "a man of substance, of flesh and bone, fiber and liquids" (3). Indeed, the Brother shares much with Ellison's invisible hero. Like Ellison's protagonist, Sayles's hero hides in plain sight. But it is not until the white slave catchers have dispatched themselves that he can truly feel free in America. Except for the white authority figures, Sayles presents a vision of America that is an indivisible blend of people.

Even though *The Brother* succeeded financially, reviews for the film were lukewarm. Donald Bogle, author of the seminal book on images of blacks in American cinema, offers one sentence about the film: "Independent white filmmaker John Sayles came up with an interesting but overrated [offbeat film] *The Brother from Another Planet*" (290). It cannot be ignored, however, that Sayles brought a film about race issues — black, brown, yellow, and white — to the screen with depth, substance, and across-the-board accessibility. Because he is not an African American filmmaker, Sayles will never achieve Bogle's definition of black sensibility. Ironically, however, a close appraisal of Sayles's film reveals that the Brother passes through all of Bogle's categorical descriptions that define the images of blacks in the American cinema. He begins as a "Tom" — enslaved, repressed, insulted — on a backward planet. He comes to Earth and assumes the guise of a jester in his torn and tattered spacesuit. For the bigoted arcade owner, Mr. Lowe, who lives up to his name, the Brother takes on the role of servant by replenishing his exhausted machines. The entire film shows the Brother as a problem person for the slave hunters. In the end, of course, he reaches a level of autonomy. In other words, he is a complex character who does not fit neatly into a package. Because Sayles is not an ostentatious filmmaker, critics often overlook the subtleties at play in his work. In *The Brother* Sayles brings a number of issues to bear in a comedy of contemporary manners told from the perspective of a black alien.

For the most part, critics were put off by Sayles's filmmaking style in *The Brother from Another Planet* — or what some considered his lack of style. "In New York City," Sayles says, "*Brother* really got pretty bad reviews, but it still broke house records" (McGhee 46). Sayles's low-key approach is unfashionable; it lacks a pigeonholing instance, a formalistic hook to entice viewers. The tone of *The Brother* stands in direct contrast to that of the hyperkinetic 1980s. In addition, the film explores relevant social issues, but it does so without inflammatory rhetoric. Sayles's taste for dry, throwaway humor with bite lacks aggression, yet it delivers the message. He does not talk down to his audience, although he does want it to think and work along with him. However, the conservative mind-set of the Reagan administration and the mood of the country in general was just beginning to be felt by Sayles. Indeed, even the word-of-mouth audience he had developed would ignore his next two films, *Matewan* and *Eight Men Out.*

Like most of Sayles's other film work, *The Brother from Another Planet* is about community. The film shows how a community reacts to an outsider, and how that outsider finds a home. At the end, when the slave hunters face the collective resistance of a dozen runaway slaves, Sayles inverts the premise of the 1950s classic *Invasion of the Body Snatchers.* He reminds us that people are not the same, and difference has its rewards. As Ed Guerrero observes, "This resolution clearly privileges the value of collective organization and resistance to oppression, and it has an allusive validity of the collective resistance of African-Americans, abolitionists, and others to historical slavery" (49). Still, Sayles is no Pollyanna. The shot that concludes the film is certainly hopeful: the Brother is happy, and smiling as he never has before in the film. He is, however, looking through a heavy-gauge wire-mesh fence at a Harlem high school. Like everything else in this wonderful film, there is a contradictory impulse at work here, an ambiguity that blunts a completely happy ending. It is a reminder that the Brother's struggle never ends. Sayles leaves his story looking ahead, to freedom, but also backward to the injustice of bondage. Once again, Sayles presents a spirited, risk-taking film that is ambitious and necessary.

8

Matewan

A lot of what I try to do in *Matewan* ... is to have the audience
spend time with people they ordinarily wouldn't spend time with,
with history they either forgot or never knew, and make it have
some bearing on what's going on today.

          — John Sayles (Popkin)

Everything John Sayles learned about filmmaking is evidenced in *Matewan* (1987), his period piece based upon the Matewan Massacre, the violent result of an attempt to unionize southern West Virginia coal miners in 1920. All the elements necessary to the creation of a film — screenwriting, production, cinematography, sound, editing, among others — are fully realized in this study of hardship, struggle, and violence. *Matewan* delivers intellectually, emotionally, and artistically.

 Matewan is more than a historical retelling of a neglected event. By examining the conservative 1920s, Sayles parallels the conservatism of the 1980s, a period dominated by the antilabor ideals of Ronald Reagan. History is vital to Sayles: "I feel that history, especially the stories we like to believe or know about ourselves, is part of the ammunition we take with us into the everyday battle of how we define ourselves and how we act toward other people" (Carnes *Past Imperfect* 11). Yet, as is the case with all of Sayles's work, *Matewan* cannot be easily categorized; it is a complex work technically, artistically, and morally. In fictionalizing the events that culminated in the Matewan Massacre, a bloody and historically accurate presentation, Sayles takes a politically unpopular stand by showing how West Virginian, black, and Italian immigrant coal miners overcome their cultural differences in their attempt to form a union. The film's unabashed support for the workers in a labor-capital conflict contradicts the conservative agenda that dominated the 1980s, where dog-eat-dog was the norm and individual accomplishment was valued over collective organization. Indeed, as Sayles points out, "Think of the big stars of the Eighties, like Arnold Schwarzenegger and Sylvester Stallone. They played Ur characters — you know, mythic characters. It was this simplistic and even heightened good-guys and bad-guys thing" (Carnes *Past*

Imperfect 24). *Matewan* refuses to present easy choices or romanticized solutions. One of Sayles's central characters is a "red," a union organizer whose job is to prevent the strike from becoming violent. In the end, however, after the strike spreads, after the struggle, after the deaths, no workers' utopia emerges.

While researching his second novel, *Union Dues* (1977), which examines how the social and political climate of the United States in the late 1960s affects a West Virginia coal-mining family, Sayles discovered accounts of the Matewan Massacre. The bloody shoot-out pitted striking miners against agents from the Baldwin-Felts Company, men employed by the Stone Mountain Coal Company to guard their mines, evict prolabor mining families, and generally keep workers in line. This event is generally considered to be the beginning of the 1920s coalfield wars in West Virginia. Yet its history is fuzzy. By most accounts, ten people lost their lives in the shoot-out: Matewan's mayor, two miners, and seven Baldwin-Felts agents.

As Sayles points out in *Thinking in Pictures: The Making of the Movie Matewan*, his detailed description about creating an independent film, "The rhetoric of both the company-controlled newspapers of the day and their counterparts on the political left was rich in metaphor but short on eyewitness testimony" (10). What intrigued Sayles were the characters involved: Sid Hatfield, a name synonymous with American violence, the chief of police in Matewan; Cabell Testerman, the mayor of the town; Few Clothes, a giant black miner who joined the strikers; and C.E. Lively, a company spy. Because these historical figures were not well documented, Sayles stayed close to the "verifiable accounts of their actions and shied away from their personal lives" (*Thinking in Pictures* 20). He personalized the story by creating fictional characters to carry the emotional weight of the film.

The history Sayles read recounted the use of imported scab labor, including blacks from Alabama and new European immigrants. Sayles was particularly interested in the pattern of immigration into West Virginia: "In 1920, one-quarter of all coal miners in West Virginia were Black. The mines in Alabama were tapped out, so those men needed the work and were often offered jobs that they had no idea were scab jobs" (Moore 6). The Italians were a different story. They went from steerage to driftmouth, never having worked in a mine. Each group was kept in a separate camp with armed guards between them. Pitting race against race, the company fueled cultural antagonisms to keep the workers divided. "That," Sayles says, "was the company solution to what they saw as the cancer of unionism" (Moore 7).

Moreover, as Jeanne Williams notes, violence was "an inevitable response for the strikers [because of] the mine operators' virtually complete control over their lives and communities" (51). Stone Mountain Coal Company at Matewan, West Virginia, operated on a feudal system, holding miners and their families in near slavery. As described in *Thinking in Pictures*, company-owned coal camps surrounded the town of Matewan. Owners told workers where to live and rented them housing at unreasonably high prices. The company rented workers the tools they needed to do their jobs, such as picks, shovels, and headlamps. The company also sold them clothing and food at inflated prices. Wages were paid in company scrip, not U.S. currency. In addition, children were used to work the mines alongside their fathers. Combined, these unfair measures kept workers in an economic vise, enveloping the entire family and preventing them from escaping the reach of the company. *Matewan* details the miners' rage at the amount of control Stone Mountain Coal had over their lives. The political implications of the story strongly appealed to Sayles.

Furthermore, Sayles recognized a visual component missing from his previous film work — landscape. There is nothing idyllic or pastoral about West Virginia; it is a land of fast-running rivers that have cut steep, rugged hills. The hills are snugly packed, creating what the indigenous people call hollers, natural pockets cut off from neighboring communities. This insulating effect attracted Sayles: "The hills hug around you — stay inside of them for a while and a flat horizon seems cold and unwelcoming" (*Thinking in Pictures* 9). West Virginia has little bottomland to farm, but it does have coal, which must be pulled from the ground. As Sayles remarks, "It's a land that doesn't yield anything easy" (*Thinking in Pictures* 9). There is nothing liberating about this landscape. The topography naturally separated workers, which served the coal companies well.

Welding together coal-company oppression, historic characters, rich story elements, and a strong sense of place, Sayles addressed larger concerns:

> All the elements and principles involved seemed basic to the idea of what America has become and what it should be. Individualism versus collectivism, the personal and political legacy of racism, the immigrant dream and the reality that greeted it, monopoly capitalism at its most extreme versus American populism at its most violent, plus a lawman with two guns strapped on walking to the center of town to face a bunch of armed enforcers — what more could you ask for in a story? [*Thinking in Pictures* 10]

Traditional history does not include stories like that of *Matewan*, as historian Howard Zinn reminds us: "Most histories understate revolt, overemphasize statesmanship, and thus encourage impotency among citizens" (574). Uncovering such history, fictionalizing it for the screen, and seeing the production through is a political act. Yet Sayles avoids the easy cynicism of the 1980s, which, in his words, sees "caring about someone you've never met ... as weakness or treachery" (*Thinking in Pictures* 38). Sayles tells the story of Matewan to resuscitate the idealism that once infused the labor movement in an attempt to make that idealism valid again, a sentiment not popular in the 1980s in the United States, a period in which the once muscular house of labor collapsed. Sayles is also interested in how people deal with new ideas: "A lot of what *Matewan*'s about is that new people were coming in, blacks and immigrants

... and, along with new people, new ideas, and one of the new ideas was forming a union" (Aufderhide *Cineaste* 12).

Matewan is not a historical documentary; it is not, for that matter, historically accurate, as Melvyn Dubofsky, a labor historian, has pointed out:

> One would think that film critics and the highly educated people who have actually viewed *Matewan* ordinarily would prefer a more nuanced, complex, and sophisticated portrait of the past than Sayles presents. Instead his heroes and heroines, as well as their villainous adversaries, are as stereotypically defined as the characters in traditional horse operas or contemporary soap operas. [488]

Criticism like Dubofsky's misses the point Sayles is trying to make with *Matewan*. Kenehan talks about "the union," a generic collective of workers. Sayles is not an advocate for a specific union; rather, he recalls a populist spirit that unions have lost over the past few decades. Moreover, as Jeanne Williams suggests, "Matewan is not so much a film about miners organizing a union as it is about miners being organized into a union" (51). Sayles made his fictional protagonist a former Wobbly to echo the grass-roots, populist ideals embodied by the Industrial Workers of the World (the IWW, its members nicknamed "Wobblies"), which was a home-grown American workers' organization. Sayles wanted to make Kenehan familiar by connecting him to the Wobbly spirit, which, as he notes, "remained alive in fact and fiction, in the Tom Joads and Woody Guthries of the Depression, in the rhetoric of Huey Long and the selling copy of the New Deal" (*Thinking in Pictures* 17). Although the American labor movement has changed since the Matewan strike, "the film's pleas," according to Eric Foner, "for nonviolence, interracial harmony, and economic justice are hardly irrelevant today. It is sobering to reflect that these ideals seem as utopian to contemporary viewers as when they were propounded by the IWW and the United Mine Workers of America nearly a century ago" (Carnes *Past Imperfect* 207).

Insistently, Sayles uses history as a foundation, adding reality to the picture, making his narrative a story about America. Not surprisingly, *Matewan* parallels the genre expectations of the classic American Western: the lone man rides into town, faces down the mob, and delivers justice. Sayles, however, makes the fictional protagonist of the story, union organizer Joe Kenehan (Chris Cooper), a pacifist, inverting tradition to question the use of violence. The Matewan Massacre temporarily put the coal company on the run, but the huge death toll of the coal wars of 1920–21 underlines Kenehan's philosophy, which follows the precepts of Martin Luther King, Jr., who understood economic oppression and the need for nonviolent revolt, not the United Mine Workers of America. Ironically, Kenehan dies because of the violence he worked to prevent.

Labor unions dramatically declined in membership and influence in the

1980s. Many Americans distrusted unions, siding, for example, with President Reagan when he broke the air traffic controllers' strike in 1981 by firing all the workers involved in the job action. Unions, of course, must share in the blame for their poor public perception. As unions matured, the accompanying bureaucratization created a gulf between officials and workers. Corruption and ties with organized crime in some unions have also affected the perception of unions as a whole. Historically, unions were never sacrosanct. According to historian Robert H. Zieger, the labor movement was "feared by the Right as un–American and radical, reviled by the revolutionary Left as reformist and opportunistic" (ix). Indeed, even one of Sayles's characters voices suspicion about joining a political group: "I don't need some hunkie in Pittsburgh to tell me what to do." Still, unions, unlike any other institution in American life, speak for working people as a class. Sayles does not analyze a labor union per se, nor does he examine its leaders. Instead, he concentrates his efforts on the workers themselves, making the film highly personal and open to various interpretations.

In addition, *Matewan* functions as a morality play that focuses on a young miner, Danny Radnor (Will Oldham), struggling to understand a cacophony of voices. The voice-over that frames the film is that of Danny as an old man called Pappy, who retells the story of the Matewan Massacre in his own words, a fact we do not learn until the end of the film. Sayles keeps Pappy's identity secret not for the sake of an O. Henry ending but to show us Danny's transformation from confused adolescent to a dedicated believer in his class, culture, and calling.

When the film opens, the miners, who are Mingo County, West Virginia, natives, strike because the Stone Mountain Coal Company dropped the price for a ton of coal. The film's plot follows the circumstances created by the miners' decision to strike to the final shoot-out, the Matewan Massacre. Joe Kenehan arrives in Matewan preaching the idea of "one big union," which Danny finds appealing. Joe's attempts to unite the fragmented workers both succeed and fail. He must contend with racial antagonisms, a company spy, a plot designed to question his own union loyalty, and the Baldwin-Felts agents, who strong-arm the workers. Sid Hatfield, the town's sheriff, a dark, violent presence, represents frontier justice, the antithesis of Joe's philosophy. Ultimately, a young striker's throat is slit by company men, and violence, the inevitable response for the strikers, breaks loose. In the gun battle, Joe is shot in the head and Danny finally comes to understand the meaning of Joe's nonviolent philosophy: Violence plays into the owners' hands because they have access to greater forms of violence — police, militia, federal troops — and can use them with impunity.

Matewan's plot line should be straightforward — all the events leading up to the gun battle. But Sayles subverts expectations. There is no single hero marching toward an inevitable climax with his antagonists. As John Alexander

Williams explains, "The Gary Cooper character in this upside down *High Noon* is divided at least two ways, between Joe and Sid, with Danny, Few Clothes, and Fausto serving as secondary moral agents at critical junctures in the plot" (349). Sayles structures *Matewan* in four distinct blocks, each detailing a victory or a defeat for Joe, the outsider, in his struggle to unionize the coal miners. His hope for nonviolent solidarity and his integrity can be seen as the moral conscience of the community. The first section examines Joe's attempts to organize the three groups — natives, blacks, and Italians — that make up the fragmented workers' camp. The next section takes up the cycle of revenge, a theme that runs throughout the film, as the strikers attempt to get back at the company, which culminates in an ambush in the woods. Then Sayles moves to C.E. Lively's attempt to discredit Joe with the miners, which is thwarted by Danny's second sermon. Finally, the exhilaration of the strikers' organizing fizzles when Hillard Elkin (Jace Alexander), another young miner, is murdered, and the revenge cycle returns, resulting in the final shoot-out.

If Sayles followed the classical paradigm — conflict, rising action, climax — we would have a generic Western. But the four movements create a sense of reality by depicting life's fits and starts, not sweeping heroic victory. When the tension finally erupts on Matewan's main street, the gun battle is plain and graphic: Confusion reigns, people shoot wildly, and most of the deaths occur at close range. When the shooting stops, it is obvious that neither side has won. Sayles deliberately avoids pat conclusions. *Matewan* has nothing in common with *High Noon* — or with any other Hollywood production that ends with the hero standing as the arbiter of moral order.

Sayles's four-movement structure gives the picture scope, a sense that the action is occurring over a long period of time, and adds psychological realism to the story by balancing life's highs and lows. By downplaying the gun battle, Sayles does not celebrate the myth of the American gunfighter. Instead, he calls into question American reliance on armed struggle to solve problems. Within each cycle, the relationship between Joe Kenehan and Danny deepens as the young miner considers Joe's words and the possibility of a union triumph. On the other hand, as Sayles points out, the "character of violence" also escalates in each section (*Thinking in Pictures* 26). When the gun battle occurs, it countervails our expectations because everyone loses. The shoot-out solves nothing, proving Kenehan's argument against violence. The conflict does not end, and as Danny in the voice of the old man tells us, the miners take the worst of it by losing their jobs, lives, and the chance to form a union, as Joe predicted they would.

Sayles indicates his intentions in the opening exposition, a visual representation of working life underground. Sephus (Ken Jenkins), a strike leader, lights his headlamp and goes to work on a coal face. Blackness dominates the mise-en-scène. We must concentrate on the image to record Sephus's actions.

(Sayles back-lighted Jenkins with a diffuse spotlight, aimed past the actor, which had to be moved in synch with his head to imitate the light from the miner's headlamp.) The shot is tight, confining, tomblike. Sephus works with a pick and a hand drill. The shots are nondramatic, providing documentary coverage of Sephus as he loads black powder into the hole he has cut into the coal face. Sayles wanted his audience to experience antique coal-mining methods and the conditions under which these men worked. Adding emphasis to the scene is the constant dripping of water, Sephus's coughing, and the lamentations of a blues harmonica.

Beginning a film with a sequence of a man working, however, lacks the hook necessary to capture an audience's interest. Sayles intercuts the shots of Sephus with shots of Danny running through the mine as he stops to whisper something to other miners, thereby adding a sense of mystery and urgency to the sequence. As Danny runs from man to man, Sephus plants a fuse in the powder-filled hole. For the sake of expediency, Sayles placed the opening credits over these shots, but the titles are quiet and do not overwhelm the images. Sephus ignites the fuse, runs for cover, and crouches at the base of a pillar with his back to the coal face. Danny trots up and slides down next to him. Both characters are covered with coal soot; only their teeth and eyes stand in sharp contrast to the darkness. Danny says, "They brung it [the tonnage rate] down to ninety cent a ton.... They got them dagoes holdin' fast in Number Three." He then asks the older miner what they are going to do. Sephus spits a stream of tobacco juice into a black puddle of water. Sayles quick-cuts to the sizzling fuse as it disappears inside the coal face. Next we see the title *MATEWAN* on screen. We hear the explosion, and the image vanishes in a flash frame like a well-delivered punchline.

Immediately Sayles establishes the plight of these workers, internal conflict, and the potential for violence with a few deft strokes. By concluding this introductory sequence with an explosion, Sayles prefigures the explosion to come: "When you see the fuse burning down until it finally explodes. That was the image I had of what happened in *Matewan*" (Moore 5). As he did with *Brother from Another Planet*, Sayles establishes the tone for *Matewan* up front. Unlike the upbeat *Brother*, however, *Matewan* is deeply pessimistic. Tight medium shots dominate the opening sequence, denoting closure, confinement, a restriction of choice. Even though this sequence ends with the miners' leaving the driftmouth of the mine as a collective body, demanding union representation, Sayles's visual composition shows the men locked in, fated to continue in their present condition — or worse.

As the men leave the mine, Sayles cuts to a shot of the West Virginia hillside, a natural physical barrier, plunging down toward the men. Moreover, a crane shot Sayles uses (which also illustrates his increased production budget) photographs the miners as they pass between railroad coal cars used by the company, depicting industrial entrapment.

One theme Sayles explores in *Matewan* is invasion, the intrusion of external forces into the West Virginia hills. The crane shot visually illustrates the size and the power of the company. Here the camera movement splits the frame in half. The shot sequence opens with a picture of an inviting, deep blue sky. The camera lingers briefly before descending. As the camera drops, we see a coal tower, the empty coal cars, and finally a medium shot of the men, who are dirty from work but obviously upbeat because of their decision to strike, passing between the cars. The mise-en-scène is unequivocal: These men are trapped. But as the miners squeeze through the tight space created by the coal cars, walking directly toward the camera, they flow to the right and left of the frame. In a single shot, Sayles moves from a closed to an open form, telling us that the story we are about to witness is too large to be limited to a narrow screen. Here Pappy's voice-over begins, describing the rock-ribbed miners and their desire to be treated like human beings.

Symbols of the industrial age — power lines, steam engines, coal towers — dominate Sayles's outdoor shots. The wilderness here is falling to technological power, which, ironically, also makes possible the miners' work. It is a time of change, even for the backwaters of West Virginia. But instead of examining the corruption of an American Eden, Sayles turns his sights on the corruption of the American ideal: Mechanical progress does not dovetail well with human progress. Industrial intrusion symbolizes disdain for the West Virginia hill culture. Every time we hear or see a car, for example, trouble follows, because the car carries representatives of the modern age, who are armed and used to getting what they want through force. Near the end of the film, Sayles shoots from ground level a rushing steam engine carrying the Baldwin-Felts agents, which suggests their relentless power. The train represents the complex, more sophisticated world beyond the holler, a world that is more than willing to exploit workers for profits.

Oscar-winning cinematographer Haskell Wexler photographed *Matewan*. As Sayles noted, "Haskell has loads of experience, including work on period pieces like *Bound for Glory* and *Days of Heaven*, and has a long-standing knowledge of and involvement in the kind of politics *Matewan* is about" (*Thinking in Pictures* 71). Wexler's own words underscore his personal commitment to the project: "My usual salary is four times what I'm making here. But I'm getting four times more in personal enjoyment. You seldom do something with your professional life that has character, dignity, and significance" (McGhee 44). Still, Wexler's task was difficult due to the minuscule budget of *Matewan*.

For the most part, *Matewan*'s mise-en-scène is dark and foreboding. The most dramatic shots occur at night, with a minimal amount of artificial lighting. Sayles and Wexler decided on a "natural look" that would add "weight and tangibility to objects and people," giving the film "psychological realism," the feeling that the image presented is as true to life as possible (*Thinking in*

Pictures 72). The mining sequence that opens the film looks authentic, especially when compared with period mine shots from other films. *The Molly Maguires* (1970), for instance, used stagy, overlit mine interiors, giving this essential setting in the film an artificial look. Of course film speeds and camera technology have advanced since then, but Sayles sought veracity for *Matewan* to enhance the poetry of his story: The dark interiors are essential to his story.

Still, 70 percent of *Matewan* was shot outdoors, much of that at night. As is the case with the coal mine interior shots, some supplemental light had to be used to reveal the characters' faces but without sacrificing the psychological realism Sayles and Wexler felt the film demanded. For instance, the light and dark tones created by both natural shadows and below-frame lighting of C.E. Lively's (Bob Gunton) face serve to remind us of his Janus nature. Half of his face is often lost in the shadows of an interior or exterior shot, giving the audience a subtle portrait of his duplicity.

Sayles and Wexler worked well together. The fireside scene between Few Clothes and Kenehan illustrates this fusion of writing and photography, the poetic nature of the psychological realism Sayles and Wexler sought. The strikers send Few Clothes to kill Joe, because Joe is suspected of being a company spy. He finds Joe alone by a fire at the strikers' camp. Few Clothes, carrying an old pistol, sits facing the fire in profile; Joe, looking into the fire, faces the camera. We are allowed to witness Joe's reaction to Few Clothes's nervousness. Few Clothes, who is distracted, unsure about carrying out his mission, stares into the fire. It is absolutely necessary for the audience to see the facial reactions of both characters, yet this is virtually impossible to accomplish under normal lighting conditions. Artificial lighting from below or off to the sides of the frame would rob the scene of its authenticity. Morris Flam, the gaffer, "rigged up a firelight unit that threw flamelike illumination on the actor's faces from below the frame line, giving Haskell enough exposure to keep them in focus and read their expressions" (*Thinking in Pictures* 78).

The flickering firelight adds a shifting effect to each character's face, highlighting the dramatic flux that propels the scene. Joe's face remains open, lacking tension, composed. Few Clothes, on the other hand, is tense, the weight of his thoughts hanging on every breath. Every time Joe speaks to Few Clothes, he seems to startle the large miner out of deep thought. Joe asks about the gun Few Clothes carries, "You ever use one of those?" Although Joe does not know Few Clothes's true purpose, his question rings with meaning. Clenching his jaw as if challenged, Few Clothes answers, "Yeah. Tenth Cavalry, in Cuba, back in ninety-eight." The men are separated by the fire, each occupying one side of the frame, indicating that they are at odds, even if one of them is unaware of that fact. Sayles's dialogue also speaks to separation: Joe is a pacifist; Few Clothes knows and understands violence.

This gulf between the violent man and the peaceful man is further accented by Sayles and Wexler. Few Clothes tries to work up hatred for Joe, asking him if he is a "Red." Wexler photographs Few Clothes in even less light, the shadows on his bulky face making him look ominous. Joe answers that he is, indeed, a "Red," which, in the age of the Palmer raids, makes him anti–American. Few Clothes asks Joe why he is not armed. Joe, whose face is bright, illuminated by the campfire flame, suggesting he has nothing to hide, says, "We carry little round bombs. Don't you read the papers?" Joe smiles. Few Clothes laughs, but his contradictory emotions return quickly to his face. Because Joe is shot in revealing light, Wexler's shots lean in his favor, which is justifiable because Joe is a committed man.

But these small exchanges have not completely convinced Few Clothes that Joe is innocent of the charges leveled against him. Joe seems, because of his pacifism, to be a walking contradiction. Sayles saves Joe's dramatic explanation of his moral philosophy for this point in the film. He tells Few Clothes about his time spent in Leavenworth prison as a conscientious objector to World War I. Joe is shot in tight close-up. Shadows from the flickering fire add to the seriousness of his beliefs. With compassion he tells Few Clothes about the federal abuse inflicted on a group of Mennonites, who also chose conscientious objector status. *Matewan* addresses the abuse of power and the limits of freedom; this soliloquy examines these themes in microcosm, with Wexler's photography adding visual metaphoric energy to the scene. The Mennonites stood up for their beliefs in the face of impossible odds. Joe's passionate admiration of their civil disobedience and steadfast conviction is obvious. Few Clothes, recognizing Joe's honesty, is nonplussed; he wants to serve the strikers, but he knows killing Joe is wrong.

Sayles and Wexler also juxtapose language and visual imagery to underline the pull violence has on the American imagination in an inventive scene involving Danny and Hillard. The boys are on their way to the coal yard to steal some coal for the strikers' camp. As they near the top of the coal hill, they turn to look at the river valley as the sun sets. Wexler's camera records the panoramic beauty of the autumn hills. Stretched out on a grassy slope, the boys take in the bucolic scene and talk. They could be Tom Sawyer and Huck Finn planning an adventure. Sayles, however, is no romantic, and the idyllic image is counterpoised by the boys' conversation.

Danny points and says, "See there, right there by the railroad trestle? 'At's where Cap Hatfield an' his boy Joe Glenn kilt three men. Boy weren't but thirteen." Danny's historic account changes the way we see the hollow. The boys see the bloody history of the landscape, not its natural beauty. Their dialogue indicates that they know the type of gun the father and son used to kill three men. Danny asks, "Think it hurts much, a bullet?" Hillard responds, "Beats dyin' in a damn coal mine." Violence is accepted, early death almost a certainty. Danny wonders how a boy of 13 could kill, but he also understands that violence is intricately linked to the West Virginia landscape.

"Cinematography," writes Sayles, "is a good model for the entire process of making a movie" (*Thinking in Pictures* 71). Balancing the technical elements — focal length, f-stop, depth-of-field, focus, movement — with the artistic elements — light and shadow, contrast, color, diffusion — makes the job of a photographer difficult. Not only do Sayles and Wexler share political values, championing progressive causes, but they share aesthetic, artistic sensibilities. James Monaco sums up a Wexler film well: It "has some guts to it, and a cinematic precision which heightens his basically naturalistic style" (119). Wexler is both a documentarist and a cinematographer, straddling the worlds of nonfiction and art, a reporter and a designer. Sayles too brings guts to his work, along with a craftsman's precision, and a desire to tell real stories. Stylistically, Wexler and Sayles communicate in an unadorned language, and both are driven by the need to tell the stories of common people. In *Matewan*, Sayles and Wexler bring their shared concerns to the screen with strength and compassion. Sayles gives Wexler credit for taking the "story off the page" and putting it "back into pictures" that are "appropriately beautiful, never gratuitously drawing you away from the story with their look" (*Thinking in Pictures* 80). Wexler, however, is quick to point out that working with Sayles is demanding. "This movie is thoroughly his picture," says Wexler. "I'm thoroughly his servant. I'm not called on for creative input; he has it so completely in mind" (McGhee 46). Sayles keeps a tight rein on his story, his technique, and his vision.

Selecting actors illustrates Sayles's total involvement in the creation of his pictures. He especially likes unknown actors, usually stage trained, people with talent but not recognition, or people who have never acted before. Indeed, the actors in *Matewan* look and sound as if they belong to the West Virginia hills. Sayles feels that an audience will forgive both artistic and technical errors in a production if "there are strong, believable characters to get involved with, and this means getting the right people in front of the camera" (*Thinking in Pictures* 45). For example, when casting the role of Joe Kenehan, Sayles had definite physical and personal traits in mind:

> We were after someone in his late twenties or early thirties, someone who seemed very American in a Midwestern, Henry Fonda–Gary Cooper kind of way, somebody who could be smart and down to earth at the same time, someone the audience and the characters would take seriously but who has some sense of humor. [*Thinking in Pictures* 47–48]

At best, a difficult task. But Sayles seeks the sort of people audiences identify with, not stars, who can change the impact of a film with their mere presence. All the actors in *Matewan* are first rate. They fill the skin of Sayles's creation.

Once again, Barbara Shapiro handled the casting for Sayles and his production team. They concentrated on the search for Joe, Elma, Danny, and

Few Clothes. Chris Cooper was cast as Joe Kenehan early on because of the naturalism he brought to his casting performance, reading the lines as if they were his, not merely typewriting on a page: Joe's voice became Chris Cooper's voice. Mary McDonnell (a relatively unknown stage actress at the time) secured the part of Elma because of her talent, experience, and the ability, Sayles notes, to "convey Elma's hard past and knowledge of a hard future without 'playing' it" (*Thinking in Pictures* 50). Shapiro discovered Will Oldham through the Actor's Theater of Louisville, which proved to be a lucky break for Sayles. "Writing a large, difficult part for anyone under twenty," says Sayles, "is a self-destructive act and I consider myself lucky to have escaped so successfully this time around" (*Thinking in Pictures* 50).

For Few Clothes, "the John Henry of the coal fields" (*Thinking in Pictures* 51), Sayles needed somebody with a physical presence and the fortitude to keep his head high in the racial climate of the rural South in 1920. Although James Earl Jones was considered for the part, Sayles's dealings with actors and their agents told him that the veteran actor was too expensive. Eventually, however, Sayles sent Jones a script with a preamble full of warnings about *Matewan*'s budget and his own brand of filmmaking. Jones returned a simple "yes" (*Thinking in Pictures* 51). In the end, casting *Matewan* was full of gambles, luck, and gut-level decisions.

The acting in the film works. As Kenehan, Cooper has to deliver the two most political and powerful speeches in the film. His rationale for non-violent action must be believable because it is incongruous with labor history. During the 1980s, many top-grossing films dealt with military subjects, a manifestation of Reaganism, increased military spending, and violence. Joe Kenehan countervails the Hollywood trend of hero worship. Joe is the mysterious stranger, a guy, according to Sayles, "trying to preach turning the other cheek in the land of an eye for an eye" (*Thinking in Pictures* 16). Cooper makes Kenehan's intellectual and emotional choices believable.

At the first meeting of the West Virginia strikers, Joe listens as C.E. Lively exhorts the men to violence against the coal company scabs; it is not difficult to sway the miners. In order to make Kenehan a believable character, Cooper must accomplish two things: He must convince his audience that he has the strength of conviction to lead a union strike, and he must counterpoise Lively's knee-jerk endorsement of violence. He begins by telling the men that they are nothing more than equipment to a coal company that does not care whether they are white or black or immigrants as long as they can dig coal, because if they cannot dig, there is always a replacement nearby. Cooper animates Kenehan's indictment of the strikers by casting unblinking looks at the group, taking full control of the room by elevating his voice, which is spiked with anger and understanding. He then points to Few Clothes (who has sought out the strikers), to illustrate the results of both racial hatred and coal-company ruthlessness. Joe says:

Matewan *(1987): James Earl Jones remains the most well-known actor to work for John Sayles. Sayles found him to be one of the best all-around actors he has ever worked with. Jones fills Few Clothes with energy, intelligence, and integrity. Photo courtesy of the Museum of Modern Art Film Stills Archive.*

You think this man is your enemy? Huh? This is a *worker!* Any union keeps this man out ain't a union, it's a goddamn *club!* They got you fightin' white against colored, native against foreign, hollow against hollow, when you *know* that there ain't but two sides in this world — them that *work* and them that *don't.* You work, *they* don't. That's all you get to know about the enemy.

Sayles's language describes the idea of unionism — to have a union, sacrifices must be made for something larger than individual well-being — and Cooper's acting gives the words backbone.

In order to drive home the problems with violence, Joe points out the fact that any armed resistance is bound to fail because not only does the coal company not want the union, neither does the state or the federal government. The use of violence will only give the opposition, which is larger and more powerful than a small band of West Virginia miners, the excuse they need to crush the strike and set an example across the country. Making his idea perfectly clear to these miners, Joe says, "You don't go shooting the solid if you can undermine the face, do you?" The mining analogy, which means that trying to dynamite the strongest part of a coal vein is a foolish waste of time, makes the strikers think. Cooper's delivery and Sayles's dialogue make Joe Kenehan real. This is not a high-toned, ideological stump speech; this is plain language, charged with common sense.

James Earl Jones carries the power of physical presence and vocal authority. Sayles notes that as an actor Jones understood the strength and intelligence Few Clothes, to whom Louis Untermyer dedicated his poem "Black Caliban of the Coal Miners," needed in order to keep his men alive so far from Alabama. When Turley, the company man, recites the cost of housing, equipment, and food to the new black miners, Few Clothes asks, "What's keeping y'all from jackin' up them prices in your store?" Few Clothes also convinces the scab miners to join the strikers during the night scene at the driftmouth. Jones, however, did not "want his character to be a revisionist black man. 'This is 1920 and he's a black man from Alabama behind enemy lines. If he talks back, he knows that the next thing to happen may be a noose around his neck'" (Carnes *Past Imperfect* 26). Still, Jones's weight and baritone voice make his scenes resonate. In addition, he brought recognizable star power to a Sayles production for the first time in Sayles's filmmaking career.

Will Oldham's Danny Radnor is a pastiche of youth and wisdom, and is still a boy yet committed to his community and its existence. As written, the character requires a versatile actor who is young, bright, articulate, able to work with adults, and, ideally, from the South. "Danny had to still be boy enough to make his preaching and organizing seem precious, had to be down to earth enough to make him believable as a coal miner," notes Sayles, "country enough to place him in West Virginia in the twenties and a good enough actor to pull off long sermons, speeches and emotional scenes" (*Thinking in Pictures* 50). Until Will Oldham auditioned, Sayles considered cutting the part back to fit the talents of the actors he had auditioned.

Thematically, *Matewan* turns on the question of violence. Because Danny is not as reactionary as Hillard, a fact that Sayles presents in the beginning of the film when the West Virginia strikers confront the black scabs, the possibility exists that he might listen to the message Kenehan tries to sell the strikers. Joe struggles to change Danny's point of view to his own; he wants Danny, in Sayles's words, to "see beyond the cycle of blood feuds and meaningless revenge the company fosters among the miners" (*Thinking in Pictures* 19). Indeed, when Danny picks up a gun at the end of the film to avenge the death of Hillard, a death so horrible that retribution seems the only course, we have to believe that the kid with the gun is the same kid we saw earlier playing catch, talking about his favorite major leaguers.

Oldham looks right, sounds right, and he can act. For example, he must show us that he can swing between the value systems of the local missionaries, the hardshell Baptists and the softshell Baptists. Essentially the groups represent Old Testament and New Testament teachings; that is, the hardshells value righteousness and retribution, the softshells value peace and justice. Two of Oldham's major scenes revolve around the Church. In one, Danny contradicts an evangelical hardshell (Sayles, himself), who equates the union movement with "Beelzebub," Satan. Danny, who is waiting his turn to preach, looks upon the hardshell with disbelief and disgust. He believes that people's earthly task is to help one another. Preaching to the congregation, Danny tells a story of unfair wages for unequal work in a biblical vineyard. Clearly, Danny is a natural born storyteller who subscribes to a moral, just society. The hardshell chases him from the pulpit.

Moral storytelling, the desire to improve life, not debase it, drives Danny's character. In the central scene of *Matewan*'s third section, Danny preaches to his congregation to save Joe's life. Oldham delivers this secular gospel with conviction, fear, and courage. He makes us believe he is facing death, contradicting a striker's order to kill Kenehan in front of two drunken Baldwin-Felts thugs. Oldham delivers Sayles's speech with intensity, his voice cracking slightly when his emotions threaten his composure.

However, Danny's most important speech and Oldham's most important acting turn comes in a confrontation with Joe. Here he boldly states the economic and political machinations at work in Matewan:

> First people come in here to help us with some money, and next we know we got no land. Then they say they gonna help us with a job and a place to live. So they put us in some damn coal camp and let us dig out their mines. Now you come in and want to help us bring in the new day. But Hillard ain't gonna see no new day. We had about as much help as we can stand. We got to take care of ourselves.

The pain in Oldham's speech stings. The Old Testament wins out. Revenge alone will relieve the pain of history Danny knows too well. Joe Kenehan, the idealist, has lost. But Danny's change from moral storyteller to destroyer is not melodramatic; Sayles and Oldham record his ambivalence vividly. Even Joe understands that he is unable to stop Danny's desire for revenge.

Danny's mother, Elma Radnor, is also pushed into violent action. Mary McDonnell conveys Elma's movement from exhaustion to retribution well. In every scene in which she appears, Elma is working — cleaning, bandaging, feeding. Wexler's photography and Nora Chavooshian's set design accent Elma's condition. Her home, a Stone Mountain Coal Company boarding-house, is visually oppressive; the expository shots of its exterior are all low-angle shots, giving the building a look of dominance, not unlike the coal tower. Indeed, Elma is surrounded by the building as the miners are by the coal mine, yet until she confides in Joe that she is exhausted, we take her work for granted. With skill, Sayles presents the condition of women in the coal camps though Elma. "I been workin'," she says. "The day they buried my husband I started and I been workin' — it don't never stop and I'm so tired sometimes and there ain't nobody." But there is no collective organizing to help Elma, or women like her. During the final shoot-out Elma kills a Baldwin-Felts agent with a shotgun blast at close range. The years of work and anger reach a violent catharsis, which denotes a complete turnaround for a woman striving to keep life under control to protect her son.

David Strathairn brings a powerful sense of menace to Sid Hatfield, who represents the film's sense of brooding violence. In the beginning of the film he looms over the other characters like a malevolent guardian angel. For example, on the first night of the strike, he is photographed in a low-angle shot on the wooden walkway of Main Street, hovering over Few Clothes, who is walking along the dirt road looking for C.E. Lively's restaurant, where the miners are meeting. Here, Hatfield dominates the mise-en-scène. Later that night, Sid greets Joe as the organizer returns to Elma's after the union meeting ends. In a reprise of the earlier shot, Sid dominates the upper half of the frame, hanging over Joe, full of vengeance. The lawman tells Kenehan, "I take care of my people. You bring 'em trouble and you're a dead man." Sid carries a sense of deep connection with the West Virginia miners, his people, whom he has sworn to protect.

Through Sayles's mise-en-scène we see Sid's distrust of any and all outsiders. He detests the Baldwin-Felts agents because of who they are and because of what they are, desperate, power-hungry men from cities and farms who would take any job for money, including killing striking miners. At a company eviction he single-handedly faces off with Hickey (Kevin Tighe) and Griggs (Gordon Clapp), two Baldwin-Felts thugs, and their helpers. After telling Hickey that he knows his boss, Mr. Thomas Felts, Sid stares the agent dead in the eye and delivers the film's only funny line: "I wouldn't pee on him if his heart was on fire." His boldness shocks Joe, who says he never saw a lawman stand up to a company gun. Sid does not even acknowledge Joe's presence. Sid Hatfield lives by his own code of honor, the knight-errant of the West Virginia coalfields.

Hickey and Griggs seem too vile to be true. History, however, validates Sayles's characterization. Baldwin-Felts agents relied on an image of invincibility to intimidate miners into submission. Coalfield violence is not uncommon in American history; it is just not recognized as essential to American classrooms. From Ludlow, Colorado, to Lattimer, Pennsylvania, to Matewan, West Virginia, American history is rife with stories of coal company terrorism. Pennsylvania's Molly Maguires were formed to combat the police who were controlled by mine owners. "There were," according to Sayles, "things that the Baldwin-Felts agents had done, things so Simon Legreeish that if I had put them into the screenplay for *Matewan* no one would have believed it" (Hodel 4). The examples Sayles cites include the lacing with kerosene of a Red Cross shipment of milk for the striking miners' children, and random shooting through coal camps to remind the workers who was boss.

Still, Hickey and Griggs represent something more than crude stereotypes. From a class perspective, they are no different from the people they have been hired to terrorize. They are working-class men who have taken on the air of urbanites. All the Baldwin-Felts agents wear suits, a mode of dress that seems incongruous in rugged West Virginia, but which definitely sets them apart from the miners, who wear the clothes of laborers. Hickey confirms his social position in a speech to Danny. After catching the boy in his room, where Danny heard about the plan to kill Kenehan, Hickey tells Danny about his experience in World War I. He recalls how he single-handedly killed a large number of German soldiers. As Tighe plays the scene, we see that Hickey enjoyed the killing and that he would kill again. Hickey understands the bloody irony in being honored by his country for killing people. For each role he created for *Matewan*, Sayles wrote up a character sheet, a Stanislavsky-inspired rumination on a character's life experience. As for Hickey, Sayles described him as Joe's foil: "In a way he has as much political analysis as Joe, it's just that he has taken the cynical rather than idealistic path and has sided with who he thinks the winners will be" (*Thinking in Pictures* 94). Hickey also stands in contrast to Griggs, who is violent to the core, a one-dimensional, dim-witted killer.

Sayles tries to work against stereotypes in all his writing, both fiction and film. In *Matewan*, with the exception of Griggs, he tried to give even the negative characters something else to play besides pure evil. For example, C.E. Lively, though a spy for the company, earns some respect for his cold intelligence. Likewise, Bass, James, and Doolin, three Baldwin agents recruited through a newspaper ad for the confrontation, are introduced as a trio of working stiffs rather than, as Sayles says, as "poker-faced grim reapers bent on murder" (*Thinking in Pictures* 22). Indeed, Doolin is a feckless innocent who has no idea what he is about to face, being just cannon fodder for the agency. The information Sayles provides about Hickey is not an "excuse or a Freudian explanation for his actions," but it is meant to give the character "room to breathe, to remind us that the man's life is not contained by this one incident in it, as well as to establish him as a guy familiar with killing" (*Thinking in Pictures* 22). However, it is necessary to Sayles's narrative to make Griggs a sociopath, so that we believe he would slit Hillard's throat without remorse or thought. Even Hickey is surprised by his partner's ruthlessness, turning away, saying "Jesus, Griggs," as Hillard jerks spasmodically while his life leaks away. Although it may be difficult for a sophisticated audience to accept absolute malevolence on the part of the Baldwin-Felt agents, it is necessary to keep in mind that the roots of coalfield oppression were political and economic. *Matewan* shows us, as Denise Giardina points out, that the "methods of economic oppression used by the exploiters of foreign, supposedly less fortunate, regions have also been common" in America (445). People like Hickey and Griggs are required to carry out the ground-level portion of such oppression.

Believability is essential to the illusion of a period piece. Without precise set design, a serious drama can become an unintended comedy. *Matewan*'s production design is impeccable, a remarkable achievement considering the $90,000 art department budget. Nora Chavooshian, who worked on *Baby,*

It's You and *Brother from Another Planet* (her first film as full production designer), made *Matewan* look real. Like most Sayles personnel, she is efficient, creative, and quick. *Matewan* was a major undertaking, and Chavooshian's work exceeded its demands.

Obviously, how a historical period is presented on film influences the story being told. Hollywood costume dramas, for example, often used the past for its value as spectacle. Or, as Sayles wryly points out, the past has been used to recall a simpler, more moral time period, which probably never existed except in private mythology. For Sayles, design is necessary for "what it evokes subjectively in the audience" (*Thinking in Pictures* 54). The images in *Matewan* show "the muscle and effort it took to build anything up in the wilderness of those hills, to feel like even the newest things were used and worn" (*Thinking in Pictures* 54). Elma's home, for instance, underscores these values.

The company's overarching presence dominates Elma, yet she displays intelligence and understanding, and she is part of the mining community. Elma contrasts with Bridey Mae (Nancy Mette), whose lonely cabin sits outside of Matewan, suggesting her desperate desire to share her life with someone as well as her dislocation from the community. Like Bridey, we are made aware of Elma's psychological makeup by the exterior and interior of her home, particularly her dining room. The outside of her home is painted in worn white and green, a color scheme used by Chavooshian to indicate the company's ownership and to suggest how the miners and their families are institutionally walled in. Elma's dining room, on the other hand, is warm and civilized, and stands in stark contrast to other interiors in the film, indicating that Elma wants to have a life beyond the coalfield, beyond the holler. Hers is not an overtly elegant eating room, but it has patterned wallpaper, tablecloths, and soft light.

Chavooshian's set design shapes the mood of *Matewan*. "The life these people led was incredibly hard," she remarks, "so the look we were going for was extremely gritty" (Seidenberg 46). Accuracy counted. Chavooshian sought dilapidated structures, trying to avoid the mistake of so many period productions, which is to use buildings that have a newer look. Nothing in *Matewan* looks new. Also important was creating the inescapable domination of the company, a necessary part of Sayles's concept of psychological realism. Sayles deliberately divorced the company owners from the film, suggesting that they would not soil themselves among the rabble, the dirty work. However, their heavy presence needed to be demonstrated. Chavooshian used color to indicate the demarcation between the Matewan power brokers and the coal miners. She used large signs that read PROPERTY OF STONE MOUNTAIN COAL COMPANY or OWNED BY STONE MOUNTAIN COAL COMPANY to dominate Main Street. All the company property is marked with the simple white and park-bench green, indicating Stone Mountain's omnipresence.

Chavooshian and her production team laid down a quarter mile of dirt with a heavy clay content to make Matewan's Main Street authentic. However, the original town of Matewan, West Virginia, proved to be too modern-looking, so Thurmond, West Virginia, was selected and redesigned to resemble Matewan. Thurmond, which sits on the floodplain of the New River and is enveloped by steep hills, retained its pre–World War I brick buildings, its water tanks, its railroad yard, and its coal-dock tower. According to Sayles, it had the "blend of natural beauty and industrial function" the production team was looking for (*Thinking in Pictures* 57). Chavooshian agreed: "This town just looked so unusual. And even though there were additions and things we had to remove, the buildings are from the mid to late 1800s; they're period-correct" (Seidenberg 45). Sayles was not interested in nostalgia, and Chavooshian delivered. Their Matewan does not ask the viewer to step into a soft, sepia-tinged photo; this town has witnessed hard times.

Cynthia Flynt's costumes, like the set design, accent the mood of the film, the characters' psychology, and they help Sayles to tell his story. Period films like *McCabe and Mrs. Miller* and *The Godfather Part II* used diffusion and film-fogging techniques to create an image that looked old to mute natural color. *Matewan* does not use these techniques. Texture, color, and design establish its period look. The costumes in the film are part of this scheme; they are old, worn, and utilitarian. Only the Baldwins and Sid wear clothes not meant for rugged work. The palette for the costumes was limited — blacks, grays, browns, rugged blues, and deep greens, which complement the environment. In addition, a fine mist of black paint was sprayed on the costumes, and everything else, to remind us that these are working people.

The mood of the set design helped the actors realize their roles. Sayles writes, "Time and again an actor would walk onto one of Nora's sets and say, 'Okay, *now* I get it'" (*Thinking in Pictures* 60). Of course the natural setting also added to the realism of *Matewan*— the montage of the tent camp, the baseball game, the ambush in the woods, the interiors of the mine.

Community, a fundamental theme of the film, is established first by sound and then by image. Each mining camp — those of West Virginian strikers, Alabama blacks, and Italian immigrants — is compartmentalized when the film begins, separated by race, culture, and armed guards. But Mason Daring's musical score recognizes no barriers: mountain fiddle and dobro mix with a blues harmonica; in turn, they mix with a mandolin. As Sayles explains, "This nonverbal musical fusion is the first step in forming a union out of people initially suspicious of each other" (*Thinking in Pictures* 109). At the outset, these few instruments, limited like the film's color scheme, seek each other out and begin to mesh. Finally, all three players come together in a single scene, playing with the intuitive understanding and awareness of musicians. This integration shot shows how music crosses racial and cultural barriers, initiating the blending of these diverse people, indicating the nascent union. In the manner of John Ford, Sayles and Daring use music to celebrate community.

Sayles uses music to boost some scenes, notably those of the men walking out of the mine, the construction of the tent camp, and the baseball and organizing montages. Each sequence is upbeat and positive, and each has a voice-over narration from Pappy Dan. They all involve group activities that lead to understanding, not division. His musical choices — a union marching song, a down-home instrumental of "Avanti Populo," an old Italian workers' song — have, in his words, "a feeling of communal energy and high spirits" (*Thinking in Pictures* 111).

Because Sayles is dealing with racial and cultural issues in *Matewan*, some established music was necessary. For example, when the scab miners turn their backs on the company and join the union during the driftmouth night sequence, Sayles and Daring wanted two versions of "Avanti Populo" to comment on each sequence and act as a transitional device. After Few Clothes and Fausto (Joe Grifasi) throw down their company shovels, Fausto whistles and then begins to sing "Avanti Populo." Joining in, the strikers sound tired and worn. The song relaxes the tension created by the possibility of violence — these are tired people. Yet, because the song is not a rousing, foot-stomping version, there is also some apprehension in the voices of the miners.

The strikers' camp, however, announces the "new day" that Joe Kenehan cleaves to so desperately. A country fiddle picks up the melody of "Avanti Populo," bringing strength and hope to Sayles's images. Clearly, the miners' prospects have changed. By using a country fiddle to play the traditional Italian tune, Sayles marks the complete integration of the ethnic groups. Visually we see the three disparate groups coalesce into a single unit. The fiddle reminds us that music was the first step in this necessary fusion.

More subtle musical comments are also heard throughout *Matewan*. For the most part, a harmonica and a dobro set the mood or announce a transition from one scene to another. Daring played the dobro. Sayles employed John Hammond, a noted Delta blues musician, to record the harmonica tracks. "Working with John," Sayles writes, "was similar to working with an actor — our discussions were about feelings and colors of emotion rather than musical technicalities, and his playing 'breathed' with the movie rather than forcing itself upon it" (*Thinking in Pictures* 111).

Music bolsters *Matewan*. Sayles recounts that during the worst days of the drawn-out fund raising, he and his production team would listen to Hazel Dickens's recording of "Beautiful Hills of Galilee," a traditional ballad heard over the final credits. Sayles also had actors listen to the ballad before they began character discussions (*Thinking in Pictures* 113).

At Hillard's funeral, the climactic emotional turning point in the film, Dickens sings Daring's "The Gathering Storm," a ballad of Old Testament retribution. Her a cappella performance is more than just background music.

Joe Kenehan listens as Danny delivers a rambling farewell to his friend, not the focused words of the backwoods preacher heard previously. Sephus tells Joe that his idea of "one big union" no longer applies to people "who can't see beyond this holler." Sephus then walks toward Sid Hatfield, who is surrounded by the other miners. Clearly, Joe has lost. Dickens's dirge becomes a lament for both Hillard and Joe. "There is a sense of tragic destiny in many hill ballads," writes Sayles, "and the expression of that resignation to doom is as palpable an antagonist to Joe as the Baldwin-Felts agents are" (*Thinking in Pictures* 113). The funeral prefigures the violence to come. When the gun battle occurs, Dickens's voice, which carries, as Sayles says, "all the mournfulness and strength of the hill tradition" (*Thinking in Pictures* 113), has prepared us for this last desperate act. With Joe Kenehan goes idealism, the possibility of human understanding, and there will be no escape from the gathering storm.

The gun battle, however, points up Sayles's development as an editor. On *Matewan* he worked with Sonya Polonsky, who also cut *Baby, It's You*. With each new film, Sayles expands his editing techniques, which is, of course, a fundamental aspect of the cinematic narrative. For example, the opening sequence of the film is cut well; it communicates the isolation of the miners and their defiance. Leaving the mine, the strikers, who are obviously happy and united, pass by reminders of the company's power — they are bookended by the coal cars, the store closes, armed guards take to the streets. While the strike represents a positive gesture on the part of the miners, the system of oppression still surrounds them. Sayles lets this sequence unfold at a controlled pace, creating a realistic sense of camaraderie sobered by the presence of the company. His editing creates the sense of real time without taking up too much film time.

In editing the night sequence before the gun battle, Sayles leaves the shots long, with few cuts, underlining the feeling of impending violence, which the film has approached numerous times but never completely realized. Now, however, full-scale violence is inescapable. We see Elma walk into her dining room holding a lamp. Sleeping company men are piled all over the room, her place of civility now overrun by thugs. The lamp comes to rest on Doolin, who stares at the camera, frozen with fear, still not sure what he is doing to earn a few dollars. The scene is slow, drawn out. Cutting away to Sid Hatfield, we see him cleaning his weapon with emotionless professionalism; this man knows he may die in the morning, but he goes about his task with precision and stoic determination.

Sayles used a similar editing technique in the driftmouth night sequence. The time between cuts is reduced, making the tension more immediate. The shots are from a hand-held camera, giving the sequence a documentary look. The camera captures the antagonism between the scabs and the strikers by cutting between close-ups of rocks and bludgeons held by burley, faceless men, to close-ups of the black and Italian scabs, who are sweating and scared. The blacks and Italians are in the same situation they have been in since the film began, caught between armed guards and strikers, waiting to be shot by either side. Something has to break. Sayles cuts to a shot of Few Clothes, a shovel in his hand, moving toward Turley and the guards. This long take changes the rhythm of the sequence and releases the tension.

Story is often enhanced by editing. Danny's sermons, for example, were made stronger by cutting back to him from a different angle. This technique strengthens these scenes, making Danny's words resonate with more power than if Sayles used a master shot. "For *Matewan*," he says, "we wanted the movie to reflect the pace of the time and the people" (*Thinking in Pictures* 117). Mining in 1920 was long, hard, slow work, punctuated only by an accident or worker unrest. By cleaving to this scheme and the natural cycle of day and night, Sayles achieved the "pace of a long, sad mountain ballad, a song of fate, revenge, and transcendence" (*Thinking in Pictures* 117).

Matewan is, in the end, a story of profound loss. After the shoot-out is over, we see a close-up of Danny's face as the camera slowly zooms in on him. Now, seeing Joe dead, he understands the organizer's ideals. Here we see the legacy of Joe's values passed on to a new generation. But, Sayles reminds us, the struggle is endless and seldom positive. Pappy's voice-over tells us about Sid's short-lived triumph. The Baldwins took their revenge by shooting him 15 times as he walked unarmed into the county courthouse: "Then C.E. Lively stepped in and put one right through his skull." The courts, Pappy tells us, ignored the murder. The Matewan Massacre and Sid's death erupted into the Great Coalfield War, which the miners lost after President Warren G. Harding brought in federal troops to break the strike. Pappy acknowledges that Joe was right: All workers can do is organize, because alone they do not stand a chance. Pappy tells us that he preached Joe's philosophy after the Matewan Massacre: "That was my religion." We see the miner's face — it is Danny. Now we understand that we have just witnessed his story.

Sayles's film poses hard questions about survival and fairness. *Matewan* is unabashedly on the side of the workers, focusing in on the moral ambiguity inherent in labor-owner conflicts. Even though the film can be criticized for small historical inaccuracies, stereotypes, and a slow pace, *Matewan* draws us into emotional lives we would not otherwise know. We experience the fear, powerlessness, and loss of the workers, who in their isolation are vulnerable to the cruelest exploitation. *Matewan* offers no easy answers. Pappy's voice-over tells us that Danny's struggle never ceased. *Matewan* deals with issues and people seldom seen on American screens. Only an independent filmmaker like Sayles would dare present such noncommercial property. As Sayles says, *Matewan* has little to make it appealing: "The story [is] political, the hero an early socialist, the ending not upbeat and there is no room for a rock soundtrack" (*Thinking in Pictures* 41). In other words, it is a John Sayles film.

9

Eight Men Out

It was really the kickoff of the Roaring Twenties. A lot of cynicism that followed was certainly helped along by the idea that even
America's game, which was supposed to be pure and good — white
ballplayers, green grass, and blue skies — could be corrupted.
                                            — John Sayles (*Premiere*)

Like *Matewan*, *Eight Men Out* (1988), John Sayles's sixth feature film,
is a period piece, which details the 1919 World Series sellout by a group of
Chicago White Sox ballplayers, who would become known as the Black Sox.
The "Black Sox Scandal," an inescapable part of American history, revolves
around traditional American pastimes: baseball and corruption. But as Louis
Giannetti and Scott Eyman point out, Sayles recalls a time when "Americans
were genuinely shocked by corruption rather than subliminally expecting it,
excusing it, and, by so doing, participating in it" (491–92). *Eight Men Out*
tells an American story of greed and loss without cynical acceptance, the chic
shoulder-shrugging common to many Hollywood productions.

Sayles explores the dynamics of the historical event with a contemporary
eye adjusted to how an abuse of power filters down from the top. "The thing
I like about [*Eight Men Out*] is that it attacks the sacred cows: the owners,"
says Studs Terkel, the journalist and author who plays Hugh Fullerton in the
film. He continues: "We think of crooked players, but not of the role of the
owners: double-crossing the players, paying them nothing.... Today we read
of players making tremendous dough. But their careers are limited. And what
about Sylvester Stallone, who hasn't a finger of talent, making $12 million [for
one film]? Or Joan Collins? We never question that" (Linfield 48). Sayles,
however, does not draw such clear lines. In fact, he does not assign guilt to
either the players or the owners; rather, Sayles, as always, allows his audience
to decide for themselves. Terkel is not so sanguine: "We're a society today
that depends upon dough. I think that the players can be bought, here and
there, today. But today a lot of fans are on the side of the owners. So this film
comes out at exactly the right time" (Linfield 48). Indeed, the story of baseball's best-known fix still resonates, for economic exploitation and corruption

are still part of the American story. Stephen Jay Gould, noted paleontologist and baseball fan, suggests that the Black Sox scandal has a continuing hold "upon the hearts and minds of baseball fans and, more widely, upon anyone fascinated with American history or human drama at its best" (xv). Among fiction writers a cottage industry has blossomed around the subject: *The Seventh Babe*, by Jerome Charyn, Harry Stein's *Hoopla*, Charles Brady's *Seven Games in October*, and Brendan Boyd's *Blue Ruin*, to name a few. American film too cannot escape the limitless possibilities the 1919 scandal offers. In *The Godfather, Part II*, mobster Hyman Roth casually sums up his appreciation for the game: "I loved baseball ever since Arnold Rothstein fixed the World Series in 1919." Rothstein, the gambler credited with organizing the fix, manipulated both players and gamblers with an invisible grace that appealed to the unassuming yet powerful Roth, who, in his own way, sought to undermine the institutional strength of the Corleone family. In *Field of Dreams* (1989), Phil Alden Robinson's adaptation of William Kinsella's novel *Shoeless Joe*, Ray Kinsella, the heroic flower child turned Iowa farmer, knows that if he builds a ballpark in his cornfield, "Shoeless" Joe Jackson, a 1919 White Sox player and one of the greatest hitters the game has ever known, will come there to play, an event that will at once recapture baseball's past and relieve this romantic farmer's guilt over his fractured relationship with his own father. Finally, John Sayles's first screenplay was an adaptation of Eliot Asinof's *Eight Men Out*, the seminal book about the Black Sox and the 1919 World Series. Such disparate writers and filmmakers, all attracted to the same material, illustrate Gould's point. For Sayles, the story of the 1919 Black Sox allowed him to comment on the power structure that surrounds the playing field and its far-reaching, insidious influence on the people who play the game.

Baseball suffers from a public, intellectual, and artistic saccharine coating. In his famous quote about America, educator and historian Jacques Barzun observed, "Whoever wants to know the heart and mind of America had better learn baseball, the rules and realities of the game" (159). Barzun's observation offers up baseball as a romantic pastoral, a game whose focus is home, played on green grass, under clear blue skies, by fresh, clean, young athletes. The late A. Bartlett Giamatti, Yale scholar and administrator and commissioner of baseball, wrote with naive eloquence about the romantic, aesthetic purity of the national game: "Repetition within immutable lines and rules; baseball is counterpoint: stability vying with volatility, tradition with the quest for a new edge, ancient rhythms and ever-new blood—an oft-told tale, repeated in every game in every season, season after season" (95). Baseball is America's romantic pasture, full of hope, celebration, and limitless possibility, enjoying an aura of innocence grounded by nostalgia.

The "Baseball Movie," a genre that has never been able to live up to its advance billing because it fails to recreate with fidelity the game upon which it is based, suffers from this romantic nostalgia, a desperate attempt to reclaim and recreate a dreamy past. According to Marvin Miller, the former executive director of the Major League Baseball Players Association, "Hollywood people know baseball from the sports press, and sportswriters are often like overgrown boys nostalgic for a past that never was" (Barra 21). Reification is delightful, but truth is better. Sayles, typically, brings a hard-eyed, realistic approach to his vision of the game. Although *Eight Men Out* is not completely free of sentimentality and romantic appeal, Sayles deliberately grafts baseball to economic and class conflicts. Sayles's game is about manipulation, big business, and cash, a perfect metaphor for the interaction between our social system and our working lives.

The average fan knows the Black Sox as a group of players who betrayed their teammates, a nation of fans, and the sacrosanct image of baseball. Historic memory, however, reserves little space for Charles Albert Comiskey, the owner of the White Sox, who, according to Gould, was "the meanest skinflint in baseball," flaunting his wealth while treating his players like peons (xvi). Arnold Rothstein, who "recognized the corruption in American society and made it his own" (Asinof *Eight Men Out* 24), remains shadowy, a figure known only to those who celebrate stealth and the unrestricted production of money. For Sayles, Comiskey (Clifton James) and Rothstein (Michael Lerner), two seemingly legitimate businessmen, are parasites who feed off the players. "The stuff that's in the movie," according to Sayles, "he [Comiskey] pulled all that and a lot worse" (Carnes *Past Imperfect* 16). Ironically, each man is historically celebrated for his own cunning brand of genius, while the players are remembered as pariahs, the men who polluted the game. It was Rothstein and Comiskey, the power brokers, along with the players they bought and abused, who pulled the White Sox apart.

Sayles based his picture on Eliot Asinof's *Eight Men Out*, first published in 1963. Originally, David Susskind hired Asinof to write a script about the scandal for television's *Dupont Show of the Month*. With help from James T. Farrell, the Chicago writer, Asinof completed his teleplay. However, Ford Frick, then commissioner of baseball, declared to the show's sponsor that the Black Sox story was "not in the best interests of baseball," and Asinof's work never made it to television. Instead, Asinof published *Eight Men Out*, and Sayles, introduced to the scandal by a Nelson Algren short story, read the book. The book's historical narrative intrigued Sayles, and he recognized its film potential. In 1977 Sayles needed an audition piece for a Hollywood film agency, so he wrote a screenplay, using Asinof's "leg-work," only to find out that the script was unusable. "When I went out to Los Angeles," Sayles recalls, "they said, we love the screenplay, we want to represent you, but forget about the Black Sox Scandal because the rights have been in litigation for twenty years" (Schlesinger 2). In 1980 the Midge Sanford–Sarah Pillsbury production team acquired the rights to Asinof's book. Still intrigued by the book's complex cinematic potential, Sayles showed them his screenplay and expressed his desire to direct the film. The producers agreed, and Sayles began what would become a long script-revision process. Both Sayles and Sanford-Pillsbury Productions were, relatively speaking, unknown at the time. In 1987, after a series of successes by both the producers and Sayles, Orion Pictures agreed to distribute the film provided that Sayles cast some young up-and-coming actors and that Sayles and the producers secure independent financial backing. So Sayles, once again, found himself working for a Hollywood studio. However, unlike *Baby, It's You*, "*Eight Men Out* was interesting," Sayles told historian Eric Foner, "in that all I had to pay — if you think you have to pay something for the price of admission to get the budget for the film — was some casting" (Carnes *Past Imperfect* 15).

Orion rejected Sayles's script for *Eight Men Out* three times, and they were not wildly supportive of his final screenplay. But because a baseball movie provides ample screentime for an ensemble cast, Sayles was able to cast the actors Orion wanted. "So," Sayles notes, "I was happy and they were happy, and I didn't have to sacrifice the story in order to — I didn't have to burn the house down in order to save it" (Carnes *Past Imperfect* 15).

Sayles's screenplay tells the story from multiple points of view — fans, players, gamblers, owners, and sportswriters — which bothered many mainstream critics, notably Roger Ebert. Usually a Sayles supporter, Ebert wrote, "Perhaps the problem is that Sayles was so close to the material that he never decided what the focus of his story really was" (196). Roger Angell, fiction editor and baseball writer for *The New Yorker*, also found the narrative difficult, acknowledging that "by the end of the picture we're worn out, like Louvre visitors, because we've lost our concentration. The picture makes it tough for anybody to focus on a particular player, or even two or three among the famous eight" (51).

Yet the narrative strategy is vintage Sayles. By this stage in his film career, the multiple perspective narrative had become his stylistic trademark. Indeed, we see it and hear it in all his films, even those focusing on one or two characters. Explaining the narrative logic of *Eight Men Out*, Sayles remarked, "I wanted to tell the whole story the way it was told in the book — as an ensemble piece rather than a star vehicle about one ball player" (*Premiere* 76). Baseball, a team game, fits Sayles's ensemble storytelling style well. By telling this story from all sides, Sayles presents a more complete picture of the Black Sox scandal. Moreover, Ring Lardner, Jr., points out that

> Sayles's screenplay does not try to simplify the complicated structure of the corruption by concentrating on a few characters or choosing one point of view from which to tell the story. Instead, he shows us that greed, the main motivation for the fix, was more or less equally distributed among gamblers, ball players, and baseball magnates, and that the consequences of their surrender to it were divided among wives, innocent players, newspapermen, and fans. [48]

Shifting perspectives create a complexity that shows us the players' culpability and, in some cases, their introspective guilt, the relationship between capital and labor, and the scandal's paradoxical outcome. Visually, *Eight Men Out* is alive with motion, a stylistic change for Sayles. Robert Richardson, the director of photography, like Haskell Wexler, had worked previously in both documentary filmmaking and the narrative cinema. Richardson, who has since shot a number of films for Oliver Stone and *Casino* for Martin Scorsese, often employs mobile camera techniques, so he and Sayles experimented with a variety of hand-held and tracking shots that add vigor to Sayles's images, visually capturing the intricate web of deception behind the fixing scheme. *Eight Men Out*'s long expository opening points up Sayles's ambitious attempt to redirect his visual style. His elaborate beginning presents the children, the players, the sportswriters, the gamblers, and all the information the audience needs to follow the convoluted fixing scheme. Sayles uses medium shots, close-ups, and fragments of dialogue to present his characters and themes. His kinetic camera, which was written into the script, clearly establishes the links in the murky fixing scheme.

As the film opens, the 1919 Chicago White Sox finish their regular season. Sayles introduces all the players, both on and off the field. For a variety of reasons, the most prominent being money, eight players conspire to throw the World Series to the Cincinnati Reds, a far less talented team. In doing so, they betray their owner, the tightfisted Charles Albert Comiskey; their fans, particularly two young boys; and a pair of watchful sportswriters, Ring Lardner (John Sayles) and Hugh Fullerton (Studs Terkel). After sportswriters, particularly Fullerton, publish the findings of their investigation into why the "best team ever" lost to a bunch of also-rans, a grand jury is called. Two players, Eddie Cicotte (David Strathairn) and "Shoeless" Joe Jackson (D.B. Sweeney), confess and sign affidavits of guilt. When the confessions mysteriously disappear, which benefits the players, Comiskey, and the gamblers, a trial jury acquits the accused players. However, the newly appointed first commissioner of baseball, Judge Kenesaw Mountain Landis (John Anderson), suspends the eight players from baseball for life, negating their constitutional right to a trial by jury, and forever branding them the Black Sox.

In many ways, *Eight Men Out* is a baseball fan's movie. Knowing something about the 1919 World Series fix, its consequences, and baseball in general makes some details of the film more revealing. Sayles works hard to present authentic play on the field, a serious flaw in most baseball films. He visually describes how baseball's team nature couples with individual play. For example, the first game image we see is a stolen base, which pits a base runner against the pitcher and catcher. Stealing a base is an individual act, displaying scrappy, aggressive play. Following this shot is a smooth double play, a defensive maneuver that requires teamwork and precision. In 1919 we experience baseball before Babe Ruth, baseball's immortal Sultan of Swat,

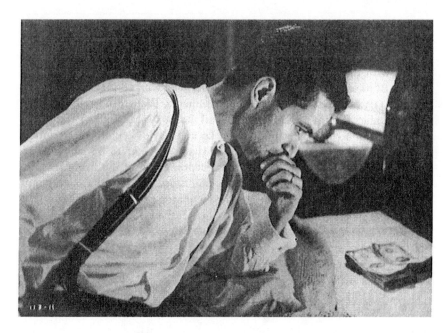

In Eight Men Out *(1988), David Strathairn's performance as Eddie Cicotte, the most intellectually ambivalent of the "Black Sox," was stark and compelling. Like most of Sayles's
conflicted characters, Cicotte is trapped in an untenable position. Although he has performed
exceptionally well for Charles Comiskey, the owner of the Chicago White Sox, the skinflint
owner will not pay his pitcher a bonus he desperately needs. Cicotte knows that his arm is
going bad and his years in the major leagues are numbered. Yet he has no legal means to challenge the parsimonious Comiskey. Here, after receiving his share of the bribe money, Cicotte
ponders what he has done.* Eight Men Out *remains the best example of what Andrew Sarris calls Sayles's "muscular Marxism." Photo courtesy of the Museum of Modern Art Film
Stills Archive.*

when the style of play was slow, one base at a time, a game dominated by
pitching. The "shine-ball" Eddie Cicotte throws throughout the film was out-
lawed after the 1919 season, as were the spitball and other trick pitches, giving the batters an advantage, and naturally increasing run-scoring potential.
Unlike today's game, home runs were not a large offensive component. Therefore, it took more than one swing of the bat, more than one person, to score
a run in 1919. The dominant, muscular, offensive weapon in Sayles's film is
the triple, which we see at both the beginning and the end of the film. As
Tom O'Brien suggests, "Sayles presents a team game and team acting because
he wants to represent a value beyond self" (85). Sayles's vision of the game is
based on teamwork and cooperation, traits of any well-functioning community.

    Still, lack of baseball knowledge does not diminish *Eight Men Out* for
the viewer. By paying close attention to the swirling chicanery of the players,

the gamblers, and the owners and their lawyers, we can appreciate Sayles's subtext without any specialized knowledge. When teamwork breaks down, trouble begins. With the team gone, chaos, confusion, and despair become the rule. Only Arnold Rothstein remains in control, behind the scenes, far removed from the field of play, financially benefiting from every error the Sox commit. In fact, from its opening scene, *Eight Men Out* signals that it is not a Hollywood baseball movie by subverting romantic convention. The film questions how we look at our world and what we are willing to accept, using corruption as its essential metaphor.

Conversely, *Field of Dreams* (1989), a Hollywood baseball movie, also deals with the 1919 Black Sox scandal, but from a Capraesque perspective. It drips with nostalgia, the stock for a Hollywood baseball stew, creating an unpolluted paradise on which "Shoeless" Joe Jackson heads a team of American Adams, the celestial team to beat all teams. Frank Ardolino calls *Field of Dreams* "New Age populism, the achievement of a personal vision that creates the miracle of restoring the guilty dead Black Sox to an innocent playing in a pastoral wonderland" (45). Here, Ray Kinsella (Kevin Costner) reconnects with his father, whom he had disavowed, by participating in the archetypical Hollywood baseball movie gesture, playing catch. Correctly, Pauline Kael saw this desire to reconstruct the past as parochial, a return to the values of the 1950s, a way of saying, "Don't challenge your parents' values, because if you do you'll be sorry. It's saying: Play Ball" ("Field of Dreams" 77).

In its simplicity, *Field of Dreams* is far more accessible than *Eight Men Out*, which challenges viewers by exposing the complex underbelly of the game. Sayles shows us baseball as it is played on and off the field, and there is nothing mystical or celebratory about this brand of hardball. The sections of games we do see are played on drab, dry ballfields, under summer's hot midday glare, places where players get dirty and dusty, where they curse and complain — hardly anyone's picture of paradise, unless, of course, their pleasure comes from playing the game. Moreover, reliable, consistent values do not exist, particularly among the people who ring the playing field. Sayles brings the complete story to the surface, acknowledging that professional ball is more than a simple game of hit, catch, and throw: It is a business that supports the values of capital over labor.

The true action in *Eight Men Out* actually occurs off the field, where the real power lies. David Scobey observes that "this is less a movie about playing games than about watching them, paying for them, and controlling them" (1143). Unlike *Field of Dreams*, baseball in *Eight Men Out* does not lead to purification: Baseball is about business, not paradise. For example, Eddie Cicotte, the senior pitching ace, is cheated out of a bonus by the miserly Comiskey. Cicotte was promised an additional $10,000 if he won 30 games. He won 29. Cicotte knew that Comiskey had him benched unnecessarily for five games near the end of the season, and he confronts the owner with this fact. But Comiskey the businessman will not budge, and so in retaliation Cicotte becomes part of the fixing scheme. Near the end of the film, after he has admitted his guilt, Cicotte, full of fear and confusion, attempts to put the reality of the fix into perspective for his innocent wife (Maggie Renzi):

> I always figured it was talent made a man big, ya know? If I was the best at something. I mean we're the guys they come to see. Without us, there ain't a ballgame. Yeah, but look at who's holdin' the money and look at who's a facin' the jail cell. Talent don't mean nothin'. And where's Comiskey, Sullivan, Attell, Rothstein? Out in the back room cuttin' up profits, that's where. That's the damn conspiracy.

This quote describes Sayles's vision of the fix, because it underscores the basic contradiction between working and the harsh, brutal realities of a compassionless system that puts money and power ahead of people.

During the opening credits, Sayles's camera glides in an upward arc across a blue sky full of puffy white nimbus clouds. The names of the actors drop from the top of the frame, falling toward earth, like angels descending — or perhaps falling from grace instead. This idyllic shot might suggest hope, a sacred look at the past, but mythic re-creation does not interest Sayles, and this unblemished blue sky comes off as an ironic comment rather than an image of regeneration and purification. In *Eight Men Out* flawed human beings share culpability, but not profit or public blame. Here, the field of play adjoins the front office, the saloon, the clubhouse, the pressbox, and the home, like any other picture of common life and labor. In an interview with Sayles, Cleveland, Ohio, sportswriter Doug Clarke summed up the contradiction of the Black Sox scandal well: "It was, of course, Pandora's box. Open it and baseball, the American order incarnate, would be in disorder. Touch it, and the taint would spoil our innocence, soiling something so intrinsically beautiful and symmetric that even the box scores become, and would remain, our article of faith. Best to leave the Black Sox Scandal musty and mythical — legend overshadowing fact" (18). Sayles, naturally, has not let the story go. It is his intention to bring it back to earth, back to hard ground for all to see.

After the credits, Sayles cuts to a street-level tracking shot of a 1919 Chicago neighborhood. A young boy runs along the street shouting, "Bucky! Bucky!" as the camera follows him. He finds his friend playing baseball on a sandlot field between two tenement buildings, where laundry hangs over a ball diamond scratched in the dirt. Sayles's mise-en-scène captures the hold the game has on these city-kids, and it begins to establish the feel of pre–Prohibition Chicago. Their desire to play their heroes' game goes without saying. The boy tells Bucky that he raised the cost of bleacher seats for the White Sox by hawking newspapers. Excitedly, they run to the park together. The Capraesque, artificial, pure blue sky gives way to working-class street life, where everyone hustles, even children, which is, in fact, a more realistic analogy for American society than the game of baseball.

Visually, Sayles and Richardson energize *Eight Men Out*. For Sayles, the camera's movement parallels the energy of baseball, especially during a World Series. Sayles uses a moving camera to depict the tenor of the times, the frenetic Jazz Age popularized by F. Scott Fitzgerald, among others. His camera sweeps among characters in the stadium, the saloon, and the clubhouse, indicating the baroque connections between various figures. Rapid movement both establishes and obscures details of the fix. We are never sure, exactly, who makes the big money from the fixing scheme. Technically, the film recalls Robert Altman's *Nashville* (1975), in which 26 roughly equal characters randomly collide. These characters are all connected to each other, whether they know it or not. For example, in the White Sox's hotel after their loss in the second game of the Series, Sayles presents a bit of visual bravura, a take he calls "the Marx Brothers sequence," where "people pop in and out of doors" (Smith 67). When the shot begins, we see the back of a man's head in close-up, moving away from us in the frame. Coming toward us is "Kid" Gleason (John Mahoney), the manager of the White Sox; the men pass shoulder to shoulder. The camera picks up Gleason, and begins moving backward. Behind him the unknown man turns, pulls out a large envelope presumably stuffed with cash, and lightly taps on a hotel room door. Gleason, who is suspicious of his players' performances, glances over his shoulder, just catching a glimpse of the man slipping into the hotel room. From the audience's perspective, this shot confirms Gleason's doubts, yet he is ironically unaware of the actions going on around him. Sayles keeps the shot going, uncut, as a number of players and gamblers and Comiskey cross paths, some aware, some not.

This elaborate long-take is smooth and clean, an indication of Sayles's increased budget and his growing visual awareness. The camera plays a more active role in *Eight Men Out* than in any of Sayles's earlier films; here, it is an indicting eye, the connective tissue between a variety of guilty parties. What the written dialogue does not spell out, the visual narrative does; it reveals the deep structure of the fixing scheme. When "Sport" Sullivan (Kevin Tighe) enters Rothstein's cavernous apartment to discuss the fix, Sayles moves the camera from an establishing shot of Rothstein eating dinner to Sullivan with hat in hand, trying to act comfortable in the presence of this big-time gambler-businessman. The slow movement of the camera links the two men, and it articulates Rothstein's intent: Sullivan, a trivial Boston gambler, will become Rothstein's pawn. As the camera reveals, the savvy Rothstein shows more interest in his food than in Sullivan's weak attempt at making a deal.

Sayles also uses multiple crane shots in *Eight Men Out*. After the final out of the third Series game, Sayles photographs Ray Schalk (Gordon Clapp), the hard-nosed White Sox catcher not involved in the fix, from above. He rises from his squatting position as the camera rises, momentarily framing him alone. With the camera rising and moving backward, taking in more of the field, Schalk runs to the pitcher's mound and embraces Dickie Kerr (Jace Alexander) as the rest of the team joins in the celebration. The master shot begins in open form, loosely framed, but evolves into a closed shot that shows us the spontaneous joy and camaraderie of the players in a brief moment of team unity on the field of play.

Sayles, however, uses another crane shot to echo and to contradict this shot of team unity. He places the crane in the center of the Chicago courtroom where the eight ballplayers are being tried for conspiracy. The people captured in the high shot are undifferentiated, like the crowd at a ball game. Sayles drops the camera to focus on Lardner and Fullerton, who discuss the mysterious nature of the trial, speculating on who has the most to gain. Then the camera rises and swings to the right, capturing the players, who enter the courtroom to a burst of applause. The players file in, looking more like criminals than a team, uncomfortable on an unfamiliar field. The crane swoops down to capture Cicotte as he passes by Lardner; the pitcher does not want to make eye contact with the writer. Instead, he ends up facing Landis, who will, of course, hand down Cicotte's final judgment. Sayles's shot choices in this extended, unedited sequence are dynamic and telling. The form of these shots is closed, showing us that the players lack the freedom they enjoyed on the ballfield. Here they are regular citizens, reduced to common criminal status. Sayles's shot selection also presents conflict on a societal level. The dialectical fluctuation is unmistakable. He introduces tiers of people differentiated by their class, jobs, and skills, vividly articulating America's social construction.

Because dialogue is Sayles's foundation, we cannot focus solely on imagery. We hear bits and pieces of conversations that ground his pictures. When the young boys enter the bleachers, the "best seats in the place," a hand-held camera follows them right to their seats, adding real-life zest to the master shot. We feel as if we are sitting in the best seats. Two men in front of the boys bet on the outcome of a batter's turn at the plate: "Two bills says he does," says one. "Two bills says he don't," responds the other. The bet is small, revealing their social class, but the casual way the line is delivered indicates that gambling is an accepted activity, a bit of common culture. It would be naive to think that the boys do not hear, see, and understand at least some of what is going on around them. Underscoring this fact, Sayles shows the boys feigning tears to hustle a man in front of them for the price of a box of Cracker Jacks.

But the boys also represent a wisp of innocence in the period before baseball became a corporate game. They are breathless when Joe Jackson, their hero, comes to bat, because they want to see him hit. Their comments express their devotion to Jackson, an athlete whose skills provide an armorlike patina. Juxtaposed with their heedless adoration are comments by a fan, a sportswriter,

Sayles's visual composition comes under constant critical attack, even in generally support-ive reviews of his films. Still, Sayles knows how to manage the frame. In this scene from Eight Men Out *(1988), the illiterate "Shoeless" Joe Jackson (D.B. Sweeney) is surrounded by a herd of journalists, all wanting his story about the Series fix. Jackson, who hardly talks to his teammates for fear of revealing his intellectual shortcomings, is trapped in a situation he has not understood from the beginning. The tight frame Sayles designed for this shot indicates Jackson's confinement. The journalists, who would never think of questioning why the owner of the White Sox pays his players so little, instead smell blood when dealing with the feeble-minded Jackson, whose single talent is playing baseball. Photo courtesy of the Museum of Mod-ern Art Film Stills Archive.*

and Jackson's own teammates about his illiteracy. The kids are free from such antagonisms; all they want is Jackson. Nothing else matters. In other words, they are the only pure observers of the game, unsullied yet by ego, gossip, or greed.

Critics see the adoring boys as one half of a Greek chorus, with Ring Lardner and Hugh Fullerton representing the older, more world-weary half. The boys are fictive; the sportswriters are based on real people. Fullerton was credited with breaking the story about the scandal. Lardner, a sports reporter and fiction writer, was known for his cynical, mordant treatments of his sub-jects. His best-known book, *You Know Me, Al: A Busher's Letters* (1916), chron-icles the life and times of Jack Keefe, a rustic pitcher whose naive ineptitude is comically endearing. We first see Lardner and Fullerton in the press box; they are photographed from behind, typewriters with copy in front of them, looking down on the playing field, commenting on the game with insiders' knowledge.

Like the boys, however, Lardner and Fullerton stand for something more: They are adults who cannot give up their fascination for a boy's game, yet they recognize and comment on the blatant corruption unfolding before them. Sayles, then, sets the pair in opposition to Comiskey. Another reporter announces, "Better get movin', boys, Commy's pourin' in the clubhouse." Lardner's deadpan response indicates his cynical, realistic awareness: "Sportswriters of the world unite! You have nothing to lose but your bar privileges." Comiskey enters the press box like a patrician: "Hello, boys. Is everybody happy?" Commy greets the pressmen by name. When he passes by Lardner, he says, "Hello, sourpuss," and pushes the writer's straw hat over his eyes, distancing himself from Lardner and his friend Fullerton, yet still displaying his control.

Sayles cuts away to a lavish spread — meats, cheeses, breads, drinks, champagne — inside the ornate clubhouse. The sportswriters follow dutifully behind Comiskey as he holds forth about his baseball team, talking like a proud father, the head of a grand American family. The writers pounce on the drinks and the food, like cattle at a feeding trough. In his book, Asinof makes it clear that the newspapermen were Comiskey's boys: "Officially they were on the staff of their respective papers, but Comiskey always made them feel as if they were working for him" (*Eight Men Out* 22). Comiskey continues to define the strengths of his players, arriving, finally, at baseball's grand illusion. "Every man for the good of the team," he happily spouts. *Eight Men Out*, however, is about the fragmentation of a team, the lack of community, so Sayles juxtaposes the artifice of the clubhouse with the reality of the field.

After turning a tough double play, the White Sox infielders run off the field. Swede Risberg (Don Harvey), the shortstop, and Chick Gandil (Michael Rooker), the first baseman, harass the second baseman, Eddie Collins (Bill Irwin), as they jog toward the dugout, taunting him by calling him "college boy" and rubbing it in that he never joins the team during their nights out. Collins tells his teammates that they would benefit from a little sleep; the Swede responds, "Shove it." Again, with only short bits of conversation, Sayles precisely captures the language of rough, male sporting life, where team unity is more of a hope than a fact. Clearly, Collins (historically a solid second baseman) is an outsider, not one of the "boys." The animosity directed at Collins is twofold: He is the highest-paid player on the team, and he has an education. By contrasting the clubhouse and the on-field scenes, Sayles begins to peel back the veneer that covers Comiskey's White Sox, and team sport in general.

Two scheming gamblers, "Sleepy" Bill Burns (Christopher Lloyd) and Billy Maharg (Richard Edson), are another essential part of the opening sequence. Sayles uses these characters to introduce the White Sox players, to promote the idea that a fix is possible, and to show his audience that *Eight Men Out* will make its statement through juxtaposition — cutting back and forth between various characters and scenes, communicating visually the byzantine structure of the fix. Burns explains to Maharg what role each player assumes on the team. Their conversation reveals that Collins's salary will prevent him from going along, that Chick Gandil might "play ball" with them, that Buck Weaver is "one of the boys" but he hates to lose, that Eddie Cicotte is the key to their scheme, and that Comiskey's incredible parsimony will sway the players to throw the Series. Moreover, Burns's appraisal establishes the close relationship the gamblers and the players share: These people know each other well. For anyone who sees baseball as a paradigm of purity, Sayles's opening wipes away any such nostalgic thinking.

Yet Sayles is doing more here than simply debunking the romance of baseball as a boy's game, free from skullduggery, a refuge of innocence. *Eight Men Out* is, for the most part, historically accurate. Baseball and betting go back a long way. According to Asinof, the gamblers were a highly visible part of the baseball world, as common in the lobbies of major-league hotels as bellhops: "Nice guys, one and all; friendly guys, ready with the warm hello and the funny yarn. They got to know the ballplayers well" (*Eight Men Out* 13). When we see "Sport" Sullivan entertaining Chick Gandil with women and drinks in a saloon, such a public meeting seems improbable by today's standards, but it was commonplace before baseball appointed its first commissioner, whose charge was to weed out corruption. With the chummy rapport between players and gamblers so blatant, many of the shots in the opening sequence are ironic, serving to point up the hypocrisy that surrounded baseball in the period during and just after World War I. Sayles does not use many long shots in *Eight Men Out*, especially in the opening sequence. Instead, most of the images are tightly framed in closed form. For example, when "Shoeless" Joe Jackson first comes to bat, Sayles places him in the center of the frame, blocking out a great deal of the background. But the midground links Jackson to the reality of what is going on behind his back. On the green waist-high wall that separates the fans from the field of play is a white lettered sign in bold caps that reads NO BETTING ALLOWED. In its composition, this shot is simplistic, perhaps even trivial, but the contrast between the foreground, where Jackson stands ready to hit with pronounced determination, and the midground, which we realize to be an empty attempt to impose a rule on the fans, suggests that what the players do not see is far more important than what they do see.

While the sportswriters are drinking, eating, and laughing with Comiskey, Sayles's camera frames the owner from a low-angle, highlighting his imperious nature, living up to his nickname, "The Old Roman." Comiskey turns his talk to Eddie Cicotte, his star pitcher: "Eddie's got the best arm I've ever seen." The background in this shot is dark, almost black. There are a few writers near Comiskey, but they are obscured by Sayles's high contrast lighting and the cigarette smoke that fills the shot. Comiskey, bathed in light, dominates the scene, and by extension the writers and the players. His words, of course, are hollow. Sayles crosscuts to Cicotte struggling on the mound. Clearly Comiskey's star pitcher is getting by on guile and desire; his playing days are all but over, age has run its course. Sayles cuts back to the pompous Comiskey, still praising Cicotte. He then quick-cuts to Lardner in a medium close-up as he whispers to Fullerton, "If he's such a fan, why doesn't he pay him [Cicotte] a living wage?"

When Comiskey addresses the sportswriters, we witness his ability to create. He controls the print image of his ballplayers. The sportswriters, with the exception of Lardner and Fullerton, never talk to the players; they take all their information from Comiskey, who fills their stomachs with food and drink. On the other hand, the gamblers, who represent a less-revered business system, one lacking a publicity machine, provide food, drink, and women for the players. Neither the players nor the writers question the motive of the forces supplying their pleasures. Sayles's camera, however, does, stitching these disparate groups together with telling precision.

Both Comiskey and the gamblers use the players for profit. In the opening sequence, after Comiskey's pennant-clinching players leave the field, they enter the clubhouse in a happy, buoyant mood, signaling victory. Victors they are. Framed by a doorway behind them, the players are photographed in a traveling shot, unified by their success. Dirty from work, but illuminated in a diffuse gold-hued light, they are emblematic of team camaraderie.

Approaching a table lined with bottles of champagne, a symbolic connection to the party going on in Comiskey's above-field clubhouse, the players, led by Cicotte, reach for the bottles with suspicion, not joy. Sayles's shot is low-angle, which again suggests a link to Comiskey by giving the players a slightly heroic presence. But this shot is not as pronounced, lacking a single dominant like the owner, and the mise-en-scène is accented by high-key lighting, and white fills the frame, undercutting the shot of Comiskey. Yet the camera distance diminishes the players. Comiskey, on the other hand, fills the frame because the camera is closer to him. Removing the cork from a champagne bottle, Cicotte inquires about the pennant bonus Comiskey promised the team. Comiskey's accountant responds, "This is your bonus." The champagne is flat; upstairs, the sportswriters toast "The Old Roman," smashing their glasses in his fireplace. These counterpoised shots underline Comiskey's fastidious thrift. He owns the team; they are his undisputed property, without any agency of their own.

The gamblers, on the other hand, merely repeat the exploitation that drove the players to the fix in the first place. Only "Sleepy" Bill Burns shows any concern for the players, when it becomes obvious to him that the money promised them will never reach their hands. Tellingly, Rothstein, who engineers the fix and, it is suggested, reaps the greatest profit, never goes near the players, who are part of the rabble from which he has extracted himself. In a marvelous re-creation, Sayles shows Rothstein and other New York businessmen watching the Series reproduced on a large tote board in a New York City hotel. A man reads from a ticker-tape account of the proceedings, while another moves cutout figures of baseball players around a painted picture of a ballfield. Only the score matters to these men, not the game. Likewise, Comiskey operates from a corporate boardroom, handing down edicts from behind an immense desk, removed from the field of play.

In Marxist terms, Rothstein and Comiskey control the players, consuming the profits these workers generate through their field performances. The players, of course, have no power, as their ill-fated, misdirected scheme to boost their pay indicates. "Sport" Sullivan sums up the players' position with metaphoric precision: "Ya know what ya feed a dray horse in the mornin' if you want a day's work out of him? Just enough so he knows he's hungry." Only Cicotte and Jackson receive any money up front. The others wait for a payoff that never arrives. In the end, with several players experiencing doubts, Lefty Williams (James Read) concludes the fix after a thug threatens his wife. Rothstein and Comiskey profit. They completely control the game and its players.

Sayles concludes his long opening with a team photo, often a standard in the Hollywood baseball movie. Buck Weaver (John Cusack) yells, "Come on, fellas, pretend it's Commy's wake." Everyone smiles. The color image turns to a black-and-white still photograph. Sayles uses a flash frame to bathe the image in white, effectively scoring the punchline. Sayles wryly points out the artificial nature of this baseball cliché: the team photo is as fake as the description of the ballplayers in the press. After all, we know that team dissension exists, gamblers are out to fix the Series, and the owner, the players' enemy, is a stingy tyrant who manipulates the press with food, drink, and talk. Only the sandlot kids exist in a state of willing innocence. Thus, baseball's romantic image is as fraudulent as this photograph full of smiling faces.

John Tintori's editing of *Eight Men Out* is crisp and sharp, using numerous quick-cuts to pace the film and to show the multilayered fixing scheme in detail. For the most part, Sayles uses editing as a counterbalancing device: The film works through juxtaposition. Sayles cuts from various individuals and groups to show contradictions and the function of power. In the courtroom scene that closes the picture, Tintori's rapid cutting technique accents the fragmentary nature of the outcome of the film and the Black Sox scandal itself. If Comiskey and Rothstein were explicitly connected up until this point in the film, the crosscut editing implicitly links the owner and the gambler. When the defense lawyer asks the prosecutor to produce his most incriminating piece of evidence, the signed confessions, he is told that the evidence is missing. Sayles cuts to Fullerton and Lardner, who speculate on the behind-the-scenes maneuvering. Lardner says, "Must have cost somebody an arm and a leg. Rothstein or Comiskey?" Fullerton answers, "Maybe Rothstein's arm and Comiskey's leg." Previously we witnessed Comiskey's lawyer and Rothstein's lawyer discussing ways to protect their employers' "business interests." Comiskey and Rothstein, apparently, fixed the trial. As David Scobey notes, "One preserves his baseball property, the other his profitable secrecy" (1144). Though never showy, Sayles's cutting technique, which Tinori provided, serves the thematic integrity of his film.

Musically, *Eight Men Out* is not as impressive as *Matewan*. In order to create an appropriate historical context, Sayles and Mason Daring chose a Chicago-Dixieland-style sound to accent the film. One tune, "After You've Gone," an ironic bit of mock praise for the fallen players that is sung to them in a saloon before the fix occurs, also closes the film, an appropriate book-ending technique that shows Sayles's sympathy for these players. Sayles and Daring collaborated on "I Be Blue," which, as its title suggests, is a fan's lament. The musical soundtrack passes judgment on the unsuspecting players, who are drawn into a web so complex that they cannot find their way out. The music surrounds them, but they cannot hear or recognize the message of the lyrics passing them by. The music, according to Frank Ardolino, ushers in "the cynicism of the Jazz Age," a decadent, freewheeling time. As the final credits roll, "After You've Gone" plays, announcing the loss felt when baseball fell from grace.

For production design, Sayles used his *Matewan* crew, led by Nora Chavooshian, to create an authentic 1919 setting. Their task was difficult, but, as in *Matewan*, they were successful. Here, their most difficult chore was filling a stadium with extras: the residents of Indianapolis, Indiana, where the baseball scenes were shot, were not interested in showing up at "their local minor league park," changing into "period clothing," and cheering for Cincinnati and Chicago teams of 70-plus years ago (Lardner, Jr. 49). So Chavooshian used cardboard cutouts scattered among real people to create a World Series–sized crowd. Cynthia Flynt's costumes, again, were period perfect, right down to the straw hats and the cigars.

Baseball movies, however, must make the actors into players, a difficult undertaking. Speed usually betrays illusion; actors, for the most part, do not have an athlete's ability to accelerate. Sayles disguised this weakness with editing and camera movement; he did not let the camera linger on players or their turns at the plate. But he also did not substitute former professional ballplayers as stand-ins for the actors either. As Roger Angell, a veteran baseball observer, says, "Sayles's feat ... is to make some of his players recognizable in the end not by their acting but by the way they look on the field" (52). Their acting, of course, has a great deal to do with the way they look on the field.

Eight Men Out shows off a stable of talent. D.B. Sweeney, who makes us feel for "Shoeless" Joe's untutored acceptance of the fix, brings the storied batter to life on the field. The actor worked for months perfecting Jackson's signature batting style, which Roger Angell describes as an "open-stance, flat-bat, left-handed cut at the ball" (52). He looks authentic both at the plate and running the bases. David Strathairn is Eddie Cicotte, a tough, veteran pitcher getting by on savvy, who, after a big hitter for the opposition drives two long foul balls, delivers a dead-on inside pitch to strike the man out. Baseball movies rely on strike-outs and home runs, the defining actions for most filmgoers, but few show pitch location. Strathairn delivers a pitch that a long-ball hitter would go for and that a true fan would recognize as ideal for that situation. Charlie Sheen is perfectly tuned to play the goofy Hap Felsch, both on the field and off. Allowing a herd of sportswriters and fans to buy him beer after beer, Felsch sits atop a bar and admits that he took part in the scheme because it was the smart thing to do. "I may be dumb, but I'm not stupid," he announces without a trace of understanding.

Sayles makes these actors believable by showing us just enough of their on-field play to establish their positions. We see John Cusack's Buck Weaver track down two hot smashes at third base, but each diving stop is edited to make the difficult play seem real. Even though Cusack lacks the speed and form of a major leaguer, he looks good holding the bat and shouting encouragement to his mates in the field.

The rest of Sayles's ensemble cast enhance the film. There are no stars here, as usual, just quality craftsmen. Kevin Tighe plays the Boston gambler "Sport" Sullivan with unctuous panache. Holding his hat in his hands talking to Arnold Rothstein, Tighe takes on the personality of a schoolboy talking his way out of some bad luck with the headmaster. Trying to look calm, with Rothstein's henchman, Monk Eastman (Stephen Mendillo), hanging over his shoulder to ensure Sullivan takes care of the fix, Tighe precisely captures the nervous tics of a man who feels mortally threatened. But when dealing with an underling, such as Chick Gandil, Tighe's slimy smile and patronizing tone capture this Boston glad-hander with pitch-perfect ease.

But it is Michael Lerner as the iconographic Arnold Rothstein, the undisputed king of the underworld, who makes the most of his screen time. His presence underlines the manipulative, inscrutable root of power behind the scenes. Rothstein focuses on business, and business alone. He is Comiskey without the veneer of legitimate business, baseball, to conceal his dealings. He stays away from the spotlight, but his shadow hangs over the playing field. He possesses a hard, trenchant point of view. Rothstein explains his truth to bagman Abe Attell, a former boxer: Fame is ephemeral, economic power is strength. Rothstein intones, "Altogether I must have made ten times more betting on you than you did slugging it out. I never took a punch." Attell responds, "I was champ." Rothstein counters, "Yesterday. That was yesterday." Lerner gives these words a resonance that carries a deeper meaning — there is only one man ever in control, Arnold Rothstein.

Control, in a word, sums up *Eight Men Out*. Charles Comiskey's lawyer defines the purpose of their mission in the inquiry against the eight White

Sox players: "Our job is to control that investigation. Make the public think you're clean." In other words, Comiskey and his men will manufacture public consent to save the business of baseball and his workers, who are, of course, necessary to his financial success. Therefore, the first rule of order is to hire a commissioner, and the owners find Judge Kenesaw Mountain Landis. In a rotogravure-style grouping of the baseball owners on a staircase, Comiskey announces their choice for commissioner in glowing, patriotic terms, like a politician making a committee appointment. Landis, the assembled reporters are told, will clean up the game for its own good. Lardner leans over to Fullerton and whispers with melancholy that Landis should "start with the birds up on the stairs with him." These men, it goes without saying, are his employers. Corruption is the rule, not the exception. The players, though guilty, are in the minor leagues compared with the owners.

Owners like Comiskey had complete legal and institutional control over the players, which gave them monopoly power. The players' actions, then, can be read as a foolish attempt at sabotage. As with the use of force against the coal company in *Matewan*, the White Sox players chose a destructive form of rebellion, one that serves the gamblers, the businessmen, and the lawyers who play by adult rules, not the rules of a child's game. By the end of the film the players recede into the background. Moving from the ballfield to the courtroom, the players become, as David Scobey notes, "pawns in an arcane struggle among Comiskey, Rothstein, the baseball establishment, and the state" (1145)—abstract powers that the ballplayers cannot comprehend. Their inarticulate, unsophisticated presence in the courtroom is emphasized by Sayles's mise-en-scène. Marginalized, they all sit around a table for the court audience to gawk at, like creatures in a zoo. None of the ballplayers, except Buck Weaver, seems to understand or care about his position. Removed from the baseball field, they lack definition. Rothstein's words, "Yesterday. That was yesterday," hang over every shot of the fallen players.

Although they were acquitted, Landis bans the players for life. His words are heard in a voice-over, contradicting the visual image of the players' team celebration at a restaurant. Sayles films the baseball team in slow motion to ensure that the pain of Landis's historic decision strikes in image and word. As major league baseball players, these men have no rights; they are the property of the league, not citizens of a democratic republic. They are in the end as they were in the beginning, talented innocents. Sayles ends *Eight Men Out* on a nostalgic note: we see Joe Jackson bat one more time. As he did in the opening sequence, Jackson hits a triple. The handful of fans present at the semipro ballpark clap, but Sayles fills the soundtrack with the applause and cheers from a big-league crowd, an aural reminder of the past. Here, Sayles shows us his own unabashed love of the game and the players. Although Sayles returns to a romanticized image of baseball, he ends the film on a realistic note. "Shoeless" Joe is pictured alone. He is not the same man he was, and he is no longer a part of the game he loved. There is no transcendence here, no field of dreams. Jackson no longer has a name, an identity. As the men in the stands speculate whether the tremendous player before them is Joe Jackson, a youngster asks his father who Joe Jackson is. The father responds, "One of those bums from Chicago, kid. One of the Black Sox." Sayles's final point is that it is the players, the visible performers, who will be committed to historical memory, not the owners or gamblers, not the power players. As Scobey points out, Sayles "vividly portrays the class conflicts that underlay baseball's growth as a commercial entertainment.... What preoccupies *Eight Men Out* is less the moral condition of its protagonists than the social construction — the making and meaning — of their actions" (1143). Sayles's narrative analyzes social and economic circumstances rather than spinning cinematic fantasy, and it asks us to take pity on the poor devils who are baseball's lost souls.

10

City of Hope

I wanted the feeling that these were parallel stories that eventually converge. The film is like a knot. Everyone is tied up together. I wanted people to be able to tell — in part by the way it is shot — that there's no way these people can avoid affecting each other, even if they never met each other.

— John Sayles, press release, 1991

City of Hope (1991) is an urban allegory. In Hudson City, New Jersey, John Sayles's fictional setting, corruption is the rule, not the exception. Depicting the natural progression of a society built on profit and greed, *City of Hope* complements *Matewan* and *Eight Men Out* nicely, continuing an American historical analysis of wealth and power: how economic space is captured and held.

Like his period films, *City of Hope* is panoramic in scope, presenting a large cast of characters connected by a nonlinear storyline that demands audience concentration. In this way it resembles a Faulkner novel with its multiple perspectives, rather than a contemporary American film. Sayles's impressive narrative reveals the inner workings of the people who populate Hudson City, while disclosing deep social criticisms that are steeped in humanism. Sayles emphasizes the systemic evils that suffocate his characters. *City of Hope* paints an authentic, complicated, relentless portrait of urban America. Sayles's political and social criticisms are clear and unambiguous: Urban relations based solely on power and money, the cornerstones of corrupt democratic politics, will lead to social fragmentation and decay.

The content of Sayles's film is both adventurous and disturbing, a risky proposition after eight years of conservative ideology dominating the country. The condition of Hudson City is a metaphor for the pitiless political ideology that dominated the 1980s. Though not highly visible, big-money players are well represented in *City of Hope*. Those on top do well: The culture of capital is robust, thriving. But Sayles's cityscape is bleak, evoking a place on the verge of collapse. The majority of the characters get by on hope alone, which is in short supply. Yet, even though profits never trickle down to street level, these people persevere. According to Sayles, "The hopefulness for me comes from some of the people from below. I don't have hope coming from above" (Demyanenko 23). While real estate deals are being cut to advance political careers and stuff bank accounts, Hudson City crumbles and burns, trapping its citizens. Here, social polarization is an ever-expanding norm, a condition met with cynical acceptance by those in control.

Sayles makes numerous stylistic adjustments to create a film that is dramatic and compassionate, analytical and politically progressive. Camera movement and expressionistic mise-en-scène bolster the content of his film. *City of Hope* also incorporates at least 50 speaking parts, a narrative strategy that makes Hollywood producers shudder. Sayles's camera intertwines all the characters as Hudson City's story unfolds over the course of three days and three nights, a time frame that provides unity and compression to a broad canvas.

City of Hope's narrative strategy and style come through in the opening credits. The credits appear in red letters on a black background, accompanied by a driving urban blues tune composed by Mason Daring. We see groups of names, never just one. The credits sweep in from the bottom of the frame, pause, and then vanish through the top of the frame, in cadence with the start-and-stop wail of a blues harmonica. As Daring's tune builds in tempo, the credits quicken. This fusion of image and sound approximates the fleeting glimpses of people and signs one sees from the interior of a subway car. Indeed, as the title of the film appears on screen, we hear the grinding, metallic sound of a train braking. Like the brief power outages experienced inside a subway car, the title CITY OF HOPE blinks on and off while the harmonica screams. The screen fades to black. Similarly, Sayles's characters do not remain on the screen for long; their stories come in fragments as the peripatetic camera moves from person to person, group to group, visually fusing these urbanities. Sayles's script resonates with city voices — raw and conventional, blue collar and white collar, street cops and detectives, lawyers and thieves — making them undeniably distinct yet interconnected, making the film very personal — people recognize one another.

Most urban dramas follow the activities of one or two people. Even Martin Scorsese, the dean of urban American filmmakers, focuses on small ethnic groups, never offering a complete, top-to-bottom urban portrait. Typically, Sayles goes against the generic grain. Each character he draws makes an imprint. This approach aptly portrays the people who make up any city. As Thulani Davis suggests, all the characters are skillfully delineated, defined so that the reasons for their actions make sense, "even if they bust kids up against a wall or assault an innocent passerby or burn people out of their homes" (22). All of the characters are dominated by corrupt city politics. Representing an outdated mode of thought, lacking the will to attack problems, driven by greed, Hudson City's government is the film's villain.

Sayles's cityscape expands quickly. His camera pans seamlessly among characters, circumstances, and places, a visual syntax Sayles wrote into his script. He deliberately avoids conventional character presentations. Each figure emerges from the hurly-burly streets of Hudson City as he or she is, without explanation, adding not only depth and richness to *City of Hope* but also humor and lyrical interludes. Sayles understands that city life is an unpredictable swirl of romance and realism, full of tension and release, mad characters, and tender moments.

For example, through a large plate-glass window Sayles photographs a television showing a Mad Anthony's electronics store commercial, recalling an image familiar to most urbanities, especially New Yorkers. Outside the frame we hear a palsied voice imitating the hyperbolic enticements of Mad Anthony (Josh Mostel). Slowly the camera pans left to reveal Asteroid (David Strathairn), a mentally disturbed homeless man. He follows Mad Anthony's every move, reprising each gesture and phrase in his own twisted dance. Wynn (Joe Morton), the only African American member of the city council, passes behind him. The camera picks up Wynn walking away from Asteroid. Coming toward Wynn are two policemen, Bauer (Stephen J. Lang) and Rizzo (Anthony John Denison), who listen to a torrent of complaints from Connie (Maggie Renzi) and Joann (Marianne Leone), a nonstop verbal tag team determined to list Hudson City's ills, blaming every problem on the minority underclass. Leaving Wynn, the camera picks up this quartet as they pass Asteroid, looking at him with pained annoyance. We follow the four until the cops get into their patrol car. Once inside, they roll up the cruiser's windows to block out Connie and Joann's cacophony of complaint. Sayles introduces all his players in a similar fashion, mixing long master shots with more typical setups. The moving camera works like connective tissue, even though each character's personal motivation is vastly different.

Inevitably, *City of Hope* invites comparison to Robert Altman's *Nashville* (1975), which also used a broad canvas and a multicharacter cast to comment on contemporary society and politics. Sayles, however, is not as oblique as Altman, and his characters are more distinct. By comparison, Altman plays it safe; his politics and intentions are sardonic, abstract. *City of Hope* is concrete: Failing American cities and corrupt politicians enjoy a long, storied history. Still, like Altman, Sayles explores politics with a skeptical eye. Like *Nashville*, *City of Hope* views the acceptance of the corruption of democratic politics as cynical and troubling. With unflinching awareness, Sayles shows how a city and a society built on bureaucratic power and profit incentive at the expense of community needs is doomed to fail. Sayles's narrative is tight, a circular tour de force that welds form with content in an ambitious, accurate account of urban decay.

Although we are led to a conclusion, *City of Hope* has no plot per se. Sayles's storyline is a Gordian knot, involving the interactive lives of more than a dozen essential characters and an even larger number of peripheral, though not unimportant, figures. Hudson City's population is urban, familiar: corrupt politicians, tough cops, real estate speculators, criminals, dopers, barflies, construction workers, professionals, street people, racial separatists. Hudson City is in trouble; it is exhausted and divisive, like most American cities. Typically, many residents of Sayles's fictive city place the blame for this collapse squarely on the shoulders of those who have the least — welfare recipients, unwed mothers, aimless, drug-addled kids, people who do not vote. Moreover, the major, unspoken divide is race, a common urban phenomenon. Sayles, to his credit, takes a broader, more radical view of urban problems: "If you mechanize and bureaucratize things and the human factor isn't involved, very often you end up with a system that doesn't serve anybody, but everybody keeps serving it" (Demyanenko 22). City Hall, where the politics of business as usual are orchestrated, is the root cause for the decay of Hudson City.

The political infrastructure has little patience or feeling for its constituents, except to shake hands and request their votes. Instead, tax abatements, luxury housing, and foreign investment are the chief concerns of this city's government. Mayor Baci (Louis Zorich), Hudson City's nominal leader, speaks for the politics of profit as he tries to appease Joe Rinaldi (Tony Lo Bianco), a successful contractor tied to city government and the Mob. "Next couple of years this town is going to be one big yard sale. And anyone with half a brain will make tracks. Let the blacks and the Spanish duke it out over what's left ... America, huh?" prods Baci. Hudson City is the end result of corrupt pragmatism.

Thus, *City of Hope* presents a bleak yet realistic view of contemporary urban corruption. The motives of the political figures here are clearly spelled out: They are their own tribe, a gang of profiteers who have been subsumed by an archaic system. As a group, the mayor and his aides, the district attorney and his staff, and most members of the city council subscribe to the politics of business as usual: Their rhetoric is full of platitudes, their public gestures are for votes, their back-room deals conveniently obscure. Real power, according to Sayles's film, comes from political control, which is where the money lies. *City of Hope* examines a worn-out urban system badly in need of change.

Place is central to *City of Hope*. Hudson City, which is being sliced up and burned down for profit, dominates the film. Sayles, who has always been more interested in character and social behavior than conventional narrative structure, uses his fictional city as a stage for his various characters, the sort of people any sentient urban dweller knows well. Each of these characters belongs to his or her own sect. "In *City of Hope*," says Sayles, "you see the black tribe, the Italian tribe, and the police force who are always their own tribe" (Crowdus and Quart 4). But Sayles is no soapbox polemicist advocating for one group against the others. Rather, he shows us what this tribalism, the factionalization of a community, does to a place.

Hudson City suffers from entropic malaise. Although any rigorous definition of entropy involves high-level mathematical considerations, the key words used in any interpretation are *randomness*, *disorder*, and *uniformity*. A schematic representation of Hudson City will help in understanding this analogy, the action of the film, and Sayles's pessimistic description of American cities. Picture Hudson City as two boxes, one contained inside the other. The interior box is the political system, tightly controlled and orderly, which influences all the activity in the surrounding box, the urban community, which is unorganized and volatile. The political system negatively influences the community, causing more and more randomness and disorder. On the other hand, the urban community has little or no influence on the system. Thus, Hudson City operates in a constant state of confusion, where nothing will upset the political system until the city is completely destroyed, finally engulfing the political system in its own chaos. As Sayles explained to Thulani Davis,

> There is this idea that inner cities are just going to be abandoned, that the money is going to be stripped from them, and whoever wants to deal with them can deal with the problems. And that people are going to have their little enclaves and take out of their own pocket to buy a police force or good schools and, in a perverted way, that's the American Dream: I'll take care of my own and fuck the rest of you. Finally, though, I think that leads to bigger crises. [22]

Even though Sayles has stated in numerous interviews that there is hope in Hudson City, signified by small, bright moments of reconciliation and repair, these glimmers of possibility are overshadowed by the pessimism that characterizes *City of Hope*. Resignation is the norm, hope the exception.

Sayles uses a more subjective and expressionistic photographic style throughout *City of Hope* than in his previous films. This dramatic change in Sayles's visual technique is announced in his first shot. Nick Rinaldi (Vincent Spano), who desperately wants to get out from under his father's shadow, is photographed from an oblique angle with the frame washed lightly in red, hinting at both his imbalance and the threat of danger to come. This shot is a fresh approach for Sayles, a switch from his signature imagery, which tends to be straightforward. The canted angle of the shot and color filter are a new visual experience for Sayles's audience. While he lacks the heightened visual flair of Martin Scorsese or Spike Lee, Sayles's awareness of visual syntax has always been in evidence throughout his directorial career, although *City of Hope* marks a significant visual change.

Sayles designed *City of Hope* around long, uninterrupted master shots that contain the entire scene, underscoring the interconnectedness of his characters. He employed Robert Richardson, who shot *Eight Men Out*, as his director of photography because of Richardson's Steadicam talent. Richardson photographs these city people with perseverance, tracking them like a anthropologist with a camera. Sayles wrote the fluid character transitions into his script, before he had decided on a cinematographer, as he remarked to Gavin Smith: "The word I used was 'trade.' I would have a conversation going, and then the stage direction would say, 'And we trade and follow these two characters. And these are the first lines that we hear, and these are the first lines that we see on camera'" (67). Using a widescreen format, Sayles and his photographic crew were able to shoot characters in the foreground and the background without losing clarity. According to Sayles, he and Richardson decided that the extra heavy Steadicam would enhance *City of Hope*. Everything, of course, comes with a price. "Bob's a hardass on his crew," Sayles explains. "He said, 'What the hell, he'll [the Steadicam operator] be in good shape when the movie's over'—I think our guy checked into a hospital" (Smith 68).

The choreography of the opening shot, for instance, is a flawless weave contrasting Nick's pessimistic confusion and Wynn's idealistic willingness to work for change. After the red wash fades from Nick's image, the camera returns to its natural horizontal and vertical axis and pulls away for a full master shot of Nick and Yoyo (Stephen Mendillo), the shop steward who, like Nick, is paid to show up but not work. Nick tries to tell Yoyo about his internal chaos, but he gives up quickly. Frustrated, he asks for cocaine to relieve his "fuckin' head." Nick then tells Riggs (Chris Cooper), the construction foreman, that he is quitting. As Nick heads for the stairs, the camera picks up Nick's father, Joe, talking to Wynn about minority hiring. After Joe denies the request because he is carrying too many union no-shows, Wynn asks, "So, we're good enough to pay rent on these apartments but we're not good enough to build them?" Frustrated, Wynn understands that he lacks real political power and thus the ability to put his people to work. Nick, who does not understand the covert system that made his father successful, begins a hopeless search to make sense of his own life.

As the camera indicates, Wynn and Nick are central to Sayles's narrative. Each is fundamental to the outcome of the film. Their parallel stories provide *City of Hope* with a framework for all the other characters as they move toward the dark conclusion of the film. Yet Nick and Wynn scarcely know each other. The opening shot is the only time they share the frame, and that is momentary. Still, like every other character in *City of Hope*, these men are inexorably linked, and this connection is Sayles's main point: Hudson City is an organic whole, and its life stories never separate. As Sidney Gottlieb points out, "Without denying the fact of individuality—people do indeed have personal goals and private desires—Sayles nevertheless insists that the primary reality of life, for better or for worse, is social" (73). Therefore, even though *City of Hope* seems epic, or panoramic, it is claustrophobic, a hermetically sealed place where no action is without consequence. Sayles's visual composition reminds us of this important point throughout the film.

In City of Hope *(1991), Councilman Wynn (Joe Morton) tries to preserve what is left of the city he represents. But he discovers that doing the right thing for his community comes with its own problems. Still, he has the support of his wife, Reesha (Angela Bassett), and ultimately of other members of the African American community.*

By contrasting the opening of *Eight Men Out*, where Sayles employed some of the mobile camera techniques, with that of the stylistically punched-up *City of Hope*, we can better appreciate his change in visual construction. Although Sayles used a moving camera in *Eight Men Out*, the connections between the characters were generally established by crosscutting, a technique that establishes and underscores the social and economic division among the characters by keeping them in separate frames. Conversely, *City of Hope*'s long, complicated takes are thematically justified and technically impressive. Sayles told Thulani Davis, "I think what I wanted to get at — in the writing and in the style of shooting — is the fact that, like it or not, people depend on each other. We're stuck with each other, and we have to deal with each other one way or the other" (21–22). While *Eight Men Out* examines the fragmentation of a baseball team, *City of Hope* examines a larger yet still personal community that is fraying badly.

From the beginning, we are thrust into Sayles's cityscape. The story unfolds rapidly, placing us on the unstable streets of Hudson City. Although Sayles never completely embraces a view of the city as a hopeless wasteland beyond reconstruction, *City of Hope* does display the characteristic film noir moods of claustrophobia and despair.

The work site is an important beginning for Sayles. It functions on a number of levels, introducing both characters and themes necessary for understanding *City of Hope*'s narrative. At the work site we see how political clout can make or break a developer, how jobs are established, and the forms corruption takes on a project that is part of Hudson City's urban renewal. The unfinished building provides both open and closed forms in which Sayles frames his characters. Initially, Nick and Yoyo are presented in closed form; they are part of the world that is constructing the building, a job, we come to find out, that is totally corrupt. Wynn, on the other hand, who wants to serve his constituents, is photographed in open form, indicating that his world has not yet become constricted. In addition, the building is a high-rise, separated from the street by height and the powerful forces that are behind its construction. Appropriately, when Nick leaves the building he enters the world of the street, the outer box, where he is not separated from the people who make up the city, and where his father's money and connections cannot easily protect him.

Nick is never allowed power or control in the frame; he exists in a labyrinthine nightmare, walled in from every side. Lost, Nick is alienated even from the corrupt world of Hudson City. Sayles places Nick in a Hamlet-like paradox: He cannot decide to stay, yet he cannot leave. Nick's scenes, then, present a bleak vision. Ironically, there is nothing for Nick to revolt against because the world around him lacks values of any kind. No positive systems of order exist, only corrupt ones. Nick's condition is as damaged as Hudson City's. Still, even though the city is corrupt, exhausted, uncaring, and racially divided, Nick in his own confused way seeks an ideal world, the sort of place that makes sense even to a confused young man.

Sayles often photographs Nick in a film noir style to indicate the character's true feelings. Nick's world is one of desolation and muddle; he resembles the city crumbling around him. On a number of occasions, Sayles photographs Nick aimlessly running through the streets of Hudson City at night, trying to escape but lacking both the will and the means to do so. In each of these sequences, Sayles places Nick in an expressionistic mise-en-scène. In the background or the foreground, pools of light dot the city's darkened streets. These pools of light suggest street lamp illumination, the sodium-vapor look so common in contemporary cities, but the amount of light is strong and direct, not diffuse. Though realistic, the lighting is also symbolic, in that its effect suggests how difficult it is for any of these city dwellers to find their way in Hudson City, especially Nick. Except for brief moments of illumination, Nick remains in the dark, suffering from emotional and intellectual turmoil.

Sayles also uses high-key lighting to jar the viewer into experiencing the cause-and-effect relationship among his characters. In a sequence recalling Scorsese's *Taxi Driver*, we see two African American teenagers, Tito (Eddie Townsend) and Desmond (Jojo Smollett), roaming Hudson City's night streets. They verbally taunt women they pass. Tito is the leader, unafraid to say anything. Desmond, a physically softer, younger-looking kid, follows Tito's lead but lacks his friend's sexually charged enthusiasm. As they pass into a pool of white light, they are suddenly pushed up against the brick facade of a building. Two cops, Paddy (Jude Ciccolella) and Fuentes (Jaime Tirelli), enter into the circle of light and begin to hassle the teenagers. Typically, Tito takes the offensive; the cops shout back. The mise-en-scène is lurid, making the characters appear unreal, nightmarish. The low-angle shot gives the cops authoritative presence and strength. Tito and Desmond are physically over-matched. Sayles highlights the racial antagonism that exists between the cops and the teenagers, examples of two distinct urban tribes. Tito shouts at Paddy, "Man, this is a free fuckin' country." The cop responds, "Where'd you hear that one. You keep your shit south of L Street." Paddy turns Tito around and pushes him toward the black part of town.

With precision, Sayles shows a transfer of power from the mouthy teenagers to the hard-edged cops who control their section of town. However, both the cops and the teenagers are in the wrong. Everyone within the frame, then, is under the hot lamp, suggesting that the cops and the teens share in a collective guilt, a manifest lack of understanding. As Tito and Desmond walk away, Fuentes suggests that they may have treated the youths too harshly. Paddy then gives his new partner some sage street advice: "If you can't get respect, you settle for fear." Yet by showing disrespect for Tito and Desmond, the cops unknowingly establish a motive for revenge, which will be carried out on a white man jogging alone in a nearby park.

Traditionally, film noir uses low-key lighting and garish high contrasts to create a shadowy world that is both sinister and inviting. Sayles, however, puts his own spin on this visual style. The high-key spotlights wash the color from his images, turning the characters into expressions of pure rage. This type of lighting becomes claustrophobic, capturing Sayles's performers within a spotlight from which there is no exit. Literally, Sayles's lighting pattern exaggerates his characters. Every move and every word demands scrutiny. In Nick's case, the lighting is ironic; he cannot see a way out of the trap that is Hudson City. The cops and the teenagers, street antagonists in a turf battle, are on display. In *City of Hope*, Sayles's lighting scheme creates the same links and disruptions as his roving camera.

Sayles also uses different evocative lighting techniques in two pivotal sequences near the end of the film: one, a confrontation between Nick and Carl (Sayles); the other, Nick's nighttime conversation with an African American man who is shooting baskets on an inner-city court. The mise-en-scène of each scene discloses thematic connections and Sayles's broader political intentions.

For all of his tough-guy posturing, Nick remains an innocent wandering though a place he truly does not understand. Memories of Tony, Nick's older brother who died in Vietnam, haunt him. Early in the film, Sayles shows

Nick looking at Tony's flattering photographs and athletic awards, kept with shrinelike reverence in his father's bedroom. These signify Tony's importance to the family, particularly his father. Tony was an all-state basketball player, a popular kid, whose life was tragically cut short. Even in death, Tony represents the traditional all–American kid, and an impossible image for Nick, a nonathletic loner, to live up to. Nick blames his father for Tony's death. According to Nick, Joe Rinaldi sent Tony to Vietnam, where he was killed. Nick, however, does not know the true story. The varnish must be stripped away from Tony's history so the truth, that Tony went to Vietnam to avoid jail, can be discovered. But discovering the truth is no panacea. Awareness, Sayles suggests, comes with a price.

Carl delivers the truth to Nick. Carl is Hudson City's fixer, the man people — cops, politicians, mobsters — turn to when they need information, fencing of stolen property, or arson work. In order to save himself from jail, Carl tells O'Brien (Kevin Tighe), a politically ambitious detective, that Nick participated in the botched burglary at Mad Anthony's electronics store. This information is used, in turn, against Rinaldi to get him to cooperate with the Mob, although Nick is unaware of his father's connection. Without thinking, Nick decides to confront Carl to exact revenge.

As he approaches Carl's garage at night, Nick's image is reflected in a darkened window, suggesting that we will now see another portion of his personality. Nick hides in the shadows as one of Carl's mechanics leaves the garage carrying a comically massive boom box blaring a heavy metal tune, "All for Nothing, Our Balls to the Wall," which precisely announces Nick's condition. Cloaked in darkness, the garage takes on a haunting look. Sayles cuts to a shot of Carl leaning up against a car inside the garage. He looks up when he hears Nick, and, looking directly into the camera says, "Well, well, well, if it isn't the fugitive." The camera picks up Nick's point of view, moving slowly around Carl, tentatively assessing the situation. Carl remains cool, calm, framed by a background that is an offbeat scheme of light and dark marked with diffuse pools of red and blue. The mise-en-scène establishes Nick's American nightmare, with the sinister Carl at its center.

Carl, a character equal to *Matewan*'s C.E. Lively in unctuous deceit, knows more about Tony and Joe Rinaldi than Nick does. Indeed, Carl inhabits a world hidden from plain view. Sayles photographs Carl in a variety of shots, but his face is always half in shadows. Clearly, Carl is a heavy who is at home in this shady world. Carl displays no surprise or fear over Nick's desire for revenge throughout the sequence.

On the other hand, Nick's face is photographed in direct light. Still, he too is framed by the background darkness of Sayles's symbolic mise-en-scène, which indicates the corruption that engulfs both these characters. Nick yells at Carl, "You rolled over on me just as you did on Tony." Carl begins to move toward Nick, reducing the visible space between them, and snarling, "Don't talk about that old shit." The camera's gaze follows Carl as he tightens the space between himself and Nick. "You think he was a fuckin' hero," Carl disdainfully shouts. Carl then reveals Tony's history, the truth behind the image: Tony was drunk, driving a stolen car when it jumped a curb, hitting a woman. In panic, Tony left both the woman and Carl, his passenger, for the cops to deal with. Nick calls Carl a liar. Carl says, "Ask your daddy, Nick." Nick than accuses Carl, who has moved away from Nick to get into his car, of torching L Street. "Like I said," Carl taunts, "ask your daddy."

Carl hits a nerve with Nick by calling Joe Rinaldi "Daddy." The implication is that Nick is unable to take care of himself and must rely on his father to get by. Nick, of course, thinks he is rebelling against his father. Now, however, Nick confronts the truth of his past and present. In a rage, he grabs a ratchet and begins to smash the windshield of Carl's car. Inside the car, which is flooded with white light, Carl reaches for a gun. As Nick opens the door, Carl raises the gun and asks Nick if he is through. "Because if you're not," he says, "I'm going to blow your fuckin' head off." Sayles spots a red light on Carl's forehead, indicating the rage and willingness behind his threat.

Illuminating the scene with a variety of lighting sources, and the symbolic reds and blues, Sayles emphasizes his meaning. Many of the characters in this film hold secrets. Rizzo, for example, never tells his partner about the existence of his young son, because the child has a physical disability. The politicians heedlessly practice featherbedding and nepotism. Nick lies about his relationship with his own sister to Angela (Barbara Williams) to make himself look better. Sayles, clearly, wants to make a comment about America's tendency toward secrecy, a form of moral corruption that has trickled down from the top. The past, the history that torments Nick, is revealed to be more complex than he ever imagined, especially his father's own corruption. Sayles's mise-en-scène exposes the hidden side of an often ugly world. Nick's inchoate rage finally takes on meaning: He has been deceived his entire life. Yet he is powerless to do anything about his condition, except face the truth.

The antithesis of the nightmare, however, follows shortly. Nick, who injured his hand while trying to attack Carl, sits near a basketball court, thinking through all that he has learned. A man shoots baskets in the background. As his basketball rolls off the rim toward Nick, he asks for a "little help." Nick obliges. The ballplayer comments on Nick's hand. Nick looks down at it and says, "My life is messed up. This is nothing." Again, Sayles's mise-en-scène is configured with reds, whites, and blues. Unlike the previous sequence, the basketball scene is outdoors, in open form. The symbolic colors do not confine these figures; rather, the colors are spread evenly among the foreground, the midground, and the background, giving the shot balance, unity. Even though it is night, the diffusion of color suggests no threat. Briefly, there is a reconciliation between these Hudson City tribal representatives. Nick and the

African American basketball player talk about his brother. The basketball player remembers how quick Tony was "for a white guy." Nick mordantly replies, "Not fast enough." Their talk is urban, good natured, and friendly. In the hands of a less serious director, this sequence could be wrung out for every drop of sentimentality. These characters only talk for a moment. Sayles plays it straight. He uses this moment to release us from the violent action of the confrontation with Carl, to highlight the fact that people in America are not as far apart as they might think.

Mistakenly, critics focus on Nick as *City of Hope*'s protagonist, seeing the progression of the film as his story. Phillip Lopate, for example, writes that *City of Hope* is at its weakest centering "on young Nick, a drug-confused young man who is simply too much of a washout to carry the film" (12). In *Cineaste*, Leonard Quart, a strong supporter of Sayles's political themes, points out that "Nick's character just can't sustain the moral and social weight that Sayles has grafted to him" (45). But Nick represents old, corrupt Hudson City; he has not been able to release himself from his father's grip. Nick, then, is Wynn's opposite. Unlike the energetic, committed city councilman, Nick is enervated, confused. Ironically, both men are searching for hope, something to make their city a better place. Nick, who has been smothered by his father, does not understand how to bring about change; his good looks and family name have always been enough. Wynn, a college political science professor turned politician, wants to be a leader, a job, he discovers, that is more difficult to perform than achieve. Wynn, in fact, occupies a more important position than Nick, for he is working to improve the condition of his community. He is more focused, more goal oriented.

Taking responsibility is a fact from which there is no escape for both Nick and Wynn. Nick's response to the problem is always visceral, ill defined. Wynn, the more cerebral character, is an idealist who, in the end, sacrifices his values for political expediency. When *City of Hope* opens, Wynn seeks change through the political system, acting in a controlled, professional way, even though he disagrees with his political peers. Eventually, Wynn realizes that his struggle comes at a price. But unlike Nick, Wynn has the ability to make a change for the common good of his people. Wynn decides to become a less high-minded, more populist leader. He takes the first steps in playing the game of politics as it has been set up in America. Leonard Quart notes, "In *City of Hope*, there is no escape from interest group politics and maneuvering, but, for Sayles, some interest groups have greater justice than others in their claims on society" (45).

After Wynn fails to convince Joe Rinaldi to hire more minority workers on his construction job, he walks to the P Street Community Center, the heart of Hudson City's black and Hispanic community, to ask Levonne (Frank Fasion), a radical community activist, and Malik (Tom Wright), a recent convert to Islam, for help that evening at a city council meeting called to vote on a school bond issue. Wynn's reformist political views clash with the more radical ideals of Levonne and the doctrinaire Malik. Wynn leaves, looking for some other means of community support. But Wynn believes in the system and in his own ability to institute change by taking the higher ground. Wynn is rankled at the thought of nepotism, quid pro quo, and the political handouts that are the foundation of the politics of business as usual.

While the world of Nick, the cops, and the teenagers is bleak, Wynn represents the opposite end of the continuum. He is idealistic and optimistic, articulate and intelligent. Sayles's camera never captures him in the indicting high-key hot lamp. Instead, we see Wynn as a hard-working, diligent, committed councilman who is just a bit unsure about how to unify his constituency. Wynn works for the passage of the school bond issue, which the white majority on the council vetoes, helps the residents of L Street who lost their homes in the arsonist's blaze, and continually appeals to Levonne for greater community support. Wynn recognizes the type of polarization that economic abandonment breeds. As he says in his defense of the school bond issue, "You pay now or you pay later." Still, he loses more than he wins: The council votes against the school bond issue, no housing is set up for the victims of the arsonist's fire, and Levonne refuses to help the man he calls "Professor Oreo." Wynn then seeks outside help from his father figure, a retired African American mayor, Errol (Ray Aranha). In a mixture of cheerful anecdotes and stern declarations, Errol tells Wynn that power always wins out over moral integrity.

In a film ripe with savvy political observations, Wynn's trip to the golf course to speak with Errol sums up the hard truth of American politics: Always take the offensive, never retreat. This conversation on a golf course, the playing field of choice for the powerful and the elite, shows Sayles at his best. Errol, who tellingly plays alone, drives his golf cart around the course with glee. He is the only African American playing the game. Moreover, Errol tells Wynn that the course was once restricted — no blacks, no Jews, and no "undesirable elements." Errol, as he says, "sued the bastards" for the opportunity to play. Wynn innocently remarks, "It must have been hard to concentrate on your game." Errol corrects him: "I never played better." Metaphorically, Sayles calls attention to the fact that those in power, the elites, traditionally run roughshod over minorities.

Visually, the golf course allows Sayles to shoot the sequence, for the most part, in open form, indicating the relative freedom that Wynn has while listening to Errol, who splices his direct comments on American politics with observations on his golf game as he moves from tee to green with the anxious Wynn in tow. Here, a quiet day on the links becomes a lesson in political reality. Wynn learns to trim his notion of justice in order to play tough politics. In doing so, Sayles confirms that no matter which tribe is in charge, a corrupt system will always prevail.

For instance, Wynn is troubled by the story that Tito and Desmond told after they were arrested for mugging Les (Bill Raymond), the white jogger. The boys told the police that Les propositioned them as they sat in the park, so they beat him. Wynn suspects the story is a lie, and so does Errol. But the incident has serious political ramifications. The Hudson City police have used extreme force in the past when dealing with the African American community. If Wynn does not support the teenagers, Levonne will see to it that his political power base, as small as it is, will disappear. In Hudson City's overheated political climate, Wynn must voice his opinion, even though the incident has been blown wildly out of proportion.

For Sayles, the circumstances surrounding this incident play themselves out practically daily in our own media-saturated political environment. As he said to Gary Crowdus and Leonard Quart,

> Whether you're a black politician or a white politician, you have to have an opinion about this kind of thing.... Every time something happens now, the media calls Dinkins [the former mayor of New York City], they call D'Amato [the junior senator from New York], they call Spike Lee, and five other people who have to have an opinion, and they don't know shit about it. They weren't there, they haven't talked to the people in the neighborhood, and half the time they haven't talked to the cops yet. [4]

Rather than any effort to discover the truth behind an incident, the politics of race dominates the discussion. Of course, the painful irony of Sayles's fictional situation is that the minority voice must be heard and developed when the corrupt majority ignores the minority's concerns. When an opportunity presents itself, a leader takes it, which is the unsettling lesson the idealistic Wynn learns from Errol.

Errol slowly narrates how his own idealism was corrupted, effectively ending his reign as mayor. But, Errol says, approaching the green, "I had twelve years in office, which is a pretty good run." Wynn responds with disbelief, "So I should lie and hope for twelve good years?" Approaching his golf ball and lining up the putt, Errol replies with a smile, "This isn't the Old Testament, Wynn. People didn't vote you in so you could test your moral fiber." Sayles shoots this section of dialogue by cutting between the two players in shot-reverse shot, keeping them in separate frames, indicating their moral and philosophical division. The background also plays a prominent role here. The golf course is bright, full of green grass and trees, balanced by a clear blue sky, removed from the mean streets of Hudson City.

Still, the golf course signifies the world of dealmakers, and with little warning, the blithe golf outing turns sinister. The tone of Errol's voice changes from that of benevolent mentor to that of political realist. He turns to look at Wynn and says, "If you're going to be a leader, lead! Take it to the man every chance you get." Sayles cuts to Wynn, who answers with a touch of anger in his voice, "This is not about a fight with white people." Sayles's camera photographs Errol in full profile, the muscles in his jaw indicating anger, as he walks toward Wynn. Sayles uses the Steadicam to film Errol in motion. Errol obscures the background, effectively creating a closed shot. He walks right up to Wynn. Staying in closed form, Sayles has Errol deliver Wynn's political education directly: "It's always about that, Wynn. If it isn't, you're just another ward heeler. You don't defend anything, you attack what's wrong. That's what a leader is."

By compressing the visual space, created by using the moving camera instead of cutting between shots, Sayles emphasizes the tense situation. Wynn and Errol are both leaders of the African American community, albeit representing two generations, but they still have to abide by the system's political rules. The incident involving Tito, Desmond, and Les is mere political fodder, the sort of stuff that could get a man elected mayor if played well. Ultimately, Wynn registers his understanding. By constricting the physical space in the frame, Sayles shows us that Wynn has no options.

Sayles then returns to the cross cutting technique he used at the beginning of the sequence to release the tension brought on by Errol's explicit definition of American politics. Wynn quietly says, "Worked so hard to get on the damn council.... I never thought about..." Wynn's loss of articulation and subdued tone also indicate how his hopeful outlook has changed. Sayles shoots him in closed form, the Steadicam wrapping around him, which indicates that Wynn has little choice regarding his public statement as to the boys' credibility. If he wants to effect political change, truth becomes relative. Errol, on the other hand, has returned to his upbeat mood. Framed in a deep-focus shot, free from political entanglements, he stands ready to make a putt: "Can't know how you're going to play the green when you stood back at the tee, Wynn," he says. "You just figure it out when you get there." Sayles ends the sequence with Errol stroking his putt, smiling ear to ear. He understands the game.

Of the two central characters, Wynn learns the realities of Hudson City politics. Nick, who attempts a different type of search, never does. Wynn convinces Les to drop the charges against Tito and Desmond, even though he knows that Les's story is true. He then goes to the P Street Community Center and delivers a rhetoric-rich, rabble-rousing speech. The citizens of his district rally around him. Wynn then leads a citizens' march to confront the mayor, who is holding a political fund-raiser with the business community of Hudson City. Wynn has changed. He now understands that to play in the game of politics, where truth and integrity are secondary, it is more important to wield power than to adhere rigidly to principles. After interrupting the mayor's pro-business speech, Wynn, basking in the lights of television cameras, says, "I brought some concerned citizens. They've been looking for you, Mr. Mayor. Got a minute?" Mayor Baci stands at the lectern speechless.

Wynn confronts Hudson City's ruling class, its private profit center, with a united public community.

While Wynn confronts the atrophied political machine head-on, Nick is lost. Nick is feckless because of Hudson City, his father, and his past. Nick views Hudson City as corrupt, lacking possibility, without hope. Wynn, conversely, is trying to reconstruct his city. He sees hope, which is signified by his attack on the entrenched political system. Change, however, comes with a price, even for the politically idealistic. Wynn sacrifices the purity of his ideals and the truth for a chance at real political power.

Wynn's triumphant citizens' march bookends Nick's possible death. Because of jealous rage, Rizzo, drunk and off duty, shoots Nick. Even though Joe Rinaldi tried to keep Nick from going to jail by using all his political "juice," the code word for doing the power brokers a favor, which, in this case, meant agreeing to burn out L Street and then sell the property to the Galaxy Towers developers, Nick could not escape the city streets. Hudson City, then, represents more than a physical space. Leonard Quart complains that "Hudson City's physical texture — its streets, buildings, and neighborhoods — are never granted a distinctive character" (45). Sayles, however, shows the contemporary city as a form of currency, to be hoarded, divided, and controlled for private profit. It is a place of compromise, where honest thought is easily subsumed by a corrupt system. And it is the system, not a specific physical space, that Sayles examines in *City of Hope*. Joe tearfully admits as much to his severely wounded son during their attempt at reconciliation at the construction site: "All my life I thought that I was the one in control. I made sure I had the juice. I had all the angles. Jesus, I'm not in control of a damn thing." As Nick slumps to the floor, Joe realizes that he truly needs help. He shouts from the open facade of his building out across the night-shrouded city for help. Sayles's camera follows Joe's cries down to the street, where Asteroid, set off by a reddish circle of light, is shuffling along. He hears Joe's cries. Grabbing the high wire fence that surrounds the construction site to anchor himself, Asteroid listens for a moment, then begins an apoplectic shadow dance, mimicking Joe's desperate calls: "Help! Help! We need help."

Here, Sayles's mise-en-scène is oblique, an echo of his opening shot. The wire fence breaks up the already skewed frame, sectioning off the lower right-hand corner of the image. The fence metaphorically cuts off Joe and Nick from Asteroid, the one person who can help them. Sayles's camera lingers on the scene. We see a master shot of Asteroid dancing around in the ghostly red light, a dominant color found throughout the film which suggests anger and violence. He flails about, repeating Joe's words, a cry in the dark for both Nick and Hudson City.

Sayles ends *City of Hope* with this disturbing, ambiguous image because Hudson City remains a place fragmented, full of rifts that cannot be repaired without serious cooperation among all the urban tribes. Still, the title of the film, given the bleak cityscape depicted, must be seen as somewhat ironic. There are characters working toward a better city and a better life here. While Sayles clearly despises the cynical nature of American politics, his own populist philosophy has enough play in *City of Hope* so we are not left with a completely fatalistic view of our cities and, by extension, our lives.

For example, Jeanette (Gloria Foster) discovers that Desmond, her son, has lied about the incident in the park. She then reminds him that in order to live properly, you must stand up for what is right; that is, live honestly. After some screen time passes, Desmond finds Les, who is about to go jogging. He apologizes to Les by saying, "I know you are not a faggot." Les responds, "We've got a long way to go." Various critics have remarked that Sayles was appealing to sentimentality with conclusions such as these, wrapping his story up like a nineteenth-century novel. But this is a jaded response. When we juxtapose these small epiphanies with the fact that the big-money people in the film get away with all their schemes at the expense of the citizens of Hudson City, it becomes clear that the point Sayles is making is that ethical behavior will not come from above. If people are going to survive with integrity, they must make individual choices to live properly within an atmosphere of massive corruption. The common citizens are Hudson City's only hope. As a coda to his multiple endings, Sayles uses a song sung by Aaron Neville and the Neville Brothers Band, "Fearless," which is both melancholy and positive, an affirmation of the resiliency of the human spirit, not a celebration of corruption.

Sayles's crew is on full display in *City of Hope*. Most of the production team and many of the actors who worked on *Matewan* and *Eight Men Out*, among other Sayles films, are at work here. Sayles wrote the parts of Wynn and Nick specifically for Joe Morton and Vincent Spano, respectively. Sayles's script is full of memorable lines, which the actors deliver with energy and style. His actors, mostly members of an unofficial Sayles repertory company, all put their talent to solid use.

For instance, Bobby (Jace Alexander) and Zip (Todd Graff), a not-too-bright pair of rock 'n' rollers who supplement their incomes by committing burglaries for Carl, are the film's comedians, postmodern Bowery Boys. Arrested and in jail after the failed electronics heist, Bobby laments, "Maybe this is hell." Zip says, "No. If this was hell, my mother would be here, reading from *USA Today* about which foods are the most mucus producing when you have a cold. Compared to my house, this is Disneyland." Kevin Tighe plays O'Brien, who works to better himself, not enforce the law, with despicable charm. Barbara Williams turns in a solid performance as Nick's love interest, who understands that taking care of her son, going to school, working, and getting enough sleep are life's key ingredients. Angela Bassett plays Wynn's loyal wife. Sayles presents her in an uncharacteristic love scene that is private, romantic, and humorous (she experiences a foot cramp while making love to Wynn). In a brief cameo, Lawrence Tierney plays Kerrigan, the local Mob boss who backs Joe's construction job. He delivers a deliberately ironic version of trickle-down economics to Joe, so the builder can understand that he is powerless: "It's the way our society works, Joe. Ya got something good, first everybody on top of ya gets a taste. Then ya share what ya got left with everybody below ya. We're social animals. Human beings, not dogs." Once again, Sayles used talented actors he knew were reliable, and who could play the kinds of roles necessary to bring Hudson City to life.

Sayles filmed *City of Hope* for less than $5 million. Raising funding for the film proved not to be as difficult as with some of Sayles's previous projects. Perhaps Sayles's name recognition had something to do with this, but, according to Sarah Green, Maggie Renzi's coproducer, the story struck a chord with many of their backers. Each one, it seemed, could relate similar stories about the cities that they lived in. For additional funding, Sayles's production team also worked out a distribution deal with RCA/Columbia for the video rights. *City of Hope* was shot on a 30-day, five-week schedule, using 40 locations in Cincinnati, Ohio, where it was cheaper and easier to move around than in New York City or Hoboken, New Jersey.

City of Hope is a brilliantly designed, troubling film. But like *Matewan* and *Eight Men Out*, it did not fare well at the box office. Sayles could not have picked a worse time to release any of the films in his American historical cycle: They reflected none of the values of the Reagan administration, were left-leaning, and were written with story in mind, not empty action. *City of Hope*, however, suffered an even worse fate than its two predecessors, which does not diminish its importance artistically or intellectually. Sayles shows us a modern city based on greed, graft, dishonesty, corruption, racism, and confusion, emphasizing the evils of a tired system. Yet we also see compassion, honesty, and love, which suggests the possibility of hope. *City of Hope* is an urban collage, and an important American film. The film reminds us not to mistake the symptoms of social breakdown for the causes.

11

Passion Fish

> I was thinking about what people do when they think they're on
> one life path and then it all gets blown in another direction.
> — John Sayles, press release, 1992

Hollywood's publicity machine declared 1992 "The Year of the Woman."
Yet only one filmmaker with commercial name recognition actually made a
film about women: John Sayles. A small story focusing on the relationship
between two willful women who understand life's pain, *Passion Fish* (1992)
revisits the intimate, domestic milieu of *Return of the Secaucus Seven* and
Lianna. Its concise narrative revolves around the sort of characters we have
come to expect from Sayles: complicated, confused, funny, functioning adults,
not people prone to cheap sentimentality or cliché. In other words, real people. Set in Louisiana, *Passion Fish* also resonates with a deep sense of place,
adding a lyrical texture to the film.

Passion Fish tells the story of two headstrong women from distinct yet
similar cultural backgrounds: May-Alice Culhane (Mary McDonnell), a privileged white Southern woman who fled her rural home for an actor's life in
New York City only to have her television career cut short by a nasty accident; and Chantelle Blades (Alfre Woodard), a privileged African American
woman whose life never met the expectations of her stern physician father,
bottoming out in cocaine addiction.

The film opens after May-Alice, a fortyish soap opera diva, has been hit
by a taxi in New York City while on her way to have her legs waxed. She is
permanently paralyzed from the waist down. Sayles's credit sequence shows
her brief, tumultuous rehabilitation period. As the credits conclude, May-
Alice returns home to the bayou country of Louisiana, where she owns her
family's old plantation house, a place she could not wait to escape while growing up. Cut off from career, friends, and ambition, the home on the edge of
a cypress swamp cocoons May-Alice; she takes up a spot on the living room
couch to drink white wine and watch television, reveling with self-destructive, masochistic pleasure in her misery.

After May-Alice runs through a series of live-in nurses, establishing her-

174

self as a full-bore bitch, Chantelle arrives at the doorstep. True to form, May-Alice attacks her new nurse with the same tough, angry, self-pitying attitude that is her only resource. Chantelle, however, is her antagonistic match; she shares May-Alice's frustrations, though not her bellicosity, keeping her personal life hidden from plain view. *Passion Fish* chronicles this testy relationship, depicting how May-Alice and Chantelle learn to trust and work with each other, a hard task for two people used to concentrating on themselves.

Unfortunately, any short description of *Passion Fish* tends to make the film sound melodramatic. Indeed, the publicity blurbs for the film did it a great disservice by comparing *Passion Fish* to the overrated but commercially successful *Driving Miss Daisy* and *Fried Green Tomatoes*, two sentimental mainstream melodramas. By comparison, Sayles's characters are fully articulated. Here, Chantelle's story carries as much weight as May-Alice's; this is not just the boss lady's tale. Sayles explains: "To a certain extent, so many mainstream movies are just consumable items. They aren't things people can remember and apply to their lives" (Dreifus 33). *Passion Fish* presents life as it is lived, not as it is imagined by the movie industry. Sayles's realist aesthetic pumps life into all his characters, allowing them to speak in raw, educated, comic, and colloquial voices, and it was a project very much on his mind:

> I had been thinking about the movie for probably close to fifteen years. I had seen Ingmar Bergman's movie *Persona*, and I had worked with hospitals and visiting nurses and heard a lot of stories about their parents and their families. I have always felt that if I was going to make an American version of *Persona* it would have a white woman in a wheelchair and a black woman pushing her around, and it would be a comedy. [Johnson *Creative Screenwriting* 12]

Passion Fish, of course, is a typically rueful Sayles comedy, which addresses issues of class and race, and how people progress as human beings.

Passion Fish just begins, introducing us to May-Alice without warning, a device that works well because she is not somebody who engenders sympathy. In a hospital room, Sayles crosscuts between close-ups of her twitching hands and her eyes. Awake, she desperately reaches for the nurse's call button but instead turns on the television. She is transfixed by the televised image, no longer seeking a nurse's assistance. Panning from the hospital bed to the television, Sayles's master shot links May-Alice with the afternoon soap opera on-screen. We hear a voice coming from the television, as the camera slowly adjusts to her point of view: "It's all so strange. All I remember was that I wasn't happy. Was I?" The camera reveals the woman speaking on the television to be May-Alice, in her soap opera persona. With focused intent, she watches herself. The television camera shifts to a reaction shot from another actress in the scene. From her hospital bed May-Alice says, "That's my close-up. He gave her my fucking close-up." Cleverly, Sayles establishes her antagonism. Without even knowing what is wrong with May-Alice, we do not like her. She lives in a small, claustrophobic condition, completely unaffected by the world around her.

Quickly, Sayles depicts May-Alice's self-infatuation. She is more concerned with how she appears on television, the length of her shot, than why she is in the hospital. Her hubris is extreme yet artificial — her emotional life comes from a televised soap opera, a choice, Sayles points out, that many people make (Smith 62). Sayles films the entire opening sequence examining May-Alice in microscopic detail. Every other figure in the frame with her is cut off. We hear their voices, see hands and body parts, but we never see a complete picture of the people trying to help May-Alice. They represent impedimenta, not people. May-Alice dominates our attention, whether we want her to or not. Here Sayles cuts against the generic grain. For the most part, Hollywood films about people with disabilities want us to feel for the patients, participate in their struggle, share the joy of their recovery.

Sayles, however, lives in the real world, the foundation of his film aesthetic. The genesis for *Passion Fish* was a stint Sayles had as a hospital orderly. He became intrigued by the dynamics between caretakers and newly paralyzed people. May-Alice, Scarlett (a sly cinematic allusion) from the daytime soaps, is accustomed to being treated like a star; she is the focus of attention, not a paraplegic in recovery. Because she is no longer the person on television, no longer independent, May-Alice flees to the dark comfort of her Louisiana home.

Visually, *Passion Fish* is far less active than *City of Hope*, since *Passion Fish* focuses on two central characters, not a population cross section from a disintegrating city. This is not to say that *Passion Fish* is any less dynamic than Sayles's urban drama; instead, it requires a different visual composition, one that Sayles and his cinematographer, Roger Deakins, accomplish with grace and beauty. Using expanding deep focus shots, a less ostentatious mobile camera, multiple exposure montages, sequence shots, lyrical master shots, and Louisiana's physical environment for an exotic backdrop, Sayles brings a style to the screen that is completely different from that of any of his previous films, indicating his understanding of cinematic grammar. *Passion Fish* lacks the gritty texture of his earlier work, and the colors are robust and inviting. He also displays a poetic use of open and closed forms, to articulate the shifting conditions in his characters' lives.

Sayles establishes the major theme of *Passion Fish* early on. May-Alice lives in a tight, insulated world — there is not much beyond herself. For almost one-quarter of the film, she is photographed in closed form to capture visually her constricted world. We are made privy to May-Alice's psychology: She cannot come to terms with the fact that she has lost her livelihood, her legs, and her notoriety. She is, to paraphrase Andrew Sarris, a Nora Desmond for the soap opera crowd (*Film Comment* 30). Sayles understands the seductive power of illusions. During her escape from New York to Louisiana, May-Alice meets two of Scarlett's fans. While asking for her autograph, they address May-Alice as "Scarlett," telling her that she will make a marvelous comeback. The unreality of the situation is not missed by May-Alice, who fights back tears behind the screen of her black sunglasses. Sayles photographs her in close-up, trembling and afraid.

Sayles's mise-en-scène thematically expresses the claustrophobia May-Alice experiences. Unlike her adoring fans, "Scarlett" knows that the world she once knew has come to an end. The multiple exposure shot that concludes the credit sequence shows May-Alice's transition from television star hiding behind sunglasses to an angry paraplegic. Yet May-Alice refuses to do anything for herself in Louisiana, except drink and watch television, the place where she once existed as a star. This self-imposed isolation, however, feeds her antagonism. Sayles runs through a comic montage of caregivers. May-Alice does whatever she can to get rid of these women. Most of them, however, are in more emotional trouble than their employer; they just do not know it. These rapid scenes show Sayles at his comic best, a reminder of his witty B-genre scripts. From the Teutonic Drushka (Marianne Muellerleile) to Lawanda (Leigh Harris), whose biker boyfriend has to have the plate in his head adjusted from time to time, these characters make May-Alice's life even more miserable. Sayles films the interaction between these women exclusively in the living room, indicating the size of May-Alice's world.

Then Chantelle arrives. When we see Chantelle, unlike May-Alice, the mise-en-scène is open. Chantelle, however, is clearly overwhelmed by her surroundings. Sayles has said that there are many factors that could keep these women apart — race, power, class (although each comes from an upper-middle-class background). Chantelle is introduced as a figure out of place in the enormous world around her; on the other hand, May-Alice is suffocated by her world. But the one thing that draws these women together is need. Still, discovering their mutual want for friendship and love will take some time.

These are two smart, bruised people. Unlike the other live-in nurses, Chantelle has little to say. Finding May-Alice on the couch with the television playing, empty wine bottles on the coffee table, and rotten eggs hanging on the wall, Chantelle immediately comes under fire from her hung-over employer, who has wet herself over the course of a long night of drinking. Chantelle helps May-Alice into her wheelchair, for her new employer, alone for days, needs a bath. May-Alice says, "Ya got any problems, personal problems, I don't want to hear them." Sayles cuts to a shot of May-Alice resting in her bathtub, and she runs through a graphic list of her own personal problems. "All the things I can't do," says May-Alice, "you do for me." Chantelle, in other words, will be a virtual servant. Chantelle, who wears a permanent look of disgust, takes none of May-Alice's caustic malice. Feeling sorry for herself, May-Alice declares: "I can't have sex I can feel. Unless I get into blowjobs. Sorry, you're probably some big Christian and I just put my foot in my mouth." Chantelle responds directly: "It's none of my business what you put into your mouth, Miss Culhane." This first riposte, which is completely unexpected, reveals Chantelle's quiet strength and elicits a faint smile from May-Alice, prefiguring their relationship.

After this exchange, however, Sayles juxtaposes these two women in their separate yet mutual loneliness. Downstairs, May-Alice sits in her dark living room, drinking and channel surfing, a perpetual ritual. Upstairs, Chantelle sits on an unmade bed. Heavy-metal posters, Lawanda's remnants, hang limply from the walls, making her more out of place than she already seems. The doorway to her bedroom creates a constricted prosceniumlike masking of the frame, as if Chantelle were locked inside a detention cell. Sayles photographs her in a medium shot, in profile, staring at nothing. Only by the paroxysms of her body can we tell that she is crying. Then she begins to gasp for air, as if sucking on an oxygen tank. These shots link the two women. Sayles's mise-en-scène is closed, claustrophobic; there is no escape from the frame. Both Chantelle and May-Alice are confined, locked in. Chantelle's background, however, remains a mystery for three-quarters of the film, although Sayles's shot selection makes us aware of their emotional linkage long before his written narrative uncovers their complete stories.

Sayles's use of open and closed form in *Passion Fish* is masterful and thematically appropriate. In fact, it is not until Sayles opens up the frame that we begin to notice a change in May-Alice. Chantelle, in a no-nonsense fashion, forces May-Alice to begin physical therapy outside the house, because she wants her employer to take responsibility for herself. Chantelle wheels May-Alice outside, literally dragging her into the light, to the edge of the lawn, which ends at a bayou slough. Predictably, May-Alice refuses to work out, dropping a dumbbell to the grass, demanding that Chantelle take her back into the house. Chantelle leaves May-Alice to wheel herself from the lawn to the house. May-Alice complains, "It's uphill!" Chantelle yells back, "So's life."

Sayles uses a wide-angle lens to photograph this exterior shot. As Chantelle retreats, May-Alice's image dominates the foreground. She is obviously upset, but from fear, not anger. Oddly, May-Alice does not turn to shout at Chantelle, the appropriate gesture considering the circumstances. Instead, May-Alice stares with tear-swollen eyes at what lies in front of her. Her wheelchair rests just at the edge of the bayou, where the muddy, brown water laps at her property. Beyond her wooden boat dock, we see a green line of cypress trees, which mark the swamp, an area neither May-Alice nor Chantelle understands. Metaphorically, the horizon before May-Alice becomes a barrier that must be crossed if her world is to expand.

In contrast to other films that use Louisiana as a setting, such as Walter Hill's *Southern Comfort* (1981), Sayles does nothing to enhance the physical environment. Instead, he records the natural terrain. May-Alice's fear comes from this open, watery country, which represents her past and a wildness she cannot control; this is, after all, the place she fled after her mother and father died. Clearly, she fears being left alone again. When Chantelle returns a few hours later, May-Alice sits transfixed looking at the dimensionless landscape of the bayou. Notably, she does not scream at Chantelle. Something has happened to May-Alice; she talks about the water's texture, the jumping fish, and the herons in flight. Here, we experience a small epiphany. We see May-Alice come to terms with a vastness outside of herself; she has begun to move away from the unreality of television by investing time in the physical world that surrounds her and by extension her own life.

Early on, May-Alice's deserted family home evokes a purgatory for these women. Chantelle and May-Alice have to adapt to the bayou country. For May-Alice, this means coming to terms with a place she never wanted to see again. Chantelle's task is different. Arriving on May-Alice's doorstep, she looks out of place. Her hair is styled in thick, black cornrows, accented by stylish gold hoop earrings that add to the beauty of her face; her clothes are fashionable, and she is clearly a far cry from the other nurse attendants May-Alice has suffered through. Later in the film, we discover that Chantelle is from a stable, upper-middle-class neighborhood in Chicago. Louisiana, then, is new, foreign terrain.

Sayles deliberately chose Louisiana to countervail May-Alice's world of television culture and Chantelle's background. When Chantelle first arrives, her bus leaves her at the side of the road. The bus recedes into the background. Behind her, white petrochemical tanks and tall, thin smokestacks rise out of the landscape. Sayles cuts to her point of view, sweeping across the area directly in front of her. We see an unpaved, crushed shell road, a rusted, empty mailbox, and a single house removed from the main road. Sayles cuts back to Chantelle in a full shot. His camera lingers on her, standing alone in the wide, flat landscape, lost. This short sequence is a model of camera placement, camera movement, and visual comment. There are no flashy techniques at work here, just a sequence shot that thoroughly conveys Chantelle's anxiety about her condition through the images of this seemingly inhospitable place.

Sayles reprises the shot later in the film, when Chantelle's estranged father and her daughter, whom she has lost custody of because of her cocaine addiction, arrive for a visit. They too arrive by bus. The camera placement is identical. Here, however, Chantelle stands on the opposite side of the road. For a moment, she simply looks at her father and daughter. Then, her daughter breaks across the road to hug her mother. Chantelle's father stands rigid, looking at his daughter and granddaughter as they embrace. This silent master shot is accented by the stark, empty background and the placement of the actors, wordlessly commenting on Chantelle's struggle to come to terms with a new life in a new place, and the amount of space she still has to cover.

Louisiana's polyglot culture spices Sayles's narrative mix, adding energetic music, appealing cuisine, and backwater folklore. *Passion Fish*'s setting
was key for Sayles: "I had been trying to think of where it should be set,
because I wanted the place to be part of what drew the woman who was paralyzed out of her shell, and was traveling through Louisiana listening to
Zydeco and Rock and Roll. When I got to Cajun country I felt it was the
perfect place to set it" (Johnson *Creative Screenwriting* 12). Mason Daring's
score includes the traditional Cajun songs of D.L. Meynard and the Balfa
Brothers, the bluesy Creole zydeco of John DeLafose and The Eunice Play-
boys, and the reggae-inspired Loup Garou. Daring himself contributed only
one number, "La Dance de Mardi Gras," which is a new interpretation of a
traditional Louisiana bayou country arrangement. In the film, Sayles balances
Daring's piece with a more traditional version by the Balfa Brothers during
the journey Chantelle, May-Alice, and Rennie (David Strathairn) take into
the bayou. Musically, Sayles indicates May-Alice's transition from the old
country she did not take time to understand to her fresh appreciation for
Louisiana.

Only Daring's musical choice for the credit sequence seems to lie outside the influence of Louisiana. The long electric guitar notes he uses underscore May-Alice's condition early on; they are loud, aggressive, and not
particularly inviting. These searing guitar licks mark transition points in May-
Alice's rehabilitation rejection, leading us to her decision to return to
Louisiana. For the most part, the music Daring and Sayles use in *Passion Fish*
is boisterous, a musical form combining African percussion, French peasant
instrumentation, Mardi Gras Indian vocals, and Southern bluegrass fiddles,
along with washboards, accordions, and sexy, provocative lyrics, which blend
to create a truly original sound found only in Louisiana.

Food is an essential part of Louisiana living, and it does not escape
Sayles's eye. At a rollicking Cajun community social, he photographs a steaming pile of crawfish being lifted from pot to plate. You know without being
told that you are on the bayou. Sayles also uses food to inject humor into his
narrative. At one point in the film, Chantelle, who cannot cook, says to May-
Alice, "Is there a rule that all black people got to know how to cook?" Applying
her best overdone Cajun accent, May-Alice responds, "Darlin', down here
there's a rule that everyone got to know how to cook." And everyone seems
to. Rennie, who displays the casual ease of someone used to the backcountry,
says, "Bird eggs. Fish. Everything out here that flies, walks, hops, or crawls
got a use. It's all good eatin'." Sugar (Vondie Curtis-Hall), Chantelle's rakish
lover, takes her to lunch at the horse track where he works as a blacksmith.
Proudly, he tells Chantelle that she is eating Boudin, a Cajun rice sausage, that
he made himself. Chantelle, trying to keep the randy Sugar at arm's length,
says the food is "fine," another indication of her uncomfortable position.

Twice Chantelle has to go to the kitchen to prepare food for May-Alice's guests, and each time she fails miserably. Sayles uses these situations for some sly humor. When May-Alice's former high school acquaintances, Precious (Mary Portser) and Ti-Marie (Nora Dunn), two screwball Southern gossips, come to see May-Alice, not out of concern but out of curiosity, Chantelle serves them Campbell's tomato soup, a cardinal sin in Louisiana. After they abruptly leave, May-Alice congratulates Chantelle for using such a clever ploy to get rid of the two pests. But Chantelle, who does not understand food, is unaware of what she has done. Moreover, when May-Alice's costars from the soap arrive, Chantelle again finds herself lost in the kitchen. We see her trying to cut a tomato with two carving knifes, one to hold it steady, the other for slicing. At the end of the film, Sayles uses Chantelle's lack of dexterity in the kitchen as a release from dramatic tension and to underline the fact that these women have come to accept their place in the bayou country. With humor, May-Alice explains, "If we're going to stay, you have to learn how to cook."

Food, however, is more than just a comic device; it adds realistic detail to the everyday lives of these women. For example, as a gesture of reconciliation, May-Alice, who is too proud to apologize to Chantelle for yelling at her because Chantelle refused to buy more wine, makes an elaborate meal of okra gumbo and jambalaya. When Dr. Blades (John Henry Redwood) and Chantelle's' daughter, Denita (Shauntisa Willis), arrive, May-Alice prepares a traditional Louisiana meal, but she gives Chantelle the credit for cooking. Dr. Blades, who does not understand the linkage between life and food in Louisiana, responds, "We've never had a cook in the family." We know without being told that he has a cold heart, even though Chantelle has created misery for him. In *Passion Fish*, Sayles uses regional cuisine not as mere local color but to add authenticity to his characters and to comment on their lives.

For the most part, Sayles's films explore the lives of ordinary people, showing their struggles and their humanity. But in *Passion Fish* he goes one step further; this film reveals a spiritual connection to the land. Sayles's form of spirituality awareness has nothing to do with religion or God; instead, he shows how people can transcend their human flaws, the natural limitations we all have, by looking at the world around them. The lyrical journey into the bayou that marks the center of the film is a metaphor for May-Alice and Chantelle's relationship. But it is also about the poetic mystery of the swamp, including its folk traditions, the pleasure of discovery, and the restorative power of the physical world.

Rennie, who grew up on the bayou, guides May-Alice and Chantelle into the watery backcountry. Chantelle is clearly uninterested in the flat, hot, wet landscape. May-Alice, on the other hand, revels in the wilderness. Sayles uses a multiple exposure montage to illustrate both the beginning of their journey and the end; in between they stop for lunch on an island named Misère, the isle of misery. Sayles uses the montage to indicate May-Alice's point of view. Here, May-Alice has just begun to take stock in the people and the place around her. Although she has been photographing the bayou from her dock, the journey inside this exotic landscape is a revelation: The land teems with life, a direct contrast to her static house. Sayles's overlapping images indicate May-Alice's reinvigoration, a renewal that takes place in a primeval world, far from the constricted vision of a soap opera. We see May-Alice reacquaint herself with what she had once known but chose to forget.

Sayles, of course, is not prone to "New Age" whimsy; he keeps his story grounded in reality. Chantelle, for example, is constantly on the lookout for snakes, which balances the sequence, keeping it from becoming overwrought with romantic sentimentality. In addition, to keep mosquitoes away, Rennie covers the women's legs with mud. But the lyrical mystery of the swamp, the sense of place that May-Alice clearly sees with fresh eyes, is never far away. Rennie, the Cajun "coonass," represents regional culture. As folklorist Suzi Jones points out, "People share a body of folklore because they live in a certain geographical area; their geographical location is the primary basis for a shared identity that is expressed in their lore, and they themselves are conscious of their regional identity" (107). May-Alice, of course, wanted nothing more than to escape Louisiana. Earlier in the film, she snidely tells Louise (Maggie Renzi), her physical therapist, that she paid thousands of dollars to get rid of her accent. Rennie and the environment change that attitude.

Rennie is laconic, friendly. He makes his living doing odd jobs, such as building May-Alice a badly needed ramp for her wheelchair. Like any real character from the backcountry, Rennie has a depth of knowledge that is prodigious yet understated. Strathairn captures this country stoicism beautifully. For example, Rennie communicates all we need to know about his wife when he says, "She got religion between the second and third babies. She got the kids in with her now. They pray for me a lot." Strathairn's quiet delivery tells us that Rennie bears life's difficulties with acceptance, not angst. Traveling on a boat at night in the mysterious bayou, Chantelle inquires, "Now are we lost?" Rennie replies, "No matter where you are, there you is." It's a response that does not sit well with the woman from Chicago, but clearly defines the easygoing Rennie, who understands life's travails and takes pleasure in the sanctuary the bayou affords, an awareness that does not need to be explained for those who know. It is Rennie's easy charm that attracts May-Alice, rekindling an old flame, and reminding her that rural Louisiana has qualities that she let herself neglect for too long. When Rennie enters May-Alice's world, her appreciation for life blooms. Rennie, then, is an important narrative catalyst. With Chantelle's presence and the possibility of seeing Rennie more often, May-Alice comes to understand that Louisiana is where she belongs.

A major theme of *Passion Fish* is the need for place in people's lives. In fact, the title of the film is wholly regional. As they watch a great blue heron take off from its perch on a tree, Rennie tells the women that his father held

Women figure prominently in most of Sayles's films; he is a feminist filmmaker. In Passion
Fish *(1992), Chantelle (Alfre Woodard, center) and May-Alice (Mary McDonnell)—pictured with Rennie (David Strathairn)—are among his finest creations. Both women are
damaged, yet they are strong, intelligent, resilient, and feminine. Like most of Sayles's female
characters, they are complex individuals. Photo by Bob Marshak.*

to the superstitions of Cajun culture, recalling how he once marveled at seeing one of those birds carrying a two-foot mud snake; for his father, this was
a sign of bad luck. As he explains to May-Alice, "Everything meant something to him. He had all them coonass superstitions. Catch somethin' in his
traps, whatever it was — turtle, gator, opossum — he'd cut open the stomach.
See what was inside. Tell the future." When Rennie stops the boat at Misère, he catches a fish for lunch. Sayles's camera watches in close-up as he guts
the fish, squeezing two smaller fish from the egg sack. Rennie calls these "passion fish," telling the women to squeeze the fish while "thinking about somebody you want some lovin' from." Chantelle responds, "You makin' this shit
up, right?" Rennie tells her that it is an old Cajun tradition; indeed, some of
his people say "that you gotta swallow them raw." Chantelle hands her fish
back, saying, "I don't need it that bad." Sayles adroitly fuses a sense of folk-
loric wonder while balancing it with his dry wit. Even Sayles's odd title suggests Louisiana — local custom defines the "passion fish," and by wishing on
them, the holder will find true romance. Of course, emotional ballast is exactly
what both of these women need.

Their return trip is photographed at night, giving the sequence a sense
of the fantastic. The cyclopean spotlight on Rennie's boat captures glimpses

of owls and alligators; it cuts the slick, black water, adding color and texture to the strange beauty of the swamp at night, a place, according to Rennie's God-fearing wife, where Satan lives because the trees do not grow straight. Clearly, May-Alice loves this wilderness. In one particular shot, Sayles focuses his camera on a cypress branch dripping with blanched Spanish moss. The branch blurs as May-Alice's profile comes into the frame, approximating the movement of the boat. The shot serves to link May-Alice to the natural world. The artificiality of her soap opera existence has completely faded. The bayou journey provides *Passion Fish* with a thematic as well as a structural center. Exploring the physical world metaphorically represents the chance both of these women have to look at life anew. The nighttime boat ride has what Sayles describes as an "otherworldly, lyrical thing going on" (Smith 64), which is abstract and stylistically distinct from most of the rest of the film.

Reinforcing the notion that May-Alice can live without her television life, Sayles introduces May-Alice's friends from her soap opera days. At this point, May-Alice, who has been forced to quit drinking by Chantelle, is emotionally strong enough to have visitors. Like her high school friends, who served to point out the cultural rift between May-Alice and her home, Dawn (Angela Bassett), Kim (Sheila Kelly), and Nina (Nancy Mette) also contrast with May-Alice's new life. These women, especially Kim and Nina, are so involved in their soap opera world that fact and fiction blend with delightful consequences, allowing Sayles to poke fun at ersatz acting methods and overzealous actors.

Nina has taken over May-Alice's role as Scarlett on the soap. She proudly announces, "I'm pregnant!" May-Alice tells her to have a seat, rest. It is, of course, Scarlett who is pregnant, not Nina. "But," responds May-Alice, "I had a hysterectomy." Nina says, "Oh, I'm sorry." "No," says May-Alice, "not me, Scarlett." Then the soap opera story, which bounces around for the sake of ratings, becomes even more bizarre, with a space alien playing the role of Scarlett's love interest, a convenient device allowing the scriptwriters to work around Scarlett's hysterectomy. Thankfully, May-Alice admits that she has not been keeping up with the program.

Like May-Alice's high school friends, the soap opera women mistakenly think that Chantelle is May-Alice's servant. After this blunder, Kim, switching gears, tries to describe the Southern environment, searching for adjectives to illustrate her feelings. "May-Alice," she says, emoting for her audience, "this country is so, it's so laden, you know ... the atmosphere ... it's..." In a wry jab at bad acting, Sayles shows us how hard it is for this woman to speak without a script. Kim tries to sum up the land in a single word, *fecund*, which diminishes the land and its history. As the sequence continues, Sayles photographs Kim whirling around near a tree, reciting a deliberately florid paean to May-Alice's ancestral place. May-Alice, who has clearly seen enough bad acting, explains, "I've had enough of that Gothic shit." The bayou, as Sayles has shown us, holds a mystery all its own, an ineffable quality that cannot be put into words. Kim does not understand where she is or why she is there. All of her experiences come from television scripts.

Still, these soap opera stars take their work seriously. In a clever, humorous parody of the process of screen testing, acting, and directing, Sayles has Nina recall her first real audition, for a "zero-budget" horror film "about people taken up into spaceships and given physicals against their will." As Kim tells the others that she will be leaving the lucrative world of soaps to go into real theatrical acting, a line they have all heard or uttered themselves, Nina says, "I didn't ask for the anal probe." The other women are mystified by her odd statement. She then goes on to recount her first screen test, which proved to be a success — she got a part. When the script arrived, Nina discovered that she had only the anal probe line — a small letdown, but Nina was determined. She created background for her character, asked her boyfriend to help her with sense memory, and waited for her big-screen opportunity, an event that proved anticlimactic. Facing an empty chair, Nina recalls how the director wanted her to speak the line in a variety of "colors," which she does, repeating the line over and over in a variety of tones and voices.

The scene is both comic and sad. Indeed, Sayles calls it "a metaphor for life, and limitations" (Smith 62). This scene is thematically deliberate, a bit theatrical, but not overdone. As Sayles related to Tod Lippy, "The character is basically talking about the theme of the movie: 'I got a raw deal, and I didn't ask for it. But what did I do? I acted like a professional, and found different ways to attack it'" (193). During this long take, Sayles's camera slowly, almost imperceptibly, zooms in on Nina. Her humiliation and sense of letdown are extreme yet balanced by her recollection, which is solid and to the point, a fine bit of acting. As viewers, we wonder how she could have subjected herself to such circumstances. Still, acting is her world, her life. Sayles captures the moment in all its natural clarity. In the world of contemporary film editing, a scene this long would never have been allowed to play itself out. But the scene is quintessential Sayles: The language is real and poignant, the camera takes us to the actor, and he allows the scene to play without interference from the editing table.

Sayles receives splendid support from his cinematographer, Roger Deakins, who has worked with the Coen brothers and David Mamet, among other filmmakers. Like Robert Richardson, Deakins is adept at moving cameras but is not as baroque. Sayles uses Deakins's talents throughout *Passion Fish*, adding more dynamic involvement to the narrative. Deakins has a solid visual style. His photography of the Louisiana landscape and backcountry richly displays his considerable skill. Having shot *Mountains of the Moon*, *Pascali's Island*, and *The Secret Garden*, all films primarily shot outdoors, Deakins understands how to photograph the natural world. Here, he carefully makes the visual elements striking, although not overly lush. The Spanish moss is gray, not emerald green. The water in the sloughs Rennie navigates is brown, uninviting. May-Alice's house is dark, but not Gothic.

But when beauty is called for, Deakins delivers. For instance, the dream sequence between May-Alice and Rennie lyrically captures her fulfillment and frustration. In her dream, May-Alice, who puts her loss of sexual ability in graphic, concrete terms throughout the film, finds herself suddenly liberated. She walks from the edge of the dock to where Rennie is working with his fishing nets. May-Alice lowers herself into Rennie's lap. Deakins's camera wraps around them as they embrace and kiss, making the scene even more intimate. Andrew Sarris called this scene "the most sweetly erotic movement of flesh toward flesh in any movie of 1992" (*Film Comment* 30). But May-Alice's pleasure is momentary. In the background someone calls her name. Looking up, she sees Chantelle and a young girl at the edge of Misère, waving and shouting, a cut that breaks her erotic reverie. Deakins photographed this portion of the sequence early in the morning, capturing the mist rising from the still water, to approximate the hazy quality of a dream and to wash away the real erotic impulse of May-Alice's subconscious. We then return to real time, and May-Alice awakens, back on her couch, in a room with the windowshades drawn, signifying her actual condition. Once again, Sayles found a cinematographer with the ability to enhance his writing through a camera lens.

Unlike most commercial feature films, *Passion Fish* focuses on the friendship between two women in complete dramatic accuracy. The film fits Molly Haskell's categorical definition of what the better women's films aspire to:

> They take the woman out of the plural into the singular, out of defeat and passivity and collective identity into the radical adventure of the solitary soul, out of the contrivances of puritanical thinking into enlightened self-interest. [162]

While Chantelle and May-Alice have separate, distinct lives, they are not completely singular. They form a community of two that is hardly utopian but it functions. In order to gain an understanding of one another, May-Alice and Chantelle fence with words. Over all their verbal bantering, these women come to appreciate each other. They combine sensitivity, wit, and toughness. But this mutual respect is earned. Chantelle is always hiding her murky past from May-Alice. May-Alice enjoys her role as demanding bitch. A small exchange between employer and employee typifies their relationship. Waking up hung-over, May-Alice says, "I kind of gross you out, don't I?" Chantelle answers, "Is this a trick question?" By not succumbing to pat Hollywood formulas — there are no big climaxes here — Sayles created two ordinary people who open up and evolve slowly into two emotionally rich people during the course of the film.

While the acting is superb, what makes these characters so exceptional is Sayles's writing. His level of realism never seems contrived or staged. We see and hear real people talking, swearing, and yelling. There is always a subtle power shift at work between the two women —first one, then the other seems to be in control. In the film's most explosive scene, May-Alice, who has been making an effort to stop drinking, confronts Chantelle in the kitchen; she is desperate for a bottle of wine. The scene starts off slowly. Chantelle softly says that she has thrown all the bottles away. May-Alice begins to lose her temper, reminding Chantelle that she hired her and that she wants her to get some wine. Again, Chantelle quietly refuses. Quickly, the tension escalates. May-Alice yells at Chantelle as if she were a common servant. Chantelle yells right back, exploding at the imperious May-Alice, calling her selfish, demanding, and impossible. Then, just as quickly, the scene ends, with May-Alice alone in her wheelchair, surrounded by the fragments of the dishes she has smashed in anger.

May-Alice and Chantelle are not stylized women. They display a complete range of feelings. Their anger is true, but they are also funny, and endearing, not mawkish. Whatever respect we give these characters, they earn it. Obviously, Sayles did not set out to make a 12-step feel-good movie-of-the-week. Whatever injuries their self-destructive behavior has caused these women, they are living with their choices. They are not victims; they are trying to figure out how to keep living, even though that choice means struggle. In other words, these woman are atypical film characters.

By interacting with the other characters, both May-Alice and Chantelle confront their own histories in order to proceed with their lives. Knowledge of the past is fundamental to many of Sayles's narratives, particularly *Passion Fish*. Each woman is trapped in what seems to be a dead end by different circumstances: May-Alice's accident and attitude, Chantelle's cocaine addiction and separation from her daughter. Neither anticipated ending up in the backwaters of Louisiana. Yet, because of the people they meet and the place in which they find themselves, May-Alice and Chantelle begin to come to terms with their past lives and each other. In other words, they are granted a second act, as Sayles makes clear:

> That's where *Passion Fish* ends: These two people have fucked up in a way. They're about to embark on a second life. So what they've done with adversity is to say, "Okay, I'm not going to roll in a ball and lie in front of the TV set drinking. Or I'm not going to go back to drugs. With reduced expectations, I'm going to throw myself into this second life." [Smith 62]

Typically, Sayles presents a fully articulated cast of characters from different races, different classes, and different generations. All the players grafted to the central story leave their mark, no matter what the duration of their screen time. Some of these characters provide Sayles's narrative with an indelible sense of the past, which helps to fashion both May-Alice's and Chantelle's history. For example, Reeves (Leo Burmester), May-Alice's uncle, recalls her father as headstrong and imperious; obviously, his daughter's father. He delivers the story of the death of May-Alice's parents with an acid-tinged Southern gentility. His disgust for his brother is undisguised. May-Alice's father died because of his own willfulness, a trait that also drove her from his home. Burmester plays this role with understated zest, every movement indicating his world-weary ennui. His performance stands out among the minor characters.

Likewise, Tom Wright, who plays Luther, Chantelle's cocaine-addicted boyfriend, leaves a mark as he fills in Chantelle's mysterious background. In his scene we see May-Alice taking pictures of the bayou. Luther steps into the frame, metaphorically obscuring the future as a glimpse of the past. Wright's body movement undermines Luther's hard, urban facade. We know that this guy is in trouble; he nervously shuffles about, with the characteristic tics of an addict. He needs Chantelle yet cannot burden her with his crippled presence. His words are clipped and staccato. Wright make us believe that we are seeing the remains of Chantelle's past, a man trapped by drug addiction.

While May-Alice is learning about Chantelle, Chantelle is learning about "Sugar" LeDoux, one of Sayles's more colorful characters, played with swaggering enthusiasm by Vondie Curtis-Hall. Sugar's role parallels that of Rennie. Like May-Alice, Chantelle seeks some kind of romance in her life. Living a humdrum existence as May-Alice's nurse, however, and fearing a return to her irresponsible ways prohibits any type of relationship. In addition, Chantelle is skeptical of men, especially a ladies' man like Sugar. The much-married Sugar, however, is different. He embraces life in his work, music, and overt sensuality. Sugar proves to be tender, understanding, and steady, all traits that make Chantelle's new life tolerable.

Curtis-Hall displays remarkable range, and he typifies the kind of actor Sayles likes: someone who is comfortable on screen or stage, willing to work for a small salary, and able to create an honest character. As an actor, Curtis-Hall has appeared as the Cuban band arranger Miguel Montoya in *The Mambo Kings*, as a barfly in Jim Jarmusch's *Mystery Train*, and as an African expatriate in *Coming to America*. Here, he is undeniably charming as the raffish, life-loving blacksmith. In a clever scene in the horse paddock, Sayles has Sugar describe his wives and his children. His daughter Albertine (Jennifer Gardner) helps him recall the names of his newest kids, as he takes a horse's hoof between his legs to shoe it. Chantelle is nonplussed, remarking that he is just like people in the movies. He says, "I'm a blacksmith." Chantelle says under her breath, "You're a black something, all right."

The three principals are excellent. David Strathairn, acting in his sixth Sayles film, again delivers a performance so natural that it is hard to believe he is acting. In fact, it is hard to think of Strathairn as the disconnected Asteroid from *City of Hope*, which indicates the talent of this underappreciated

Vondie Curtis-Hall (left) and Alfre Woodard in Passion Fish *(1992). Writing in a 1996 issue of* Cineaste, *Cliff Thompson defined John Sayles's ability to create realistic African-American characters: "Virtually alone among black movie characters, who are largely either walking history lessons (*Glory *or* Malcolm X*), second-banana types whose jobs are to marvel at the daring of white heroes (*Die Hard *with a Vengeance or the* Lethal Weapon *series), or nameless, small-time criminals (you name it), blacks in John Sayles's movies are what real blacks know themselves to be: flesh-and-blood people" (32). Sayles has called himself a conduit for voices, and his ability to cross race, class, and gender lines is unequaled among contemporary filmmakers. Photo by Bob Marshak.*

artist. Sayles once remarked that Strathairn's physical dexterity is comparable to Steve McQueen's. Like McQueen, Strathairn communicates a raw masculinity, bringing an ease to his film work, a natural, unactorish ability that is poised, controlled. In *Passion Fish*, he is always doing some task that gives his character believability — pounding nails, fishing, or just slapping his hat to his knee. Usually these are small, easily missed gestures. For example, as he steers his boat into the swamp, we see him quietly whistling while playing with a wild flower. Each unemphatic gesture serves to indicate Rennie's quiet, peaceful charm.

Sayles wrote the part of May-Alice with Mary McDonnell in mind. For her work, she received an Academy Award nomination for best actress. In order to prepare for the part, McDonnell did physical and emotional background work, visiting with physical therapists and paralysis patients. An actress at home in film or theater, McDonnell has acted in *Dances with Wolves* (1991), *Grand Canyon, Sneakers,* and *Matewan.* Her best scenes are often silent. For example, when she attempts, in vain, to get her body to respond sexually to touch while cloaked in the darkness of her deserted living room, with only the flickering eye of her constant companion, the television, bearing witness, she produces real emotion. McDonnell also conveys May-Alice's nastiness well; she is easy to hate. Still, she shows us the cost of pride and independence. May-Alice's appearance is unadorned, plain, not glamorized in any way. The closest she comes to a love scene with Rennie is quiet, creating heart-felt sentiment. At the Cajun community social, she says, "Rennie, you don't have to have a job or something to fix to come out and visit." He says, "Yeah, well, I'll do that then." She adds, "Do it real soon." These are two people who find each other after too many years and too many mistakes. Even though Rennie is below May-Alice socially, she now sees what we have seen in him from the beginning — an attractive, sweet man. As Caryn James points out, "A complex fabric of influences come together in the scene — sexual need, the difficulty of communication, the fear of rejection, class barriers — yet none of them are expressed directly" (11). The scene shows us how two talented actors work.

Of all the performances in *Passion Fish*, however, Alfre Woodard's is most striking. She plays her role with gusto, making Chantelle nasty, kind, and sexy, a complete, complex, unique woman. The personal touches Woodard brings to her role are remarkable, her comic timing is excellent, and the acidity she adds to her lines gives Sayles's language multiple meanings. Woodward's film credits include *Grand Canyon*, *Remember My Name*, *Health*, and *Crooklyn*. Like all good actors, Woodard does not tell us she is acting; she is Chantelle. In the beginning, Woodard keeps Chantelle in check. Of course, because of the early bedroom shot, we know that she is holding a secret. But like her smiles, her tears are not on public display. She plays it tough. At the community social, when Sugar leaves the bandstand to ask her to dance, Chantelle communicates the presence of her strict father with just her eyes. Sugar catches the cue and asks Chantelle's bespectacled little girl to dance instead, which, as Andrew Sarris says, takes "this musical tableau into the emotional stratosphere" (*Film Comment* 30). The silent exchange between Curtis-Hall and Woodard exhibits the professional strength of these two talented actors. For her work, Alfre Woodard received the Best Supporting Actress Award from Independent Feature Project/West, the largest nonprofit group of independent filmmakers in the nation, which is rapidly becoming a hipster's version of the Academy Awards organization.

Passion Fish just ends, leaving May-Alice and Chantelle floating on the bayou water. We know that they will stay in Louisiana and that they are "stuck with each other." They have learned to live together. May-Alice will not return to the soap opera world in New York, and Chantelle will continue on for now as her nurse. What makes this moment in the film so special is that it ends too soon. Sayles has paced this film with a languid quality that fits the characters. *Passion Fish* shows the lives of two ordinary, yet exceptional women. Their lives are so rich, so complicated as to be real.

Sayles used his production team, loose ensemble of actors, and ability as a director and a writer to create an emotionally charged film about women's lives, free from melodrama, superfluous action, and an overly dramatic climax. In other words, he examines adult problems with adult eyes. *Passion Fish* is a small, intimate film full of personal observations. After seeing this film, Andrew Sarris, not always a strong supporter of Sayles's work, wrote, "Sayles has directed, written, and edited the most accomplished, the most nuanced, and most lyrical English-language movie of the year" (*Film Comment* 30).

12

The Secret of Roan Inish

> I think that magic realism has to do with telling a story that is not
> literally true; it's not literally possible. It may have elements of fan-
> tasy to it, but it actually gets to deeper truths than you might by
> documentary means.
> — John Sayles (*Charlie Rose* interview, 1995)

Stories lie at the heart of every John Sayles picture, but *The Secret of Roan Inish* (1995), his ninth feature film, stresses the power of storytelling. Sayles structures the film's narrative around a group of interconnected stories — some mythic, some oral history — told to Fiona Coneelly, an independent ten-year-old who, as she searches for her lost brother, connects with forces of nature conspiring to return her family to their rightful home, Roan Inish, an island off the west coast of Ireland. These stories link many generations of Coneellys and reveal "deeper truths" about the clan's connection to Roan Inish and its environment. The stories intertwine like braids, convincing Fiona that the remaining Coneellys must return to Roan Inish. *The Secret of Roan Inish* is Sayles's most poetic film, weaving oral stories with stunning visual composi-tions to reveal the magic possibility of an ordinary world.

The Secret of Roan Inish presents two new creative directions for Sayles: This is his first picture shot outside the United States, and it is his first chil-dren's story. It is also a screen adaptation, something Sayles usually avoids in his own filmmaking. The movie's complicated narrative, however, is clearly designed to appeal to adults as well. Maggi Renzi introduced Sayles to his source material, *Secret of the Ron Mor Skerry*, a novel by the recently deceased British writer Rosalie K. Fry, which revolves around a young girl's encounter with "selkies" (seal people). Renzi believed that Fry's book, long out of print, could be made into a movie. Sayles decided to adapt the story for a simple reason: "I've always liked stories of children raised by animals" (Holden "In a Departure..." 13). Yet Renzi revealed in Skerry Movies' production notes that Sayles took some convincing: Even though he liked the book he found it "rather slight" (Skerry Movies Corp. 2). Before starting *City of Hope* (1991), Sayles asked Renzi to research the book's screen rights. Even though Fry had published 52 books, she was not especially well known; it took the production team six months to locate Fry, and another year to secure the rights to *Secret of the Ron Mor Skerry* (Skerry Movies Corp. 9).

Renzi, however, was undeterred, determined to prove the book's integrity and relevance. She field-tested it on friends' kids and a grammar school class in Massachusetts (Skerry Movies Corp. 2). She discovered that the children were moved by the idea of a lost sibling: "This compulsion to look for your little brother really belongs to kids ... siblings are the important companions with whom they share their day-to-day lives" (Skerry Movies Corp. 3). Moreover, Renzi believes that adults are also interested in stories that revolve around early childhood: "I think tapping into your childhood is generally a good idea but some people need to be reminded of that. I am sure that's why we love to see Cillian [Byrne], who plays Fiona's lost brother, tearing across the beach; his delirious sense of freedom is so affecting because we know we can never be that carefree again. It's good to spend time with children" (Skerry Movies Corp. 3). Indeed, Renzi and Sayles are friends with and serve as a surrogate aunt and uncle team to an expanding circle of children and young adults, so they felt an obligation to make a solid movie for them. Children, according to Renzi, are an underserved audience.

For his screen adaptation, Sayles fleshed out the history of the Coneelly clan, using two flashbacks, including one about the mythological selkie woman, which help explain the Coneellys' connection to Roan Inish and the natural world. The selkie legend is Celtic in origin. It tells of a creature who can be either a seal or a woman: A man captures the seal skin of a selkie who has transformed into human shape, claiming her for his own; she bears him many children, mixing the blood of man and beast. But one day she finds her seal skin, transforms back into a sea creature, and returns to the sea, her true home. Although Sayles left the spine of Fry's plot intact, the beauty of his retelling lies in the visual descriptions, the moody atmosphere, the garrulous people, and the wondrous happenings that surround Fiona, all combining to create a cinematic tapestry quite unlike any other Sayles has constructed.

Sayles's tale unfolds with an unhurried grace, much like a spoken story. Set in Ireland in 1949, *The Secret of Roan Inish* revolves around ten-year-old Fiona Coneelly (Jeni Courtney), sent by her widowed father, a laborer who lives in an industrial, oppressive city, to live with her grandparents, Hugh (Mick Lally) and Tess Coneelly (Eileen Colgan), on the west coast of Ireland. From their cottage, Roan Inish (Gaelic for Seal Island) can be seen in the distance but only by those who know it well. It has been three years since the Coneellys abandoned Roan Inish. Through a series of stories told by several people, Fiona hears her family's compelling history. Fiona connects the film's desperate characters, binding them to their history and their land. We experience everything though her eyes, ears, and imagination. Sayles's narrative places demands on the audience, who must listen as carefully as Fiona to assemble the magical story of the Coneellys.

The film opens with a silent shot of a fishing boat coming toward the camera, which sits just above the water line; this shot presents a seal's point of view. The sea creature floats just on the top of the water, watching the approaching boat, which carries Fiona. The seal then dives into the water. Sayles's camera cuts to another perspective, closer to the passing boat. We see Fiona, a pale, thin, blonde child, quietly standing on the deck of the boat; she is reserved, yet with a trace of melancholy in her soulful brown eyes. She looks directly into the camera. Sayles reverses the shot, and we see a seal resting on a rock from Fiona's perspective. Visually, then, Sayles reveals the secret of Roan Inish from the start of the film: Fiona and the seals share a vital link. As the narrative develops we come to understand why.

Fiona arrives at her grandparents' home, and they all discuss the city and the jobs that drew the younger Coneellys away from Roan Inish and the life of the sea. Hugh says, "Ah! City indeed. Nothin' but noise and dirt and people that's lost their senses. Couldn't tell the difference between a riptide and a raindrop if you shoved their face in the water." For Tess, the island remains a sad memory. From the cottage window, Hugh points out Roan Inish to Fiona. He is pleased when she sees the island, a sliver of green on the endless blue horizon. Eamon (Richard Sheridan), a cousin, arrives and hints at the mystery of Roan Inish — tales of lights seen at night. It is a place the other fishermen fearfully avoid, even though Hugh always fills his nets fishing its shoals.

That night, Hugh tells Fiona the first of many stories about her ancestors; this one explains how his great-grandfather, Sean Michael, an independent Irishman forever at odds with British rule, kept the Coneelly name alive after escaping a drowning death at sea during a storm that killed all the other male members of the clan. According to the tale, Sean Michael was saved by a seal, which plucked him from the raging sea and carried him safely to shore. Found unconscious on the beach by a group of women, Sean Michael was revived by a series of ancient methods, including being placed between two cows to restore his body temperature. Later that night, unable to sleep, Fiona stares out the window in the direction of Roan Inish, where she sees the mysterious light. "The light!" she whispers in wonder.

The next morning, Fiona asks Hugh about the day the Coneellys evacuated Roan Inish, the day Jamie, her infant brother, was lost, washed out to sea in his wooden cradle. As Hugh recalls the day for her, Fiona imagines the gulls and the seals collaborating to steal Jamie away, making him their own. Later, at the quay, Eamon tells Fiona that there are stories of Jamie being sighted near Roan Inish floating on the sea in his cradle, sitting upright in the stern like a miniature sailor. Excited by these tales, Fiona persuades Hugh to take her to Roan Inish when he goes fishing. Alone on the island she explores one of the abandoned cottages and discovers traces of life: fresh ferns on the bed, hot embers in the fire. Later, strolling on the beach, she sees small footprints in the sand, which are quickly washed away by the tide.

The following day Fiona meets Tadhg (John Lynch), another cousin, one of the "dark" Coneellys, labeled "daft" by the locals. He also has a tale for Fiona, the story of Liam Coneelly, who centuries ago made an intimate connection with the natural world, which lingers forever in the Coneelly blood. When the Coneellys first arrived on Roan Inish, according to Tadhg, the "seals and birds moved aside to make room for them." Walking on the beach one day, Liam, a loner even among his own, saw a selkie transform into a woman by shedding her seal skin, which he claimed, thus making her his own. They married, even though the family was suspicious of this strange woman, who spoke an ancient form of Gaelic. When her first baby was born, the selkie woman, who called herself Nuala (Susan Lynch), asked that the baby's cradle be made from the "wood of a ship that sailed the ocean." Liam obliged, making a cradle that resembled a ship, carved with shells, fish, and seaweed. Nuala said that the cradle would rock all her children on the "motion of the sea." Together the couple had many children, living in relative peace.

Yet Nuala, with her wild, black, Pre-Raphaelite hair and dark sensual looks, remained a stranger, an outsider among the island people. Often she would spend days sitting on the beach, gazing at the sea, listening to the sounds of the waves, gulls, and seals. Nothing could disturb her. One day, Nuala's oldest daughter, also named Fiona, asked her mother about the "leather coat" her father kept hidden in the roof of their home. With her seal skin secured, the selkie resumed her original form and returned to the sea, her natural home. According to Tadhg, the selkie always kept watch over her children from the water; and from the day she returned to the sea, no seal was ever harmed near Roan Inish. Every generation, Tadhg says, a "dark" Coneelly is born. These family members are fearless sea travelers and exceptional fishermen, profoundly connected to the water. He finishes his story by whispering, "Welcome back, Fiona Coneelly. We've been waitin'." Fiona is mystified by Tadhg. Tess says that Tadhg exists "between earth and water," that odd demarcation line that perfectly describes a selkie's condition. Tadhg's story reveals the Coneellys' connection to the natural world.

Fiona asks Eamon to take her back to Roan Inish, where she falls asleep and dreams of the selkie woman. In the dream Nuala rises from the sea, turns directly toward Fiona, and with her hand beckons the child. The gesture signifies that it is time to come home. The dream startles Fiona awake. Walking through an open field, she finally sees Jamie from afar. He is naked, picking wildflowers on a bluff near the sea; he is beautiful and strong, with spools of wild black hair springing from his head. When Fiona calls to him, Jamie runs away in fear, escaping to the sea in his cradle-boat, which moves effortlessly through the water, propelled by an unseen force.

The Secret of Roan Inish *(1994) resonates with stories and storytelling. The central tale is that of Liam Coneelly (Gerard Rooney) and Nuala (Susan Lynch) the selkie woman. Here Nuala's first born rests in the cradle-boat that will pass through generations of Coneellys; it is an object that symbolically connects the clan to the sea. Sayles's shot composition reveals the importance of women in the film: Nuala dominates the foreground, Liam stands slightly behind her, and deep in the background of the shot stand other members of the community, who visually illustrate how removed they are from the Coneelly clan. Photo by David Appleby.*

Due to a dense fog the next day, Hugh refuses to take Fiona fishing. As Fiona stands alone on the quay, an oar-less boat inexplicably floats to her, and she boards. Surrounded by seals, the boat moves through the thick fog seemingly under its own power. She is deposited on Roan Inish. There she again falls asleep and dreams of the interior of a cottage. She imagines the cradle-boat rocking gently and crabs scurrying about. Fiona awakens. She runs to the abandoned cottage, peeks through a window, and sees Jamie and a seal engaged in a mock tea party, a game Fiona used to play when she lived on Roan Inish. Fiona watches from the window until the boy and the sea creature become aware of her. Jamie looks up, his blue eyes wide and full of fear. He runs to his cradle-boat and escapes to the sea again, with the seal in fast pursuit. That night, Hugh and Eamon rescue Fiona. She tells them about Jamie. Hugh is curious but decides that Fiona has dreamed about Jamie. Still, he cannot explain how the boat magically navigated a course to Roan Inish.

Fiona is now convinced that if she brings the Coneellys back to Roan Inish the seals will return Jamie to the family. She plots with Eamon to refurbish the abandoned cottages. They work hard for many days, without seeing Jamie but being observed by the gulls and the seals. On the mainland one night, watching rain clouds collect, Fiona nonchalantly says, "I hope Jamie comes in out of the storm." Tess demands to know what she means, and Fiona fervently tells her that Jamie is alive and living with the seals; she has seen him with her own eyes. Hugh dismisses her idea as a fanciful dream. Surprisingly, Tess believes Fiona. Hugh and Eamon watch with disbelief as Tess quickly packs for a trip to Roan Inish. Clearly, Tess has always felt that Jamie was alive. On Roan Inish, the small group settles into one of the restored cottages, preparing a fire and seaweed soup, a recipe Nuala left the family, according to Coneelly lore. As the storm breaks, Jamie is pulled ashore by a family of seals. The seals take Jamie's cradle-boat and refuse to let him back into the water, slapping their bodies against the beach to prevent his return to the sea. Finally, Jamie runs into Tess's arms. In the end, Hugh, Tess, Eamon, Fiona, and Jamie are reunited as a family back on Roan Inish, where the natural balance has been restored.

The Secret of Roan Inish underscores how difficult it is to pigeonhole Sayles as a filmmaker. Although certain issues — history, community, place, work, politics, class, gender — are recognizable in all of Sayles's work, including *Roan Inish*, the critical impulse to describe him as a particular type of filmmaker collapses under the weight of his versatility. As Sayles remarked to George Hickenlooper, a writer and documentary filmmaker, in response to a question about the director's eclectic range, "It's always interesting to me to try and put myself inside people's heads — that's part of why my stories are so different" (308). And, as Maggie Renzi warns, "I actually think people make a mistake when they try to describe John's career in a linear way" (Skerry Movies Corp. 4). Still, to many critics this film marked a departure for Sayles, a moving away from his realist's aesthetic. After all, Sayles's reputation as a filmmaker who makes muscular political pictures stands at odds with a fey, mythic tale that points up the need to return to one's roots. Sayles has delved into the fantastic before, in 1984's *The Brother from Another Planet*, a film idea that came to Sayles in a dream. But the issues of race and inner-city life, as seen through the eyes of "the Brother," were based on reality. *The Secret of Roan Inish* is more an extension of *Passion Fish*, where the transcendent power of the natural world informs the entire picture. Still, the underlying story in *The Secret of Roan Inish* presents people trying to regain control of their lives by coming to terms with their roots, a theme that also surfaces in *Return of the Secaucus Seven, Baby, It's You, The Brother from Another Planet*, and *Passion Fish*.

Sayles, of course, steadfastly remains a storyteller, someone intrigued by how other people, even children, see things. *The Secret of Roan Inish* is no exception. Children's stories often contain powerful lessons. In *Don't Tell the Grown-ups: Subversive Children's Literature*, Allison Lurie reminds us that "children's literature suggests that there are other views of human life besides those of the shopping mall and the corporation. They mock current assumptions and express the imaginative, unconventional, noncommercial view of the world in its simplest and purest form" (xi). Fiona's awareness of the connection between humanity and nature allows for the presentation of a different experience, one removed from contemporary cultural signposts. Sayles makes Fiona a complex youngster trying to make sense of her world, and, in turn, that of her ancestors.

Fiona's story is complex and sophisticated; she is no ordinary ten-year-old. When he was asked in 1995 by Charlie Rose, the PBS talk-show host, if this story would appeal to children, Sayles compared *The Secret of Roan Inish* to a "pre–Disney Hayley Mills movie, or *To Kill a Mockingbird*." Although Sayles admitted that *To Kill a Mockingbird* was not necessarily a children's movie, the analogy fits. Fiona, like Scout, guides us through the narrative; moreover, both children bring an unspoken moral seriousness to their stories. As he does in his adult dramas, Sayles expects his audience to linger over the sight and sound of this film. Children (or adults) accustomed to MTV-like edits, silly humor, and the whirling images spawned by video games will need to get used to the calm pace of Sayles's film. Sayles, who also edited the picture, cut *The Secret of Roan Inish* to replicate a storyteller's style of speech, as he described to Rose: "Somebody sits down. They begin to speak. We begin to see what they're talking about, and their voice may fade out or it may stay on the screen, but I want the movie to have a more kind of oral tradition feeling to it. That's a risk" (11). Assembling the film as a series of oral tales is indeed risky, but the images that Sayles constructs to illustrate the spoken word are mesmerizing, and his unhurried folktale offers a valuable, albeit complicated message, a characteristic missing from most Hollywood pictures designed for children.

Yet although *The Secret of Roan Inish* celebrates the imaginative and unrestricted agenda of childhood, its poetic goodwill does not neglect adult sensibilities. While Sayles shows us the world as Fiona sees it, taking her side instinctively, *The Secret of Roan Inish* reaches adults willing to concentrate and follow Fiona into a world of stories that carry universal power and meaning. "The story has more resonance than just an animal story," Sayles remarked. "Where so many Irish songs and stories are about leaving Ireland, this was about people making the decision to go back to their roots. It became an exploration of roots in general and what they mean to people" (Holden "In a Departure..." 13). Exploring her own roots, Fiona comes to trust and communicate with the gulls and seals, and the sea and the land. Sayles allows us to see these fantastic connections, seemingly unusual territory for him, which align to create a magic realist tapestry that appeals to both children and adults.

Describing a central theme of the film, Sarah Green underscores this magical connection: "Like children we can plug into the greater forces of nature; we can rekindle our relationship with the natural world" (Skerry Movies Corp. 3). Fiona easily believes in the magic of a world free from socially imposed restrictions, as Green details:

For me it's about trust and faith. I have a strong belief that kids grow up with a natural sense of spirituality which they forget as they are socialized into a busy world. Fiona is at that age when she can choose to forget because everyone is saying "you didn't hear this," or "that seal did not talk to you," or she can choose to keep her faith and she does." [Skerry Movies Corp. 3]

It is fitting that two young people, unfettered from a changing world, plot the Coneelly family return to Roan Inish, and exhilarating when Tess, the naysayer, drops her adult resistance to Roan Inish and its terrible memories when she realizes her suppressed belief that Jamie is alive may be true.

Yet Sayles's film resonates with substantive ideas meant for both children and adults. Children naturally enjoy the idea of taking control and changing the attitudes of the adults around them. Fiona's search for Jamie, which is a traditional quest, holds universal appeal; the scenes between Fiona and Jamie are deeply emotional, especially her anguish when he runs from her. When Fiona successfully reunites Jamie with the family, the film hints at a sympathetic charm but avoids becoming saccharine. The scene is at night, bathed in deep, mysterious blues, and Fiona thanks the seals before returning to the cottage, reminding us of the Coneelly connection to the natural world. And Sayles does not end with a warm shot of the family, an image adults have seen often enough; rather, he concludes with a freeze frame of a seal — one last reminder that nature remains inscrutable yet an essential part of existence. The image provides a fleeting moment of poignance that underlines the power of the natural world and the balance that has been restored on Roan Inish. Ireland, especially the western shore and off-coast islands, functions for Sayles as Louisiana does in *Passion Fish*. It is a place of rough, mysterious beauty; a vestigial place, shaped by memories and legends; a reminder that a rugged life has not been entirely eradicated. In *The Secret of Roan Inish* nature has a consciousness and a power to control human events. The gulls and the seals conspire to steal Jamie away from his family because the Coneellys break their centuries-old covenant with the physical world by evacuating Roan Inish. *The Secret of Roan Inish*, like *Passion Fish*, observes the power of women. When Sean Michael is revived, woman save the Coneelly family line from dying out. When we see Sean's picture of "heaven," Sayles's camera pans across the faces of peasant women (including Maggie Renzi), people with the knowledge and ability to bring the young man back to life. Nuala, the selkie woman, represents the spiritual center of the Coneelly family. Finally, Fiona, with an ultimate push from Tess, re-establishes the entire family on Roan Inish, their spiritual and natural home. In addition, *The Secret of Roan Inish* is about the loss of tradition, the loss of language, the loss of place, the loss of self, and the hard work required to reassemble missing pieces of one's culture. While *Roan Inish* can reach a child on an imaginative and adventurous level, it can stir deep emotions in adults, asking them to ponder their own connection to the earth.

The Secret of Roan Inish is grounded by Sayles's practical touch and literary taste. Sayles works to capture the mystery behind the concrete reality of his story, using an ancient form of storytelling, one that informed generations, to get his essential point across. As Sayles explained in a 1995 *Charlie Rose Show* interview, "Somebody tells somebody who tells somebody who tells somebody. So the story is not just a story, it's also a link with who you are in the world, and where you came from." It is, in other words, an organic form, communicating values, mores, and knowledge of the physical world. Although Sayles holds critics at arm's length by noting that *Brother from Another Planet* also embraces the fantastic, *The Secret of Roan Inish* does a better job of wedding the magical and the real. It can, in fact, be described as magic realism.

Magic realism, a critical term that suffers from a voguish contemporary usage to describe fiction, theater, and film, describes a certain approach to subject matter and style found in the fiction of a number of Latin American novelists, notably in the work of Gabriel García Márquez, author of *One Hundred Years of Solitude, Chronicle of a Death Foretold,* and *Love in the Time of Cholera.* American writers such as John Cheever, Robert Coover, and William Kennedy have also used magic realism in their novels and stories. Magic realism blends the fantastic and the real, often transforming the latter into something extraordinary. Sayles, like Márquez (a writer he admires), understands magic realism to be first and foremost based in the everyday, not the remarkable. Life's mysteries are part of daily reality, territory Sayles knows well. *The Secret of Roan Inish* suggests that we take notice of the world around us, that we see through the eyes of an enlightened child, and that we be guided by her imagination and the powerful forces of nature.

Sayles uses magic realism with quiet restraint, never overloading the frame. The film's visual composition is beautiful yet ordinary, what you would expect to see in northwest Ireland. But the magic is there, below the surface. For example, the seals and the gulls are treated as characters in the film, not props, even though the animals propel the mythic part of Sayles's narrative. They exist as natural components of the environment. Fiona, of course, realizes that the animals are more than just pretty to look at: Their power over the Coneelly family is natural, part of the spiritual connection the Coneellys have to Roan Inish. Their desire to re-establish the Coneellys on Roan Inish, no matter how bizarre, is meant to be seen as perfectly acceptable, part of the bargain Liam and Nuala established centuries ago; it's as natural as a mother wanting her children close to home. Only Fiona, however, can imagine the connection between the Coneellys and Roan Inish: She sees the gulls and the seals steal the infant Jamie away; she sees a perfectly sunny day turn to dark, thundering rain. In other words, Sayles allows us to witness the fantastic elements of his story through Fiona's imagination; it is part of her reality, but Fiona must convince the rest of her family that the mystery of Roan Inish is part of their shared history. In the end, of course, they have no problem believing that a family of seals and gulls, and indeed the entire natural environment, can raise a healthy human baby.

Filming *The Secret of Roan Inish* removed Sayles from the United States, a major endeavor for an independent filmmaker. Ireland, of course, has tugged at many well-known directors, such as John Ford and John Huston, also filmmakers with literary sensibilities. Sayles, who is half Irish, had only been in the country once, spending one day in Belfast. The untamed coastline of County Donegal, which proved to be both enchanting and burdensome, added a historic literary and cinematic background to *The Secret of Roan Inish*. Irish literature is thick with myth, struggle, and exile, often capturing William Butler Yeats's vision of the country's "terrible beauty," his famously descriptive observation of Ireland as a beautiful battle zone. The typical Irish film, however, presents a different perspective, one dominated, until recently, by cobalt skies, green fields of Shamrocks, thatched cottages, and little people guarding pots of gold. These romantic images were usually created by foreigners, particularly Americans. Writing in *Film Comment*, Harlan Kennedy succinctly summed up the popular Irish cinema: "Romantic movies from *The Quiet Man* (1952) to *Far and Away* (1992) hint at a never-never Golden Age, a time of simple pastoral integrity, Church-blessed community spirit, heroic faith in the Irish struggle" (24). Continuing, Kennedy defines two dominant generic strands within Irish cinema: the political — *Willy Reilly and His Colleen Bawn* (1920), *The Informer* (1935), *Odd Man Out* (1947)— and the bucolic — *Darby O'Gill and the Little People* (1959), *Young Cassidy* (1964), *Finian's Rainbow* (1968).

Although *The Secret of Roan Inish* has some standard Irish ornamentation — cottages, drink, green fields, a rugged seacoast — Sayles's Ireland melds picturebook beauty with the reality of a working existence. We see how cottages are thatched, why men drink, and the reasons why the Irish are known for their practicality and strength in the face of adverse conditions. Sayles's characters have dirt under their fingernails, and work — cutting peat, whitewashing cottages, sealing a boat hull with pitch, fishing — defines who they are. These people are committed to the land and the sea through hard work, not romantic fancy.

Movies set in Ireland have a rich cinematic history. By switching the film's setting from Fry's Scotland to Ireland's western seacoast, Sayles adds a literary patina to his story by overturning an established tradition. Sayles avoids romanticizing the country by mixing pastoral beauty with honest reality. After all, Fiona and Eamon restore the family home through extremely hard work. These children take a pragmatic, responsible approach to their own lives and that of their family, creating a community based on shared labor. By combining Harlan Kennedy's generic categories, Sayles creates a grown-up fairy tale in which a motherless child finds spiritual guidance through stories, hard work, the natural world, and her own family's unique genetic history.

We need look no further than Sayles's mise-en-scène to recognize and understand how he employs magic realism to show us Fiona's world, and her oddly endearing history. Sayles and his crew deliberately kept the fantastic in check. When the mysterious selkie woman transforms from a seal into a human being, for example, the shot could easily have been lost to special effects. What we see is a woman slipping off an artificial seal skin, as a diver might peel off a wetsuit. The selkie woman is shot in close-up to reduce the amount of territorial space she has in the frame, a composition choice designed to illuminate her beauty and to hint that her freedom is about to be lost. Sayles opted to present the transformation in a "fairly mechanical, simple way ... about the same way they would have done it in the silent movie days. It was labor intensive. A lot of KY Jelly" (Johnson *Creative Screenwriting* 10). In other words, he did not want the transformation to overwhelm the union between the selkie woman and Liam Coneelly. Although Sayles does not ignore the scene's magic veneer, the linkage between the Coneellys and the natural world outweighs anything a special effects department could do. Instead, Sayles opts for a simple, straightforward look, underlined by close-up sensuous photography.

Haskell Wexler photographed the film, and its lyrical beauty cannot be ignored. Wexler, a three-time Oscar winner, called Sayles and asked to be the director of photography for *The Secret of Roan Inish*, knowing full well that he would have to commit to a reduced salary. For him, working with Sayles is a rare, welcome opportunity:

> After I worked with John on *Matewan*, I came away with great respect for his views and his abilities. Marketing, advertising and demographics seem to be the motive power of our business now, and it's possible to come up with a lot of films aimed at the lowest common denominator. But with John, no matter what you think of his films, he makes his own pictures. [Gritten F20]

Sayles, on the other hand, credits Wexler: "One of the things that Haskell excels at is maintaining consistency when the weather is changing every hour or every few minutes, especially when you are shooting part of the scene on one day and the rest on another" (Skerry Movies Corp. 5). Camera movement and color add a dreamy, otherworldly quality to the film, illustrating the magical power of the physical world. Visually experiencing the stories told to Fiona, we are reminded of Sayles's manifest skill as a filmmaker. Wexler's practiced, artistic shots provided the director with a film overflowing with commanding beauty.

Set against the wild coastline of County Donegal, Ireland, the film features an evocative visual composition, designed to illustrate Fiona's experiences through finely choreographed pictures. Sayles and Wexler crafted a visual style to match the film's narrative material. As his characters tell their stories, Sayles illustrates their words with wonderfully conceived images from

Fiona's imagination. Sayles adjusts the visual composition with grace and skill, adding rich textures to this odd Celtic tale. Yet the most troublesome aspect of the *Roan Inish* shoot was the environment that the film celebrates. Weather on the coast of Ireland varies wildly, which means that the light is subject to fluctuation, a headache even for an Academy Award–winning cinematographer. Still, Haskell Wexler's photography frames the damp beauty of the region skillfully.

In 1949 northwestern Ireland was removed from the world, a place out of step with the postwar industrial boom. As we see early on in the film, Fiona travels between two worlds: the industrial, unnatural city, and the untamed, natural west. Sayles's use of a short, two-part flashback — her mother's burial and her city life — contextualizes Fiona's journey to her grandparents' home. Sayles juxtaposes the beauty of the west, even in a time of death, with the alienation of the city through mise-en-scène, which comments on Fiona's condition. Even though Fiona is unaware of where she belongs as the film opens, Sayles, with Wexler's help, visually describes where her true home is and why.

After the opening credits, we see Fiona alone on a fishing boat. Sayles's camera tracks in on her, capturing the young girl in a medium close-up. Then he cuts to a flashback of the recent past, starting with a slightly low-angle medium shot of the younger-looking Fiona holding a bouquet of wildflowers. A priest, who is reading a burial prayer, stands to her right, and her father stands to her left. A stone cross, part of her mother's headstone, dominates the foreground of the frame, effectively sealing Fiona into a constricted space within the frame, indicating the impact of her mother's death. This shot gives way to Fiona's point of view. The camera pans slowly from a slightly low angle, and through her eyes we see her father and her older brother, who holds a crying baby, grouped around the grave. These shots are closed, and her father and brother seem to loom over Fiona. Her gaze then shifts to the headstone, which reads BRIGID CONEELLY: 1910–1946. The camera slowly pans away from the headstone, out across the graveyard to the open sea, which gleams in the morning sun. The continuous movement of the camera, which preserves Fiona's place within the frame and the story, countervails the somber burial scene. If Sayles had cut to a separate shot of the sea, we would not understand Fiona's spatial interrelationship with her family, Roan Inish, and the sea. Sayles's choice of an open shot underscores the natural physical beauty of Ireland's seacoast. Moving from the burial ground to the sea also suggests a connection between these two places; indeed, the earth and the sea provide the Coneellys with the only life they know, one full of sweeping beauty yet grounded by harsh realities. Each shot is beautifully photographed, filled with various shades of blue and brown. More important, however, we are silently made aware of Fiona's pivotal role in the film's narrative design.

The grandeur of the sea dissolves into a harsh urban scene. Sayles's soft

Haskell Wexler (left) and crew shooting a scene from The Secret of Roan Inish. *Photo by David Appleby.*

edit illustrates how quickly the natural world can fade from view. Natural light gives way to darkness, steaming machinery, and sweaty workers. The frame is severely restrictive and highly formalistic, which represents Fiona's dislocation. A tension exists between Fiona, with her blonde hair and bright dress, and the bleak, dark, steam-filled laundry room where her older brother and father work.

Through a cloud of white steam, Fiona wanders into the shot from the right side of the frame. The camera tracks her through the cavernous commercial laundry room. She is looking for her father. Sayles's camera stays on Fiona as she moves through the noisy, crowded room. For the most part, the workers who pass her are anonymous. Because the camera holds to Fiona in a tight medium shot, we see only parts of the workers' bodies. She is directed by her brother to the pub where her father stands drinking at the bar. As she enters, Fiona is referred to by amorphous voices as a "sprat," a "creature," as "pale as a fish's belly," analogies that suggest Fiona's true character.

Sayles makes it clear that the unhealthy, waiflike Fiona is completely alone. Even her father does not acknowledge her presence; he too is a victim of this polluted world, although he announces that he cannot go back to the west coast due to the lack of work. The island, he says, is finished. The female bartender pleads with Jim Coneelly to look at his little girl, who is in need of something more than he can provide. Conspicuously, Sayles places Fiona between her father and his drinking partner, both standing at the bar dressed in old work clothes. Cigarette smoke and pints of brown stout also work to constrict Fiona's space within the frame. She can hardly see above the bar. The men are truncated: two bodies bookending her at the bar, people we never fully see, only hear. Fiona is trapped, outside her element. This shot, of course, recalls Brigid Coneelly's burial. For the most part, Sayles shoots this two-part flashback in oppressive closed form. In each case, therefore, the mise-en-scène details Fiona's powerlessness. Still, Sayles's positioning of Fiona vis-à-vis the camera draws our sympathy: She is the dominant, the brightest character in the frame, and her eyes communicate all we need to know about her emotional condition. The only other appealing image in this flashback sequence is the loosely framed shot of the sea, shown from Fiona's point of view. Efficiently, Sayles and Wexler have visually represented the contrast in Fiona's life. Clearly, the physical world lies at the thematic core of the film.

With speed and economy, Sayles introduces all the film's major thematic elements and its central character. Sayles uses Fiona, whose point of view dominates the film, to celebrate storytelling. Fiona's beguiling tale disguises some of the film's more astute observations about childhood and the influence of history. Because Fiona Coneelly exists outside the modern world, time and place are important character elements, for they allow Sayles to create a character free from our hyperactive culture. "With Fiona's character in *Roan Inish*," Sayles told Mary Johnson in an interview for *Creative Screenwriting*, "I wanted her to be somebody who had never seen a TV show or a movie. So in her imagination when she illustrated a story in her mind, her references weren't Disney movies, they were things in the natural world that she had seen" (9). While living with her grandparents, Fiona imaginatively translates all the stories she hears, making her unlike many children we see in the movies: She is curious, intelligent, and responsible. We are immersed in Fiona's innocent view of the world, and we experience her transcendence, that moment when she becomes completely aware of her connection to Roan Inish, which is not presented with lavish fanfare but as the direct result of her intellectually connecting all the stories and experiences she has taken in.

Fiona is free from external influences. Her full range of imaginative possibility has not been saturated by artificial images. Fiona is our filter, our guide; over and over throughout the film someone tells her a story, and her imagination creates vital links to the language. Sayles explores the nature and power of storytelling through Fiona, who intently listens as each tale is told. Sayles feels that America's oral tradition has slipped away, having been replaced by an artificial, media-generated history, devoid of real people and real drama: "I think it's a very strange thing to look to ... network television to figure out who you are in the world; whereas, if your ... grandparents are telling you a story that happened to their grandparents — that has a much more organic thing to with who you are than *The Brady Bunch*" (*Charlie Rose Show* inter-

view [1995]). *The Secret of Roan Inish* reminds the audience that stories transmit history and truth, and feed the imagination.

Even though the film revolves around spoken stories, Sayles and Wexler
show viewers the water, the rocky green landscape, and the sea creatures, all
essential to the Coneelly environment; this view is evident every time Fiona
looks toward Roan Inish, always shot in an open, inviting form, suggesting
limitless possibility and honest natural beauty. What elevates the mise-en-
scène into the realm of magical realism is point of view, a device established
in the film's credit sequence, which is a mysterious, ephemeral journey through
a watery field of luminous blue. This brilliant blue denotes wonder, and it
prepares the viewer for the magic to follow. When the credits end, Sayles cuts
to a shot just at the water's surface, where a small steamship, belching black
smoke, moves toward the camera from right to left. The kinetic pattern here
is strange, moving against the grain. Our expectation is to see a subject move
from the opposite direction, just as we read words on a page — from left to
right. But Sayles wants us to realize that something odd, something magical
is happening. In fact, we are looking through a seal's eyes. The creature
watches the ship that is carrying Fiona, who is completing her journey home.
The seal, it seems, has been waiting for her return. Once the creature sees
her, it dives into the sea, and Wexler's camera takes us along.

Wexler fills *The Secret of Roan Inish* with infinitely variable light, and it
rebounds from the screen frame after frame: the glimmering mackerel blue
water along the Irish seacoast, the fresh whiteness of newly restored cottages,
the detailed dark tones in a prescient dream, the mysterious shadows formed
by heavy fog, the bright earthy look of a fishing quay, the soft morning light
that suffuses Fiona's bedroom, the gorgeous blue flowers on a field of green
grass lit by a brilliant sun. Yet there is nothing ornate about these shots. All
the visual choices Sayles and Wexler make strengthen the film. In *The Secret
of Roan Inish*, Sayles's images speak as clearly as his characters. With Wexler's
artistic input, Sayles used the color and light of Ireland to highlight his story
of magic possibility.

Sayles, however, still comes under regular attack for his visual style: many
film critics recognize him as a writer only. Such a reductive view of Sayles as
a complete filmmaker has followed him since he started making movies. For
example, critic Michael Atkinson, writing in Baltimore's *City Paper*, observed,

> There's so much that's ravishing and original in *The Secret of Roan Inish*, it's
> a crushing shame John Sayles directed it. Never a graceful filmmaker, Sayles
> is best at male-oriented political combats like *Matewan* and *Eight Men Out*.
> Projects like *City of Hope*, *Passion Fish*, and "Roan Inish" require a subtle
> touch, a visual fluency and an emotional tenor that Sayles apparently lacks.
> [25]

Atkinson believes that Sayles is incapable of creating a visually poetic film.

This type of misreading stems in part from the popular critical notion that Sayles is not a visual artist, but it also ignores a major stylistic component of his films, including *The Secret of Roan Inish*. Sayles approaches each film differently, fusing the look of a film to its story. His pictures match his language. Sayles takes a pragmatic approach to each of his films, weighing budget limitations, considering the story, and understanding the talents of his director of photography. The visual style of each Sayles film is tailored to enhance its story, theme, and mood. Without apology, Sayles displays no personal visual signature, which bewilders most film critics trained to focus on the director as the major creator of film art. Even though the magical aspects of the visual narrative are presented in a low-key style, *The Secret of Roan Inish* is still full of beautiful, well-choreographed images, but they all stand in service to the story, Sayles's primary concern.

Sayles also uses natural sounds to push the magical aspects of *The Secret of Roan Inish*. "The soundtrack," according to Renzi, "will creep up on you so that you become aware that the waves are making more noise; that the wind has increased and suddenly there is too much bird song. There will be all these indications that it is not just the seals or the gulls, but nature in general which is conspiring to let Fiona know what she needs to know" (Skerry Movies Corp. 3). The waves, the wind, the birds, and the seals all add their natural music to the narrative. As he has done in the past, Sayles makes sure the sound complements the images. For example, as Hugh tells Fiona Sean Michael's story, Sayles uses blowing wind nonsynchronously, enhancing the drama of the tale. The increased wind also allows Sayles to make an auditory cut from an interior shot of Fiona listening to Hugh to the images of a thrashing sea conjured by her imagination and to segue from the Coneelly cottage to the pictures Fiona sees in her imagination.

In addition to the aural cues on the soundtrack, Mason Daring again composed all the music for the film. Working with Sayles has provided Daring an opportunity to explore a variety of musical forms, including traditional Celtic ballads. For *The Secret of Roan Inish* Daring used traditional arrangements, his own compositions, and the Irish lyricist Maire Breatnach to comment on and accent the atmosphere of rich mystery that Sayles desired. "Fiona's Lullaby," a traditional arrangement by Daring, performed by Eileen Loughnane, illustrates how Daring's research and musicianship fuse to embellish a sequence in the film. The gentle lyrics encourage Fiona to sleep in maternal security:

> Little one, little one,
> Sleep, sleep … Beside my bosom, beside my bosom,
> Sleep, sleep,
> Peacefully serene, peacefully serene.

On screen, we see Fiona fall asleep inside the deserted family cottage, a

Sayles's first feature film shot outside the United States, The Secret of Roan Inish *(1994) is about the power of storytelling. Here, Fiona (Jeni Courtney) listens to her grandfather Hugh (Mick Lally) spin a tale while she keeps an eye on an unusual sea gull that seems to trace her every move. Photo by David Appleby.*

building Jamie uses as a shelter. Daring's score and Sayles's mise-en-scène combine to describe an intense feeling of maternal safety and peace. Daring used mostly Irish musicians to perform his score, and they played traditional Irish instruments — flutes and whistles, fiddles, uilleann pipes, bouzouki, Celtic harp, bodhran, mando-cello — to underscore the authenticity of Sayles's film.

Sayles also worked for the first time with a group of foreign actors. His talent as a director transferred well. Sayles draws strong yet earthbound performances from his cast, all of whom were either trained Irish actors or unknowns who answered an open casting call. They deliver Sayles's words in actual Irish speech, never resorting to stagy mock Irish. Ros and John Hubbard served as casting directors, chosen because of their fine work on *The Commitments* (1991) and *Into the West* (1993), films that required the recruitment of unknowns. For his picture, Sayles sought unknown actors for the roles of Fiona and Eamon, key characters.

Over 1,000 young girls were tested for the role of Fiona. The physical description for the role, which appeared on Irish television and in local newspapers, called for a young girl: "Thin, underweight, pale complexion, but perky and not afraid of water" (Skerry Movies Corp. 16). Elaine Courtney thought her daughter, Jeni, fit the description. Jeni, who had never acted before, was selected because of her looks, her love of the water, and her raw talent. Jeni fit right into the world of filmmaking, showing an uncanny calm in front of the cameras. Sayles was pleased because Jeni was a natural actor, someone who took pleasure in the process of creating a film. Jeni Courtney presents Fiona as caring and intelligent, using her face to communicate fear, hope, or frustration. She makes Fiona a believable ten-year-old, one free from the modern world.

Richard Sheridan also came with no professional experience. But he too proved to be a real find for Sayles. His genuine, youthful enthusiasm, coupled with a quiet reserve, allows Eamon, who is a bit skeptical of Fiona and her ideas, to be at once reserved yet willing to take a chance. As Sheridan told an interviewer, however, he has little in common with the character Sayles created: "I am more like Fiona — very impulsive." Answering the newspaper ad for actors was indeed a rash move for the young man. "Wise boy wanted for film. Big lumps need not apply" read the headline announcing the open casting call. According to Ros and John Hubbard, Sheridan is more accurately described as "tall and coltish" (Skerry Movies Corp. 15). Nevertheless, they decided on Sheridan with one week to go before shooting. Although he seems a bit stiff the first time we see and hear him on-screen, Sheridan fills out the role nicely. By the time he agrees to help Fiona rebuild the cottages at Roan Inish, we accept his every move. Both of these young actors committed themselves with grace and subtlety, and they clearly enjoyed working under Sayles's direction.

The remaining players in the film are accomplished Irish actors, many of whom work regularly in the theater, including Eileen Colgan, Mick Lally, and John Lynch. Colgan, who trained under Shelagh Richards, the Abbey Theatre actress and director, sees Tess as an archetypal Island woman. Says Colgan, "Women at that time were used to their children emigrating and never seeing them again. They were resigned to loss and carrying a fair amount of pain" (Skerry Movies Corp. 11). Tess, of course, is strong and wise, gruff and tender. Colgan uses her talents to bring out all of Tess, who seems to be the only truly practical member of the Coneelly family, until she realizes that Jamie is alive. Like many actors who have worked with Sayles, Colgan took the part because the script was intelligent and because Sayles is an actor's director. According to Colgan, Sayles is "concerned primarily with the performance and making actors feel as though they are being catered [to] rather than concentrating on things technical which can be the case with others" (Skerry Movies Corp. 12). Colgan sees the message of *The Secret of Roan Inish* as an anodyne for spiritual ennui: "We have an expression in Ireland which we use when we say good-bye, which is 'Keep the Faith' and I feel that, in a sense, this is its message. In other words, if one does not close doors, if one keeps hope alive, then things can happen" (Skerry Movies Corp. 12).

Mick Lally also sees a deeper truth at the center of the film: "There is a theme running through the film about the importance of traditions and how modern-day life and developments should not require us to discard or jetti-son our heritage. It is telling that we cannot divorce our selves from the past" (Skerry Movies Corp. 14) Lally, due to his extensive work on stage and in film and television, knows a good role when he sees one. And Hugh Coneelly was a role he could not ignore. Filling young Fiona with stories from the past, which reveal her family to her, appealed to Lally's sense of tradition. Lally's Hugh Coneelly brims with honesty, either when he is telling Fiona a tale or when he visually communicates the pain he feels at losing his seaside cottage. Lally's range as an actor comes across under Sayles's direction. Moreover, Lally relished working with Sayles: "What struck me reading the script for the first time was that John's dialogue is very accurate and true to the way Irish peo-ple speak which is unlike what most overseas screenwriters put into our mouths in terms of what they assume we say" (Skerry Movies Corp. 5). Lally appre-ciated the fact that Sayles took time to research the region, the people, and the culture of rural Ireland.

In Pat O'Connor's *Cal* (1984), John Lynch found the type of notoriety that generated roles in television, film, and theater. Recently, Lynch worked with Daniel Day-Lewis in Jim Sheridan's *In the Name of the Father* (1993), a film that drew favorable attention in the United States. Lynch, then, is per-haps the best-known actor in *The Secret of Roan Inish*. His role as Tadhg, though small, is memorable, especially his fishing technique. What Lynch brings to the screen is a sense of darkness, the feeling that suggests his char-acter has been places, and that he carries an awareness others cannot possi-bly share. He fits Tadhg, who seems to be at odds with everyone, with tailor-made precision. Lynch appreciated Sayles's film work and wanted the chance to work with the writer-director: "He's great, he's different. He has an honesty and a sense of commitment that I respond to. On set he gives clear, concise direction, managing to convey in simple terms, very complex ideas" (Skerry Movies Corp. 17). Sayles's ability to connect with his actors, to write a literate screenplay that would appeal to Irish actors, and to convey his own sense of integrity and commitment helped to make *The Secret of Roan Inish* a picture full of solid performances.

Most of the film's primary photography was done in County Donegal, concentrated at Kate's Strand, Rosbeg. According to Renzi and Green, the search for the right location was difficult. Green noted, "John was looking for beauty, but of a more harsh, rugged kind" (Skerry Movies Corp. 9). Sayles used Fry's original line drawings from her book as a visual reference for the film (Skerry Movies Corp. 5). Sayles also had to work closely with produc-tion designer Adrian Smith to achieve the appropriate period look for the film, "since a lot of what the story is about is people who come out of the land and have to carve their homes out of the land" (Skerry Movies Corp. 5). The frame is not overwhelmed with color, underscoring the harshness of the land and the sea, so we remain focused on the stories being told. Natural lighting was used whenever possible. Sayles chose Ireland for his film because it is a beautiful land made famous by immigration, clashing cultures, and improbable stories. Like *Passion Fish*, *The Secret of Roan Inish* is about place, and how place shapes people.

The seals and the gulls proved a challenge for the production crew. According to Sayles,

> It's the logistics of the place that are tough. It's not that the seals didn't do what we wanted them to do, it was a question of positioning them in a suitable but natural looking environment in which they could swim around. However, as it is impossible to confine them to a particular area, they had to be filmed in a pen, so not seeing the pen was a problem. [Skerry Movies Corp. 6]

R. Paul Miller, the associate producer, was largely responsible for the wildlife units. In order to achieve a realistic look, his solution was a threefold design: He used environmental footage shot by Jeff Goodman, trained-seal footage, and shots using animatronic seals. Sayles edited these disparate shots to create a realistic-looking community of seals. Working with the birds proved to be much more difficult, but in the end dedicated teamwork paid off. What we see on the screen looks natural, as if the seals and the gulls responded to acting cues.

Although the local Donegal communities supported the filmmakers, loving the idea of participating in the filmmaking process and of ultimately seeing their village on-screen, one major mishap occurred, and it almost scuttled the entire project. As reported by David Gritten in the *Los Angeles Times*, "A mentally unstable young local man employed as a laborer on the film set fire to three thatched cottages, built by the crew on the beach" (20). Insurance covered the cost of the damage, but for a film that got off the ground with shaky financial backing to begin with, a setback like this one could have stopped the entire picture. But the filmmakers persevered, with increased help and support from the locals.

The Secret of Roan Inish has proved to be a popular success, particularly on the video market. Its crossover appeal, reaching both children and adults, has helped to turn a solid profit for Sayles. But he had a difficult time selling the picture. "Our timing couldn't have been worse," Sayles recalled for Stephen Holden. "It would have been better had we started a year earlier. That was when studios would buy anything with sprocket holes that they could call a children's film" ("In a Departure..." 13, 21). The completed film sat for almost two years before First Look, a West Coast company owned by the Overseas Film Group, agreed to handle the property ("In a Departure..." 21).

The film cost $5 million to make, a modest sum by studio standards, especially for a foreign location shoot, but more than most of Sayles's films, exceeding his average budget by $2 million. Just raising money to produce the film was problematic. Sayles invested considerably more of his own money in the film than he had intended, although he finally reached an agreement with the Denver-based Jones Intercable, a deal secured two weeks into filming in 1993. "Getting money for [*The Secret of Roan Inish*] was a huge hassle," revealed Renzi, "a really ugly experience. At one point John said he just wanted enough money to pay the crew severance and send them home" (Gritten F12). Thankfully, that scenario never occurred.

After completing *The Secret of Roan Inish*, Sayles wrote two original screenplays and, to pay off his initial debt, worked on a number of Hollywood film scripts: *Apollo 13* for Ron Howard, *The Mummy* for Universal, a basketball movie for Disney, and two drafts of a film about the 1960s for Rob Reiner, which was never produced. While working with Reiner, Sayles established a relationship with people from Castle Rock Entertainment, a Turner company. Castle Rock expressed interest in backing Sayles's next project, a story about a Texas sheriff trying to solve an old murder.

13

Lone Star

> In my movies, very often there's a spine, which is the genre story,
> that's almost generic, but not quite. Here it's a detective story. But
> it's only a spine, it's not the most important thing. It's like the
> difference between Dashiell Hammett and Raymond Chandler.
> Hammett is very thin on the page, and it really is about who did
> what to whom, whereas with Chandler it's about the trip. When
> you can join the two of them — which is why *Chinatown* is such a
> good script — you're really doing something good.
>
> —John Sayles (Lippy)

John Sayles's *Lone Star* (1996) is a sprawling, complicated film about the
burden of history and the rifts caused by arbitrary borders drawn between people and cultures. The story focuses on the interactions of three ethnic groups —
Mexican, Anglo, African American — in the fictional town of Frontera, Texas,
located on the Rio Grande. *Lone Star* is a remarkable fusion, part murder
mystery, part domestic saga, part love story, part Western. Using more than
50 speaking characters, Sayles's elaborate screenplay makes demands on his
audience, a trait that separates his independent films from the script work he
does for Hollywood. As the narrative expands, taking in multiple perspectives, the central story tightens, cinching Sayles's characters both literally and
metaphorically.

The U.S.–Mexico borderland has always interested Sayles, especially in
Texas, a place with which he was somewhat familiar, having hitchhiked
through the state during his itinerant college days and having watched his
breakthrough script, *Piranha* (1978), shot on location in San Marcos. But, as
Sayles explained to public television's Charlie Rose, the idea for his multi-
generational border history sprouted from an extremely different place:
"Although it's set on the Texas-Mexican border, a lot of what I was thinking
about when I was writing it was Yugoslavia and how do you wake up one
morning and have somebody come to your house and say, 'Well, here's a gun.
You're a Serb. Let's go kill your next-door neighbor'" (*Charlie Rose Show* interview [1996]). The variegated histories and three principal storylines that color
Lone Star allow Sayles to explore the tangled thinking that separates people.

Because Sayles wanted to set his story on the border in Texas, Maggie Renzi and fellow producer R. Paul Miller set up a reconnaissance vacation in Del Rio, Texas, where the trio rented a houseboat on Lake Amistad and explored the borderland. Sayles started right to work on the screenplay. Originally, the filmmakers planned to shoot closer to Austin, Texas, a convenient place for cast and crew. But the borderland south of Del Rio had a look Sayles could not ignore: "There's kind of a Wal-Mart feel to everything: it's all about commerce, about signs — layers of signs" (Lippy 51). Although Del Rio, Texas, site of several recent movies — including *Lonesome Dove* and *The Return of El Mariachi*— was considered, Eagle Pass, Texas, and Piedras Negras, Mexico, connected by a busy international bridge, became the film's central location. "What we had in Eagle Pass," said Renzi, "was the real resonance you get when you're making a movie about a place. The extras look exactly right, the accents of the local actors are right, the costume department can shop locally" (Castle Rock 7). In addition, Eagle Pass and Piedras Negras sit on the Rio Grande, a physical borderline between the United States and Mexico. Symbolically the river calls to mind the problem of illegal immigration, currently a contentious political issue. The international border between Texas and Mexico provides an appropriate stage for Sayles's dynamic multicultural drama.

One week after returning to New York, Sayles was ready to make the movie, a complicated layering of stories from three distinct border communities — Anglo, Mexican, and African American. Sayles wrote the script in four months, from September to December 1994. He began filming in April 1995.

In contrast with the *Roan Inish* experience, finding financial backing for *Lone Star* was rather easy, due to Sayles's association with Castle Rock Entertainment, a production company owned by Ted Turner. "This was one-stop shopping," Sayles indicated to Tod Lippy. "I'd worked for Castle Rock as a screenwriter, working with Rob Reiner, so I kind of knew some of the people there, and asked them if they wanted to look at the screenplay when I was done, and they did, and said, 'Yeah, why not'" (Castle Rock 194). The budget for *Lone Star* was $5 million, the same as for *The Secret of Roan Inish*. Considering the scope of Sayles's picture, this amount of money is incredibly small. Moreover, Castle Rock, like Miramax, knows how to promote its products, and *Lone Star* was energetically promoted.

Lone Star, Sayles's tenth feature film, was nominated for an Academy Award for best original screenplay, his second nomination, and the film generated a large, mostly positive, critical reception. Shot in wide-screen Super 35 mm, the film looks like none of Sayles's other pictures. Yet even with its high production values, heavy promotion, and commercial recognition, *Lone Star* remains a John Sayles film, powered by carefully drawn characters, personal stories, and revealing history.

Lone Star extends some of the themes Sayles investigated in *The Secret of Roan Inish*: familial roots, the power of history, oral storytelling. *Lone Star* is, however, a vastly different film in look and intent. Like Sayles's more overtly tough-minded pictures —*Matewan*, *Eight Men Out*, *City of Hope*—*Lone Star* examines social stratification and political ideology from multiple perspectives. Various film critics noted the similarity between *Lone Star* and *City of Hope*, Sayles's take on city life and competing political camps. *City of Hope* inter-weaves characters whose lives collide even if they do not know one another. The characters in *City of Hope* share the film frame from time to time, which is not true of *Lone Star*. As Sayles remarked to Tod Lippy in an interview for *Scenario*, "*City of Hope* is very much a snapshot of the present" (51). Unlike Sayles's urban drama, *Lone Star* seamlessly connects the present and the past in a lavish visual style. Indeed, the film illustrates William Faulkner's famously accurate assessment of history: "The past is never dead. It isn't even past."

Set in Frontera, Texas, part of Rio County, the narrative glides between two primary time frames, 1957 and the present. In 1957 the Anglo popula-tion controlled the town, but in the present, the Anglo power base has eroded and the Mexican majority is emerging politically, economically, and cultur-ally. *Lone Star* focuses on the current and past lives of three main characters: Sam Deeds, Pilar Cruz, and Delmore Payne, each representing one of the major ethnic groups that make up Frontera. Sam, the current Anglo sheriff of Rio County, attempts to solve the 40-year-old murder of Sheriff Charley Wade, an old-fashioned "bribe-or-bullets" lawman who terrorized Rio County. Sam believes his late father, Buddy Deeds, who was Wade's deputy, murdered Charley Wade. After Wade vanished, Buddy Deeds succeeded him as sheriff of Rio County, and he became a local legend. Pilar, the daughter of a prominent Mexican restaurant owner and now a high school history teacher, was Sam's teenage love, but Buddy forcibly ended their relationship, an act for which Sam never forgave his father. When the story begins, Sam and Pilar have been separated for more than 20 years.

Army Colonel Delmore Payne, an African American career officer who grew up in Frontera, is only peripherally connected to Sam and Pilar. His father, Otis Payne, however, played a major role in Charley Wade's death. But Sam and Delmore are thematically linked: both suffer from damaged father-and-son histories. Typical of a Sayles independent script, *Lone Star*'s robust narrative is filled with fully realized secondary characters who estab-lish emotional, intellectual, and historic lines of connection among his pri-mary figures.

These characters provide *Lone Star* a rich backdrop, making for a labyrinthian narrative, just what you would expect from a murder mystery. More important, however, the residents of Frontera, Texas, are evocatively realistic. They expose the multicultural community dynamics that exist in America today. Sayles is not interested in the mechanical design of a crime story; rather, he wants to explore how this diverse group of people interact among themselves as part of a larger community. Sayles's assembly of voices connects races, classes, and cultures.

The film opens in the 1990s, and the first image we see is desert fauna, sunbaked and uninviting. As the camera slowly pans to the right, we see Cliff (Stephen Mendillo), an army career man, cataloguing the local vegetation. In the background, we see Mikey (Stephen J. Lang), also an army officer, sweeping a metal detector over the dry desert floor, looking for spent bullet casings, which he uses to form into metal sculptures that resemble the work of Frederic Remington. Mikey discovers a Masonic ring, a skull, and then a corroded sheriff's badge. These are the remains of Big Charley Wade (Kris Kristofferson), the corrupt, violent sheriff who ran Rio County with an open palm and a quick gun. Wade disappeared in 1957, after a public argument with his deputy, Buddy Deeds (Matthew McConaughey).

Sheriff Sam Deeds (Chris Cooper) begins an investigation to determine how Charley Wade ended up buried on an abandoned army rifle range 40 years ago. Sam, long estranged from his father, believes that Buddy murdered Charley Wade.

At the Cafe Santa Barbara, a well-known Frontera eatery, Sam asks Hollis Pogue (Clifton James), the current mayor of Frontera and also a former deputy to Wade, to recall his version of the night Wade vanished. Hollis obliges, and the narrative shifts to 1957. We are in the same restaurant, but it appears to be smaller, darker. The confrontation between Buddy Deeds and Charley Wade erupts over the mordida the restaurant owner pays to Wade in order to keep mojados (wetbacks) working in his kitchen. Buddy refuses to pick the money up for Wade, telling the sheriff that the entire county has had enough of his tactics and it is time he left. The argument is tense, serious. Each man threatens the other with death. Buddy Deeds, however, holds his ground against the notorious Sheriff Wade, as a terrified young Hollis (Jeff Monahan) watches from the background. We return to the present, and Hollis declares that Wade "went missing the next day, along with ten thousand dollars in court funds from the safe at the jail" (*Scenario* 12). Buddy then became the sheriff of Rio County, and his legend was born. According to Hollis, Buddy ran Rio County in a different manner: "Money doesn't always need to change hands to keep the wheels turning" (*Scenario* 13). Unlike Wade, Buddy was admired by the Mexican community for being fair. He became legendary for his ability to keep Frontera's economy running smoothly, even though the three ethnic communities remained separate.

The scene shifts to the local army base, which is scheduled to close. We are introduced to Colonel Delmore Payne (Joe Morton) as he addresses his officers. His language and demeanor indicate that Del is a spit-and-polish, by-the-book military man, an inflexible career soldier who takes his command seriously: "You may have heard rumors that I run a very tight ship. These rumors are not exaggerated" (*Scenario* 13).

Chris Cooper as Sam Deeds in Lone Star *(1996): Cooper also appeared in* Matewan *and* City of Hope. *Cooper is a reticent performer who brings a grace and dignity to his roles. Like many of the members of Sayles's loose repertory company, Cooper is terribly underappreciated. Photo by Alan Pappé.*

That night, at Big O's Roadhouse, the black community's gathering place, owned by Del's father, Otis Payne (Ron Canada), a wailing blues tune and loud talk fill the air. Everyone is having a good time. We follow a teenager, Chet Payne (Eddie Robinson), Del's son, into the tavern. Chet focuses his attention on Big O, who is working behind the bar, smiling, laughing, and serving drinks. Chet pulls a crumpled piece of paper from his pocket, a label for Big O's barbecue sauce, with a picture of Otis the Chef on it. Chet looks from the label to the man behind the bar, making a visual connection. Behind him, an argument suddenly turns violent. Two men fight over a woman, and one of the men is shot. Athena (Chandra Wilson), a black army private, kneels over the bleeding man. She screams for help. Otis appears behind Chet, wraps his large arm around the teenager's shoulder, and calmly declares, "You weren't here tonight, were you?" Chet responds, "No, sir" (14). Otis tells Chet to exit though the back door, then he turns his attention to the chaos in his bar.

That same evening, at a parent-teacher meeting, members of the Anglo and Mexican communities debate how history should be taught at the high school. The argument revolves around Pilar Cruz's (Elizabeth Peña) pluralistic approach to teaching, which runs counter to the prescribed textbook. Paloma (Carina Martinez), Pilar's daughter, brings word that her brother,

Amado (Gonzalo Castillo), has been arrested. Pilar exits the meeting and rushes to the county jail.

There, Sam, who is dealing with the troubling discovery in the desert and the shooting at Big O's, sees Pilar from a distance. His lingering gaze and body language make it clear that they know each other well. Sam retrieves Amado for Pilar. Their dialogue reveals that Pilar is widowed and that she is trying to raise her children alone.

In order to compress time, Sayles employs a languid tracking montage dominated by close-ups detailing the forensic examination. We see the gathered bones of the skeleton being tagged, photographed, and measured. The camera glides over the bleached-out remains, concluding with a tight shot of a container half full of fizzing rusty liquid. A pair of tongs remove the badge, which reads SHERIFF—RIO COUNTY.

Ben Wetzel (Richard A. Jones), a Texas Ranger, then meets Sam in an empty bar. He holds the forensic report, which confirms that the remains are those of Charley Wade. Ben, who grew up in Rio County and who remembers Wade well, tells Sam that he will "keep names out of [the investigation] till we got some answers or hit a dead end" (*Scenario* 17). Sam now has time to find out if his father killed Charley Wade, a suspicion he firmly believes and wants to prove. Sam continues to ask questions around town about Charley and Buddy and their final confrontation.

That same day Minnie Bledsoe (Beatrice Winde), whose husband, Roderick (Randy Stripling), used to own the roadhouse, eventually selling it to Otis, tells Sam more about Wade's abuse of power and something about how the African American community felt about Buddy Deeds's political style. The narrative glides into the past, taking us back to the roadhouse in 1957. We see young Otis (Gabriel Casseus) working as a waiter. He walks toward Charley Wade's table, where the imperious sheriff and young Hollis sit watching over the patrons. From Wade's point of view we see a man slip money — a gambling debt payment — into Otis's shirt pocket. Clearly, young Otis is running numbers out of the club. Because he did not cut Wade in on the illegal profits, the sheriff beats the young man. For good measure, he then shoots up Roderick's club.

When the narrative returns to the present, we are no longer on Minnie's front porch; instead, we are in the roadhouse, where Otis, not Minnie, concludes the story for Sam. Otis calmly defends Buddy: "I don't recall a prisoner ever died in your father's custody. I don't recall a man in this town — black, white, Mexican — who'd hesitate a minute before he'd call on Buddy Deeds to solve a problem" (*Scenario* 21). Neither Otis nor Minnie has anything bad to say about Buddy Deeds; rather, they have the utmost respect for his methods, which Sam, who is searching for moral truth, finds questionable.

Sayles cuts to the kitchen of Cafe Santa Barbara, where Mercedes Cruz (Miriam Colon) and Pilar argue about the past. Mercedes refuses to return to Mexico even for a short visit, a choice that disturbs Pilar. Mercedes bitterly responds, "You want to see Mexicans, open your eyes and look around you. We're up to our ears in them" (*Scenario* 23). Later that night, as Mercedes gets into her large, expensive Buick, Enrique (Richard Coca), a recently immigrated employee, admirers the vehicle: "Es muy lindo, su coche." Mercedes scolds him, "En inglés, Enrique. This is the United States. We speak English" (*Scenario* 23).

At the roadhouse the next day, Otis and Del have their first meeting in almost 40 years. Because of the shooting the night before, the colonel has come to threaten to make Big O's off limits to army personnel. Otis, who abandoned Del when he was eight years old, tries to explain the significance of the bar to his son: "There's not enough of us to run anything in this town — the white people are mostly out on the lake now and the Mexicans hire each other. There's the Holiness Church and there's Big O's place." Del says derisively, "And people make their choice." Otis replies, "A lot of 'em choose both. There's not like a borderline between the good people and the bad people — you're not either on one side or the other" (*Scenario* 25). The remaining conversation reveals Del's unhappiness over having to return to his hometown, a place that he has been trying to erase from his memory, and his bitterness toward his father, who abandoned him and his mother, moving three houses away to live with one of his mother's best friends. Otis and Del do not communicate in this exchange. Maintaining a cold, professional distance, Del informs Otis that he will be receiving official notification of the impending ban.

We next see Sam in the middle of the night in his office, searching through piles of old Sheriff's Department records. A series of dissolves illustrates a paper trail of payroll reports, real estate transfers, many with Buddy's signature, autopsy reports, eviction notices, a map of Perdido, and Sam's handwritten notes. This paper trail uncovers the extent of Wade's legally sanctioned brutality and raises questions about Buddy Deeds's hirings at the county jail and his real estate holdings.

Later that morning, Sam crosses the Rio Grande to Ciudad León, Frontera's sister city. There he meets Chucho Montoya (Tony Amendola), who tells Sam about the death of Eladio Cruz (Gilbert R. Cuellar, Jr.), a young day-laborer brutally and senselessly murdered by Charley Wade for smuggling Mexicans across the border. The narrative shifts to the 1956. We now see and hear how Charley Wade conducted business. Wade tricks Eladio into showing him the shotgun the young man keeps in his truck. As soon as Eladio turns to touch the shotgun, Wade shoots him in the back of the head. Sickened and shocked, the young Hollis gasps, "You killed him!" In a matter-of-fact tone Wade responds, "You got a talent for statin' the obvious" (*Scenario* 34). As the narrative glides into the present, we see Sam looking over the site of Eladio Cruz's murder, standing just above the spot where the young Chucho Montoya (James Borrego) hid from the savage Wade.

Marisol (Lisa Suarez), the high school principal's secretary, jokes with Pilar about working too much, not having a lover. She says, "How 'bout the sheriff ... the old-high-school-heartthrob sheriff. I thought you were crazy about each other. He's available, you're available." With difficulty, Pilar mutters a response, "Nobody stays in love for twenty-three years" (*Scenario* 36). The narrative cuts to 1972. At a drive-in a B film, *Black Mama, White Mama*, a low-rent version of *The Defiant Ones*, plays on the screen. We see Buddy and young Hollis striding through the lot, searching the cars with their flashlights. Buddy discovers young Sam (Tay Strathairn) and young Pilar (Venessa Martinez) groping each other in the backseat of a car; he rips them apart. In a rage, young Sam screams and curses at his father, while young Pilar begs Hollis not to tell her mother. The narrative returns to the present, where Sam stands alone by his car in the lot of the long-abandoned drive-in. After he drives away, a crane shot lingers on the derelict screen.

After an impressionistic montage shows Sam driving at night, thinking about Pilar and what Buddy Deeds did to them, he ends up at the high school where Pilar is working late. Separately they drive to her mother's restaurant. Alone inside the Cafe Santa Barbara Sam and Pilar talk briefly, then dance. The scene illustrates their deep romantic connection, alive even after 23 years. Then they make love in Sam's empty apartment.

The next day, after a scene between Chet and Otis Payne, Sayles cuts to the Cafe Santa Barbara, where Hollis sits eating breakfast. Sam arrives and reminds the mayor that he needs to know more about the night his father refused to be Charley Wade's bagman. Sam tells Hollis that he is going to San Antonio and that he would like an answer when he returns.

Sam then drives to San Antonio to see his ex-wife and retrieve a box from her garage that holds Buddy's personal papers, which he hopes will shed some light on Buddy's real estate transactions and, perhaps, Wade's death. Along the way, he stops to talk with Wesley Birdsong (Gordon Tootoosis), a Native American who sells curios at a roadside stand near where Buddy Deeds grew up. Wesley knew Buddy before he became a law enforcement officer. "If he hadn't found that deputy job," Wesley tells Sam, "I believe Buddy might've gone down the other path, got into some serious trouble. Settled him right down. That and your mother. 'Course he had that other one later" (*Scenario* 36). This news stuns Sam, and he asks for the woman's name, but Wesley feigns amnesia; however, he warns Buddy, metaphorically, to stop digging into the past.

Back at the military base, Del begins to upbraid Athena for breaking the drug policy and for her involvement in the shooting at Big O's. But before he starts, Del wants to find out why she joined the army. Athena declares, "It's their country. This is one of the best deals they offer." The remark troubles Del, who believes in service to his country. He asks, "How do you think I got to be a colonel?" Athena says, "Work hard, be good at your job. Sir. Do whatever they tell you." Del then asks her why "they" let blacks in on the military opportunity. She says, "They got people to fight. Arabs, yellow people, whatever. Might as well be us" (*Scenario* 40). Del is obviously affected by Athena's description of the military; its social and economic implications are sobering. Del straightens Athena's cap and tries, half heartedly, to explain the type of community the army can generate. Then he dismisses her. The camera lingers on him as he leans against his desk, gently slumping, staring straight ahead, mulling over Athena's words.

In San Antonio, Sam asks Bunny (Frances McDormand), his manic-depressive, football junkie ex-wife, for his belongings still in her garage. He finds a love letter from the "other woman" to his father, and he learns that Buddy had had a baby girl with Mercedes Cruz, his longtime lover. Sam then realizes that by breaking up his teenaged romance, Buddy Deeds was trying to prevent his children from committing incest. Still, Sam remains convinced that his father murdered Charley Wade.

Del, dressed in civilian garb, pays an unexpected visit to Otis's house. Carolyn (Carmen de Lavallade), Otis's current wife, shows Del the shrine Otis has kept of his son's academic and military achievements over the years. Shaken and confused, Del says, "My mother said he never asked about me." Carolyn smiles slightly and replies, "He never asked her" (*Scenario* 43).

That same night, Mercedes, while resting in a chaise lounge on her patio, is startled by Enrique, who emerges from the dark without warning. He is soaked and in need of help; his fiancée broke her leg as he was helping her and some other illegal immigrants cross the Rio Grande. Mercedes reaches for her phone to call the border patrol, but quickly changes her mind, deciding instead to help the young people.

When he arrives home, Del immediately goes to Chet and tells him that military life is not for everyone. With some discomfort, Del tells Chet that he would be happy with any decision that the young man might make concerning his own life. After some uneasy small talk, Chet asks if they are ever going to see Del's father: "He lives here, right?" Del acknowledges that he does. Then he suggests awkwardly that the two families could get together for a barbecue. Chet grins, "Cool. He makes his own sauce" (*Scenario* 45).

The narrative cuts to 1945. A young Mercedes stands in the middle of the Rio Grande, abandoned, terrified. Eladio Cruz, her future husband, comes to the river's edge with a lantern in his hand. He says, "Me llamo Eladio Cruz. Bienvenido a Tejas" (*Scenario* 44). Mercedes's memory reveals that she, like the young people she is now helping, crossed into Texas illegally, a fact she has kept secret for decades.

Later that same night, Sam angrily confronts Hollis and Otis at the roadhouse. He accuses them of having witnessed Buddy murder Charley Wade. Otis and Hollis finally tell Sam the truth. The narrative returns to Roderick Bledsoe's roadhouse. Young Otis is conducting a card game when Charley and young Hollis arrive ahead of schedule for the monthly payment. Wade briefly looms over the table, then knocks it over. He kicks and punches Otis, beating him into submission. Wade then commands Otis to turn over the gun kept over the bar in a cigar box. Stunned and bloodied, Otis obeys, falling into the same setup Wade used to kill Eladio Cruz. As Otis reaches for the gun, Charley Wade takes aim at the center of his back. Framed by the doorway of the roadhouse, Buddy Deeds shouts at Charley Wade. Two shots ring out, and Sheriff Wade, blood pouring from his body, falls to the floor. Young Otis looks over the bar at the dead lawman. We see Wade's blood spattered over the cash on the bar. Sayles's camera cuts to Buddy Deeds, and pulls back as he approaches the bar, watching the scene carefully. The smoking gun comes into the frame, and we realize the focus of Buddy's attention. As Sayles's camera continues to pull back, we see a stunned Hollis holding the gun. Otis concludes the story: "Sheriff Charley had some real big friends in politics then, and if the truth come out it wasn't going to go easy on Hollis. I don't know why I trusted Buddy with it — don't know why he trusted me. The first time I ever talked with him was right there, and then with a dead white man leakin' blood on the floor between us. He could charm the scales off a rattler, Buddy Deeds" (*Scenario* 48). Now Sam must choose between the truth and the legend of his father. Hollis says, "Word gets out who that body was, people are gonna think Buddy done it." Sam, visibly relieved at knowing the truth replies, "Buddy's a goddam legend. He can handle it" (*Scenario* 48).

The next day, Sam and Pilar meet at the deserted drive-in. Sam reveals that Buddy was also her father, that he bought the restaurant for Mercedes with the missing $10,000, and that he paid the hospital bill when Pilar was born. Mercedes was Buddy's longtime lover. Pilar is stunned and angry, not because of Sam's discovery but because she does not want to lose him again. Sam and Pilar must face the future knowing that their happiness together can only be achieved if they turn their backs on social norms and on their shared past. "Forget the Alamo," Pilar says, suggesting that they will escape history and stay together (*Scenario* 49). Sayles concludes the film with a wide shot of the drive-in. Sam and Pilar sit side by side holding hands on the hood of his car, looking at the blank screen.

Lone Star's complex structure borrows from two masters of American crime fiction. What begins as a straightforward Dashiell Hammett–like detective story slowly opens up into a Raymond Chandler–like journey, in which numerous points of view collide, revealing the sociocultural condition of Frontera, Texas. Hammett, the great progenitor of realist American detective fiction, concentrated on linear plotting; Chandler, who despised plotting, concentrated on atmosphere and character. Chandler created self-contained scenes, placing a cinematic template over his work. Sayles follows both models. *Lone Star* seems baroque, yet the film is well plotted and direct. Still, the atmosphere and the characters Sayles creates make *Lone Star* more than an intriguing whodunit. Like Chandler, Sayles vividly renders the actualities of American life by moving through various social tiers. Like Hammett, Sayles works from a specific outline, and he shows us why all the stops in the film are necessary. Overall, of course, *Lone Star* is driven by characters, the voices Sayles so convincingly creates for the screen.

Sayles's large ensemble cast infuses *Lone Star* with a rich subtext, adding a sociological and psychological depth to *Lone Star* not usually seen in commercial films. As Gavin Smith suggests, the struggles these people face allow Sayles to comment metaphorically on the "racial stratification and cultural conflicts of contemporary society" (58). For example, *Lone Star* countervails the conservative notion of America as a melting pot. In response to a question from writers for *Cineaste* magazine about his interest in Latinos and Hispanic American cultures, Sayles defines his view of the United States:

> Where I'm coming from, in fact, is pretty much the opposite of Pat Buchanan's idea of this monoculture which is being invaded. English-speaking culture is just one of many cultures. It has become the dominant culture or sub-culture in certain areas, but it's a subculture just like all the others. American culture is not monolingual or monoracial. It's always been a mix. As one character [Cody, a bartender] says, "We got this whole damn *menudo* down here." [West and West, "Borders" 15]

Sayles's tripe stew uses history as its stock, the essential ingredient that binds all the major and minor characters, people from different generations, different ethic communities, with different moral agendas who reveal their flaws, strengths, fears, and passions throughout the course of the film.

Frontera, Texas, is the place all these people share, and it serves Sayles well because it is a nondescript place, much like the fictional Hudson City he used in *City of Hope*. Both fictive locations are nowhere and everywhere, isolated yet representative of the strained borders that exist between race and race, class and class, and gender and gender throughout the United States. Indeed, borders, real and imagined, are a central theme in *Lone Star*: "Within the movie there are lines between people that they choose either to honor or not to honor. It may be this enforced border between Mexico and the United States, it may be one between class, race, ethnicity, or even military rank" (West and West, "Borders" 14). Because of its unique history, the Texas borderland supplies Sayles the proper milieu to comment on the arbitrary quality of all borders.

In Frontera, the Anglo minority has used the border to protect its own values and to seal its own political power. At the curriculum meeting, for instance, one of the parents declares his definition of the border: "I'm sure they got their own account of the Alamo on the other side, but we're not on the other side, so we're not going to have it taught in our schools" (*Scenario* 14). The Anglo speaker sees Mexico as a defeated foreign country, lacking political and economic might. From his perspective, Mexico was finished in

1836 with the formation of the Texas Republic. And, as he says, "Winners get the bragging rights, that's how it goes" (*Scenario* 14). However, his argument ignores the culture in which his daily life is immersed, a mixture of both Mexican and American perspectives. For Sayles, this character illustrates the tribalism at the core of Frontera's social structure. The speaker's tribe, the Anglo winners, are in control, so it is their job to dictate the rules of the game by presenting a heroic history of the state, not a messy, complex look at historical events. Pilar, the history teacher at the center of the curriculum discussion, argues for a more inclusive view of history, one that grows from both sides of the debate, one that includes multiple perspectives, a distinct change from the prescribed "textbook" curriculum. Pilar desires, as she says, to show "cultures coming together in both negative and positive ways" (*Scenario* 14). Pilar's view challenges the status quo interpretation of history by adding perspective, reshuffling the deck to offer a more realistic view of history.

Sayles's most overt comment on the Mexican-American border comes from Chucho Montoya, El Rey de las Llantas (The Tire King), in Ciudad León, Mexico. Montoya, who lived in the United Sates for 15 years, was transported secretly across the border by Eladio Cruz, and he witnessed Charley Wade's murder of Cruz. Chucho mocks the notion of borders of any kind. Drawing a line in the dirt with a Coke bottle, he challenges Sam to cross the line. Sam obliges. Chucho responds: "Ay, que milagro! You're not the sheriff of nothing anymore — just some tejano with a lot of questions I don't have to answer" (*Scenario* 33). Sam's power, sanctioned by the United States, no longer exists in Mexico. Facetiously, Chucho suggests that Sam has been magically transformed by crossing an arbitrary line drawn in the sand.

But Chucho is not finished. "Bird flying south," he says, "you think he sees that line? Rattlesnake, javelina — whatever you got — halfway across that line they don't start thinking different. So why should a man?" (*Scenario* 33). Speaking metaphorically, Chucho indicates that the natural world holds to no boundary; in other words, an invisible line drawn in the sand cannot decide ownership. Although he understands Chucho's bitterness, Sam points out that Mexico has "always been pretty happy to have that line. The question's just been where to draw it —" (*Scenario* 33). Chucho, however, has little patience for the world of politics, which, from his perspective, causes more harm than good: "My government can go fuck itself, and so can yours. I'm talking about people here — men" (*Scenario* 33). Clearly, the symbolic and physical borderline has bred a malevolence that Chucho sees as poisonous. He then tells the story of the killing of Eladio Cruz, a consequence of crossing the international border illegally and challenging Charley Wade's power. Charley Wade murdered Eladio because he was nothing in the lawman's eyes, just, as he says, a "little greaser sonofabitch … running a goddam bus service" (*Scenario* 34). Wade's form of justice is arbitrary and capricious, a fictional reminder of Texas Rangers who abused their power. Chucho's story has the thematic strength of a border ballad, in which Eladio is the defenseless innocent and Charley Wade a brute who exploits Mexicans. Chucho's story asks why men use borders as lines of power. According to Sayles, "I think that's one of the reasons that people like borders — they can say, 'South of this line, I'm a big guy, and I run things here.' Or it may be as literal as, 'This is my land and, if you come on it, I can shoot you'" (West and West, "Borders" 14).

Each of the primary characters in the film confronts far more personal borders, those found in their family histories. In *Lone Star* the thorny relationship between fathers and sons informs Sayles's screenplay. The generational conflicts that exist between Buddy and Sam, and Otis and Del and Chet tell a political story that adds a deep personal resonance to Sayles's film. For Sayles, the personal is the political.

"I spent my first fifteen years trying to be just like Buddy and the next fifteen trying to give him a heart attack," Sam says to Pilar as they walk together along the Rio Grande (*Scenario* 28). Early on, Sam, like everyone else in Rio County, revered Buddy Deeds, the archetypal Texas frontier lawman: brave, fair, honest — heroic in proportion to other men. The first time we see Buddy on screen underlines his larger-than-life persona. Staring out at Charley Wade from under the brim of his cowboy hat, Buddy refuses to become one of Wade's lackeys. Self-contained and forceful, Buddy stands in stark contrast to young Hollis, who fears the sheriff. When Buddy places his Colt .45 six-shooter on the table, daring Charley to draw on him, shades of the Western hero, virile, brave, and forthright, arise. Because he threatened violence against an enemy of the community, indeed an Anglo man, Buddy's legend took firm root.

Although it is only implied in Sayles's film, Buddy fills a natural patriarchal role common to the borderland. As Americo Paredes, noted scholar of lower border culture, describes it: "The original settlements had been made on a patriarchal basis, with the 'captain' of each community playing the part of father to his people.... Obedience depended on custom and training rather than on force" (*With His Pistol* 11). Following the brutal reign of Charley Wade, Buddy was embraced by the community because people credited him with Wade's disappearance. Even though Buddy was not completely honest and carried on an extramarital affair, the residents of Frontera felt protective of him and were willing to ignore his indiscretions because he rid the town of a monster. However, even though Buddy is memorialized as a great man, Sam, who uncovers his father's graft, the shady real estate deal, illegal uses of prisoners for private work, and infidelity, sees him as more of a hypocrite than a hero. Because of his deep animosity toward Buddy for destroying his love with Pilar, the information Sam finds helps him paint an ugly picture of his father. Sam wants to prove that his father killed Charley Wade so that he can collapse the legend of Buddy Deeds.

Sam's deepest anger, though, comes from his belief that Buddy was a racist who deliberately fractured his relationship with Pilar because she was Mexican. The drive-in scene suggests that miscegenation is what the Anglo community fears most, and Buddy, Frontera's moral arbiter, appears to uphold this unwritten law. But as he deepens the murder investigation, Sam discovers more about himself and his father than he could ever have anticipated. Buddy was, in fact, attempting to prevent his son from committing incest, an ancient taboo. Buddy could not, of course, reveal this fact to his son because to do so would have exposed his own blood ties to the indigenous Mexican community.

What Sam uncovers represents a generational microcosm of Texas border history. Charley Wade sees the Mexican population as inferior, expendable. Therefore, he feels justified in exploiting Mexicans and killing them if necessary. Buddy Deeds, on the other hand, represents a generation that recognized the presence of the Mexican population, and he worked with them (and the black community) to ensure his power. Yet Buddy's relationship with the Mexican community is best witnessed through his relationship with Mercedes Cruz. Buddy could not, for generational-cultural reasons, make his love affair known, nor could he admit to being Pilar's father, although he took tacit responsibility for the child. Revealing his intimate connection with Mercedes would have eroded Buddy's public standing. As the third generation sheriff, Sam displays a more compassionate connection to the Mexican community. He understands how his neighbors were exploited throughout the history of Frontera, which gives him an outsider's perspective on his hometown. When Sam discovers that his relationship with Pilar is incestuous, it is a galvanizing moment in *Lone Star*, creating a metaphor that draws attention to how closely tied the Mexicans and Anglos truly are: everyone is involved in the mix, and it is almost impossible to separate oneself completely.

The situation of Otis, Del, and Chet is more traditional and more straightforward. Unlike Sam, in his relationship to his father, the three generations of Payne men have the opportunity to change their relationship; moreover, because they are all alive, their reconciliation is a possibility. Unlike his father, Chet seeks information from the past. He is curious about his grandfather, and, therefore, his family history. Del, on the other hand, wants nothing to do with his father, considering Otis irresponsible for abandoning and embarrassing him and his mother. For example, the scene where Chet sneaks into the back room of Big O's, where Otis keeps his black Seminole Indian exhibit, reveals a great deal about generational relationships. Chet admits to his grandfather that Del is a difficult father: "Every time he moves up a rank, it's like he's got to tighten the screws a little more" (*Scenario* 39). Chet shows an interest in Otis's collection, and he asks Otis why he got involved with such an arcane hobby. Otis says, "These are our people." Chet asks, "So I'm part Indian?" Otis responds, "By blood you are. But blood only means what you let it." Chet responds, "My father says the day you're born you start from scratch, no breaks and no excuses, and you got to pull yourself up on your own" (*Scenario* 40). Otis is visibly disturbed by this remark. Not only does it echo conservative dogma, but it also suggests that Del has turned his back on both his race's social history and his family's personal history.

The encounter with Athena, however, forces Del to face truths that he has never allowed himself to consider. Athena, as her name suggests, offers wisdom on the conditions of life and contemporary warfare. When Del discovers that his father was actually deeply proud of his accomplishments, he makes an extraordinarily difficult personal decision to reclaim his past. He realizes that his ties to the military are nothing compared with the deep, albeit troubling, personal history shared by a father and son. Even though the relationship of Otis, Del, and Chet is not as dramatic or as surprising as Buddy and Sam's, it does serve to show how important it is to understand one's historical roots, both from an individual perspective and from that of the group.

The women in this picture, Mercedes, Pilar, and Bunny, struggle with history as well. As mother and daughter, Mercedes and Pilar are rich, diverse female characters, women who are intelligent, complex, and troubled. History is the taproot of their problems. Mercedes has completely divorced herself from her roots; she calls herself Spanish, not Mexican. Ironically, Pilar teaches history at the local high school, and her son, Amado, shows a deepening interest in Tejano culture. At the outset, Mercedes represents a conservative Mexican attitude, one that suggests that it is appropriate to slam the immigration gate once one has crossed the border. Pilar sees Mercedes as cold and secretive; indeed, Mercedes seems most comfortable when she is alone on her back porch, drinking scotch and water, waiting for sleep to take her away. Even here, however, Mercedes is not content, as Sayles's camera indicates. When we see her in these early shots, Mercedes is photographed in a canted angle, suggesting that something is unbalanced, unfinished. We learn, of course, that Mercedes has entered the United States illegally. According to Sayles, she is "very closed about [her past] because in the culture in which she lives, there's a certain amount of shame in being a *mojado*, a wetback" (West and West, "Borders" 16). Mercedes is an important member of the Frontera business community, her restaurant is well known, and she is a member of the city council. In other words, Mercedes's economic ties run deeper than blood relationships. Americanized to a fault, she has everything to lose if her real history is revealed.

Understandably, Pilar runs into roadblocks every time she attempts to find out about her own family history, particularly her supposed father, Eladio Cruz. Pilar's personal history is full of the loss of men, her father, her first love (young Sam), her husband, Fernando, and her son Amado, who rejects the education she reveres. Under these conditions, it is easier to accept her willingness to commit to an incestuous future with Sam. Unlike Mercedes, Pilar has little left to lose.

Bunny too struggles under the yoke of history; in her case, however, we know that her father is a dominant force in her life. Unlike most of the characters in *Lone Star*, Bunny will never escape her father's reach. We witness Bunny and Sam's entire relationship in one short, intense scene that is both funny and sad, and we understand why Sam had to flee from Bunny and her father. As Sayles described the scene to Tod Lippy in *Scenario*, "It has the arc of a play; there are two acts in it, almost, because she gets that second wind. And she has incredible insight, and can be charming, but at other times she's completely crazy. But above all, she's going to be there complaining about Daddy even after he's dead" (193). Because Bunny cannot escape her own history, the scene serves to underline an essential theme in the film.

Historical interpretation reflects one's personal agenda. Some, like Cody (Leo Burmester), the ornery redneck bartender, who questions the eroded lines of "demarcation," cleave to idealized stories and idealized heroes. He tells Sam that the bar is the last stand, an overt link to the Battle of the Alamo, a pivotal event in Texas's history. Cody then tells Sam that Buddy "stood for something," as though all that was truly good and valuable is gone. Sayles's use of the Alamo is deliberate: "When Sam goes down to Mexico, the Mexican guy [Chucho Montoya] draws a line in the sand, which refers to a famous moment from the history of the Alamo, when [William] Travis drew a line" (West and West, "Borders" 14). These historical signposts help to set the Anglo community off from the Mexican community, for they are specific to the history of the Republic of Texas. Yet the context in which Sayles uses the images reveals much about how he presents history in the scene. Leo embraces the same sorts of values as the father at the curriculum meeting, seeing history in a series of large, swaggering images. As Sayles presents these characters, he raises questions about how his audience sees history, what its agendas are. History, of course, is not tidy, and Sayles's narrative underscores this fact.

Ideally, the true history of the border should be presented from multiple points of view. As Americo Paredes reminds us, "Texas-Mexicans died at the Alamo and fought at San Jacinto on the Texas side" (*With His Pistol* 19). Even Cody, who does not understand the diversity of his community, sprinkles his speech with Spanish. Moreover, the black community stands as a reminder of Texas's slave-holding past, a bit of history that Pilar passes along to her high school students but a fact that history books tend to ignore. Sheriff Charley Wade, for example, who represents oppression on multiple levels, tells the young Otis Payne the first time they meet that black people in Frontera stay in their place and stay quiet. Big O's place is the only location where blacks can feel at ease, and the army base is the only place where they can find meaningful work, as Athena notes, and protection from the chaos of contemporary cities. Wesley Birdsong, the only Native American in Sayles's Western, chooses not to live on the reservation because he "couldn't take the politics" (*Scenario* 34). He has deliberately marginalized himself, living between

"Nowheres and Nothin' Much," a situation that pleases him. Still, these disparate ethnic representatives are all connected, sharing a past that will not leave them.

As he did in *City of Hope*, Sayles uses the camera to remind us of the interconnections among his characters. Unlike the earlier film, *Lone Star* uses wonderfully choreographed elisions from one time frame to another which reinforce the power of history, a thematic technique Orson Wells used in *Citizen Kane*, albeit with much more flash. Cinematographer Stuart Dryburgh, known for his work with director Jane Campion, particularly in *The Piano* (1993), served as Sayles's director of photography. Like Sayles, Dryburgh had never worked in Super 35 mm, wide-screen format. Super 35 uses normal lenses, allowing for greater horizontal dimension, instead of anamorphic lenses, which squeeze the total image horizontally (Wilson 66). To capture the long, flat look of the borderland, Super 35 was a logical choice.

The results are evident in Dryburgh's photography. When Sayles's characters speak about the past, the camera slowly tracks in toward the speaker. The camera reinforces the importance of history that suffuses Sayles's film as it slowly glides into the past. Sayles used a similar device in *City of Hope*, employing a lurching Steadicam to weave the diffused, hyperactive citizens of Hudson City together. In *Lone Star*, the transitions are poetic, languid, designed not to speed up present time but gently to compress decades.

Sayles wrote these visual transitions into the script for Lone Star, as he did in his screenplay for *City of Hope*. Achieving these elisions required creative teamwork. With Dryburgh and Dan Bishop, the production designer, Sayles used stagecraft and lighting to achieve the seamless transitions that we see throughout the film. More than just stylistic flashes, these transitions thematically contribute to the story. For example, when Chucho Montoya tells his version of Eladio Cruz's murder, he walks toward the left side of the frame, passing in front of a bright yellow sign, part of the mise-en-scène of the tire yard. The sign is lit in high key, so it attracts our attention. The camera follows Chucho from a personal distance. As he reaches the border of the sign, the camera rises above it, lifting us into a crane shot, to reveal Eladio Cruz 40 years earlier repairing a flat tire on his truck, which rests on a bright, sunny bridge spanning an arroyo. The cinematographer had to match two different lighting keys: Chucho in the tire yard, and the wide-angle shot of Eladio Cruz on the bridge. Sayles's production crew had to erect a small version of the tire yard near the bridge. Combined, these two filmmaking units created a visually tantalizing transition into the past. Eladio's clothes and the make of his truck tell us that we have crossed four decades. Yet the shift in screen time is borderless, transporting the audience into the past in a cinematic, fluid, organic fashion.

An edit cuts, or breaks, the film strip. *Lone Star*, which is about the psychological power of history, the inability to break away from the stories that affect each character and the entire community, uses the editing process thematically. On the visual level Sayles attempted to avoid breaks of any kind, particularly when moving into or out of the past. "In *Lone Star*," Sayles told Gavin Smith, "I didn't even want a dissolve, which is a soft cut, I didn't want that separation if I could avoid it" (63). For the most part, shifts into the past are smooth, without an editor's interference.

Still, to achieve the fluid movement we see on the screen, the filmmakers had to move backgrounds and often shoot two halves of a set in different places. This technique, however, adds vigor to Sayles's composition. His camera typically takes us to a personal distance from the speaker, inviting us into a private world, then allows us to see an event from a subjective point of view. Thus, Sayles deepens the psychological complexity of the film. Removed from the frame by a slow pan, the speaker still remains with us — we see that person's story, his or her struggle with the past

At times, Sayles starts a story in the voice of one speaker and concludes it in the voice of another; for instance, when Minnie Bledsoe describes Charley Wade to Sam, the flashback ends with Otis telling the story. Shifting the storyteller connects Minnie and Otis, even though they never appear together on the screen. Sayles also uses editing to link his characters. For example, when Pilar mutters that no one stays in love for 23 years, Sayles suddenly cuts to 1972, forcing his audience to make an abrupt leap in time, deliberately more jarring than the gliding visual elisions. Pilar is no longer telling the story — the intrusion of the past is out of balance stylistically. The drive-in sequence ends with a shot of Sam, in a medium shot, standing next to his car in the abandoned parking lot of the defunct drive-in; it is his memory we have witnessed. The harsh cutting into and out of the past underscores Sam's feelings. The glides into the past serve as a visual metaphor representing the memory of the speaker; the edits, which are abrupt, announce a memory that a character has internalized, something he or she is unwilling to share with others.

Sayles's mise-en-scène also reinforces the role of history in the film. The opening scene, in fact, is a good illustration of how the director uses the frame to transmit story ideas. The first image we see is a medium shot of the Texas scrub, cacti, yuccas, and other indigenous plants. Then, the camera slowly moves to the right, expanding the frame. In the foreground we see Cliff looking over the local vegetation; he dominates the shot as the camera glides over him, moving from left to right, capturing the flat horizon line of southwest Texas scrub country. Cliff fills the left side of the frame, but the camera carries us toward Mikey, an insignificant figure in the background, who will shortly uncover the bones of Charley Wade. Sayles accomplishes a number of things with this shot. First, the vegetation indicates an uninviting place. Second, he introduces us to the gently moving camera that he will incorporate at significant moments throughout the film. Finally, Mikey's position in the frame metaphorically suggests to us that history is never far away.

Visually, Sayles also goes against the grain of convention. *Lone Star*, which has some of the trappings of a Western, is clearly a revisionist film: Sayles takes a skeptical look at the popular values celebrated in classical Westerns. For instance, Sayles does not stun his audience with the epic grandeur of the western United States, as did John Ford in the majority of his Westerns. When we see Cliff and Mikey, they are on an abandoned rifle range. The arid, inhospitable desert is not an enemy to be conquered. Just the opposite. The rifle range has been tamed and abandoned. The colors in this opening shot are not vibrant; rather, they are washed out, deliberately made unappealing. Cliff and Mikey stand out because of the odd clothes they wear, looking like guys from New Jersey, not Westerners. Sayles presents a different look at the Western, one less heroic, less romantic than is typical of the genre. In fact, when the ostensible hero of the film, Sam Deeds, enters the picture, the first thing we notice is that he does not carry a weapon of any kind, a costuming choice that marks Sam's character. Because he lacks the primary piece of law enforcement equipment, a gun, we must question his position as a peace officer; this is not a conventional lawman.

Another illustration of Sayles's use of the frame occurs at the end of the film, when Sam tells Pilar that they share the same father. Sam and Pilar, sitting on the hood of his car in the abandoned drive-in, are shot from a personal distance, which is in balance with most of the master shots that we have seen throughout the film. The proxemic pattern within the frame is intimate, the distance of physical involvement, appropriate for lovers. Everything within the frame suggests an honest connection between these people. They are, of course, closer than either of them ever imagined. After Sam presents Pilar with the photograph of Buddy and Mercedes playing in the water years ago, Sayles cuts to a wide shot taken from a slightly low angle. Sam and Pilar are now in the middle of the frame, no longer dominating it. Instead, the empty movie screen, long neglected, hangs over them. The mise-en-scène is suggestive. Sam has accepted his past; it no longer plays like a bad movie in his head. Although he hated his father and wanted to convince the community of Frontera that Buddy murdered Charley Wade, Sam has instead uncovered the truth. Buddy did not want his son committing incest with his daughter, and he covered up the murder of the corrupt Charley Wade to save the life of the kind yet feckless young Hollis Pogue. While not truly at peace with his father's memory, Sam can now walk away from the cover-up. He can also, if Pilar is willing, walk away from their shared past and cross the social borders set up against incest to create their own new story. The images of history no longer loom over them.

Sayles, however, is not one for pat endings. As he suggested to Gavin Smith, the empty screen can suggest something less positive: There is a sense at the end of the film "that they are looking at the screen as if something may come up, but the screen is wasted" (62). Their love, their relationship, which is antisocial by common definition, cannot be projected, cannot be sanctioned by society; it is beyond the boundary of socially acceptable behavior. Therefore, they have to create their own story, create their own pictures, but in isolation. Nothing can remain in Frontera for Sam and Pilar if they stay together.

This final shot displays Sayles's use of the wide-screen format. "What I wanted to do … was to make everything more visual," said Sayles, "because there wasn't much action in the film" (Lippy 195). Mercedes Cruz serves as a good illustration of how Sayles uses the frame and the camera to comment on his characters. "With Mercedes," Sayles remarked, "she's first seen out-of-focus in the background — this little woman Hollis briefly refers to in the cafe scene. Then you see her in the restaurant kitchen, and even though she's still small, she's giving orders, and every time you see her she gains stature, literally. So that by the time you see her alone, we're below her, and she seems bigger" (Lippy 195). Mercedes too has evolved by the end of the film. No longer willing to exist in a world of shadows and secrets — underlined by the canted night shots in her backyard — Mercedes decides to help Enrique and his fiancée (Maricela Gonzalez), an act of compassion Mercedes seemed incapable of earlier. Sayles, then, uses the frame and the camera to depict how Mercedes has adjusted her life.

Colonel Delmore Payne, on the other hand, is introduced as a forceful figure the first time we see him. His face fills the frame as he tells his officers exactly who he is and what he expects. Sayles cuts this scene to reinforce the colonel's presence, balancing close-ups of Del with reverse angles of his officers in a medium shot. We know who is in control. Yet as the story builds, Del falls from the center of the frame, moving to the margins. Moreover, Del begins to share the frame with others, and he is usually dressed in civilian clothes, removed from the military base, his seat of power. When Del speaks with Chet at the end of the film, he is once again photographed in a close-up. But this time the detailed shot reveals an emotional and intellectual change. Del understands that his version of military life has separated him from his father, his son, and even his troops. Sayles's compositional progression show us how his character has changed. Sayles deliberately establishes proxemic patterns within the frame to indicate positions of power among his characters.

Dryburgh and Sayles designed a stylistically significant shot to detail Sam's emotional life, which works like the nocturnal boat ride in *Passion Fish*. The montage is dominated by dissolves, which add a lyrical quality to the images, a formalistic touch within a realistic film. We see Sam driving down a deserted highway, the broken white line of the road reflected on his windshield. Other cars, their headlights reflected in his windshield, pass him by. But we see only their headlights and the movement of Sam's eyes to his rearview mirror to indicate the presence of another driver. The imagery here provides a different look at Sam, a subjective take on his mysterious love for Pilar.

For most of the film, Sam just asks objective questions like any good investigator. This montage, however, because it is stylistically distinct from the rest of the film, communicates something different about Sam: "This is the part of Sam's life that he has a chance to change," Sayles explained. "This is the part that, if it goes right, is outside of society. I wanted something about what's going on inside him, which has got to be very hopeful" (Smith 64). For the most part, the frame is dark, except for Chris Cooper's face, which is lit in high contrast. As the sequence unwinds, the camera moves closer to Cooper, until he appears in close-up. Sam's conflicting emotions are transmitted by the actor's look of concern and confusion. With only the haunted sound of Little Willie John's voice singing "My Love Is" to describe Sam's condition, Sayles and Dryburgh silently communicate his character's desires.

Dryburgh used a variety of visual techniques in *Lone Star*. We see the ethereal nature of Sam's love for Pilar, sunbaked natural history footage of the scrubland, Steadicam shots, and one or two shots that look like documentary footage. But it is the powerful, unedited glides into the past that mark the visual style of *Lone Star*. Remarkably, some critics, bound to see Sayles as a writer only, still belittle his visual compositions. For example, Hal Hinson, the *Washington Post*'s film critic, suggests that "his directing style hasn't grown much beyond that of a first-year film student. Perhaps his literary roots make him suspicious of Hollywood slickness, but as an alternative, Sayles foregoes style altogether. Visually, his films are inert, dead on the screen" (6). Using standards that apply to Hollywood filmmakers working without budgetary restraint does not do Sayles justice. "I'm totally uninterested in form or style for its own sake," Sayles remarked. "But I am interested in the technique of how to tell a story" (Smith 67). Each of Sayles's films has a distinct look, a deliberate stylistic design, often dictated by financial limitations. Sayles believes that he does not have a signature visual style, which is part of his filmmaking philosophy: "I've been able to work with different DPs [directors of photography], and haven't always tried to work with the same person. I've tried to work with ones who don't have a recognizable style, but kind of go with the subject" (Smith 67). For Sayles, the story reigns supreme, and the look of each of his films reflects that aesthetic. *Lone Star* is about history, and Sayles's camera reproduces history's power with clarity and panache.

Music too is fundamental to Sayles's cinematic storytelling. As Sayles told Megan Ratner, one of the reasons for *Lone Star*'s large budget was so that he could buy music: "Music costs have quadrupled since I made *Baby, It's You* ... there were some songs we just couldn't get ... it went down from 27 songs. But that's all right, it was never meant to be *Casino*, where the soundtrack is a great double album" (34). Once again Sayles sat down with Mason Daring to design the musical soundtrack.

Certainly subject dictates the type of music Sayles selects for his films. Daring remarked, half jokingly, to an interviewer on National Public Radio that Sayles loves all music and that he intends to use all of it in his movies (Dowell). Daring segued from melancholy Celtic arrangements of *The Secret of Roan Inish* to the music of the Anglo-Mexican border country, akin to quitting The Chieftains to join Los Lobos. Essentially, *Lone Star*'s soundtrack aurally illustrates the three dominant cultures represented in the film: Mexican, Anglo, and African American. For Sayles music was a primary part of his research: "I learned more from listening to songs — both Spanish and English — than from the literature I read" (Lippy 51). Daring's music is wide ranging, a collection of broad musical styles. In the 1950s rhythm and blues music still had a large listening audience, even as it was transforming into rock 'n' roll. American genres like blues, gospel, and country and western combined easily with ranchera boleros (country ballads), conjunto (ensemble harmonizing), and corrido (traditional Mexican folk songs revolving around a heroic figure) music from Mexico. The wailing harmonica of bluesman Marion "Little Walter" Jacobs, for instance, sounds like the saxophones heard in early rock tunes. Ivory Joe Hunter, a piano crooner, who wrote "Since I Met You Baby," witnessed the transformation of his song into a major Mexican hit sung by "El Rock 'n' Roll Kid," Freddie Fender. "Desde Que Conozco" was a major Spanish-language hit for the young San Antonio singer, who would go on to become one of Texas's best-known musicians. Little Willie John's "My Love" seals the emotional impact of Sam's nighttime drive; Ruben Mendez's "Mi Unico Camino," announces Sam's quest during the opening credits, albeit in Spanish. Daring selected Lucinda William's "The Night's Too Long" and Rudolfo Olivares's "Juana La Cubana" to add a dash of the 1990s to his soundtrack. Like the movie itself, the music Sayles and Daring chose offers a rich take on cultures from different decades. More important, the music spices *Lone Star*'s story and its visual composition.

For example, the master shot of Sam and Pilar in Cafe Santa Barbara illustrates how Sayles uses music in *Lone Star* to comment on the history of his characters. The scene opens with Sam and Pilar sitting in chairs, gazing out into the night. Sayles then cuts to a shot of them in profile. They are on the right side of the frame and the alignment of their faces leads us toward a dominant feature of the mise-en-scène, an old-fashioned jukebox glowing brightly in the background. Pilar rises and walks toward the jukebox. She looks at the selections and says, "My mother hasn't changed the songs since I was ten" (38). She puts a quarter in the machine and punches in her selection, "Desde Que Conozco," sung by Freddie Fender. Earlier in the film, when Del walks into Big O's, Sayles uses Ivory Joe Hunter's original version, "Since I Met You Baby." Using two versions of the same song, Sayles provides a cultural anchor for both the black and Mexican characters in the film: "It was a song that was a hit on black stations, and then it was the first hit for Freddie Fender, the first Hispanic rock-and-roll guy. He took rock-and-roll, black music that was becoming used by white people, and brought it to

Latin America" (Smith 64). The mixture of cultures that percolates all through *Lone Star* also informs Sayles's choice of music; it too crosses borders.

Sayles and Daring also use music traditionally — commenting on characters, establishing settings, advancing the story — and to suggest the mood and spirit of *Lone Star*. "Mi Unico Camino" plays over the opening credits, to help set the locale. The Spanish lyrics, accordion, and guitar work indicate that we have crossed a border. The title of the song, "My Only Road," indicates Sam's reason for returning to Frontera, which is to renew his love for Pilar. On-screen we see his police cruiser cutting through the Texas scrub toward the place where Charley Wade's remains were found. The song, then, transports us, suggests Sam's affair of the heart, and ironically comments on the unexpected road Sam has taken, one that could prove his father murdered Charlie Wade. To reinforce the fact that America is, from Sayles's point of view, a multilingual country, the song comes without translation. In contrast to this traditional recording, the next major selection, "Juana La Cubana," announces a generational distinction. The song is heard as we watch Amado Cruz hooking up a stolen CD player, while a deputy sheriff watches. Performed by Fito Olivares, the instrumentation is electronic, bass driven, indicating a contemporary situation; indeed, on-screen we see young, aimless teenagers bopping to the beat of the song blasting from a boom box, a subtle comment on the economy of this Texas border town.

Big O's also comes with its own music, the rousing rhythm and blues of Little Walter, whose harmonica screams out the pleasures of a night away from work. "Boogie" foreshadows the shooting about to occur at Big O's, capturing both the joy and the violence of the blues. Duke Levine's sonic electric guitar riff on "Papertrail," which overlays Sam's review of the old police files, underlines Sam's attempts at connecting the pieces of the murder mystery and, more importantly, the facts of his own history. The guitar lick returns when we move from the close-up of young Chucho Montoya hiding near the bridge where Eladio Cruz was murdered to a shot of Sam Deeds standing on the bridge itself 40 years later. Levine's guitar calls attention to connections Sam is making in his head.

Little Willie John's "My Love," used to articulate Sam's love for Pilar, contains a reverb effect and fades out slowly, adding to the transcendent quality of Sam's nighttime drive toward Pilar. "Sam and Pilar," written by Mason Daring and performed by Duke Levine and Mike Turk, fuses blues harmonica and Spanish folk guitar to highlight the combination of cultures represented by Sam and Pilar's love.

Typically, Sayles and Daring did their homework when it came to selecting music for *Lone Star*. By the time the crew started shooting, Sayles already had the soundtrack (Ratner 34). The primary example of his careful planning is Charley Wade's murder scene, which contains no words, only images, an unusual dramatic choice for Sayles. He selected Little Walter's "Blue and

Lonesome," a tune dominated by a searing guitar and wailing harmonica flourishes. "There's a great internal violence to it," Sayles remarked, "a pounding
rhythm and a kind of inevitable feeling" (Ratner 34). As filmed, the sequence
is impressionistic, full of canted angles, and marked by abrupt cuts. We do
not hear from the characters. Instead, the music carries us through the
sequence. Sayles breaks the tension enhanced by the music with Buddy Deeds
shouting at Charley Wade from the doorway of the bar. The gunshots punctuate the scene's inevitable conclusion. Even the song heard over the closing
credits, Patsy Montana's "I Want to Be a Cowboy's Sweetheart," provides an
ironic coda for the romanticized cowboy life.

Music augmented Sayles's story, one that would be larger than a physical border. Sayles and Daring filled *Lone Star*'s soundtrack with music that
works on multiple levels, crisscrossing generic borders. Their collaborative
work as a team continues to be an indispensable part of Sayles's cinematic
storytelling.

Lone Star features many familiar faces, actors who have worked with
Sayles before. Sayles actually wrote some of the parts with specific actors in
mind: "I had Chris Cooper in mind to play Sam, and Elizabeth Peña as Pilar.
And I also had Steve Lang [Mikey] in mind" (Lippy 194). In addition, once
Sayles created Bunny, he immediately considered Frances McDormand for the
part. Because of the respect many actors have for him, Sayles still attracts talented yet little-known performers, people who can, according to Sayles,
inhabit a "character and really listen" (Zucker 329).

All three of the leads, part of Sayles's loosely affiliated repertory company, had previously worked with Sayles. Joe Morton, who has enjoyed the
longest working relationship with Sayles, first appeared as the charming alien
in *The Brother from Another Planet*; later Morton appeared in *City of Hope* as
the idealistic young city councilman, Wynn, who learns that truth and
integrity are characteristics that a strong political leader cannot afford. Chris
Cooper, whose performance as Sam Deeds perfectly matches *Lone Star*'s quiet
style, first appeared in *Matewan* as the pacifist union organizer, Joe Kenehan,
and then as Riggs, a construction foreman, in *City of Hope*. Elizabeth Peña,
although never previously involved in one of Sayles's film projects, worked for
him in *Shannon's Deal*, his short-lived television drama, as Lucy, a woman who
became Shannon's secretary because she could not afford to pay him for his
legal services. In addition to the three leads, some of the other cast members
who have worked with Sayles include Miriam Colon (*City of Hope*), Clifton
James (*Eight Men Out*), Leo Burmester (*Passion Fish*), Stephen Mendillo
(*Lianna, Eight Men Out, City of Hope*), and Stephen Lang (*City of Hope*).

As is his practice, Sayles wrote short biographical sketches for each of
the 50-odd speaking parts in the film. Although recognized as an actor's director, Sayles allows little creative leeway on the set: "I don't want to be on the
set and find them playing something in a certain way, and when I ask why,

they say, 'Oh, my uncle burned me with an iron when I was 5 years old.' Because actors will do that, they'll fill it in if they think they need to. So I'd rather fill it in for them, so they're grounded" (Lippy 52). The biographical sketches ensure that Sayles's own vision of the film reaches the screen, free from improvisational indulgences. Moreover, the sketches allow each actor to understand his or her character fully and adjust easily to minor script changes. The sketches also help conserve Sayles's budget: There are fewer takes, no rehearsals. Because Sayles knew so many of his main actors, he spent more time with the secondary performers, people who always figure prominently in a Sayles film. This connection allowed Sayles to get the best performances as quickly as possible: "So much of movie acting is about the moment. If they know where they're coming from before we start shooting, then they can really play the moment. Especially with a low budget, where you're not going to want to do it a million times" (Lippy 52).

Morton, who grew up in a military family, turns in another strong piece of work for Sayles, who is obviously comfortable working with Morton, now an accomplished character actor. Because of Morton's professional background and personal history, Sayles expanded Del's role in the film, a revision tactic he often employs: "If it seems the [actor] might [take the part], it influences what I do. Usually I think I might expand the part because the actor is so good or can bring something personal to it.... So when [Morton] took the role of Delmore and got to the set of *Lone Star*, he was the guy who knew who saluted who" (Nechak 25). Unfortunately, even though he turns up in major Hollywood films from time to time, Morton remains an underappreciated actor. In *Lone Star* Morton gives a superb performance. Moreover, as Cliff Thompson observes, Morton plays a black man "within the larger society," yet not reduced to a simplistic stereotype, so often the picture received by the American moviegoing public (32–33).

Delmore Payne, who cleaves to ruling authority without question, must change as *Lone Star* progresses, bending to the realities he has previously ignored. His father, Otis, has little regard for formal rules and laws, but he does understand how the game of life is played, an awareness Del comes to late in his own life. Morton must transmit Del's new understanding without the aid of dialogue, because even though Del changes internally, he is still not well practiced at articulating his emotions. Therefore, Morton must use his eyes and body to make the audience recognize Del's modulated conversion. When Athena reveals her take on the military to Colonel Payne, his carefully constructed world visibly shifts. In the scene, Morton drops the ramrod-straight posture that has marked his character since the opening of the film; he sags just a little, his eyes move downward slightly, communicating a change in his perception. In addition, Morton silently reveals the compassion beneath Del's military-hardened exterior when he tells his son that the military might not be his best career choice. As he did in *The Brother from Another Planet* and *City of Hope*, Morton shows us a complex, intelligent man who is troubled and compassionate.

When Sayles told Chris Cooper that he had written the part of Sheriff Sam Deeds specifically for him, the actor was staggered. "Thirty or forty minutes into the story I realized this is not a small part," Cooper noted (Ryan "Mr. 'Last Minute'..." 11). Ironically, Sayles almost passed over Cooper for the role of Joe Kenehan in *Matewan* because of the actor's quiet seriousness, a trait that fits Sam Deeds well. Still, Sayles cast Cooper a bit against type: "I don't think anybody has thought of Chris as a romantic lead, but he has that side" (Ryan "Mr. 'Last Minute'..." 11). Like Morton's Delmore Payne, Sam Deeds is haunted by a flawed father-son relationship. In Sam's case, according to Sayles's character description, "when he was an adolescent, a guy [Buddy] he used to idolize turned out to be a hypocrite." Sam drives himself to expose that hypocrisy to a community that deified Buddy.

Psychologically, Sam is riveted to the past, to Buddy's mythic figure. Yet, while Buddy Deeds profited from a conveniently arranged real estate deal, Sam discovers that his father was an honorable man who understood the rules of the game and held to his own code of integrity. Cooper, then, must play a deeply conflicted character without relying on the histrionics often associated with confused men. Instead he uses silences, gaps in dialogue, to speak for him. Sam Deeds unfolds slowly. By the end of the film we come to believe that he has made peace with his past. Andrew Sarris, the noted film critic, observed that Cooper's "Sam Deeds is the antithesis of the flamboyant stereotype of Texas heroes. There is no swagger in him, only a soft-spoken authority, and a cautious tread through the still-hot embers of his troubled adolescence" ("At the Movies..." 28). Cooper offers a low-key performance, which underlines his talent. Elizabeth Peña may be the most recognizable of Sayles's leads, having acted in *Down and Out in Beverly Hills*, *La Bamba*, *Jacob's Ladder*, and *Free Willy 2: The Adventure Home*, among other Hollywood films. A theater-trained actress, Peña is perfectly cast as Pilar Cruz, who unlike the male leads does not overtly struggle with her past. For Pilar the present is the challenge, particularly her son, her mother, and Sam Deeds. The role demands that Peña mix the reserve of a high school teacher, the worry of a troubled mother, and the sexuality of a long-lost lover. She makes Pilar believable, an honest portrait of a woman laboring with her life as a daughter, mother, and widow.

Peña jumped at the chance to work with Sayles again, not realizing that she was cast as the female lead. Nevertheless, she was gratified to play a nuanced, complex Latina. Peña brings a sad-eyed eloquence to her character; she is also asked to express more visible anger than other characters in the film. Peña's Pilar is rational, stern, and loving. With the firm support of Sayles's writing and direction, the lead actors deliver their lines with believability and integrity, while marking their characters with small gestures that make them human.

Lone Star *(1996): Director Sayles and Frances McDormand, who plays Sam Deed's ex-wife, Bunny, chat before shooting her scene. The set design underscores Bunny's most American obsession: football. Photo by Alan Pappé.*

The central characters do not foreground a Sayles picture. The secondary characters typically carry just as much weight as the leads, frequently understanding more than the people who are the focus of the film. Clifton James communicates Hollis Pogue's troubled spirit, stained by a past he cannot detach himself from. He adds intrigue and ultimately empathy to a character whose role grows with the film. Matthew McConaughey, now a bankable Hollywood star, looks like the legend Buddy Deeds is supposed to be; his demeanor is cool, collected, and dangerous. His dark eyes hint at a willingness to kill. Kris Kristofferson plays Charley Wade with unrestrained malice, yet, due to his skills as an actor, we can see an intelligence at work: He makes us understand that Wade thinks he is justified in his actions. When he tells young Otis Payne that "runnin' numbers without I know about it is both illegal and unhealthy" (*Scenario* 20), Kristofferson bites out the words, and we know the young man is in deep trouble. Eddie Robinson's Chet Payne stands in stark contrast to his stern father by showing us how willing he is to discover his own roots; he looks and acts like the graphic artist he longs to be. Miriam Colon hides Mercedes Cruz's compassionate heat beneath a hard exterior with skill. Gabriel Casseus shows us young Otis's cockiness through smirks and sideward glances, and he maintains his pride when overpowered by the vicious Sheriff Wade. Finally, Frances McDormand delivers an incredible cameo as Bunny, a not-so-atypical American manic-depressive football addict.

Lone Star carried Sayles's screenwriting talents to a much wider audience than he had ever reached before. The film deserved the Academy Award nomination it received because *Lone Star* reminds us that language in film can be as complex as it is in literature. Sayles's ability to keep multiple story lines moving toward a believable and startling conclusion raises him above most American filmmakers — independent or commercial.

Sayles also makes a few cinematic references in *Lone Star*, notably to *Chinatown* (1974), *Citizen Kane* (1939), and *Touch of Evil* (1969), all films dealing with history and its complexity. When Charley Wade kills Eladio Cruz, out of the frame emerges a brief glimpse of Edwin S. Porter's *The Great Train Robbery* (1903), a Western that ends with a close-up of an outlaw firing his pistol at the audience. Sayles even reminds us of his B movie roots when he places *Black Mama, White Mama* on the screen during the drive-in scene. *Lone Star* also revises the Western, updating the genre with a skeptical eye on the past and a clear eye on the present. The death of Charley Wade, for example, looks and feels like a traditional Hollywood Western showdown. With Kristofferson playing Charley Wade, shades of Sam Peckinpah haunt the frame. Of course, Sayles's story is about real conditions, not ghosts from Hollywood's past, and the shoot-out sequence shows how he tips the Western upside down. We do not expect the ineffective young Hollis to step into the conflict, yet he does, and he kills Wade in a style far more historically accurate than that of most of the deaths we have witnessed in countless Westerns. Hollis shoots Wade in the back. Sayles's remarkable tapestry, moreover, reflects contemporary life on the border and throughout the United Sates, matching current conditions to his fictional account of community dynamics in Frontera, Texas. As Andrew Sarris observed, "What begins as a murder mystery ends as an Oedipal conundrum with two double-whammy revelations of Sophoclean grandeur" ("At the Movies..." 28). Sayles wrote, directed, acted in (his part, that of Zack, a border patrolman, was cut), and edited *Lone Star*, which stands as his most commercially successful achievement to date.

When asked in 1995 by Stephen Holden of the *New York Times* to comment on being a well-known director, Sayles noted that only a "small minority" of moviegoers actually recognize a director's name and that an even smaller number recognized his name. *Lone Star* changed that assessment. Because of his talents, Hollywood's inability to produce films tailored for adult sensibilities, and the financial backing and public relations machine of Castle Rock Entertainment, Sayles reached a broader audience than he ever had in the past. He appeared on "Late Night with David Letterman" to promote the film and at the Academy Awards ceremony, two places seemingly outside his world. In addition, Sayles opted to include *Lone Star* in a package of movies — including *Space Jam*, *Michael*, and *Mars Attacks!*, all commercial Hollywood films — that will run on TNT and TBS. Sayles struck a rich deal with Turner's company, which agreed not to cut the film's running time. Clearly, *Lone Star* elevated Sayles's commercial name recognition.

Yet Sayles, always cutting across the grain, had already started working on his next film, even while he was being advertised to mainstream filmgoers. Shooting for *Men With Guns* (*Hombres Armados*), his Spanish-language film based loosely on the Guatemalan civil war, began in January 1997 and wrapped in late February. Working outside the English language is chancy, but taking chances is what Sayles's brand of filmmaking is all about.

14

Contributing More

Very few people get to make more than a couple of independent films without either starting to work for the studios, or giving up, turning into an underground filmmaker.

—John Sayles (Chute)

Film is a collaborative art. As Louis Giannetti observes, "Film is a more complex medium than the traditional arts because movies synthesize many language systems simultaneously, bombarding the spectator with literally hundreds of symbolic ideas and emotions at the same time, some of them overt, others subliminal" (*Understanding Movies* 468). The process of making a film is difficult, expensive, and long. There are no easy decisions in filmmaking. However, for the most part, audiences take movies for granted. They are interested in how movies look, not how they are made. Most viewers do not even know who directed the movie, let alone who the editor was. Even John Sayles was not immune to this condition: "I didn't even know that people made movies until I was in college. I just went to them, and it was not a John Ford movie, it was a John Wayne movie" (Zucker 343). Now, after making 11 of his own pictures, Sayles knows well what goes into making a movie: writing, planning, directing, and editing, combined with the collaboration of a cast and crew, which somehow meld to realize his independent vision.

Sayles enjoys the fusing of ideas, attitudes, and styles that filmmaking demands. Although a movie set is far from being a democracy, Sayles makes every effort to keep his film crew operating as a cohesive, relatively democratic unit. As he wrote in 1987, "Getting people to work with rather than in spite of each other can be difficult, and whenever possible we try to appeal to people's sense of collaborating on a shared project rather than retreat behind the safe formula of rank" (*Thinking in Pictures* 105).

Sayles is truly an independent filmmaker, unlike most of his contemporaries. Asked in an interview about his reputation as the champion of independent filmmaking, Sayles responded, "I hope it means that my independence from the studio structure is not just physical, but aesthetic. I hope that with my work I can encourage other people to make films on their own without the pressure of the studio telling them to change the story or cast somebody who's an untalented schmuck" (Hickenlooper 309). Sayles presents his stories in his way, without outside interference. Although Sayles has profited from Hollywood's budgets by writing scripts and doctoring screenplays, when it comes to his own films, he does not function well under the aegis of a studio. Sayles wants to put his own vision on the screen — like John Cassavetes, for example — and not a corporate vision beholden to test audiences and ratings boards.

Viewing Sayles's film work from *Return of the Secaucus Seven* (1980) to *Men With Guns* (1998) we witness the rapid and astonishing growth of an independent film artist, a rarity in the American cinema where so much depends on the marketplace and the promotion that the studios provide. It is entirely possible that Sayles will be the last truly independent filmmaker of our time. Movies demand money; money determines the images. Even some of the new and exciting filmmakers on the scene today — Quentin Tarantino, Nick Gomez, Robert Rodriguez, Leslie Harris, Hal Hartley — look to studios for financial help to make their movies.

Unlike the work of many of his independent peers, all of Sayles's work is marked by language. "Talk is cheap," he explains, "and action is expensive" (*Thinking in Pictures* 6). Sayles creates talking prose, capturing the essence of people through their speech, which makes them full, believable characters. He is intrigued by people who keep going in the face of long odds and uncertainty. Many critics wrongly suggest that he celebrates "outsiders" or "losers," weak nouns used to classify ordinary people, folks who are not physically perfect, wealthy, or connected. Sayles's characters seem exceptional because few films revolve around the lives of regular people. As Louis Giannetti correctly points out in his review of *Matewan*, "There are few American filmmakers who demonstrate such decency and compassion toward ordinary people, people who would be astonished at the suggestion that a movie could be made about their lives. That's Sayles's greatest strength as an artist — he can see the poetry in our souls" ("John Sayles' Ordinary People" 10). For the most part, contemporary directors lack the ability and perhaps the desire to do so. Sayles's blue-collar ties show through in his characters. He is one of the few contemporary directors (or fiction writers, for that matter) concerned with issues of class and work. Sayles can capture the speech of a lawyer or a mechanic, a bayou fishing guide or a soap opera star, a faculty housewife or a big-city mayor with impeccable precision. A Sayles script delivers honest, concrete language, created for real characters, a stylistic trait that attracts quality actors to his low-budget productions.

Sayles is eclectic in his subject matter, so he defies popular critical labels. However, certain threads weave through all of Sayles's film work. From sports to cooking, Sayles knows how to present small, carefully researched details to add regional flavor and a sense of place to his work. For example, his musical interests move from rock 'n' roll to urban blues to folk. He uses music to enliven and define his films, not merely to manipulate our emotions. Music helps Sayles enhance his ideas without telling his audience how to think; it establishes mood, reveals character, and enriches emotion.

The tension that exists between an individual and the community comes through in all of Sayles's film work. Often, his film narratives explore how difficult, and perhaps undesirable, it is to fit into prescribed social groups. For example, at the conclusion of *The Brother from Another Planet*, we see the Brother, who has been liberated from slavery, standing alone in front of a chain-link fence. Although he has discovered a community of his own, other escaped alien slaves, that he stands by himself at the end of the film signals his triumph, although the fence is an uncomfortable reminder that there is still work to be done. *City of Hope* magnifies the troubling fact of urban tribes, whether they be ethnic or job related, and only when characters break from their insular groups do they achieve autonomy, usually at great cost. *Passion Fish* too comes to an ambiguous, uncertain finish: Are May-Alice and Chantelle, two women who have spent considerable time with each other throughout the film, truly friends? *Lone Star* also raises questions about where and how people from different cultures and races can and cannot mix. Rather than exclusively bringing people together, Sayles's films also focus on how people are cut off from different ethnic groups, different cultures, and different ideas.

What we remember best are Sayles's characters, who range from college friends on the cusp of 30 to a black extraterrestrial to an amorous Louisiana blacksmith to the hard-bitten "Tire King" of Ciudad León. In each case, the details Sayles employs to embellish his creations — the games they play, the food they eat, the music they listen to — describe them and enhance his film narratives. Before the actors arrive on set, for example, Sayles provides them with short biographies of their characters. In his own detailed outline, Sayles knows how each of his characters interact and connect with other figures in his story. The mosaic that he creates is impressive: His characters look, act, and sound the way spectators expect them to. His stories are always multi-layered, full of voices that we hear daily. Sayles's ability to pick up the peculiarities of speech is extraordinarily keen.

A lot of negative criticism has been directed at Sayles's presumed visual limitations. *Return of the Secaucus Seven*, for example, is technically raw, not an unusual trait for debut films. Yet in a 1996 poll conducted by *Filmmaker*, the magazine of independent film, Sayles's *Return of the Secaucus Seven* was voted the fifth most important independent film of all time. As most independent filmgoers realize, his production budget interfered with his ability to enrich its visual composition. But Sayles is not interested in visual pyrotechnics to enhance the form of his work. At heart, he is a storyteller whose style is concrete, direct. He knows that stylistic virtuosity can interfere with the complicated pulse of his narratives. His visual compositions vary from film to film, but Sayles has become an assured filmmaker, as *Passion Fish*, *The Secret of Roan Inish*, and *Lone Star* clearly prove. Ironically, when Sayles deliberately adjusted his visual style for *City of Hope*, using a relentless Steadicam, he was taken to task by some critics because he tried to be visually innovative. Sayles's rationale for the relentless motion was to articulate visually the tenuous condition of our cities, to stress the interconnectedness of Hudson City's citizens, and to underscore the collective nature of urban life. In a backhanded way, the criticism leveled at Sayles stems from his narrative talent. Critics of his first seven films liked for the most part what he had to say, but they wanted more visual stimulation, the sort of stylistic dazzle that mainstream films use to capture audiences' attention.

Men With Guns (*Hombres Armados*) (1998) marks a return to more overtly political concerns, yet like all of Sayles's work, the film's focus is people:

> The idea for this particular story came from two different friends. Both had family who had been involved in international programs in Latin America. One was a doctor who trained other doctors, and the other was an agronomist who trained people in growing corn. Both had these experiences in helping people out. The very people they helped became suspect in the eyes of their own government, basically because they were helping Indians, and that was something that only a communist would do. They discovered that most of the people they had trained were murdered within a few years. (Johnson 10)

For this film, based loosely on the Guatemalan civil war, which ended recently after 36 years of fighting, Sayles wrote his screenplay in Spanish and then translated it to English. *Men With Guns*, the English-subtitled version of the film, was released in the United States and in Europe, where audiences are more receptive to multilingual films. Sayles put up close to half the production money ($1 million) himself (Simon *passim*). Sayles's scripts-for-hire work, boosted even more by the success of *Lone Star*, paid his share of the production.

Men With Guns follows Dr. Fuentes (Federico Luppi), a physician who attends the ruling class in an unidentified Latin American country, as he travels to see how the young students he trained to work as doctors for the rural poor have fared. Fuentes's well-meaning mission soon turns horrific: He discovers that all of his students have been murdered by men with guns — government troops who brutally suppress the indigenous population. Having moved beyond his society, Fuentes begins to face his own ignorance. As Fuentes travels, he is joined by a plucky boy (Dan Rivera Gonzáles), a soldier (Damián Delgado), a priest (Damián Alcazar), and a mute woman (Tina Cruz). All have been marked by the men with guns, and they exist in a ghostly reality. Together these desperate travelers, all seeking enlightenment, cross paths with numerous people who enhance their knowledge of themselves and the horrendous political reality that surrounds them. Finally the group reaches Cerca del Cielo ("Close to Heaven"), the place "where rumors go to die," the place that exists outside politics, and the place where Fuentes's heart gives out. Upon his death, Fuentes's medical bag is passed on to the soldier, who must assume the doctor's work. Sayles's final shot, a view of a higher mountain seen from the perspective of the mute woman, suggests that the journey toward enlightenment is a continuous struggle, more than a walk up a single mountain. Sayles's allegorical treatment of Fuentes's movement away from ignorance illuminates the film's fundamental theme: Political awareness is a responsibility.

The film, which echoes some of the ideas Sayles covered in *City of Hope*, revolves around the character of Dr. Fuentes, who was created out of stories told to Sayles by friends, including the novelist Franciso Goldman, whose *The Long Night of White Chickens* weaves elements of Guatemalan history into a murder investigation. *Men With Guns* displays Sayles's visual maturity and establishes him as the most daring American director working today. Sayles uses open and closed forms in his mise en scène to define the plight of Fuentes and the rural people. The narrative explores war, responsibility, and the weight of history. Sayles frames his narrative with a dash of magic realism, which forces his audience to question the reality of all the characters and situations in the film. Sayles reaches, once again, for universal elements in his cinematic storytelling. He does not want his viewers to see only a nameless Latin American country on the screen; rather, he paints conditions that exist all around the globe. Slawomir Idziak's cinematography captures the lush jungle environment. Mason Daring's score creates an audio accompaniment that enhances Fuentes's journey. And, as always, the performances are first rate, especially the work of rural people who, as Janet Maslin points out, had "never seen a film before they appeared in this one" ("Profile: John Sayles" B29). Finally, this is a film about not giving up, about fighting off easy cynicism, issues that Sayles will continue to examine in his next project, *Limbo*.

Sayles is still a young man. His output to this point in his career has been astounding, a fertility unmatched by almost any other independent or commercial filmmaker. He has accomplished all his own work outside of Hollywood or its celebrity. Sooner or later the value of his work will be accepted by mainstream filmgoers because Sayles is determined to continue telling stories about the lives of ordinary people. However, he appears uninterested in fame for himself, unspoiled by his stature as America's premier independent filmmaker, not to mention ace rewrite man. Speaking with Shelley Levitt, Sayles defined his own sense of reward:

> Every time out, people like your movie or they don't like your movie.... It makes a lot of money or it doesn't. I don't take any of that personally. For me, it's such a triumph just to get a movie financed and made, that the very existence of these movies is success enough. [90]

Filmography

The Films of John Sayles

Return of the Secaucus Seven   1980

Libra Films. *Producers:* William Aydelott and Jeffrey Nelson, for Salsipuedes Films. *Director:* John Sayles. *Screenplay:* John Sayles. *Editor:* John Sayles. *Cinematography:* Austin de Besche. *Music:* Mason Daring. *Songs:* Adam Le Fevre. *Running time:* 106 minutes.

Principal characters: Mark Arnott (Jeff); Gordon Clapp (Chip); Maggie Cousineau-Arndt (Frances); Adam Le Favre (J.T.); Bruce MacDonald (Mike); Jean Passanante (Irene); Maggie Renzi (Katie); David Strathairn (Ron); Karen Trott (Maura); John Sayles (Howie).

Lianna   1983

United Artist Classics. *Producers:* Jeffrey Nelson and Maggie Renzi, for Winwood Company. *Director:* John Sayles. *Screenplay:* John Sayles. *Editor:* John Sayles. *Cinematography:* Austin de Besche. *Art director:* Jeanne McDonnell. *Music:* Mason Daring. *Running time:* 110 minutes.

Principal characters: Linda Griffiths (Lianna); Jane Hallaren (Ruth); John DeVries (Dick); Jo Henderson (Sandy); Jessica Wight MacDonald (Theda); Jesse Solomon (Spencer); John Sayles (Jerry); Maggie Renzi (Sheila); Stephen Mendillo (Bob).

Baby, It's You   1983

Paramount Pictures. *Producers:* Amy Robinson and Griffin Dunne, for Double Play Productions. *Director:* John Sayles. *Screenplay:* John Sayles. *Editor:* Sonya Polonsky. *Cinematography:* Michael Ballhaus. *Story:* Amy Robinson. *Music:* Joel Dorn. *Songs:* The Supremes, Lou Reed, Bruce Springsteen, Frank Sinatra, Bobby Vinton, The Shirelles. *Running time:* 105 minutes.

Principal characters: Rosanna Arquette (Jill); Vincent Spano (Sheik); Joanna Merlin (Mrs. Rosen); Jack Davidson (Dr. Rosen); William Raymond (Mr. Ripeppi); Matthew Modine (Steve); Robert Downey, Jr. (Stewart).

The Brother from Another Planet   1984

Cinecom International. *Producers:* Peggy Rajski and Maggie Renzi, for A-Train Films. *Director:* John Sayles. *Screenplay:* John Sayles. *Editor:* John Sayles. *Cinematography:* Ernest Dickerson. *Production design:* Nora Chavooshian. *Art director:* Steve Lineweaver. *Music:* Mason Daring. *Running time:* 110 minutes.

Principal characters: Joe Morton (The Brother); Darryl Edwards (Fly); Steve James (Odell); Leonard Jackson (Smokey); Bill Cobbs (Walter); Maggie Renzi (Noreen); Tom Wright (Sam); Dee Dee Bridgewater (Malverne Davis); Caroline Aaron (Randy Sue Carter); Jamie Tirelli (Hector); John Sayles, David Strathairn (Bounty Hunters); Fisher Stevens (Cardsharp Magician).

Matewan   1987

Cinecom Entertainment Group. *Producers:* Peggy Rajski and Maggie Renzi, for Red Dog Films. *Director:* John Sayles. *Screenplay:* John Sayles. *Editor:* Sonya Polonsky. *Cinematography:* Haskell Wexler. *Production design:* Nora Chavooshian. *Art director:* Dan Bishop. *Costume design:* Cynthia Flynt. *Music:* Mason Daring. *Running time:* 132 minutes.

Principal characters: Chris Cooper (Joe Kenehan); Will Oldham (Danny Radnor); Jace Alexander (Hillard); Ken Jenkins (Sephus Purcell); Bob Gunton (C.E. Lively); Gary McCleery (Ludie); Kevin Tighe (Hickey); Gordon Clapp (Griggs); Mary McDonnell (Elma Radnor); James Earl Jones ("Few Clothes" Johnson); James Kizer (Tolbert); Michael Preston (Ellix); Jo Henderson (Mrs. Elkins); Nancy Mette (Bridey Mae); Joe Grifasi (Fausto); Ronnie Stapleton (Stennis); David Strathairn (Sid Hatfield); Ida Williams (Mrs. Knights); Maggie Renzi (Rosaria); Thomas A. Carlin (Turley); Tom Wright (Tom); Josh Mostel (Mayor Cabell Testerman); Davide Ferrario (Gianni); John Sayles (Hardshell Preacher).

Eight Men Out   1988

Orion Pictures. *Producers:* Sarah Pillsbury and Midge Sanford, for Sanford/Pillsbury Productions. *Director:* John Sayles. *Screenplay:* John Sayles. *Editor:* John Tintori. *Cinematography:* Robert Richardson. *Story: Eight Men Out,* by Eliot Asinof. *Production design:* Nora Chavooshian. *Art director:* Dan Bishop. *Costume design:* Cynthia Flynt. *Music:* Mason Daring. *Running time:* 120 minutes.

Principal characters: John Cusak (Buck Weaver); Don Harvey (Swede Risberg); John Mahoney (Kid Gleason); James Read (Lefty Williams); Michael Rooker (Chick Gandil); Charlie Sheen (Hap Felsch); David Strathairn (Eddie Cicotte); D.B. Sweeney ("Shoeless" Joe Jackson); John Sayles (Ring Lardner); Studs Terkel (Hugh Fullerton); Christopher Lloyd (Bill Burns); Clifton James (Charles Comiskey); Jace Alexander (Dickie Kerr); Gordon Clapp (Ray Schalk); Bill Irwin (Eddie Collins); Richard Edson (Billy Maharg); Kevin Tighe (Sport Sullivan); Maggie Renzi (Rose Cicotte); Stephen Mendillo (Monk); Tay Strathairn (Bucky).

City of Hope   1991

Samuel Goldwyn Company. *Producers:* Sarah Green and Maggie Renzi, for Esperanza Films. *Director:* John Sayles. *Screenplay:* John Sayles. *Editor:* John Sayles.

Cinematography: Robert Richardson. *Production design:* Dan Bishop and Dianna Freas. *Costume design:* John Dunn. *Art director:* Chas. B. Plummer. *Music:* Mason Daring. *Executive producer:* John Sloss. *Running time:* 129 minutes.

Principal characters: Vincent Spano (Nick); Joe Morton (Wynn); Tony LoBianco (Joe); Anthony John Denison (Rizzo); Barbara Williams (Angela); John Sayles (Carl); Bill Raymond (Les); Angela Bassett (Reesha); Josh Mostel (Mad Anthony); Jace Alexander (Bobby); Todd Graff (Zip); David Strathairn (Asteroid); Kevin Tighe (O'Brien); Daryl Edwards (Franklin); Ray Aranha (Former Mayor); Stephen Mendillo (Yoyo).

Passion Fish   1992

Miramax. *Producers:* Sarah Green and Maggie Renzi, for Atchafalaya Films. *Director:* John Sayles. *Screenplay:* John Sayles. *Editor:* John Sayles. *Cinematography:* Roger Deakins. *Production design:* Dan Bishop and Dianna Freas. *Costume design:* Cynthia Flynt. *Music:* Mason Daring. *Executive producer:* John Sloss. *Running time:* 138 minutes.

Principal characters: Mary McDonnell (May-Alice); Alfre Woodard (Chantelle); David Strathairn (Rennie); Vondie Curtis-Hall (Sugar); Maggie Renzi (Louise); Angela Bassett (Dawn/Rhonda); Sheila Kelley (Kim); Nancy Mette (Nina); Tom Wright (Luther); Leo Burmester (Reeves).

The Secret of Roan Inish   1995

First Look Pictures. *Producers:* Sarah Green and Maggie Renzi, for Skerry Movies Corporation. *Associate Producer:* R. Paul Miller. *Director:* John Sayles. *Screenplay:* John Sayles. *Editor:* John Sayles. *Cinematography:* Haskell Wexler. *Production designer:* Adrian Smith. *Costume design:* Consolata Boyle. *Music:* Mason Daring. *Executive producer:* John Sloss. *Running time:* 103 minutes.

Principal characters: Jeni Courtney (Fiona); Eileen Colgan (Tess); Mick Lally (Hugh); Richard Sheridan (Eamon); John Lynch (Tadhg); Cillian Byrne (Jamie); Susan Lynch (Nuala).

Lone Star   1996

Castle Rock Entertainment. *Producers:* R. Paul Miller and Maggie Renzi, for Rio Dulce Productions. *Director:* John Sayles. *Screenplay:* John Sayles. *Editor:* John Sayles. *Cinematography:* Stuart Dryburgh. *Production designer:* Dan Bishop. *Costume design:* Shay Cunliffe. *Music:* Mason Daring. *Songs:* Patsy Montana, Walter Jacobs, Lucinda Williams, Little Willie John, Big Joe Turner, Freddie Fender, Conjunto Bernal. *Executive producer:* John Sloss. *Running time:* 137 minutes.

Principal characters: Chris Cooper (Sam Deeds); Elizabeth Peña (Pilar Cruz); Joe Morton (Delmore Payne); Kris Kristofferson (Charley Wade); Clifton James (Hollis); Stephen Mendillo (Cliff); Stephen J. Lang (Mikey); Richard Coca (Enrique); Miriam Colon (Mercedes Cruz); Matthew McConaughey (Buddy Deeds); Eddie Robinson (Chet); Ron Canada (Otis); Gabriel Casseus (Young Otis); Leo Burmester (Cody); Tony Amendola (Chucho Montoya); Gordon

Tootoosis (Wesley Birdsong); Frances McDormand (Bunny); Gilbert R. Cuellar, Jr. (Eladio Cruz); Tay Strathairn (Young Sam).

Men With Guns (Hombres Armados) 1998

Sony Pictures Classics. *Producers:* R. Paul Miller and Maggie Renzi, for Anarchists' Convention Inc. *Director:* John Sayles. *Screenplay:* John Sayles. *Editor:* John Sayles. *Cinematography:* Slavomir Idziak. *Title photography:* Luis González Palma. *Production designer:* Felipe Fernández Del Paso. *Costume designer:* Mayes C. Rubeo. *Casting director:* Lizzie Curry Martinez. *Music:* Mason Daring. *Executive producers:* John Sloss, Doug Sayles, Jody Patton, and Lou Gonda. *English subtitles:* Helen Milsted Eisenman. *Running time:* 126 minutes.

Principal characters: Federico Luppi (Dr. Fuentes); Damián Delgado (Domingo, the Soldier); Dan Rivera González (Conejo, the Boy); Damián Alcazar (Padre Portillo, the Priest); Mandy Patinkin (Andrew); Kathryn Grody (Harriet); Tania Cruz (Graciela, the Mute Girl); Iguandili López (Mother); Nandi Luna Ramírez (Daughter); Rafael de Quevedo (General); Carmen Madrid (Angela Fuentes); Esteban Soberanes (Raul, Angela's Fiancé); Roberto Sosa (Bravo); Dionisios (Salt Man); Lolo Navarro (Blind Woman); Maggie Renzi (Tourist by Pool); David Villalpando (Gum Person); Oscar García Ortega (Sergeant); Guadalupe Xocua (Modelo Woman); Celeste Cornelio Sánchez (Raped Girl); Nazario Montiel (Guerrilla).

Limbo in process

Production Company: Anarchists' Convention Inc. *Director:* John Sayles. *Screenplay:* John Sayles. *Editor:* John Sayles.

Principal actors: David Strathairn; Mary Elizabeth Mastrantonio; Kris Kristofferson; Vanessa Martinez.

Screenplays by John Sayles

Piranha 1978

Producer: John Davidson, for New World Pictures. *Executive producer:* Roger Corman. *Director:* Joe Dante. *Screenplay:* John Sayles. *Editors:* Mark Goldblatt, Joe Dante. *Cinematography:* Jamie Anderson. *Art direction:* Bill and Kerry Mellin. *Music:* Pino Donaggio. *Special effects:* John Berg. *Running time:* 92 minutes.

Principal characters: Bradford Dillman (Paul Grogan); Heather Menzies (Maggie McKeown); Kevin McCarthy (Dr. Robert Hoak); Keenan Wynn (Jack); Dick Miller (Buck Gardner); Barbara Steele (Dr. Mengers).

The Lady in Red 1979

Producer: Julie Corman, for New World Pictures. *Director:* Lewis Teague. *Screenplay:* John Sayles. *Editors:* Larry Block, Ron Medico, Lewis Teague. *Cinematography:* Daniel Lacambre. *Production design:* Philip Thomas. *Set decoration:* Keith Hein. *Music:* James Horner. *Sound:* Anthony Santa Croce. *Running time:* 93 minutes.

Principal characters: Pamela Sue Martin (Polly Franklin); Robert Conrad (John

Dillinger); Louise Fletcher (Anna Sage); Robert Hogan (Jake Langle); Laurie Heineman (Rose Shimkus); Glen Withrow (Eddie); Rod Gist (Pinetop); Peter Hobbs (Pops Geissler); Christopher Lloyd (Frognose); Dick Miller (Patrick); Nancy Anne Parsons (Tiny Alice); Alan Vint (Melvin Purvis).

Battle Beyond the Stars 1980

Producer: Ed Carlin, for New World Pictures. *Executive producer:* Roger Corman. *Director:* Jimmy T. Murakami. *Screenplay:* John Sayles. *Editors:* Allan Holtzman, Bob Kizer. *Cinematography:* Daniel Lacambre. *Set decoration:* John Zabrucky. *Music:* James Horner. *Miniature photography:* C. Comisky. *Miniature design:* Mary Schallock. *Running time:* 104 minutes.

Principal characters: Richard Thomas (Shad); Darlanne Fluegel (Nanelia); Robert Vaughn (Gelt); John Saxon (Sador); George Peppard (Cowboy); Sybil Danning (St. Exmin); Sam Jaffe (Dr. Hephaestus); Morgan Woodward (Cayman); Steve Davis (Quopeg); Earl Boen, John McGowans (Nestor #1 and #2); Larry Meyers, Laura Cody (Kelvin); Lynne Carlin (Nell); Terrence McNally (Gar); Ansley Carlin (Wok).

Alligator 1980

Producer: Brandon Chase, for BLC. *Executive producer:* Robert S. Bremson. *Director:* Lewis Teague. *Screenplay:* John Sayles. *Cinematography:* Joseph Mangine. *Running time:* 92 minutes.

Principal characters: Robert Forster (David Madison); Dean Jagger (Slade); Perry Lang (Kelly); Bart Braverman (Newspaper Reporter); Robin Riker (Marisa); Henry Silva (Colonel Brock); Michael Gazzo (Chief of Police); Jack Carter (Mayor).

The Howling 1981

Production: Michael Finell, Jack Conrad, for Avco Embassy. *Director:* Joe Dante. *Screenplay:* John Sayles, with Terence H. Winkless. *Cinematography:* John Hora. *Editors:* Mark Goldblatt, Joe Dante. *Art direction:* Robert A. Burns. *Special effects:* Roger George. *Special make-up:* Rob Bottin. *Music:* Pino Donagio. *Sound:* Ken King. *Running time:* 91 minutes.

Principal Characters: Dee Wallace (Karen White); Patrick Macnee (Dr. George Waggner); Dennis Dugan (Chris); Christopher Stone (William [Bill] Neill); Belinda Balaski (Terry Fisher); Kevin McCarthy (Fred Francis); John Carradine (Eric Kenton); Slim Pickens (Sam Newfield); Elisabeth Brooks (Marsha); Robert Picardo (Eddie); Margie Impert (Donna); Dick Miller (Bookstore Owner).

The Challenge 1982

Production: Robert L. Rosen, Ron Beekman, for CBS Theatrical Films Group; released by Embassy Pictures. *Director:* John Frankenheimer. *Screenplay:* John

Sayles, with Richard Maxwell. *Cinematography:* Kozo Okazaki. *Editor:* John W. Wheeler. *Art direction:* Yoshiyuki Ishida. *Music:* Jerry Goldsmith. *Running time:* 106 minutes.

Principal characters: Scott Glenn (Rick); Toshiro Mifune (Toru Yoshida); Donna Kei Benz (Akiko); Atsuo Nakamura (Hideo); Calvin Jung (Ando); Clyde Kusatsu (Go); Sab Shimono (Toshio as an adult); Kiyoaki Nagai (Kubo); Kenta Fukasaku (Jiro); Shogo Shimada (Father of Yoshida); Yoshio Inaba (Instructor); Seiji Miyaguchi (Old Man); Miiko Taka (Yoshida's Wife).

Enormous Changes at the Last Minute   1983

Production: Mirra Bank, for Ordinary Lives, Inc.; released by ABC Video; TC Films International. *Directors:* Mirra Bank, Ellen Hovde, Muffie Meyer. *Screenplay:* John Sayles, with Susan Rice (based on short stories by Grace Paley).

Principal characters: Ellen Barkin (Virginia); David Strathairn (Jerry); Ron McLarty (John); Sudie Bond (Mrs. Raftery); Lynn Milgrim (Faith); Jeffrey DeMunn (Ricardo); Zvees Schooler (Pa); Eda Reiss Merin (Ma); Fay Bernardi (Mrs. Hegel-Shtein); Maria Tucci (Alexandra); Kevin Bacon (Dennis); John Wardwell (Doc); Lou Criscuolo (George).

Clan of the Cave Bear   1986

Production: Jon Peters, Peter Guber, for Decade-Jones; released by Warner Bros. *Producer:* Gerald I. Isenberg. *Director:* Michael Chapman. *Screenplay:* John Sayles (based on the novel by Jean M. Auel). *Cinematography:* Jan De Bont. *Editor:* Wendy Green Briemont. *Production design:* Anthony Masters. *Art design:* Guy Comtois, Richard Wilcox. *Set design:* Kimberly Richardson. *Costume design:* Kelly Kimball. *Special effects:* Gene Grigg, Michael Clifford. *Make-up:* Michael G. Westmore, Michele Burke. *Music:* Alan Silvestri. *Running time:* 98 minutes.

Principal characters: Daryl Hannah (Ayla); Pamela Reed (Iza); James Remar (Creb); Thomas G. Waites (Broud); John Doolittle (Brun); Curtis Armstrong (Goov); Martin Doyle (Grod); Adel C. Hammoud (Vorn); Tony Montanaro (Zoug); Mike Muscat (Dorv); John Wardlow (Droog); Paul Carafotes (Brug); Janne Mortil (Ovra); Lycia Naff (Uba); Rory L. Crowley (Durc); Colin Doyle (Young Boy).

Wild Thing   1987

Producers: David Calloway, Nicholas Clermont, for Atlantic Releasing Corp. *Executive producers:* Thomas Coleman, Michael Rosenblatt. *Director:* Max Reid. *Screenplay:* John Sayles. *Cinematography:* René Verzier. *Editors:* Battle Davis, Steven Rosenblum. *Music:* George S. Clinton. *Sound:* Henri Blondeau. *Production designer:* Ross Schorer. *Costume designer:* Paul-Andre Guerin. *Special effects:* Jacques Godbout. *Running time:* 92 minutes.

Principal characters: Rob Knepper (Wild Thing); Kathleen Quinlan (Jane); Robert Davi (Chopper); Maury Chaykin (Trask); Betty Buckley (Leah); Guillaume Lemay-Thivierge (Wild Thing, 10 yrs); Clark Johnson (Winston); Sean

Hewitt (Father Quinn); Terry Abner (Rasheed); Summer Francks (Lisa); Sean Levy (Paul); Robert Bednarski (Free/Wild Thing, 3 yrs); Neil Affleck (Detective Walt); Tyrone Benskin (Detective Maury).

Breaking In   1989

Producer: Harry Gittes, for Samuel Goldwyn Company. *Executive producers:* Andrew Meyer, Sarah Ryan Black. *Director:* Bill Forsyth. *Screenplay:* John Sayles. *Cinematography:* Michael Coulter. *Editor:* Michael Ellis. *Music:* Michael Gibbs. *Sound:* Les Lupin. *Production designer:* Adrienne Atkinson, John Willett. *Special effects:* Larry L. Fuentes. *Costume design:* Louise Frogley. *Running time:* 91 minutes.

Principal characters: Burt Reynolds (Ernie); Casey Siemaszko (Mike); Sheila Kelly (Carrie); Lorraine Toussaint (Delphine); Albert Salmi (Johnny Scat); Harry Carey, Jr. (Shoes); Maury Chaykin (Tucci); David Frishberg (Nightclub Singer); John Baldwin (Sam the Apostle); Eddie Driscoll (Paul the Apostle); Stephen Tobolowsky (D.A.); Richard Key Jones (Lou); Walter Shane (Boss); Tom Laswell (Bud).

Men of War   1994

Producer: Arthur Goldblatt, Andrew Pfeffer, for Grandview Avenue Pictures; released by Dimension Films. *Director:* Perry Lang. *Screenplay:* John Sayles (Original Title: *A Safe Place*), with Ethan Reiff and Cyrus Voris. *Cinematography:* Ronn Schmidt. *Editor:* Jeffrey Reiner. *Line producer:* Jason Clark. *Costume designer:* Ileane Meltzer. *Music:* Gerald Gouriet. *Production design:* Steve Spence, Jim Newport. *Casting:* Risa Bramon Garcia. *Make-up effects:* Mony Monsano. *Executive producer:* Moshe Diamant, Stan Rogow. *Story:* Stan Rogow. *Running time:* 103 minutes.

Principal characters: Dolph Lundgren (Nick Gunner); Charlotte Lewis (Loki); B.D. Wong (Po); Jimmy G (Anthony John Denison); Ocker (Tom Guinee) Nolan (Don Harvey); Tiny "Zeus" Lister, Jr. (Blades); Tom Wright (Jamaal); Catherine Bell (Grace); Trevor Goddard (Keefer); Kevin Tighe (Merrick); Perry Lang (Lyle).

Uncredited Screenwriting

The Quick and the Dead   1995

Production: Joshua Donen, Allen Shapiro, and Patrick Markey, in association with Japan Satellite Broadcasting and IndieProd; released by TriStar Pictures. *Director:* Sam Raimi. *Screenplay:* Simon Moore. *Cinematography:* Dante Spinotti. *Editor:* Pietro Scalia. *Production design:* Patrizia von Brandenstein. *Art design:* Steve Saklad. *Set direction:* Hilton Rosemarin. *Casting:* Francine Maisler. *Sound:* Dennis L. Maitland. *Costume design:* Judianna Makovsky. *Music:* Alan Silvestri. *Running time:* 103 minutes.

Principal characters: Sharon Stone (Ellen); Gene Hackman (Herod); Russell Crow (Cort); Leonardo DiCaprio (Kid); Tobin Bell (Dog Kelly); Roberts Blossom (Doc Wallace); Kevin Conway (Eugene Dred); Keith David (Sergeant Cantrell); Lance Henriksen (Ace Hanlon); Pat Hingle (Horace the Bartender); Gary Sinise (Marshall); Woody Strode (Charles Moonlight); Jonothon Gill (Spotted Horse).

Apollo 13   1995

Production: Brian Grazer, for Imagine Entertainment; released by Universal Pictures. *Director:* Ron Howard. *Screenplay:* William Broyles, Jr., Al Reinert. *Cinematography:* Dean Cundey. *Editors:* Mike Hill, Dan Hanley. *Production design:* Michael Corenblith. *Art direction:* David J. Bomba, Bruce Alan Miller. *Music:* James Horner. *Running time:* 140 minutes.

Principal characters: Tom Hanks (Jim Lovell); Bill Paxton (Fred Haise); Kevin Bacon (Jack Swigert); Ed Harris (Gene Kranz); Gary Sinise (Ken Mattingly); Kathleen Quinlan (Marilyn Lovell); Joe Spano (NASA Director); David Andrews (Pete Conrad); Xander Berkeley (Henry Hurt); Clint Howard (ECOM White); Tracy Reiner (Mary Haise).

Mimic   1997

Production: Bob Weinstein, B.J. Rack, and Ole Bornedal, for Dimension Films. *Director:* Guillermo Del Toro. *Screenplay:* Matthew Robbins, Guillermo Del Toro (based on the short story by Donald A. Wolheim). *Cinematography:* Dan Lausten. *Editor:* Patrick Lussier. *Music:* Marco Beltrami. *Production designer:* Carol Spier. *Running Time:* 105 minutes.

Principal characters: Mira Sorvino (Dr. Susan Tyler); Jeremy Northam (Dr. Peter Man); Charles S. Dutton (Leonard); Josh Brolin (Josh); Giancarlo Giannini (Manny); Alexander Goodwin (Chuy); F. Murray Abraham (Dr. Gates).

Teleplays

A Perfect Match   1980

Production: CBS/Lorimar. *Director:* Mel Damski. *Teleplay:* John Sayles. *Cast:* Bonnie Bartlett (Judge Greenburg); Michael Brandon (Steve Triandos); Collen Dewhurst (Meg Larson); Charles Durning (Bill Larson); Marilyn Kagan (Lisa); Linda Kelsey (Miranda McLloyd); Lisa Lucas (Julie Larson).

Unnatural Causes   1986

Production: NBC/Image Entertainment. *Director:* Lamont Johnson. *Teleplay:* John Sayles. *Cast:* Patti LaBelle (Jeanette Thompson); Marie McCann (Phillipa); John Ritter (Frank Coleman); John Sayles (Lloyd); John Vargas (Fernando 'Nando Sanchez); Alfre Woodard (Maude DeVictor).

Shannon's Deal   1989, 1990

Broadcast History: 1989, Pilot; April 1990–May 1990, Series. *Producer:* Stan Rogow. *Director:* Lewis Teague. *Teleplay, episodes 1 and 4:* John Sayles. *Music:* Wynton Marsalis. *Legal Consultant:* Alan Dershowitz. *Cast:* Jamey Sheridan (Jack Shannon); Elizabeth Peña (Lucy Acosta); Jenny Lewis (Neala Shannon); Richard Edson (Wilmer Slade); Miguel Ferrer (D.A. Todd Spurrier); Martin Ferrero (Lou Gondolf); Ralph Waite (Jack Shannon's Father); Michelle Joyner (Country & Western Singer).

Bibliography

Primary Sources

FILMS

Sayles, John, director, screenwriter, editor, and actor. *Return of the Secaucus Seven*. Salsipuedes Productions, 1980.
_____, director, screenwriter, editor, and actor. *Lianna*. Winwood Production Company, 1983.
_____, director and screenwriter. *Baby, It's You*. With Vincent Spano, Rosanna Arquette. Paramount Films production in association with Double Play Productions, 1983.
_____, director, screenwriter, editor, and actor. *The Brother from Another Planet*. A-Train Films, 1984.
_____, director, screenwriter, and actor. *Matewan*. Red Dog Films, 1987.
_____, director, screenwriter, and actor. *Eight Men Out*. Sanford/Pillsbury Productions, 1988.
_____, director, screenwriter, editor, and actor. *City of Hope*. Esperanza Films, 1991.
_____, director, screenwriter, and editor. *Passion Fish*. Atchafalaya Films Production, 1993.
_____, director, screenwriter, and editor. *The Secret of Roan Inish*. Skerry Movies, 1995.
_____, director, screenwriter, and editor. *Lone Star*. Rio Dulce Productions, 1996.
_____, director, screenwriter, and editor. *Men With Guns (Hombres Armados)*. Anarchists' Convention Inc., 1998.
_____, director, screenwriter, and editor. *Limbo*. Anarchists' Convention Inc., in process.

NOVELS

Sayles, John. *Pride of the Bimbos*. New York: Atlantic–Little, Brown, 1975.
_____. *Union Dues*. New York: Atlantic–Little, Brown, 1977.
_____. *Los Gusanos*. New York: HarperCollins, 1991.

SHORT STORIES

Sayles, John. *The Anarchists' Convention.* New York: Atlantic–Little, Brown, 1979.
_____. "The Halfway Diner." *The Atlantic Monthly* 259 (June 1987): 59–68.
_____. "Treasure." *Esquire* 109 (March 1988): 168–80.
_____. "Peeling." *The Atlantic Monthly* (Sept. 1993): 69–74.
_____. "Keeping Time." *Rolling Stone* 9 (Dec. 1993), 48–52, 82–84.

NONFICTION

Sayles, John. *Thinking in Pictures: The Making of the Movie Matewan.* Boston: Houghton Mifflin, 1987.
_____. *Sayles on Sayles.* Ed. Gavin Smith. New York: Faber and Faber, 1998.

ESSAYS AND REVIEWS

Sayles, John. "At the Republican Convention." *The New Republic* 2, 9 (Aug. 1980): 20–25.
_____. "Goldman, Biro, and Nyuk-Nyuk-Nyuk." Review of *Adventures in the Screen Trade,* by William Goldman. *Film Comment* 19 (May/June 1983): 72–73.
_____. "Pregame Jitters." *Esquire* 105 (June 1986): 55–57.
_____. "Cassavetes's Sources Seemed to Be Our Own Doubting Lives." *New York Times* 12 May 1991.
_____. "The Big Picture." *Mother Jones Magazine Interactive* (May/June 1996): On Line. Internet. Available http://bsd.mojones.com
_____. "Chicago Guy: Nelson Algren." *Conjunctions.* "Tributes: American Writers on American Writers." Ed. Martine Bellen, Lee Smith, and Bradford Morrow. Annandale-on-Hudson, N.Y.: Bard College, Fall 1997.

INDEPENDENT SCREENPLAYS PUBLISHED

Sayles, John. "Lone Star." *Scenario* 2:2 (Summer 1996): 6–49. Published script.

STUDIO SCREENPLAYS

Sayles, John, screenwriter. *Piranha,* directed by Joe Dante. New World Pictures, 1978.
_____. *The Lady in Red,* directed by Lewis Teague. New World Pictures, 1979.
_____. *Battle Beyond the Stars,* directed by Jimmy T. Murakami. New World Pictures, 1980.
_____, with Frank Ray Perilli. *Alligator,* directed by Lewis Teague. BLC, 1980.
_____, with Terence H. Winkless. *The Howling,* directed by Joe Dante. AVCO-Embassy, 1981.
_____, with Richard Maxwell. *The Challenge,* directed by John Frankenheimer. CBS Entertainment, 1982.
_____, with Susan Rice (based on short stories by Grace Paley). *Enormous Changes at the Last Minute,* directed by Mirra Bank, Ellen Hovde, and Muffie Meyer. TC Films International, 1983.

_____. *Clan of the Cave Bear* (based on the novel by Jean M. Auel), directed by Michael Chapman. Warner Bros., 1986.
_____. *Wild Thing*, directed by Max Reid. Clermont Pictures, 1987.
_____. *Breaking In*, directed by Bill Forsyth. Samuel Goldwyn Company, 1989.
_____. *Men of War*, directed by Perry Lang. GrandView Avenue Pictures, 1994.

UNCREDITED SCRIPT WORK

Sayles, John. *Apollo 13*, directed by Ron Howard. Universal Pictures, 1995.
_____. *The Quick and the Dead*, directed by Sam Raimi. TriStar Pictures, 1995.
_____, with Steven Soderbergh. *Mimic*, directed by Guillermo Del Toro. Dimension Films, 1997.

SCREENPLAYS WRITTEN BUT NEVER FILMED

Sayles, John. *Night Skies*, 1980.
_____. *Blood of the Lamb*, 1981.
_____. *Terror of Loch Ness*, 1982.

SCRIPTS COMMISSIONED

Sayles, John. "Bob Merriman, the American Leader of the International Brigade." For TriStar.
_____. *SS Indianapolis*, 1991. For Jonathan Demme.
_____. *The Fifth Child*, 1996. For Maggie Renzi and Paul Miller.
_____. *Tom Mix Died for Your Sins*, 1996. For Sydney Pollack.
_____. *Brother Termite*, 1997; in process. For James Cameron.
_____. *Gold of Exodus: The Discovery of the True Mount Sinai*, 1998; in process. For Castle Rock.

MUSIC VIDEOS: DIRECTOR

Born in the USA, Bruce Springsteen and the E-Street Band, 1985.
Glory Days, Bruce Springsteen and the E-Street Band, 1985.
I'm on Fire, Bruce Springsteen and the E-Street Band, 1985.
Mountainview, with Marta Renzi. Music program for PBS, 1989.

TELEPLAYS

Sayles, John, writer. *A Perfect Match*, directed by Mel Damski. CBS, 1980.
_____. *Unnatural Causes*, directed by Lamont Johnson. NBC, 1986.
_____. *Shannon's Deal*, directed by Lewis Teague. NBC, 1989.
_____. *Shannon's Deal*, two episodes; series run: 1990.

UNPRODUCED TELEVISION WORK

Sayles, John. Pilots for *The Brother from Another Planet* as a television show.
_____. Adaption of Peter Mathiessen's *Killing Mr. Watson*. For TNT.

PLAYS

Sayles, John. *New Hope for the Dead.* Produced Off Off Broadway, 1981.
_____. *Turnbuckle.* Produced Off Off Broadway, 1981.

Secondary Sources

American Cinematographer 64 (April 1983): 85–86, 88. John Sayles interview.
Andrews, Terry L. Review of *The Brother from Another Planet. Magill's Cinema Annual 1985.* Englewood Cliffs, N.J.: Salem Press, 1985.
Angell, Roger. "No, But I Saw the Game." *The New Yorker* 31 July 1989, 41–56.
Ansen, David. With Katrine Ames. "Doing What Comes Naturally." *Newsweek* 11 April 1983, 78–79.
Ardolino, Frank. "Ceremonies of Innocence and Experience in *Bull Durham, Field of Dreams,* and *Eight Men Out.*" *Journal of Popular Film and Television* 18 (1990): 43–51.
Asinof, Eliot. *Eight Men Out.* 1963. New York: Henry Holt, 1987.
_____. "John Sayles Interview." *Directors Guild Magazine* (December 1997/January 1998). On Line. Internet. Available http://www.dga.org/magazine/v22-5/john_sayles.html
Atkinson, Michael. "The 26th Annual Baltimore Film Festival." Review of *The Secret of Roan Inish. City Paper* 5 April 1995, 25.
Aufderheide, Patricia. "Filmmaking as Storytelling: An Interview with John Sayles." *Cineaste* 15 (1987): 12–15.
_____. "Journals: Sayles in Harlem." *Film Comment* (March/April 1984): 4, 6.
Auster, Al, and Leonard Quart. *The Cineaste Interviews.* Chicago: Lake View, 1983.
Barra, Allen. "Hollywood Keeps Striking Out on Real-Life Baseball." *New York Times* 28 April 1991, 13H, 21H.
Barzun, Jacques. *God's Country and Mine: A Declaration of Love Spiced with a Few Harsh Words.* Boston: Little, Brown, 1954.
Bazin, Andre. "An Aesthetic of Reality." *What Is Cinema?* Berkeley: University of California Press, 1971, pp. 16–40.
Beale, Lewis. "He's the Lone Wolf Behind *Lone Star.*" *Daily News* 19 June 1996, 38.
Bogle, Donald. *Toms, Coons, Mulattos, Mammies, & Bucks: An Interpretive History of Blacks in American Films.* 2d ed. New York: Continuum, 1993.
Bonetti, Kay. *The American Audio Prose Library,* 1982. John Sayles interview.
Bourjaily, Vance. "A Revivalist of Realism." *The New York Times Book Review* 1 April 1979, 15, 33.
Broeske, Pat H. Review of *The Howling. Magill's Cinema Annual 1982.* Englewood Cliffs, N.J.: Salem Press, 1982.
Canby, Vincent. "Film View: Mixed Adventures." *The New York Times* 21 June 1981, II 17.
_____. "Long in the Tooth." Review of *Alligator. The New York Times* 5 June 1981, C8.
_____. "Lycanthropophilia." Review of *The Howling. The New York Times* 13 March 1981, C10.

_____. "Of Shaggy Dogs and Logarithms." Review of *Breaking In. The New York Times* 9 Oct. 1989, C18.

Carnes, Mark C., general editor. With eds. Ted Mico, John Miller-Monzon, and David Rubel. *Past Imperfect: History According to the Movies.* New York: Henry Holt, 1995.

_____, ed. "A Conversation Between Eric Foner and John Sayles." *Past Imperfect: History According to the Movies.* New York: Henry Holt, 1995, pp. 11–28.

Caro, Mark. "Telling Stories: John Sayles Reveals What Makes Him So Independent-minded." *Chicago Tribune* 2 April 1998, 5:4.

Carr, Jay. "Sayles' Lone Star Shines with Mystery." *The Boston Globe* 28 June 1996, 45, 52.

Carson, Gerald. "The Saloon." *American Heritage: The Magazine of History* (April 1963): 25.

Castle Rock Entertainment. "*Lone Star*, Production Notes." Beverly Hills, Calif., 1996.

The Charlie Rose Show. PBS talk show. WNET, New York. 15 March 1995.

_____. WNET, New York. 26 June 1996.

Chute, David. "John Sayles: Designated Writer." *Film Comment* (May–June 1981): 54–59.

Clark, John. "Filmographies." *Premiere* (Sept. 1991): 120.

Clarke, Doug. "Sympathy for the Poor Devils." *The Cleveland Edition* 22 Sept. 1988, 18.

Connors, Joanna. "Irish Family's Tales Take Sea, Saw Trail in Myth." *The Cleveland Plain Dealer* 31 March 1995, 6, 7.

Cooper, Carol. "Soldier's Story Salute." *Film Comment* (Nov./Dec. 1984): 17–19.

Crouch, Stanley. "New Films Plumb True Depth of the Melting Pot." *Daily News* 26 June 1996, 27.

Crowdus, Gary, and Leonard Quart. "Where the Hope Is: An Interview with John Sayles." *Cineaste* 18:4 (1991): 4–7, 61.

Daring, Mason. *Lone Star.* With Duke Levine, Tim Jackson, Larry Luddecke, Mike Turk, and Evan Harlen. Daring Records, CD3023, 1996.

_____. *The Secret of Roan Inish Soundtrack.* With Cormac Breatnach, Maire Breatnach, Roan Browne, and Gerald Foley. Daring Records, CD3015, 1995.

Davis, Thulani. "Blue-Collar Auteur." *American Film* (June 1991): 19–22, 49–50.

Dekoven, Marianne. "To Bury and Praise: John Sayles on the Death of the Sixties." *Minnesota Review* 30:3 (1988): 129–47.

Demyanenko, Alex. "One Man Out." *Village View* 1–7 Nov. 1991, 22–35.

De Witt, Karen. "Ideas & Trends: Incest as a Selling Point." *The New York Times* 30 Marck 1997, E6.

"Dialogue on Film: John Sayles." *American Film* 11 (May 1986): 13–15. John Sayles interview.

di Caprio, Lisa. "Liberal Lesbianism." *Jump Cut* 29 (1984): 45.

Dominguez, Robert. "'Guns' Maker Sayles Aims for Originality." *Daily News* 4 March 1998, 38–39.

Dowell, Pat. "The Secret of Roan Inish." *Morning Edition.* NPR.WITF, Harrisburg. 17 February 1995.

Dreifus, Claudia. "The Progressive Interview: John Sayles." *The Progressive* (Nov. 1991): 30–33.

Dubofsky, Melvyn. "Matewan." *Labor History* 31 (1990): 488–90.

Dyer, Richard. "Rejecting Straight Ideals: Gays in Film." *Jump Cut: Hollywood, Politics, and Counter-Cinema.* Edited by Peter Steven. New York: Praeger, 1985.

Ebert, Roger. *Roger Ebert's Video Companion.* Kansas City, Mo.: Andrews and McMeel, 1993.

Ellison, Ralph. *Invisible Man.* 30th anniversary ed. New York: Vintage, 1972.

Epel, Naomi. *Writers Dreaming.* New York: Vintage, 1993, pp. 221–28.

Farber, Stephen. "Five Horsemen After the Apocalypse." *Film Comment* 21:4 (1985): 32–35.

Felperin, Leslie. "Walking Alone." *Sight and Sound* (Sept. 1996): 22–24.

Ferrante, Anthony J. "The Independent Spirit." *Scr(i)pt* 2:4 (July/Aug. 1996): 6–9.

"Filmmaker." *The New Yorker* 23 March 1981, 30–31.

Giamatti, A. Bartlett. *Take Time for Paradise: Americans and Their Games.* New York: Summit, 1989.

Giannetti, Louis. "John Sayles' Ordinary People." *The Cleveland Edition* 15 Oct. 1987, 10.

_____. *Understanding Movies.* 7th ed. Englewood Cliffs, New Jersey: Prentice Hall, 1996.

_____, and Scott Eyman. *Flashback: A Brief History of Film.* 2d ed. Englewood Cliffs, N.J.: Prentice Hall, 1991.

Giardina, Denise. "Union, Mines, and Mountains." *Christianity and Crisis* 47 (1987): 443–45.

Goldman, Francisco. *The Long Night of White Chickens.* New York: The Atlantic Monthly Press, 1992.

Goodman, Mark. "Sports Today: John Sayles Interview." *Z Magazine* (October 1988): 71–74.

Gottlieb, Stanley. Review of *City of Hope. Magill's Cinema Annual 1992.* Englewood Cliffs, N.J.: Salem Press, 1992.

Gould, Stephen Jay. Introduction to *Eight Men Out* by Eliot Asinof. xv–xviii. New York: Henry Holt, 1987.

Gritten, David. "Sayles' Little 'Secret': A Film for Children." *Los Angeles Times* 30 July 1993, F12, 20.

Guerrero, Ed. *Framing Blackness: The African American Image in Film.* Philadelphia: Temple University Press, 1993.

Haskell, Molly. *From Reverence to Rape: The Treatment of Women in the Movies.* 2d ed. Chicago: University of Chicago Press, 1987.

Hickenlooper, George. *Reel Conversations: Candid Interviews with Film's Foremost Directors and Critics.* New York: Citadel Press, 1991.

Hinson, Hal. "*Lone Star:* Stagnant Sayles." *Washington Post* 12 July 1996, F6.

Hodel, Martha Bryson. "Mining Matewan's Past." *The Cleveland Plain Dealer* 8 April 1993, C4.

Holden, Stephen. "In a Departure, John Sayles Turns a Myth into a Hit in 'Roan Inish.'" *The New York Times* 5 March 1995, H13, 21.

_____. "Real Men, an Endangered Species on Film." *The New York Times* 7 July 1996, H9.

Holmlund, Christine. "When Is a Lesbian Not a Lesbian? The Lesbian Continuum and the Mainstream Femme Film." *Camera Obscura: A Journal of Feminism and Film Theory* 25–26 (1991): 145–78.

Howe, Desson. "John Sayles's Bright Star." Review of *Lone Star*. *Washington Post* 12 July 1996, "Weekend," 39, 41.

Jacobs, Diane. *Hollywood Renaissance*. New York: A.S. Barnes, 1977.

James, Caryn. "*Passion Fish* Nourishes the Grown Ups." *New York Times* 24 January 1993, H11.

Johnson, Mary. "Profile: John Sayles." *Creative Screenwriting* 3:1 (summer 1996): 5–12.

Johnson, Sharon. "John Sayles Remains an Outsider." *Harrisburg Patriot News* 8 Sept. 1996.

Johnson, Timothy. "Review: *Return of the Secaucus Seven*." *Magill's Cinema Annual 1983*. Englewood Cliffs, N.J.: Salem Press, 1983.

Johnston, Trevor. "Sayles Talk." *Sight and Sound* (Sept. 1993): 26–29.

Jones, Suzi. "Regionalization: A Rhetorical Strategy." *Journal of the Folklore Institute* 13 (1976): 107.

Kael, Pauline. "Field of Dreams." *The New Yorker* 1 May 1989, 76–77.

_____. *Movie Love: Complete Reviews, 1988–1991*. New York: Dutton, 1991.

Kauffmann, Stanley. Review of *Lianna*. *New Republic* 188 (14 March 1983): 24–25.

Kelley, R.S., "The John Sayles Border Stop." On Line. Internet. 21 April 1997. Available http://www~scf.usc.edu/~rskelley/film/film.html

Kemp, Philip. Review of *Passion Fish*. *Sight and Sound*, Sept. 1993, 51–52.

Kenan, Randall. "Miami Vice." *The Nation* 24 June 1991, 856–58.

Kennedy, Harlan. "Irish Cinema: Idyll & Ideology." *Film Comment* (May–June 1994): 24, 35–40.

King, Stephen. *Danse Macabre*. New York: Everest, 1981.

Kipen, David. "'Roan Inish' Is Latest Product of Saylesmanship." *Los Angeles Daily News*, rpt. *The Cleveland Plain Dealer* 31 March 1995, 6, 7.

Klawans, Stuart. "Films." Review of *Lone Star*. *The Nation* 29 July/5 Aug. 1996, 34–36.

Laermer, Richard. "John Sayles, an Interview." *Films in Review* 36 (Feb. 1985): 105–6.

Lardner, Ring, Jr. "Foul Ball." *American Film* (July/August 1988): 45–49.

Lawson, Steve. "John Sayles: A Man for All Media." *New York Times Magazine* 17 April 1983, 108–18.

Levitt, Shelley. "Bio: John Sayles." *People* 8 March 1993, 86–90.

Linfield, Susan. "Studs Terkel: World Serious." *American Film* (July/August 1988): 48.

Lippy, Tod. "A Talk with John Sayles." *Scenario* 2: 2 (summer 1996): 50–53, 192–96.

Lopate, Phillip. "With Pen in Hand, They Direct Movies." *New York Times* 16 Aug. 1992, H7–13.

Lurie, Alison. *Don't Tell the Grown-ups: Subversive Children's Literature*. Boston: Little, Brown, 1990.

Maltin, Leonard. "Writers Guild Foundation Career Achievement Award." Interview. On Line. Internet. 13 February 1998. Available http://www.wga.org/pr/0298/sayles.html

Marney, Angela. "*Lianna*: A Move Toward Better Things." *Off Our Backs* (April 1983): 18.

Martesko, Karol. "The Fifty Most Important Independent Films." *Filmmaker* 5:1 (fall 1996): 40–42, 45–47, 51–60.

Martin, Wallace. *Recent Theories of Narrative*. Ithaca: Cornell University Press, 1986.

Maslin, Janet. "Sleepy Texas Town with an Epic Story." Review of *Lone Star*. *The New York Times* 21 June 1996, C1, C16.

_____. "Swordplay." Review of *The Challenge*. *The New York Times* 23 July 1982, C8.

_____. "An Unsuspecting Traveler Loses His Illusions, Step by Harrowing Step." Review of *Men With Guns* (*Hombres Armados*). *The New York Times* 6 March 1998, B29.

Mast, Gerald. *The Comic Mind: Comedy and the Movies*. 2d. ed. Chicago: University of Chicago Press, 1979.

_____. *A Short History of the Movies*. Rev. by Bruce F. Kawin. 5th ed. Chicago: University of Chicago Press, 1986.

McGhee, Dorothy. "Solidarity Forever." *American Film* 12 (Sept. 1987): 42–46.

Merck, Mandy. "*Lianna* and the Lesbians of Art Cinema." *Films for Women*. Edited Charlotte Bronsdon. London: BFI, 1986, pp. 172–73.

Minsky, Terri. "Sayles and Bargains." *Premiere* (Sept. 1991): 38, 40.

Monaço, James. *American Film Now: The People, the Power, the Money, the Movies*. 2d ed. New York: Plume, 1984.

Moore, Marat. "Where the Rubber Meets the Road: John Sayles Talks About His Coal Mining Movie *Matewan*." *Now and Then* 5:1 (spring 1988): 5–8.

Navarro, Vincente. "The Lincoln Brigade: Some Comments on U.S. History." *Monthly Review* 38 (1986): 29.

Nechak, Paula. "Rapping with John Sayles." *MovieMaker* 3:20 (July/Aug. 1996): 25–27, 49.

Neff, Renfreu. "Writing in Tongues." *Creative Screenwriting* 5:3 (summer 1998): 32–36.

Nichols, Bill. *Ideology and the Image: Social Representation in the Cinema and Other Media*. Bloomington: Indiana University Press, 1981.

O'Brien, Tom. *The Screening of America*. New York: Continuum, 1990.

Osborne, David. "John Sayles: From Hoboken to Hollywood — and Back." *American Film* (Oct. 1982): 31–36, 68.

Pally, Marcia. "Women in Love." *Film Comment* 22 (March/April 1986): 35–39.

Paredes, Americo. *A Texas-Mexican Cancionero: Folksongs of the Lower Border*. Urbana: University of Illinois Press, 1976.

_____. *With His Pistol in His Hand: A Border Ballad and Its Hero*. Austin: University of Texas Press, 1996.

Popkin, Daniel. "High School Class Perspectives: An Interview with John Sayles." *Cineaste* 13 (1983): 39–40.

Premiere (Oct. 1988): 76. John Sayles interview.

Pribram, E. Deidre. "Review Essay: *Apollo 13*: Rewriting History." *Creative Screenwriting* 3:1 (summer 1996): 13–16.

Quart, Leonard. Review of *City of Hope*. *Cineaste* 18:4 (1991): 44–46.

Ratner, Megan. "Borderlines." *FilmMaker: The Magazine of Independent Film* 4:4 (summer 1996): 32–35.

Rauzi, Robin. "The Indie Icon." *Los Angeles Times/Calendar* 1 March 1998, 7, 76.

Ravo, Nick. "Ernest Dickerson Would Rather Be Called Director." *New York Times* 18 April 1993, H19.

Rea, Steven. "*Clockers*' Author Thrives as a Script Doctor." *The Philadelphia Inquirer* 17 Sept. 1995, G7.

_____. "Sayles Concocts a Texas-Size Murder Mystery in *Lone Star*." Review of *Lone Star*. *The Philadelphia Inquirer* 12 July 1996, "Weekend," 3.

Rizzo, Cindy. "John Sayles Interviewed." *Gay Community News* 10:30 (1983): 8.

Rosen, David, with Peter Hamilton. *Off-Hollywood: The Making and Marketing of Independent Films*. New York: Grove Weidenfeld, 1990.

Russo, Vito. *The Celluloid Closet: Homosexuality in the Movies*. New York: Harper & Row, 1987.

_____. "A State of Being." *Film Comment* 22 (March/April 1986): 32–34.

Ryan, James. "Mr. 'Last-Minute' Gets a Plum Role." *The New York Times* 30 June 1996, 11, 16.

Ryan, Susan. "*Men With Guns*: Review." *Cineaste* (summer 1998): XXIII: 3, 43–44.

The Samuel Goldwyn Company. "*City of Hope*, Production Notes." Los Angeles, Calif., 1991.

Sarris, Andrew. At the Movies with Andrew Sarris: John Sayles' *Lone Star* a Texas-Sized Marvel." *The New York Observer* 17 June 1996, 28.

_____. "Baby, It's You: An Honest Man Becomes a True Filmmaker." *Film Comment* (May–June 1993): 28–30.

Schlesinger, Tom. "Putting People Together." *Film Quarterly* (1981): 2–8.

Scobey, David. Review of *Eight Men Out*. *The American Historical Review* 95 (1990): 1143–1145.

Seidenberg, Robert. "*Matewan*: Nora Chavooshian Creates Major Miners." *Theater Crafts* 21 (1987): 45–48.

Simon, Joel. "John Sayles, Long a Director at the Edge, Crosses a Border." *The New York Times* 9 March 1997, H15, 20.

Simpson, Janice. "Neck-Deep in the Culture." *Time* 5 Aug. 1991, 64.

Skerry Movies Corporation. "*Secret of Roan Inish* Production Notes," 27 Oct. 1993, 1–30.

Skolnick, Dylan. "John Sayles." *Films in Review* (Jan./Feb. 1997): 26–28.

Smith, Gavin. "John Sayles: 'I Don't Want to Blow Anything by People.'" *Film Comment* (May–June 1996): 57–68.

Snyder, Michael. "Man with Guts." *Salon*. On Line. Internet. 13 March 1998. Available http://www.salon1999.com

Sony Pictures Classics. "*Men With Guns*: Production Notes." On Line. Internet. 6 March 1998. Available http://www.spe.sony.com

Stempel, Tom. *FrameWork: A History of Screenwriting in the American Film*. New York: Continuum, 1991.

_____. "Sons and Daughters of *Return of the Secaucus Seven*." *Creative Screenwriting* 3:3 (winter 1996): 96–102.

Sterngold, James. "At the Movies." *The New York Times* 20 February 1998, 6.

Suarez, Ray. "Talk of the Nation: Representation of Filmmaking" NPR. WAMU, Washington, D.C. 20 December 1995. (On Line. Internet. Available http://www.npr.org)

Summer, Jane. "Sayles Explores Border Culture." *The Boston Globe* (reprint from *Dallas Morning News*) 28 June 1996, 52.

Thompson, Cliff. "The Brother from Another Race: Black Characters in the Films of John Sayles." *Cineaste* 22:3 (1996): 32–33.

Thompson, David. *A Biographical Dictionary of Film*. 3d ed. New York: Knopf, 1995.

Turan, Kenneth. "Master of the Possible: Director John Sayles Exhibits a Determined Vision." *The Los Angeles Times* 13 May 1996, F1, 6.

Twitchell, James B. *Dreadful Pleasures: An Anatomy of Modern Horror*. New York: Oxford University Press, 1985.

Unger, Sanford J. "Film View: Immigrants' Tales, in Subtle Shades of Gray." *The New York Times* 23 June 1996, 15, 28.

Valen, Mark. "John Sayles." *Films & Filming* 360 (Sept. 1984): 10–12.

Wadhams, Wayne N. "Taking Sound for Low-Budget Features." *American Cinematographer* 64 (April 1983): 81–83, 88–96.

West, Dennis, and Joan M. West. "Borders and Boundaries: An Interview with John Sayles." *Cineaste* 22:3 (1996): 14–17.

_____, and _____. Review of *Lone Star*. *Cineaste* 22:3 (1996): 34–36.

Williams, Jeanne. Review of *Matewan*. *Cineaste* (1988): 51–52.

Williams, John Alexander. "John Sayles Plays the Preacher." *Appalachian Journal: A Regional Studies Review* 15 (1988): 344–52.

Wilson, Anton. *Cinema Workshop*. Hollywood, Calif.: A.S.C. Holding Corp., 1983.

Worth, Larry. "Sayles Effort Really Pays Off." *New York Post* 5 March 1998, 53.

Young, Josh. "Mr. Rewrite's Return." *Esquire* (June 1996): 36.

Zieger, Robert. *American Workers, American Unions, 1920–1985*. Baltimore: Johns Hopkins University Press, 1986.

Zinn, Howard. *A People's History of the United States*. New York: Harper Perennial, 1990.

Zucker, Carole. *Figures in Light: Actors and Directors Illuminate the Art of Film Acting*. New York: Plenum, 1995, pp. 327–44.

Index

Academy Award nominations 4, 18, 240
actors 6
Alexander, Jace 120, 146, 172
Algren, Nelson 14, 139
Alligator (1980) 12, 15, 35, 41–44
Altman, Robert 69, 145, 158
American Film 85
American Video Award 6
The Anarchists' Convention (short story collection) (1979) 13, 53
Anarchists' Convention, Inc. 4, 18
Anderson, Sherwood 57
Andrews, Terry L. 98
Angell, Roger 140, 152–53
Apollo 13 (1995) 4, 13, 15, 50–51, 212
Ardolino, Frank 143, 152
Arquette, Rosanna 6, 86–87
Asinof, Eliot 18, 19, 138–39, 149
Atkinson, Michael 206
The Atlantic Monthly 12, 18
Atlantic Monthly Press 11–13
Auel, Jean M. 47–48
Aufderheide, Pat 98

Baby, It's You (1983) 16, 70, 84, 85–96, 131–132, 140, 197, 233
Bacon, Kevin 47, 51
Ballhaus, Michael 92–95, 103
Barzun, Jacques 138
Baseball (1994) 16
baseball in literature 138
"The Baseball Movie" 13–39, 143, 151–53
Bassett, Angela 6, 162, 172, 184
Battle Beyond the Stars (1980) 12, 32–34
Bazin, André 58
Bergman, Ingmar 175
The Big Chill (1983) 70
The Birds (1963) 24, 43

Bishop, Dan 6, 229
Black Mama, White Mama (1972) 220, 240
The Black Sox 137, 139, 141, 155
Bogle, Donald 113
borders 223–25, 228, 236
Bourjaily, Vance 9
Brady, Upton 11–12
Breaking In (1989) 48–49
Bridgewater, Dee Dee 112
Broeske, Pat 39
The Brother from Another Planet (1984) 16, 17, 96, 97–114, 121, 132, 197, 200, 236, 237, 244
Burmester, Leo 187–88, 228, 236
Burns, Ken 16

Cameron, James 51
Canada, Ron 217
Canby, Vincent 35, 43–44
Carson, Gerald 111
Cassavetes, John 57–58, 61, 70, 81, 243
Casseus, Gabriel 218, 239
casting 110, 125–26, 208–9
Castle Rock Entertainment 212, 214, 240
The Challenge (1982) 5, 45–46
Chandler, Raymond 213, 222–23
Chaplin, Charlie 6, 107–8
characters 243–44
The Charlie Rose Show 192, 198, 200
Chavooshian, Nora 6, 100, 129, 131–33, 152
Cheever, John 200
"Children of the Silver Screen" 3
Chinatown (1974) 240
Chute, David 28, 37
Cineaste 53, 72, 80, 115, 167, 223
cinematography 92, 94–95, 103–6, 122–

267

23, 125, 129, 133, 135–36, 144–146,
149–50, 152, 154, 157–58, 160–61, 165,
168, 170–71, 176–79, 186, 194, 203–6,
214, 218, 229–31
Citizen Kane (1941) 21, 229, 240
City of Hope (1991) 4, 14, 16–17, 156–73,
176, 188, 192, 206, 215, 217, 223, 229,
236, 238, 244–45
City Paper 206
cityscape (setting) 162
Clan of the Cave Bear (1986) 47
Clapp, Gordon 6, 57, 70, 130, 145
Clarke, Doug 144
Colgan, Eileen 193, 209
Colon, Miriam 219, 236, 239
Columbia Pictures 72
Cooper, Carol 104
Cooper, Chris 6, 118, 126, 161, 216–17,
233, 236, 238
Coover, Robert 200
Comiskey, Charles Albert 139, 141–44,
154
community 133–34, 159, 162, 226
Coppola, Francis Ford 6
Corman, Roger 3, 12, 19–22, 26, 35
Courtney, Jeni 193, 208–9
Crane, Stephen 9
Creative Screenwriting 97, 205
Crowdus, Gary 169
cuisine 180–81
Curtis-Hall, Vondie 16, 180, 188–90

Dante, Joe 12, 16–17, 19, 21, 26, 35, 37,
39
Daring, Mason 6, 47, 70, 112, 133–34,
152, 157, 180, 207–8, 233–36
Davis, Thulani 11, 14, 18, 157, 160,
162
Deakins, Roger 176, 185
DeLillo, Don 14
Demme, Jonathan 6, 16
Denison, Anthony John 50, 158
DeVries, Jon 73
di Caprio, Lisa 72
Dickerson, Ernest 98–99, 103–6
Directors Guild of America 18
Doel, Frances 19–20
Dreifus, Claudia 10–11
Dryburgh, Stuart 229, 232
Dubofsky, Melvyn 118
Dunne, Griffin 85
Dwan, Allan 30
Dyer, Richard 79

Ebert, Roger 140
Edson, Richard 148
Eight Men Out (1988) 4, 16, 17, 114, 137–
55, 156, 160, 162, 172, 206, 215
Ellison, Ralph
Enormous Changes at the Last Minute
(1983) 46–47
Esquire 13
Eyman, Scott 137

Faulkner, William 156, 215
feminism 60–61, 72
Field of Dreams (1989) 138, 143
Film Comment 13, 18, 21, 35, 79, 98, 201,
242
film noir 162–63
Filmmaker 244
financing 74
Fitzgerald, F. Scott 145
Flynt, Cynthia 6, 133, 152
Foner, Eric 85, 118, 140
Ford, John 134, 201, 231, 242
Forsyth, Bill 48–49
Frankenheimer, John 15, 45
Fry, Rosalie K. 192–93

Giamatti, A. Bartlett 138
Giannetti, Louis vii, 137, 242–43
Giardina, Denise 131
"Golden State" 12
Goldman, William 13
Goodman, John 17
Gottlieb, Sidney 161
Gould, Stephen Jay 138–39
The Great Train Robbery (1903) 240
Green, Paul 14
Green, Sarah 6, 173, 198–99, 210
Gridlock'd (1997) 16
Griffiths, Linda 73–74
Gritten, David 211
Guerrero, Ed 114
Los Gusanos (1991) 13–14

Hammett, Dashiell 213, 222–23
Hammond, John 134
Hanks, Tom 50
Hard Choices (1986) 16
HarperCollins 14
Haskell, Molly 61, 75, 186
Hatfield, Sid 116
"Heisenberg's Uncertainty Principle" 76

Hickenlooper, George 10, 197
High Noon (1952) 120
Hinson, Hal 233
Holden, Stephen 211, 240
Holmlund, Christine 77
Howard, Ron 50, 104, 212
Howells, William Dean 75
The Howling (1981) 12, 15, 16, 35–42, 44
humor 113–14
Huston, John 201

"I-80 Nebraska, m.490–m.205" 12
Invisible Man 113
"Irish Cinema" 201

James, Clifton 139, 216, 236, 239
Jaws (1975) 12, 20, 25–26, 41–43
John Steinbeck Award 18
Johnson, Mary 205
Johnson, Timothy 69
Jones, James Earl 6, 126–28
Joyce, James 201

Kael, Pauline 5, 49, 143
Karten, Terry 14
Kasden, Lawrence 70
Kauffmann, Stanley 75
Keaton, Buster 97, 108
"Keeping Time" 18
Kelly, Gene 3
Kelly, Sheila 49, 184
Kenan, Randall 14
Kennedy, Harlan 201
Kennedy, William 200
King, Stephen 22
Kipen, David 15
Klawans, Stuart 5
Kristofferson, Kris 216, 239–40

The Ladd Company 73
The Lady in Red (1979) 2, 28–32
Lally, Mick 193, 208–10
landscape (setting) 117, 124, 176, 178–79, 181–82, 184–86, 199, 205
Lang, Stephen J. 158, 216, 236
Lardner, Ring 147
Lardner, Ring, Jr. 140
Lee, Spike 16, 55, 98, 160, 169
Lerner, Michael 153
Levitt, Shelley 245
Lianna (1983) 16, 70, 72–84, 86–88, 92–93, 98, 110

Library of Congress National Film Registry 18
Limbo 17, 245
Lippy, Tod 185, 214–15, 228
Little, Brown and Company 12
Little Vegas (1990) 16
Lloyd, Christopher 6, 31, 148
Loach, Ken 61
London, Jack 9
Lone Star (1996) 4, 6, 14, 17–18, 213–41, 243–44
Lopate, Phillip 167
Los Angeles Film Critics Award 55
Los Angeles Times 211
Lurie, Allison 197–98
Lynch, John 195, 209–10
Lynch, Susan 195–96

MacArthur Foundation 17, 96
MacDonald, Bruce 5
"Magic Realism" 14, 192, 198, 200, 206
Malcolm X (1992) 16
Maltin, Leonard 16
Mantell, Michael 6
Marney, Angela 72
Márquez, Gabriel García 14, 200
Marsalis, Wynton 15
Martin, Wallace 56
"The Marx Brothers Sequence" 145
Maslin, Janet 46
Mast, Gerald 5, 41, 98, 107
Matewan (1987) 4, 13, 16, 17, 96–97, 114, 115–36, 137, 154, 156, 165, 172, 189, 202, 206, 215, 217, 236, 238, 243
Matewan Massacre 115–16, 118–19, 136
Mathnet (1992) 16
Matinee (1993) 16, 17
McCarthy, Kevin 22, 27, 37, 40
McConaughey, Matthew 216, 239
McDonnell, Mary 6, 126, 129, 174, 183, 189
McDormand, Frances 221, 236, 239
McQueen, Steve 189
Men of War (1994) 50
Men With Guns (*Hombres Armados*) (1998) 4, 14, 17, 241, 245
Mendillo, Stephen 6, 153, 161, 216, 236
Mette, Nancy 6, 132, 184
Meyer, Russ 3, 31
Miller, Dick 17, 23, 29, 38
Miller, Marvin 139
Miller, R. Paul 6, 211, 214
Mimic (1997) 4

Miramax 214
Monaco, James 125
Morton, Joe 6, 97, 103–4, 107–9, 112, 158, 162, 172, 216, 236–38
Mostel, Josh 6, 158
The Mummy 212
Murakami, Jimmy T. 32
My Life's in Turnaround (1993) 16

Nashville (1975) 69, 145, 158
The Nation 5
National Book Award 9
National Book Critics Circle Award 9
Nelson, Jeffery 59, 72
New Hope for the Dead (1981) 14
The New Republic 13, 75
New World Pictures 3–4, 12, 19–21, 30, 34–35, 40, 50, 53
New York Times 240
The New Yorker 140
Newsweek 86
Next Wave Films 18
Night Skies 72

O. Henry Award 12
O'Brien, Tom 142
Oldham, Will 126, 128–29
Orion Pictures 140
Osborne, David 55

Paley, Grace 46–47
Pally, Marcia 79
Paramount Pictures 85–86
Paredes, Americo 225, 228
parody 12, 20, 25–26, 28, 32, 41–43, 100
Passion Fish (1994) 4, 6, 17–18, 174–91, 197, 199, 206, 211, 232, 244, 245
"Peeling" 18
Peña, Elizabeth 6, 15, 217, 236, 238
A Perfect Match (1980) 15
Persona (1966) 175
Personal Best (1982) 74, 77
Piranha (1978) 3, 12, 15, 16, 19–22, 24–28, 41–43, 213
Poe, Edgar Allan 101
Polonsky, Sonya 92, 135
Popkin, Daniel 80
Premiere 137
Pribram, E. Deidre 50–51
Pride of the Bimbos (1975) 12–13
production 6–7, 10

Quart, Leonard 167, 169, 171
The Quick and the Dead (1995) 50

Rajski, Peggy 6, 18, 98
Ratner, Megan 233
Rea, Steven 50
Reagan, Ronald 70, 102, 112, 114–15, 119, 126, 173
realism 9, 56, 74, 122, 132–33, 186, 211
Reed, Lou 89
Reid, Max 48
Reiner, Rob 212, 214
Renzi, Maggie 6, 11, 19, 192–93, 197, 207; as actor, 6, 57, 70, 144, 158, 182; as producer, 6, 70, 72, 98, 173, 199, 210, 212, 214
Resnais, Alain 77
Return of the Secaucus Seven (1980) 9, 13, 18, 34, 53–72, 75, 83–84, 88, 92, 174, 197, 243–44
Reynolds, Burt 49
Richardson, Robert 141, 145, 160, 185
Rizzo, Cindy 78, 81
Robinson, Amy 85
Robinson, Eddie 217, 239
Rosen, David 59, 70
Rothstein, Arnold 138–39, 143
Russo, Vito 72, 74, 79, 81

Sanford-Pillsbury Productions 139–40
Santitos 18
Sarris, Andrew 5, 18, 21, 142, 176, 186, 190–91, 238, 240
Sayles, John vii, 3–4, 10–18, 58, 110, 245; and acting 16, 58–59, 107, 109, 125, 152–53, 236–39, 240; as actor 16, 57, 79, 100, 103, 109, 128, 141, 164; and character sheets 131, 236–37; dialogue, 23–25, 45, 51–52, 60–62, 64, 70, 107, 110–111, 119, 121, 123, 127, 129–30, 144, 146, 148–49, 151, 153–55, 157, 159, 161, 164–66, 168–71, 177–78, 180, 182–88, 194–97, 210, 216–22, 224–26, 244; and editing 91–92, 135–36, 148–52, 169, 175, 177, 179, 185, 218, 229–30; and history 115, 118, 130, 137, 149, 215, 223–24, 228, 233; and mise-en-scène 67, 82, 92–95, 104, 120–21, 130, 147–51, 154, 157, 160, 163–66, 171, 177–79, 196, 202–4, 206, 230–31, 233–34, 239; and music 15–16, 80, 88–89, 90, 94, 106, 112, 133–34, 136, 152, 165, 172,

180, 233–36, 243; and "psychological realism" 122, 132; storytelling of 3, 9–18, 119, 129, 157, 163, 192, 198, 200, 205–6; visual style of 5–6, 66–67, 80, 94, 117, 121–22, 141, 143, 160–61, 163–64, 166, 168–70, 176–78, 181–84, 193–94, 200, 202–3, 206, 213, 215, 229–34, 244–45
Scenario 213, 215, 228
Schlesinger, Tom 21
Scobey, David 143, 152, 154–55
Scorsese, Martin 92, 141, 157, 160, 163
screenplay 139–40, 213, 215–23, 243–44
Secret of Roan Inish (1994) 5–6, 14, 17, 192–212, 214–15, 234, 245
Secret of Ron Mor Skerry 192–93
"Selkie Legend" 193
Seven Samurai (1954) 32
Shannon's Deal (1990) 15, 16, 236
Shapiro, Barbara Hewson 6, 110, 125
Sheridan, Richard 194, 209
Siemaszko, Casey 49
Sinatra, Frank 87, 90–91, 93, 96
Skerry Movies Corp. 192
Sloss, John 6
Smith, Gavin 34, 161, 223, 230–31
soap operas 175–77, 184–85
Somebody in Boots 14
Something Wild (1986) 16
Sony Pictures Classics 4
sound 88, 207
Spano, Vincent 6, 86–89, 160, 172
Spielberg, Steven 15, 72, 98
Springall, Alejandro 18
Springsteen, Bruce 6, 15, 90–92; *Born in the U.S.A.* (1984) 6; *Glory Days* (1985) 6; *I'm on Fire* (1985) 6
Sragow, Michael 5
Star Wars (1977) 32
Straight Talk (1992) 16
steadicam 160–61, 170
Steele, Barbara 27–27
Stempel, Tom 54
Stone, Oliver 55, 141
Stone, Robert 14
Strathairn, David 6, 11, 17, 46–47, 57, 63, 70, 100, 103, 109–10, 130, 141–42, 153, 158, 180, 183, 188
Strathairn, Tay 220

Takemine, Go 16
Tanner, Alain 57

Teague, Lewis 35, 41, 44
television 6, 15, 16, 110, 243
Terkel, Studs 137, 141
Them! (1954) 26, 41–42
Thinking in Pictures: The Making of the Movie Matewan (1987) 13, 19, 66–67, 86, 91, 116
Thompson, Cliff 189, 237
Thompson, David 19, 22, 32
Tierney, Lawrence 173
Tighe, Kevin 6, 50, 130, 145, 153, 165, 172
Tintori, John 151
Touch of Evil (1958) 240
Turnbuckle (1981) 14
Twentieth Century–Fox 85
Twitchell, James 26, 36, 39

Union Dues (1977) 9, 12–13, 96, 116
Unionism 115–16, 118–20, 126–27, 134–35
Unnatural Causes (1986) 15
Untamagira (1990) 16
Untermyer, Louis 128
urban politics 157–60, 173

violence 119–20, 123–24, 128, 130
visual composition (defined) 233

Wadhams, Wayne 88
Washington Post 233
The Well of Loneliness 79
Wexler, Haskell 6, 122–25, 129, 141, 202–6
Wild Thing (1987) 48
Williams, Jeanne 116, 118
Williams, John Alexander 119–20
Williams, Marco 99
Williams College 11
The Wolf Man (1941) 36, 38–39
Woodard, Alfre 174, 183, 189–90
Wright, Tom 6, 167, 188
Writers Guild Foundation 18

"The Year of the Woman" 174
Yntema, Peggy 12

Zieger, Robert H. 119
Zinn, Howard 117